THEY PLAYED WITH

BOBBY MOORE

THE WEST HAM YEARS

By Tim Crane

Foreword by Sir Geoff Hurst

First published in England in October 2014 by

Tim Crane

Tel: 07798 934 824

tcrane183@gmail.com

©Copyright Tim Crane

Photographic credits:

Players and families

EX Hammers Magazine (www.ex-hammers.com)

Dave Alexander (www.footballwanted.com)

Steve Marsh (www.theyflysohigh.co.uk)

Kent Gavin (kentgavinassociates.com)

Albert York

Designed by Paul Scott

Grays, Essex

Tel: 01375 371064

paul716scott@btinternet.com

Printed by The Printing House

3rd Floor , 14 Hanover Street , London, W1S 1YH

Tel: 0203 291 3258

Distributed by Tim Crane

183 Westcombe Hill, Blackheath, London, SE3 7DR, England

Distribution email: tcrane183@gmail.com

ISBN 978-0-9930286-0-1

To Mum

Thank you

CONTENTS

FOREWORD
BY SIR GEOFF HURST

It is always a pleasure to talk about Bobby Moore. He is West Ham United's greatest ever player and the memories from all those who played with him should never be forgotten. It is a personal high to know that I was fortunate enough to play with Bobby on more occasions than any other player and indeed I have also lined up with most of the 89 Hammers in this book.

Seeing the extraordinary array of photographs of them in the West Ham shirt takes me back to that fantastic time in my life. It is even more poignant, and tinged with sadness, now that we have recently lost the likes of Phil Woosnam, Andy Malcolm, Ernie Gregory and John Bond to add to the other greats we have lost down the years such as Noel Cantwell, Malcolm Musgrove, John Dick, Budgie Byrne and, of course, Mooro himself. It is a tremendous effort to preserve their memories and keep alive the contribution of West Ham and England's greatest ever player.

A lot of people ask me who I looked up to as a kid and I surprise them by saying: 'Bobby Moore,' because he was only eight months older than me. The reason for this is because he graduated to both West Ham United's first team and the England team much quicker than me. His first World Cup was 1962 in Chile and mine was 1966, so, in terms of advancement and self-development, he was closer to four years ahead of me. He lived his life to be the best he could be on the day. On the pitch you wouldn't even think about Mooro because he was usually the best player out there. However, you would think about him all the time if he was missing from a match for whatever reason.

The thing about Mooro for me is that when he joined West Ham he was a tubby little kid and didn't fall into the group of naturally gifted individuals. If you look at the 1966 World Cup squad for instance, as a kid, Bobby wasn't as gifted an individual as, say, Bobby Charlton or Jimmy Greaves. But, Bobby had two fantastic qualities: He could read a game almost telepathically and, in addition to that, he was always very composed. If there is one single moment which underlines just how composed he was as a player it would be the final seconds of the 1966 World Cup final. He was playing in the biggest game ever, in one of the world's biggest stadiums, against one of the best teams in the world and he was playing as though it was a Sunday morning match on Hackney marshes. Who has ever chested the ball down in his own penalty area when 3-2 ahead with the opposition laying siege and then calmly played a 50-yard ball with pinpoint accuracy out of defence for the striker to seal the game? Magnificent!

Only recently, I saw a defender in the Premier League trying a similar thing and he mis-timed the ball, which hit his shoulder and set up the opposition striker for a goal. You can see similar aberrations in leagues all over the world and these are just club matches and not the super-charged occasion of a World Cup final.

People can argue long into the night about who the best defender is but we have never had anyone anywhere near the quality of Bobby Moore. His leadership, command, composure, responsibility and delivery with either foot mark him out as the undisputed, greatest ever defender. Not just one of the greats – the one and only great.

I have so many memories of Mooro but even now I see things that I hadn't noticed previously, particularly in old film footage. I saw a clip recently of the 1962 World Cup in Chile and Mooro is taking a free kick. Back then, corners, free-kicks and throw-ins were taken by the senior pros but it was typical of Mooro that he wanted to take responsibility at such a young age. This typified his desire to control things on the pitch which is why you could guarantee he would play well in the big games like the semi-finals and finals. Yes, you could really guarantee it.

Bobby wasn't a big shouter or screamer on the pitch and preferred the raised eye approach to leadership. It was a subtle but highly effective way of communicating his dissatisfaction with something you were doing in a game. Similarly, he wasn't in the habit of giving away compliments that easily so when you did receive one it made you feel 10 feet tall and you never forgot it. A good example is the moment when Gordon Banks made the greatest save the world has ever seen, against Pele in 1970. Mooro recognised the brilliance with a gentle slap on Banks' shorts. Banksy has never forgotten it.

I also remember one such time when I was in a particular purple patch. As a striker you have five or six years when your youth, talent and experience all combine and overlap to give you a terrific run in both your own playing and scoring ability. We were playing up at Sunderland and had won 4-2. I scored one and set up another for 'Budgie' Byrne. After the game I was in the bath and Bobby came over and said: 'You're effing brilliant at the moment, you know you are. You are absolutely effing brilliant!' I will always remember that compliment from the great man. For me, the fact that he swore makes it even better!

If I had to underline the man's greatness to future generations it would be to take one of the most devastating moments in England's footballing history – Maradona's brilliant second goal during the 1986 World Cup quarter-finals. When you watch that goal there is a point when you can envisage Mooro intercepting the ball and keeping that goal out of the record books. Only Mooro could have stopped Maradona that day and that is the difference between him and every other defender that has ever pulled on a football jersey. Mooro stopped bad history.

He was simply the greatest. The player to look up to. The best captain West Ham and England has ever had – and there have been some decent ones – but Bobby will never be replaced. Absolutely unbelievable and we will never see another like him. Impossible. It was a privilege to play alongside him.

West Ham fans will love reading this book. Another vital piece of the puzzle.

Sir Geoff Hurst
Cheltenham, 2014

The author with Sir Geoff Hurst.

ACKNOWLEDGEMENTS

Given the sheer number of helpful people I have met along the way a complete list of names would simply be too long to render them meaningful. It has simply been a case of West Ham people helping West Ham people.

I catapult my sincere gratitude to all the players, families and friends for their time, effort, photos and recollections. This book is your body of work.

A few names simply have to be recognised not least my better half, **Helen Kensett**, for her unerring support which I am hoping will kick in soon! Her tireless mothering of our three children – **Emily, Hannah** and **Gracie** – freed up the valuable time required to complete such a book.

My mother, to whom this book is dedicated. Another layer of support from the great woman.

My sisters, Sally and **Jackie**, for the laughs and memories down the years. Let's not lose sight of each other.

Uncle Sid – Gone but always here. **My best friend Stuart Liddell** – Here but always gone!

My good friend **Tony McDonald**, editor of the *EX Magazine*, for his advice, support and an email in 2002 asking me to spend the rest of my life tracking down *EX Hammers* (or their descendants) from any period between 1895 and now. It has been Christmas Day, every day ever since!

The rest of the team at EX – **Terry Connelly, Terry Roper, Roger Hiller, Neil Humphreys, Henry Gunton** and my absolute favourite superstar – **Susie McDonald**, whose culinary treats have offset the gloom of far too many Betfair losses!

Steve Blowers and **Danny Francis** for their keen eye, grasp of the English language and patience in proof-reading 250,000 words. Unforgettable.

Paul Scott – 'the Ronaldo of print design' – who possesses an attention to detail not seen since Michelangelo. I have truly benefited from his professionalism and expertise.

Gary Firmager, long standing editor of popular fanzine *Over Land and Sea* for giving me my first chance in writing. I believe *Taking the Press* is still widely discussed by West Ham cognoscenti...

Rob Jenkins, veteran West Ham physio of some 1400 first team games between 1966 and 1990. He possesses a perfect blend of warmth, humour and knowledge which I have benefited from in our pre-match gatherings in his cosy Green Street clinic opposite the main gates of the Boleyn Ground. Through Rob I have enjoyed the memorable company of his good friends and true Hammers **Bert Wilson** and **Peter Gurr**.

Hilary Pratt, daughter of ex-Chairman, Reg Pratt, for her supportive words, warmth of character and keen interest.

Brian Dear for his special West Ham heart and expertise in keeping alive all that is good and wholesome about the club.

Sir Geoff Hurst for his enthusiasm and time in contributing so many fine stories as well as the book's foreword. It is my constant worry every four years that someone may match or better his unique World Cup achievement. His photo sits on our mantelpiece on every occasion.

Tony – *'Mr Who's Who of West Ham United'* – Hogg for his rich, multi-coloured character. Also for his beautiful response to the general enquiry; 'How was your Weekend?' – 'It was weak and then it ended!'

John Northcutt – heavyweight Hammers historian, published author of major statistical works on West Ham United and a dependable source of knowledge on the club.

Richard Miller for his spellbinding knowledge of Bobby Moore and dedication to the statistical accuracy of the great man. If Bobby Moore has a number one fan, Richard would be a serious contender having viewed his performances from the terraces on no fewer than 540 occasions.

Steve Marsh – 'the Victor Watson of the West Ham collecting world' – who, along with his good friend Stuart Allen, ensure the very best handling of West Ham United's proud history.

Finally, jolly Joe Durrell for the twinkling pride in his eyes when hearing he was one of only 89 Hammers to have played with Bobby Moore. The journey would not have been made without him.

West Ham people helping West Ham people.

INTRODUCTION

89 Hammers played first team football with Robert Frederick Chelsea Moore during his 16-years in the senior side at West Ham United. Their recollections of the great man between 1958-1974 form an integral part of the Bobby Moore story. For the record, Bobby also played with 92 England internationals and 35 Fulham team-mates.

I must concede that it was never my intention to write a book about Bobby Moore. The definitive work – *The Life and Times of a Sporting Hero* - by Bobby's official biographer, Jeff Powell, is simply the best on the shelf. Similarly, the dedicated and tireless undertaking of Phil Daniels, in his book *Moore Than a Legend*, has also ensured a thorough and expert handling of the subject. My own reasons for writing this book have a different impetus.

Since 2002 I have written for the *EX Hammers* magazine, a publication which has its heritage in preserving the contribution made by former players of the club. It is the only magazine to recognise their valuable role in the club's history – in small or large measure – and provides a guarantee in print that West Ham players will never be forgotten.

Naturally, during my experience of tracking down and interviewing past players, I have heard many stories about Bobby Moore along the way and the experience has provided layers and layers of material relating to his time at West Ham United and beyond. It was during one such interview when the idea to write this book was hatched.

The interviewee was Joe Durrell, a Stepney-born Hammer who played six first team games on the left-wing, during 1971-72. When researching the interview it came to light that Joe, who still lives in Stepney, was one of those 89 Hammers to have lined up with Bobby Moore in West Ham's first team. The impact and pride this news had on Joe engendered a flow of 'Mooro' stories deserving of the widest possible audience.

The experience left me in no doubt that I was very well placed to ensure that these, and the myriad of other Bobby Moore tales from the 89 Hammers, were preserved for present and future generations of fans. That became my quest.

The journey has been extraordinary and it is a pleasure to lay before all Bobby Moore fans, so many original stories and unpublished personal photographs.

The experience of researching and writing this book has had its fair share of good fortune. Bertie Lutton made a very rare visit from his home in Australia and readily gave his time to be interviewed. Similarly, both Trevor Dawkins and Ted MacDougall visited from the United States, Clyde Best from Bermuda, Tommy Taylor from Finland and, perhaps most fortunate of all, both John Sissons and Roger Hugo made rare returns to these shores from South Africa.

Other overseas Hammers, Jim Standen, Bobby Howe and Ade Coker in the United States as well as the highly elusive Tony Scott and former keeper, Bobby Ferguson both in Australia, were equally generous with their time.

Unfortunately, there have been a few lows along the way, with the club losing several of its most decorated and fondly remembered stars.

The sad passing of John Bond and his big, charismatic approach to life, was a particularly black day. John played in Moore's debut game – against Manchester United in 1958 – and formed part of the defensive line-up when the Hammers beat Preston North End in the 1964 FA Cup final. John was very supportive of the *EX Hammers* magazine and had always been so very willing to support our efforts in any way he could.

Andy Malcolm, another member of Bobby Moore's debut line up, died in South Africa on Boxing Day, 2013. It was a bitter blow having enjoyed his lovely character over a series of interviews in the months prior to his sad passing. Just four days earlier Phil Woosnam, another key contributor to the proud history of West Ham United, passed away in Atlanta, Georgia. His legacy lives on with every game of soccer which takes place in the United States of America.

Sadly, this takes the number of surviving Hammers down to 62 from the 89 who played in the first team with Bobby Moore. Thankfully, the families and friends of those that are no longer with us have ensured their legacies are kept alive within the pages of this book. All have been so very helpful with their memories and photographs.

The recollections have been both touching and enduring. Many recalled Bobby's stature on the pitch and his generosity and compassion off it while others highlighted Bobby's great sense of humour and immaculate approach to everything he did. As a consequence, the high regard for the man has been bolstered further.

During a number of background interviews with former staff of West Ham United many first class stories came to light. Former club physio Rob Jenkins recalled a time when West Ham were playing in Bermuda in the early 1970s. 'We were having a couple of drinks in a bar and this young woman came over and pointed at Bobby and said that she recognised him from somewhere. Now, Bobby wasn't the type to say 'Well I did lift the World Cup a few years ago' and instead feigned confusion. Anyway, later in the evening the woman returned: 'I've got it! I've got it!' she said – 'You're the drummer in the hotel band!' Bobby was eating a meal at the time and just pretended to play the drums with his knife and fork!'

Even those players who did not play with Moore were still affected by his aura. 1970s midfielder, Anton Otulakowski, recalled the moment when he signed for the club. 'John Lyall picked me up at King's Cross and the first thing he did was drive me to see Bobby Moore's house.'

One of the most poignant Bobby Moore moments came when interviewing former Hammer of the Year, Lawrie Leslie, who is suffering from a long illness as well as having to cope with gradual memory loss. I sat alongside our gallant goalkeeper and set down photos of every Hammer with whom he played. He stared intently at them all. The great names in West Ham's illustrious past fell under his gaze and his doting wife, Janette, looked on with interest. 'I can remember the way they moved' he said, in his lilting Scottish brogue. 'But I can't remember their names.' Then, after a long pause, he pointed and said: 'But I know that's Bobby.'

Tim Crane – October 2014

___

Ted Fenton – Bobby Moore's first manager.

CHAPTER ONE
1958-59

Bobby Moore's total appearances (July 1958-June 1959): 63 games (3 goals)

Reserves: 21 (1 goal), **Youth Cup:** 8 (1 goal), Friendlies: 7, Switzerland Youth Tour: 6 (1 goal),
League Division One: 5, **Metropolitan League:** 5. **Mid-week League:** 5, **Southern Junior Floodlit Cup:** 2,
LFA Cup: 2, Southern Floodlit Cup: 1, England Youth International: 1

There are various ways of running a football club. The two extremes are when on the one hand a club relies solely on the cheque book to secure established 'stars' or on the other hand when a club develops its own youngsters into a successful team. It is obvious which must be the more satisfying.
Reg Pratt, Chairman of West Ham United Football club throughout the Bobby Moore era

When Bobby Moore signed professional forms for West Ham United in May 1958, the club had just gained promotion to the top-flight after an absence of 25 years. Prior to the achievements of that unforgettable 1957-58 campaign, it was the surviving members of the Hammers first-ever FA Cup final line-up of 1923, who represented legendary status at the club.

Ted Hufton, George Kay, Jack Tresadern, Billy Moore, Jimmy Ruffell and Victor Watson were household names amongst the West Ham faithful. They personified a golden age in the club's history, when participation in the first-ever Wembley cup final and promotion to the top flight, for the first time, were achieved in a single season.

Those men from 1923 were the unforgettable generation but, in 1958, a new era of heroes was established. Players such as John Bond, Ken Brown, Noel Cantwell, Malcolm Musgrove, Andy Malcolm, John Dick and Vic Keeble had been cemented into the claret and blue consciousness for evermore. The eternal era of Moore, Hurst and Peters was still yet to come.

One of the greatest photographs in the history of West Ham United depicts a scene from a promotion dinner, which took place at the Café Royal, Regent Street on July 12, 1958.

West Ham United's 1958 promotion dinner at the Café Royal. Bobby Moore at the back.

West Ham United 1958-59. Back in the big time!

Seated at the far end is a 17-year-old Bobby Moore. Next to him is his good friend and Colts team-mate, Andy Smillie, while his future defensive partner, Ken Brown, sits behind him. Ken would be voted the Hammer of the Year at the end of Moore's first season in the senior team.

The image simply oozes 'family club' and beneath a huge Hammers crest sat some 300 invited guests. There was a considerable number of former players who attended, including the 1923 FA Cup final team and cult-hero Danny Shea, who was one of a number from the pre-First World War Southern League era. The axiom 'Once a Hammer always a Hammer' carried tremendous gravitas and the room was bristling with people to whom West Ham United meant so much more than just a name.

Chairman Reg Pratt galvanised the audience with a rousing speech: 'We regard our present success not so much as an end but as a new beginning, a challenge, a spur to greater efforts. We will give everybody the opportunity to prove their worth.'

The formation of an Old Players' Association formally established the importance of the club's past. The unwritten message to every ex-Hammer who had pulled on the claret and blue shirt since the club's formation in 1895 was crystal clear: The club is entering a new and exciting period and you are an intrinsic part of it.

This was the club to which Bobby Moore was about to make such a successful and lasting contribution. There would be many more celebratory dinners to come.

The sporting landscape of 1958 was a world apart from the present incarnation of the so-called 'beautiful game.' Players lived in the same neighbourhood as the supporters, used the same shops, frequented the same pubs and travelled on the same buses and trains. Every club was a product of its community and not a play-thing for the wealthy. Overseas

signings were an alien concept and Brian Dear, leading scorer in West Ham's 1965 European success, often regales Hammers supporters at various nostalgia evenings when declaring: 'Billy Bonds was the club's first overseas signing in 1967. He was bought from Charlton Athletic...!'

The 1958 World Cup, hosted by Sweden, had a tremendous impact on the nation. It was the first to be shown on television and with England, Scotland, Wales and Northern Ireland all qualifying, most people with a TV set were sitting in front of it during the rather dull and wet summer of 1958.

The collective talent of Brazil, with Pele, Garrincha, Didi, Vava et al was so fresh and innovative that a new type of football connoisseur was born throughout the world. Bobby Moore's youth team-mate, John Cartwright, was particularly affected and, to this day, is still known by his close friends as 'Didi' after Brazil's midfield maestro.

Players' earnings were constrained by the maximum wage, which had just been increased to £20-per-week. This was still three times higher than the average working man's weekly wage. There was simply no need for an agent to help negotiate a better deal.

There was certainly not the yawning cash chasm which exists today and the standard of living enjoyed by footballers in 1958 was marginally better than the supporters, who paid to watch them. Once again, a humorous perspective is offered by Dear: 'My first house cost £5,200 and the monthly repayments were 28 quid and I still fell behind with them. I didn't get my first personalised number plate until I was 60!'

When Bobby Moore witnessed the successful promotion team of 1958 he was cheering on working class heroes not show-business millionaires. A season ticket was around the ten pound mark, as opposed to the £1,000 sought today.

However, times were soon to change immeasurably and Bobby Moore would be at the very forefront of dramatic

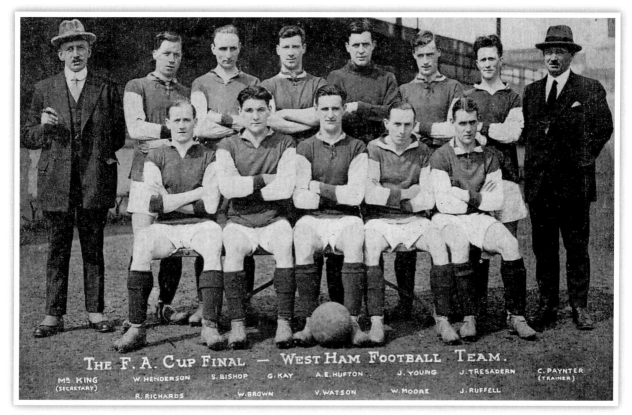

THE F. A. CUP FINAL — WEST HAM FOOTBALL TEAM.

MR KING (SECRETARY)   W. HENDERSON   S. BISHOP   G. KAY   A.E. HUFTON   J. YOUNG   J. TRESADERN   C. PAYNTER (TRAINER)

R. RICHARDS   W. BROWN   V. WATSON   W. MOORE   J. RUFFELL

The West Ham legends when Bobby Moore joined the club in 1956.

changes in the landscape of both football and society. The game was modernising. The tools of the trade were changing. Cotton replaced wool, short replaced long, light replaced heavy and the era of Stanley Matthews, Billy Wright, Tom Finney and Nat Lofthouse was to be replaced by the emerging talents of Johnny Haynes, Bobby Charlton, Jimmy Greaves, George Best and, of course, Moore himself. Most tellingly, West Ham manager Ted Fenton would, in a few year's time, be replaced by Ron Greenwood.

Similarly, society would soon be having its music and fashion tastes re-defined by the irrepressible rise of rock 'n' roll and the Carnaby Street culture. Elvis Presley, Buddy Holly, Jerry Lewis, Fats Domino, Chuck Berry, The Everley Brothers and Paul Anka reigned supreme in the local palais, dance hall and teenage bedroom. In just a few years' time The Beatles and the Rolling Stones would eclipse everything.

The private life of Bobby Moore was also completely transformed in 1958, the year in which he met Christina Dean. Their four-year courtship was under way and, initially, it had none of the celebrity, Hollywood movie star status which would soon define their daily existence.

Despite 1958 being a landmark year for Moore, it was tainted with bad news. The one player, with whom Bobby had a unique affinity, was about to leave the club. Malcolm Allison announced his retirement from the game and would soon take up his first post in football management – with

amateur side, Sutton United. He would eventually go on to enjoy memorable successes with both Manchester City and Crystal Palace.

Allison stands as one of the most influential characters, not just in Bobby's life, but in the history of West Ham United. His £6,000 move from Charlton Athletic, in 1951, is one of the great transfer master-strokes during the Ted Fenton era.

Tragically, Malcolm contracted tuberculosis while at West Ham, which resulted in the removal of a lung. He was never again able to reach full fitness and never played in the top flight for the Hammers after pulling on the first team shirt some 300 times. 21,600 attended his testimonial against an All Star XI at the Boleyn Ground on November 17, 1958. Bobby Charlton, Brian Clough and Peter Brabrook were amongst those who played. Bobby Moore sat in the stand.

West Ham United was going through a number of both large and small scale changes during 1958, with a ground development programme being top of the agenda. Interestingly, the club only bought the freehold of the Boleyn Ground in April 1959 after maintaining a landlord-tenant relationship, which dated back to the move from the Memorial Grounds in 1904. Chairman Reg Pratt negotiated the freehold purchase from the Roman Catholic Archdiocese of Westminster for £30,000. Covering of the North Bank would be one of the first priorities.

Moore would witness changes to each stand, including the complete replacement of the 'Chicken Run' in 1968. There was also a desire to increase the ground capacity to 48,000. Sadly, this figure was never achieved and the club's record home attendance remains at 44,417 for the visit of Tottenham Hotspur in the FA Cup third round on January 8, 1927. The game ended 3-2 courtesy of a hat-trick from the peerless Victor Watson. The post-war record also came against Spurs – 42,322 – for a 2-2 draw on October 17, 1970.

Match days were also seeing a few cosmetic changes in 1958. A new-style programme was launched which was smaller and more expensive. However, the increase in price to sixpence for first team matches and fourpence for reserve team games was no hardship for the halcyon period the club was about to enter.

There was a feeling that something significant was brewing at the club and this was best reflected most of all in ticket sales. For the first time in the club's history, it was announced that applications for season tickets were oversubscribed and an announcement was published in the programme to prevent any further applications. Match tickets for adults ranged between three shillings (15 pence) for the Chicken Run, three shillings and sixpence (17½ pence) for the West Stand and seven shillings and sixpence (37½ pence) for a seat in C Block, which purportedly afforded the best view of all.

By 1958, Moore had been at the club for two years, having signed amateur forms at the start of the 1956-57 season. He had played for the Colts alongside team-mates Joe Kirkup, Harry Cripps, John Lyall, Andy Smillie and John Cartwright. His football lineage had seen him play for both Barking and Essex, while he earned his first England Youth cap – versus Holland in Amsterdam – at just 16 years of age. He would eventually gain 18 caps at England Under-18 level, which set a new record.

Moore had made his reserve team debut against Birmingham City at the Boleyn Ground on December 7, 1957 and was in the Colts team, which beat Arsenal in the final of the Southern Junior Floodlit Cup at the end of that campaign. He would make 21 reserve-team appearances during the 1958-59 season. A typical line up for the reserves would include many of the following players: Brian Rhodes, Joe Kirkup, Malcolm Pyke, John Lyall, Eddie Bovington, Bill Lansdowne, Doug Wragg, John Smith, Geoff Hurst, Billy Dare, Harry Obeney, Brian Dear, Andy Smillie and Tony Scott.

Bobby captained the Colts in the FA Youth Cup final at the end of the 1958-59 season, eventually losing over two legs against Blackburn Rovers. In the fifth round of that particular cup run, West Ham earned a draw at Aston Villa and Bobby's performance was described as having: 'All the hallmarks of greatness.' He was just 18-years-old. There was some consolation for losing the Youth Cup final, when winning the Southern Junior Floodlit Cup for a second time – beating

Manager Ted Fenton and assistant Bill Robinson with West Ham's Youth Team trophies.

Directors' trophy for Bobby Moore

A MODEST YOUNG GIANT BY THE NAME OF BOBBY MOORE STOLE MOST OF THE LIMELIGHT AT WEST HAM'S YOUTH PRESENTATION DINNER ON FRIDAY. BIG MOMENT FOR THE 17-YEAR-OLD CENTRE-HALF – RATED BY MANY THE BEST TEENAGE PROSPECT IN BRITAIN—CAME WHEN HE WAS PRESENTED WITH THE DIRECTORS' TROPHY FOR BEING HAM-MERS OUTSTANDING YOUTH PLAYER IN 1957-8.

In the words of club chairman Mr. Reg Pratt, J.P., Moore received the award "because of his great character and the lustre he has brought to West Ham."

For Bobby it really was a night to remember. From Mr. Ray Osborne, the F.A. Youth Section's number one official, he received 12 youth international caps. Mr. Osborne also presented youth international caps to Tony Scott, Andy Smillie and Peter Reader.

Moore's five games for England in the recent international youth tournament — for which caps are

not awarded—enabled him to set up a record of 17 England youth appearances.

Referring to West Ham, Mr. Osborne told the four youngsters: "This is one of the finest clubs in the game, if not the finest."

'Tremendous pride'

Mr. Henry Welsh, next season's vice-chairman of the English Schools' F.A., had this to say of West Ham's talented teenagers: "In a few years' time these young stars will shine just as brightly as the seniors are now. In the last two

years nine of them have played for England."

He added: "We have a tremendous pride in these boys here to-night." Season 1959-60 will see Mr. Welsh as chairman of the Schools' F.A. – first West Ham man to achieve this honour.

After thanking the youngsters for their efforts last season, Mr. Pratt said: "Our juniors are now juniors in a First Division club, and we expect a great deal more from them because of that."

Genial youth section manager Bill Robinson later took up this point to say: "I realize that being a First Division club our efforts must be greater—but, with reference to the first team, Wally St. Pier must be very proud that so many of the players have come up through the junior team."

During the evening Southern Junior Floodlight Cup plaques were presented to Earl, Kirkup, Cripps, Moore, Keetch, Hurst, Woodley, Scott, Bovington, Norcott, B. (K.) and Lyall.

Press plaudits for a rising star.

Chelsea Colts, 1-0, at Stamford Bridge. Interestingly, seven players from that line-up gained England Youth honours: Moore, Hurst, Smillie, Scott, Cartwright, Peter Reader and Derek Woodley.

Remarkably, Moore had already made his first team debut over six months prior to that FA Youth Cup final. It came just four months after signing professional forms with the club. He would eventually make five senior appearances during the 1958-59 season, playing with 13 lucky Hammers along the way.

At the time of Bobby Moore's debut versus Manchester United, there were several members of the backroom staff, who were instrumental in the development of the impressionable young captain of the youth team.

There was Bill Robinson, who was responsible for the youth team section and had been promoted to assistant-manager under Ted Fenton. Also, Albert Walker who had recently taken over reserve team responsibilities following the departure of Harry Hooper snr. Furthermore, Wally St Pier, the chief scout, whose eye for a player ensured a conveyer belt of talent throughout Bobby Moore's time at West Ham United. All three would be watching the blond-haired boy from Barking as he ran out on that September evening.

The most influential voice of all was that of Noel Cantwell, whose famous words: 'Play the kid,' in response to Ted Fenton's enquiry about whether to play Malcolm Allison or Bobby Moore, marked a new era of glory at West Ham United.

Bobby Moore, aged 17, ran out for his first-ever senior appearance in the West Ham United shirt. It was seven o'clock on the evening of Monday September 8, 1958 and the visitors were Manchester United, still in mourning following the Munich air disaster some seven months earlier. The 10 Hammers, who lined up alongside Moore to overcome Matt Busby's Reds 3-2 and top the league, all stand tall in West Ham United's history.

Some won trophies and others achieved legacies that are indelibly printed on the memories of West Ham United supporters the world over. Those 10 men form a big part of Bobby Moore's journey. A path which would end some 16 years and 89 first team players later.

Bill Robinson and Wally St Pier – Bobby Moore's early influencers.

These 'debut boys' witnessed Bobby's first game out on the hallowed turf of the Boleyn Ground. Some later lined up alongside him at Wembley Stadium, while one stood alongside him on his wedding day as his best man. They are the initial 10 of those 89 Hammers, who played first team football with Bobby Moore.

Here is their story...

BOBBY MOORE'S DEBUT

The Boleyn Ground, September 8, 1958

Attendance: 35,672

Line Ups
West Ham United: Ernie Gregory, John Bond, Noel Cantwell, Andy Malcolm, Ken Brown, Bobby Moore, Mike Grice, John Smith, Vic Keeble, John Dick, Malcolm Musgrove

Manchester United: Harry Gregg, Bill Foulkes, Ian Greaves, Freddie Goodwin, Ronnie Cope, Wilf McGuinness, Colin Webster, Ernie Taylor, Dennis Viollet, Bobby Charlton, Albert Scanlon

Result
West Ham United 3 (Dick, Smith, Musgrove)
Manchester United 2 (Webster, McGuinness)

1 – ERNIE GREGORY
November 10, 1921 – January 21, 2012

Born: Stratford, London

Position: Goalkeeper

Games played with Bobby Moore: 3 (1958-59)

Games played for West Ham United: 406 (1946-59)

Ernest Gregory was Bobby Moore's first goalkeeper. He was almost 37 years of age when taking his place between the sticks for Bobby's debut. The difference in age between the young lad from Barking and the experienced professional from Stratford was almost 20 years. It would be the first of only three games in which Ernie would line up with Bobby before his retirement as a player in 1960.

Gregory was one of West Ham's greatest ever servants. He enjoyed over 70 years of service as a player, coach and occasional visitor to the Boleyn Ground towards the end of his life.

Bobby Moore would have seen Ernie almost every day of his 16 years at West Ham and Ernie would have witnessed Bobby mature into a world class World Cup winning England captain. We can safely assume that tremendous respect existed between the two men.

Ernie joined the club in 1936 and signed professional forms in 1939 although the Second World War delayed his first team debut – v Plymouth Argyle – until December 1946. He won an England B cap against France in 1952.

Ernie's 406th and final game came at home to Leeds United on September 5, 1959.

In October 1960 he was granted a testimonial game against Costa Rican side Ligo Deportiva Alajeulense. He benefited to the tune of £2,100 and spent the next 30 years as part of West Ham's coaching staff.

Ernie always had the greatest of respect for pre-War Hammers and revered former team-mates such as Dick Walker and Len Goulden. On many occasions after Ernie had helped the Hammers to promotion in 1958 he was often mobbed at the gates for his signature. He would sometimes make his way to the match with 1923 FA Cup final goalkeeper, Ted Hufton, who worked in the club's press room for many years. Ernie's respect for the his predecessors was steadfast and he would say to everyone within earshot. 'It's not me you should be asking for an autograph its Ted, the club's greatest ever goalkeeper.'

Ernie Gregory passed away on January 21, 2012, aged 90. He was pre-deceased by both his wife, Yvonne, and their daughter, Lorraine.

Ernie was cremated at the City of London cemetery. Amongst the congregation were over 50 ex-Hammers straddling seven decades. Current chairman and former youth team player, David Gold, ensured the club was well represented.

Most fittingly, five former first team goalkeepers – Alan Dickie, Phil Parkes, Peter Grotier, Mervyn Day and Allen McKnight – all paid their respects and there was no shortage of memories to be shared. Brian Dear delivered a most poignant, humorous and heartfelt eulogy.

We need to extend our sincere thanks to Ronnie Boyce for providing an insight into the type of relationship Ernie shared with Bobby Moore. 'Ticker' Boyce was Ernie's friend of over 50 years and the man who visited him up until the very end.

Following are his recollections along with many other interesting anecdotes, many of which Bobby himself would be nodding at in knowing recognition.

When the team sheet went up every Friday, there would be a big crowd of players all craning their necks to take a look. Ernie would be sitting down away from it all: 'Take a good look,' he would say, 'if you're not on the front have a look on the back!' He would also say: 'the line-up for tomorrow is Ink, Stink, Pen and Ink, Freeman Hardy and Willis!'
Ron Boyce

West Ham were looking for a replacement for Ernie Gregory and I was playing for Hendon as an amateur at the time. I played in a competition between senior amateur clubs and the reserve teams of London professional clubs. It was called the London Challenge Cup and Hendon played West Ham. Ernie was in goal for West Ham and I must have played well because he met me on the half way line at the end of the game and asked me if I had ever considered turning professional. A short while afterwards I signed for West Ham.
Peter Shearing

Ernie Gregory, John Bond and Noel Cantwell were like the three musketeers when I joined the club. Malcolm Allison

had already left and Bobby Moore was something of a D'Artagnan-like figure.
Alan Dickie

When I first joined I was a bit naïve, Ernie called me over and told me he was timing all the young lads to see how quickly they could get to the kiosk on the corner outside the ground and would I pick up a packet of 20 Bachelors for him. I belted out the ground and flew to the kiosk and back with my lungs bursting. 'How quick was that?' I gasped. 'Oh I forgot to set the timer' he replied, taking the fags from me! Another time we were playing a reserve team match at Bristol Rovers and Ernie had given up smoking for a few weeks. I wasn't playing but I was sitting on the bench. Dave Llewelyn, who was a prolific striker in the reserves, was put clean through but put it wide and Ernie was bursting with exasperation. 'Grote, Grote!' he shouted, 'Go and get me some fags!'
Peter Grotier

Ernie was absolutely brilliant to me. I was a Chelmsford boy and not part of the East London intake and, to be fair, he toughened me up. He was old-school and on my very first day of pre-season training in 1973 he took my weight and height and then asked to see my hands. I showed him and he said 'They are too soft. Now go in the toilet and piss on them every day for a month and that will liven them up!' He would never let me wear an under shirt and in the coldest weather I was only allowed to wear a thin, cotton, goalkeeper's shirt, shorts and socks. He just about allowed me to wear gloves every now and again!
Mervyn Day

We were playing Portsmouth, I think, and before the game he had said to me; 'Son I don't like the way that sun is coming up over there so I want you to win everything in the air.' So I'm battling away for all I'm worth but they won a penalty and this fella hits a belter and Ernie threw himself, full length and pushed it around the post for a corner. It was a smashing save and I was so excited I ran up to him and said 'Ernie that was brilliant, well done, what a save!' Anyway, he pushed me away and said; 'Calm down, son, I should have caught it.'
Ken Brown

Ernie had this comb that he'd take out of his pocket while standing in front of the mirror.

He would run the comb through his hair and say 'It's not fair that I should have everything and everyone else has nothing.'
Frank Lampard senior

I used to room with Ernie. He looked after me and I called him my uncle. He was a top man. I used to go and see him at his house when he wasn't doing so well and he loved to talk about the old days. He was West Ham through and through.
Bill Lansdowne senior

He used to have a white Hillman car and you could eat your dinner off the engine. Anyway, a few of the lads put some stones in the hub cap. It was three days before he realised and we were rolling around every time he was asking people

Clockwise from top left: Bond, Cantwell, Gregory and Keeble.

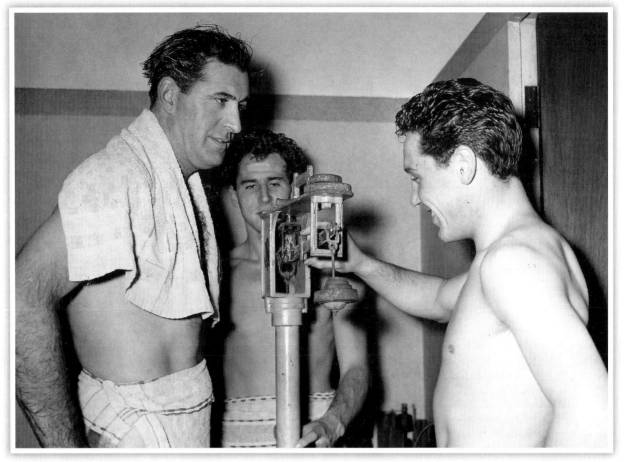

Big Ern' with Bill Lansdowne and Eddie Lewis.

what it might be. He was so opinionated about the quality of a player and had so many funny phrases which I'll never forget. Everyone will remember Ernie saying: 'If he's a player, Crippen was innocent.'
Mick McGiven

Out of everyone at West Ham, John's favourite was Ernie Gregory. He absolutely loved him. On one occasion when Ernie was in hospital for something, John and Brian (Dear) went to visit him. John said that when they walked in Ernie said 'Here are my boys!' he was so proud of them both.
Carol Charles

Dear old Ernie, I was like Manuel to his Basil Fawlty. He would always be slapping me around the head! He was such an impressive man and wouldn't hurt a fly. He was the guardian angel of every goalkeeper at West Ham.
John Ayris

The first thing I did at West Ham was run down the shops to get Ernie some cigarettes.
Joe Durrell

Ernie looked after the reserves and would give the goalkeepers plenty of stick if they got beaten at the near post or from distance.

One day, I found an old newspaper cutting in a drawer at home and it showed Ernie being beaten from 60 yards in a game at Plymouth from 1947. Coincidentally, we were playing Plymouth and on the coach home I showed it to Ernie – it read: 'No one was more surprised than goalkeeper Ernie Gregory when the ball sailed 60-yards over his head and into the back of the net. You could tell he was mortified and dismissed it by saying: 'I don't remember that game at all!'
Trevor Hartley

Ernie wouldn't let any of the ground staff touch his boots. He would take them home and clean them himself. I can see him now with them wrapped up in a brown paper parcel under his arm walking out of the stadium.
Terry McDonald (FA Youth Cup finalist 1957)

When I joined West Ham from Sheffield Wednesday, Ernie asked me if I knew Derek Dooley. Now, I knew Derek Dooley really well. He is a big legend up at Hillsborough, scoring 64 goals in 63 games and he still holds the record for most goals in a season at the club – 46.

His career was cut tragically short after having part of his leg amputated. He broke his leg in a game against Preston and gangrene set in. All of a sudden Ernie started removing his shirt to reveal this horrible scar on his chest where studs had cut into him. They were like two tram lines down his chest. 'Derek Dooley 1952,' said Ernie!
Peter Eustace

Ernie gave me the nickname 'Les' because he had played with a Les Bennett in the 1950s. It just stuck and all the old players still call me 'Les' to this day.
Peter Bennett

Ernie was great. I played and coached with him at West Ham. When I joined the club he was just coming out of the army. There was Ernie and George Taylor vying for the first team shirt. He was very friendly with Dick Walker, they were great pals.
Jim Barrett

Ernie said to me that once I had established myself as centre forward for West Ham then I'd be the club's striker for the next 10 years.
Micky Beesley

Everyone loved Ernie. I didn't hear a bad word about him. He was never down. To all intents and purposes he was a goalkeeping coach and I had never heard of such a thing. He was probably the first.
Bobby Gould

...and the final word goes to Ron Boyce;
If Ernie was here now I'm fairly certain he would find some little fault with Bobby Moore and go on about that. He didn't really have a good word for anyone but that was Ernie. There was no harm intended but he wasn't the type to say; 'He was marvellous!' He was more likely to say '£45 quid a week for him! You've got to be joking!'

The only players he ever said anything good about were old Dick Walker and Lenny Goulden. He absolutely loved them both.

Ernie in action with Malcolm Allison in close attendance.

2 – JOHN BOND

December 17, 1932 – September 25, 2012

Born: Dedham, Essex

Position: Right-back

Games played with Bobby Moore: 156 (1958-65)

Games played for West Ham United: 429 (1951-65)

Honours with Bobby Moore:

1964 FA Cup winner

1964 FA Charity Shield (shared with Liverpool)

Jonathan Frederick Bond was one of the great characters at West Ham United and served the club with honours over a 16 year period from 1950-1966. He played at right-back but on several occasions fulfilled the role of a very capable, deputy striker. In fact, John scored a hat-trick in a 4-2 victory over Chelsea at the Boleyn Ground in February 1960 – it was the first hat-trick Bobby Moore saw scored by a Hammer in the first team.

Eight years older than Bobby, John developed a lasting friendship with his club captain. Nicknamed 'Muffin' on account of his ferocious, mule-like, kicking ability, John had been playing for the first team since 1952, a full six years before Bobby broke into the first team. Indeed, at the time of Bobby's debut, John had already played almost 170 games for the club.

John signed professional forms for West Ham United on September 9, 1950, after former manager Charlie Paynter recommended him to newly appointed manager, Ted Fenton.

Bond made his league debut at Highfield Road, Coventry, on February 9, 1952. In 1955 he first partnered Noel Cantwell in what was to become one of the most fondly regarded scoring full-back partnerships in the club's history. Former team-mate, Eddie Presland, recalls John and Noel going together like 'fish and chips.'

The right back's eight goals during 1957-58 played a big part in the team's long-awaited promotion to the top flight. He ended up scoring 33 league goals in 382 league appearance for the club.

Muffin's crowning moment in the claret and blue came in 1964, when the Hammers overcame Preston North End, 3-2, in the FA Cup final. At the time, he was the longest-serving player on the club's books. In various interviews, John was also very fond of his one and only goal in Europe – a 30-yard strike against Sparta Prague in the successful European Cup Winners Cup campaign of 1964-65. Sadly, John missed the final due to injury and Joe Kirkup took his place.

On May 11, 1966 the club honoured John with a testimonial. He had signed for Frank O'Farrell's Torquay United just a few weeks earlier.

John qualified as a Football Association coach whilst at West Ham, which would keep him in good stead after his playing days. His knowledge, experience and larger than life character and irrepressible optimism served him well, primarily during his managerial career at Bournemouth, Norwich City and Manchester City, respectively.

John Bond passed away on September 25, 2012, after a battling against prostate cancer. We extend our gratitude to his lovely wife, Janet, for the following recollections:

When Bobby Moore first joined West Ham he roomed with my John. They were a good match because John's mother Lily Kate was pristine in everything she did and John was the same. He would bring his washing home folded up and everything had to be immaculate. Sometimes, he would come home and start re-arranging my earrings and necklace on my bedside table. I would ask him what he was doing but he would just laugh. Whenever we visited a friend's house John would wait for them to leave the room before levelling up a picture! He would tell me how Bobby would arrange all his loose change and I bet Bobby was telling Tina the same things about John!

John and I were very close to Bobby and Tina and we would go round to their house and wait for them to get ready to go out on a Saturday night. John was a bit impatient and would say: 'Come on, Mooro!' before sitting down and keeping his eye on their cat, which was called Pele. John didn't like cats and one night Pele jumped on his lap and tore a hole in his best suit.

West Ham went on tour to America in the early 60s and the wives stayed at home to look after the children. I used to get on well with Tina, Lisa Standen and Doreen Brabrook. We decided to have our own holiday so we packed up the kids, the dogs and the kitchen sink and went to Margate for a week. The boys couldn't believe it but we had such fun.

Both Bobby and John worshipped Noel Cantwell. In later life, when Noel was very ill, he was asked to take part in a television documentary about Bobby Moore but he didn't want to do it because of his illness. His wife Maggie called up John and asked if he would talk to Noel about doing it because she knew he would listen to John. In the end John went over to their house and they filmed Noel and him together. It's a lovely moment with the pair of them reminiscing about their days at West Ham.

Noel was a Catholic and he would drag John to midnight mass at Christmas. He was single when we first met him and he used to come out with us. Anyway, one night he kept saying: 'Let's go up west to the Dorchester Hotel' but John never wanted to go all that way. Noel was adamant because he had met Maggie, his future wife, who was the resident singer in the hotel. She used to finish at 1am and Noel would meet her. We all loved Maggie's voice and once at a party at Bobby and Tina's house, the boys would wind up Noel by getting Maggie to stand on a chair and sing every Protestant song she knew!

When our son Kevin had finished playing for Seattle Sounders in the North American Soccer League we went to watch the New York Cosmos play. Before the game the teams came out and kicked loads of footballs up in the stands and Kevin caught one. After the game, I was standing near the dressing room with the ball and who should come along but Pele. Well, I thought it's now or never and asked him to sign it for Kevin. We had a chat and I said that my husband played football with a very good friend of his. He asked who it was and I said: 'Bobby Moore'. Well, no sooner had I said it than he took the ball and got it signed by Chinaglia, Carlos Alberto and all the others playing for the Cosmos at the time. When he returned it he asked me to give Bobby his warmest regards. Kevin has still got the ball.

When John was manager of Bournemouth he arranged a big charity sportsman's ball and Bobby and Tina came along to that. They were always helping each other out.

John loved Bobby and talked about him wherever he went. He always said that winning the FA Cup with West Ham was his proudest achievement in football.

I miss John terribly, he was such a big man and we were blessed with a long, happy life together.
Janet Bond

The following player recollections will add further insight into the type of character Bobby Moore would have remembered.

A terrific full-back with a tremendous kick. Another of the club's great characters and always had the habit of squeezing his nose and rubbing his face. A great striker of the ball.
Sir Geoff Hurst

The thing with Bondy was that he knew the people in charge

John's finest moment in the West Ham shirt.

of him were not very good and he said what he thought. Ted Fenton had this megaphone which he used to bark orders with from the stand and John used to tell him to stick it up his arse! He was so unruly at that time and it took Ron Greenwood to get the best out of Bondy.
John Cartwright

I remember we played Notts County after West Ham had sold Ken Tucker to them. He was in the line-up to face us and Bondy was in the dressing room saying: 'Don't worry about Tucker, I'll have him. He's only got one leg and I'll put the other one into touch'. We ended up losing 1-4 with Ken scoring one and setting up two!
Harry Obeney

Coach Bill Robinson (right) puts John Bond, Bobby Moore, John Dick and Vic Keeble through their paces.

They called him Muffin because he had a kick like a mule and he hated it. I only played six times for West Ham in 1960 but John played up front and scored in one of them – Blackpool in a 3-3 draw. Bobby Moore marked Stanley Matthews in that game.
Peter Shearing

I was a cheeky little sod with Bondy. They played him up front even though his regular position was right-back. The 1959 youth team had beaten Aston Villa in the quarter final and I had scored a couple. I was in the bath and Bondy walked in and I shouted: 'That's how you play centre-forward, Muffin!' He put me in my place with a few well-chosen words! He tried to take me to Bournemouth as a coach but I was only 29 at the time and wanted to carry on playing.
Micky Beesley

West Ham sent me out on loan to Torquay and I used to spend a lot of time with John. He would drive me down there in his Jaguar. I also played for him at Bournemouth and one day I went to see a specialist because I was having a problem with my back. They took some x-rays and when I went for the results the doctor simply asked me if I could do anything else other than football. It wasn't very tactful but he said I would

end up in a wheelchair if I carried on playing. John was terrific about it and helped to arrange a testimonial for me. John called up West Ham and they brought a team down to play, Mooro, Hursty, the lot. I couldn't play because of my back but the boys really looked after me.
Bill Kitchener

John Bond was my favourite player when I was a kid at school. I used to go over to Plashet Park with my friend, Terry Campbell, and like most kids we would call ourselves after a famous footballer. Terry would be Noel Cantwell and I would be John Bond. I loved the way Bondy ran and the way he struck the ball. There was an air of arrogance and confidence about him when he played and he was the first player who caught my eye. I always remember in the warm-up before a game he would kick the ball up in the air and sit on it as it came down.
Roger Cross

When West Ham got relegated in 1978 I didn't want to play in a lower division and I knew John Bond was interested in me at Norwich so I went to see him and he offered me a good deal. On the way home I realised I was an East End boy and

not a farmer and I didn't fancy the distance so I stayed at West Ham. It was a reality check really and made me realise just how well off I was at West Ham.
Frank Lampard

I played for John at Bournemouth in the early 1970s and he changed the club. He brought proper football to Bournemouth. There was one funny moment soon after he joined the club when he sat us all down and played the 1964 FA Cup final on the screen. West Ham beat Preston and he obviously wanted to use it as an example of how to play a good passing game and highlight the things Bobby Moore could do on a pitch. It soon became noticeable that every time Bondy got the ball he was hoofing it up field. In the end all the lads were shouting 'Boom!' every time Bondy got the ball.
Trevor Hartley

I played under John at Bournemouth. What a terrific man! He took the team on a round the world trip. We went to Iran, Singapore, Australia, New Zealand, New Caledonia, Tahiti and Los Angeles. Simply unbelievable. The spectators were wearing grass skirts and garlands in Tahiti! We lost our first game and Bondy went mad. He said we weren't going to get paid unless we won our next nine games. So we just went out and duly won our next nine games. He used to wear the best suits and smoke the biggest cigars and he always made sure that we travelled in the best coach. We felt unbeatable playing for John.
Keith Miller

He came down here and managed Shrewsbury Town but it didn't work out that well. The bookmakers were pleased he came, though!
Jimmy Lindsay

John was a good player – calm, cool and collected. He was my best mate and I was his. We roomed together and were two of a type. We used to take the piss out of people and they would take it out of us but we didn't care. He was a great laugh. My wife Doreen and I would go round to John and Janet's house two or three times a week for a drink or a meal. We used to have such a laugh.

One night Bondy asked me to go to Walthamstow greyhounds because he had been given a dog to back. I drove and it was a filthy night, icy, rainy and foggy. I lost control of the car and smashed into a pylon. I was wedged in and John could just about squeeze out. Anyway, I eventually got out and looked around for Bondy but he was gone! He had ran back home to avoid the police and any publicity. Ron would have gone mad with us but we managed to keep it out of the press. I still don't know if that dog won!
Peter Brabrook

John (left) at the unveiling of the Bobby Moore statue at Wembley in 2007 with Ken Brown, Sir Geoff Hurst, Kenny Lynch and Peter Brabrook.

3 – NOEL CANTWELL
February 28, 1932 – September 8, 2005

Born: Cork, Republic of Ireland
Position: Left-back
Games played with Bobby Moore: 27 (1958-60)
Games played for West Ham United: 263 (1952-65)

Noel Eucharia Cornelius Cantwell was Bobby Moore's great friend and had the honour of being best man when he wed Tina in 1962 at the Church of St Clemence, Ilford. They played 27 times together in the claret and blue before Noel's transfer to Manchester United in November 1960. The experience was priceless to Bobby and he learned lessons about the great game which would serve him well throughout his career.

Best man Noel at Bobby and Tina's wedding.

Whether it was on the training ground, field of play or around the salt and pepper pots in Cassettari's Cafe, Cantwell would have been sharing his deeply held beliefs on the game. Both Cantwell and Moore were greatly impressed by Malcolm Allison, one of the most influential players in West Ham's history.

Big Mal imbibed those keen to learn with a simple concept – that attacking football should start with the goalkeeper and flow through defence, midfield and attack with the ultimate objective of breaching the opposition's goal. Noel himself was a great reader of the game, knew where to be on the pitch, which players to watch and where to put the ball. Perhaps most significant of all Malcolm's advice was the wholehearted belief that there was no substitute for hard work and ball practice. Bobby Moore was his most dedicated student.

Noel was almost nine years older than Bobby and had been at the club since 1953, eventually playing over 250 games. He recommended Moore over Allison which gave the 17-year-old blond lad from Barking his first game for West Ham United.

By the time Bobby set foot on the hallowed turf at the Boleyn Ground for his debut against Manchester United, Noel had already played over 150 games for the club and was an established Republic of Ireland International. He would eventually gain 17 caps whilst a Hammer.

Noel lifted the FA Cup as captain of Manchester United in 1963, one year before Bobby emulated the achievement with West Ham United. They remained great friends throughout Bobby's lifetime. The Hammers were blessed to have Cantwell, Moore and Bonds serve as club captains over a 30 year period.

Noel Cantwell passed away on September 8, 2005 and we owe an enormous debt of thanks to both his wife Maggie and their daughter Kate, for the kind loan of photographs from their private collection. Personal thanks are also extended to Noel's very good friend, Dave Spurgeon, who shared the following recollections.

Noel used to tell a story about the time when, after the World Cup, Bobby put it to Ron Greenwood that West Ham needed to build a team to consistently challenge for honours and one that was more difficult to beat. Bobby knew from his

Captain Noel being held aloft by his team-mates after promotion in 1958. L-R Musgrove (partly obscured), Fenton, Pyke, Bond, Keeble, Smith and Nelson. Kneeling down are Grice and Gregory.

England training with Jack Charlton, Paul Reaney and Norman Hunter that the versatile Paul Madeley of Leeds United was frustrated at not being able to establish a regular first team place despite excellent performances at either right-back, centre-half or in a midfield ball-winning role. Bobby clearly rated the skill and attitude of Madeley who was a good tackler, good passer of the ball and had the hard 'they shall not pass' streak instilled by Leeds manager, Don Revie.

According to Noel, Bobby told Ron that if Leeds were approached, he was certain that Madeley would jump at the chance to sign for the Hammers. Once again, however, he was rebuffed and no signings were made to beef up the defence until the 1967-68 season, when Bonds, John Cushley and goalkeeper Bobby Ferguson were signed. It is interesting to note that in Jeff Powell's book on Bobby Moore, Mooro named Madeley as his preferred right-back in his all-time England line-up. One might have reasonably expected George Cohen or the very stylish and consistent Jimmy Armfield to have been his choice. Testimony to how much Bobby rated Madeley as a player.

During the 1965-66 season Bobby approached Ron and urged him to sign Cantwell's former Manchester United team-mate, Maurice Setters, then at Stoke City. Noel had privately sounded Maurice out and Moore went to Ron knowing Maurice would gladly join West Ham. Ron rebuffed Bobby by saying somewhat curtly: 'Not interested, Bobby, we don't kick people.' The first thing Noel did when taking over as manager at Coventry City at the start of the 1967-68 season was to sign Maurice Setters.

Once Bobby had committed his loyalty to the club with a new contract he urged Ron Greenwood to sign two other players before the start of the 1966-67 season. Bobby knew that his great pal Johnny Byrne was never going to recapture his pre-1965 knee injury form and that was sadly to be the case. Bobby was also greatly impressed by a classy young centre-forward from Sheffield United named Mick Jones, averaging nearly a goal every other game in a very ordinary Blades' side.

Jones was still only 21 in 1966 and to quote Noel, Bobby

said to Greenwood: 'This boy has great potential, great attitude and would kill to play alongside Geoff Hurst to further his international chances. And by the way, Peter Bonetti is in a contract dispute with Chelsea and thinking of putting in a transfer request. That's why Tommy Docherty has signed Alex Stepney from Millwall, as an immediate replacement.'

History tells us that Jones forged a lethal partnership with Allan Clarke at Leeds United and Bonetti resolved his pay dispute with Chelsea. Noel and Bobby would reminisce about a West Ham team that could have included Jones and Hurst up front, with Madeley alongside Bobby at the back and Bonetti behind them. As the old song goes: 'Fortunes always hiding . . .'

When, in 2003, Prince Andrew unveiled The Champions statue opposite The Boleyn pub, both Noel and England World Cup-winner Ray Wilson were chatting together in the lounge back at the ground. Ray was reflecting on his Everton days and saying how they loved to play West Ham because it would be a pure football skill contest and Everton had skilful players and played the same attacking, entertaining ethos as Ron Greenwood. 'The big difference was that when we had to mix it against the likes of Leeds,' said Ray. 'We had players like Jimmy Gabriel and John Morrissey who could do just that, as well as be skilful and creative with the ball, but West Ham never did.'

Noel could only agree, because he often reflected on his own West Ham playing days when we returned to the old First Division in 1958: 'When we went to places like Bolton, Burnley and Blackburn, they would f*****g batter us! They saw us as 'southern softies', as aristocrats with our continental low-cut boots, short-sleeve shirts and short cut shorts and loved to turn West Ham over.'

After he had retired in the 70s, Bill Nicholson told Noel that he could have persuaded the Spurs board to pay £160,000 for Bobby Moore – staggering in the context that the £110,000 Everton paid to Blackpool for Alan Ball in 1966 set a British transfer record that had the football press of the day making sensational comments about the size of the fee and asking the question: 'What next . . . a £125,000 player?' Well, that came two years later courtesy of the Spurs' cheque book, when Nicholson signed the England Under-23 centre-forward Martin Chivers from Southampton.

Nicholson told the Spurs board, when courting Bobby's services, that the defensive rock of 21-year-old keeper Pat Jennings, centre-half Mike England and Bobby Moore would form a defence that no amount of money should be able to buy and, according to Noel, that prospect clearly excited Bobby.

In the late 1960s Matt Busby had informally offered Noel a coaching role at Old Trafford, indicating that Noel would be his successor. Based on the trust of this information Noel

Iron Man Noel supporting Phil Woosnam, Andy Smillie, John Cartwright, Mike Grice and Malcolm Musgrove.

actually declined the offer to manage Aston Villa, who had just been relegated from Division One. Such impending changes often sparked dressing room revolts and several players, fearing for their United futures under a Cantwell-led regime, voiced serious concerns to their manager. Busby eventually persuaded Noel to take the manager's job at Coventry City to 'cut your teeth on' in readiness for the United role. As we know, that coveted position subsequently went to another ex-Hammer, Frank O'Farrell and Noel was never appointed.

At a former Manchester United players' dinner in 1999, the question was posed to Noel: 'What would you have done if you had taken over the manager's position in 1972?'

Noel answered that he would have signed Bobby Moore knowing that West Ham were due to release him on a free transfer at the end of the 1972-73 season, as had been agreed with Ron Greenwood. Noel would have negotiated a nominal transfer fee to have brought that forward and made sure his pal got a signing-on fee as well. He would have also approached Stoke City to enquire after one of their recent signings, a certain Geoff Hurst, and would have gone to Coventry City for two young players he nurtured in his time there, Willie Carr and Dennis Mortimer.

Not so well known is the influence Noel had on how Bobby wore his kit. The habit that Bobby had of rolling the waistband of his shorts over to shorten the length came from Noel. After West Ham adopted the more continental style kit of short sleeve, V-neck cotton shirts and shorter shorts in 1956, Noel liked his as short fitting as possible, to the degree that his wife, Maggie, actually cut and sewed Noel's shorts to shorten them.

Noel even took his own shorts on international duty. He often said that the ones provided for the Irish team were extra-large in size, making some of the smaller players like Johnny Giles look like they were wearing cut-down parachutes! Smart and immaculate personal appearance on and off the pitch was second nature to both Noel and Malcolm Allison, and a habit Bobby easily followed.

Bobby and Malcolm actually played pool and darts several times for Noel's pub teams when he and Maggie ran the New Inn in Peterborough.

When asked about his greatest disappointment in football, Noel replied that it was Ireland's failure to qualify for the 1966 World Cup in England, after losing a group play-off to Spain, 1-0, in Paris. His dream for that tournament was to potentially walk out at Wembley leading Ireland against England, looking across to the opposing captain whom he had nurtured as a 17-year-old boy at West Ham United.
Dave Spurgeon

Following are memories from Noel's former West Ham team-mates and close friends:

Noel was a fantastic full-back and a great captain. A steal at £29,000 when he went to Manchester United and was yet another Hammer who got heavily into coaching. I met up with him on a few occasions later in life. A smashing guy.
Sir Geoff Hurst

We all called him 'SOS'. Noel was a brilliant fella. I hadn't been long in the team and we had a tour of Ireland. Anyway, one night everyone

had gone to bed and he knocked on my door and said, come on we're going out. Well, we went out and everyone seemed to know him and was buying us drinks all night. I don't know how we got back. It was lovely to be with Noel.
Ken Brown

Noel was a lovely guy, a super guy. He was hard but had a lot of skill and was very knowledgeable.
Vic Keeble

Noel was a quiet guy that thought a lot about the game. He had a lot of time for people and got on well with Malcolm Allison.
John Cartwright

I played for Noel when he managed Peterborough. He was a brilliant manager and we had some fun. I remember once we beat Wycombe Wanderers in the FA Cup. I think they were in the Southern League at the time but on the way back Noel told the directors we were going to stop off for a drink at the Haycock Hotel which was a top class hotel. It was as though we had won the final itself!
Dave Llewelyn

One of the chaps from my golf club went back home from South Africa many years ago and bumped into Noel at a train station on his way to watch an international game. Noel took the time to quickly write me a lovely letter which my friend brought back with him.
Andy Malcolm

Noel's favourite photo – with son Robbie and great friends, Malcolm Allison (far left) and Bobby Moore.

4 – ANDY MALCOLM
May 4, 1933 – December 26, 2013

Born: Upton Park, London

Position: Wing-half/Midfield

Games played with Bobby Moore: 64 (1958-61)

Games played for West Ham United: 306 (1953-62)

Andrew 'Andy' Malcolm won the inaugural Hammer of the Year award in 1958. He had been an ever-present player in the club's promotion season and would eventually play in over 300 league and FA Cup games for the club.

Malcolm was eight years older than Bobby Moore and had been in the first team for five seasons by the time Moore made his debut against Manchester United in September 1958.

Malcolm's football journey saw him captain Romford Schoolboys and Essex County. He also gained three England Youth caps – the first ever gained by a West Ham United player.

Andy signed professional forms for West Ham in the summer of 1950 and made his first team debut on December 5, 1953 at home against Notts County.

He was one of a very few number of Hammers to have played in over 100 consecutive games for the club, being ever present in 1957-58, 1958-59 and lining up in the first 26 games of 1959-60. Interestingly, it was Bobby Moore who first wore Andy's Number 4 shirt at the end of that run – versus Bolton Wanderers on January 23, 1960.

Malcolm laid a strong claim to being the hardest player West Ham United has ever produced. He had a stout reputation for nullifying the attacking intentions of star players such as

Training at Grange Farm with Dave Dunmore and a young Bobby Moore.

Johnny Haynes, Jimmy Greaves and Denis Law.

Unsurprisingly, when Ron Greenwood joined West Ham in 1961 Andy's very physical approach to the game did not form part of his style plan. He was soon transferred to Chelsea for £10,000. Blues striker Ron Tindall also joined the Hammers as part of the deal. Andy was a year short of what would have been a richly deserved testimonial.

When researching this book, Andy was so very generous with his time and humble in his manner. His recollections of Bobby were low key and genuine and the several conversations we shared are a personal highlight of this journey. He was extremely modest and his trademark laugh was never too far away. It was such a blow when the news broke that he had died at his home in Port Elizabeth on December 26, 2013. He was 80. Andy was the ninth Hammer from Bobby Moore's debut line-up to pass away. Both Ken Brown and Vic Keeble continue to carry the flag.

I was a senior pro when Bobby Moore joined the Upton Park ground staff. The club had an influx of young boys who would soon define the future of West Ham United and England. There was Bobby Moore, Geoff Hurst, Martin Peters, Ronnie Boyce, John Lyall, John Cartwright, Andy Smillie, Brian Dear and quite a few others who were really good for their age. It was no surprise when they all went in to the first team. Those days seem to have gone and you don't see so many youngsters coming through at West Ham.

They were good boys, they knew what they were doing and Bobby always had this aura about him. He looked like he was going to be a good player and he became exactly that. You could see he had a certain class about him even at that young age. He was keen to learn and improve himself.

After West Ham won promotion up at Middlesbrough in 1958, there was a tremendous crowd waiting for us on the platform when we returned to King's Cross Station. I'll never forget that. So when Bobby got into the team the following season the club was beginning

to go places. I played in Bobby's first game – at home to Manchester United – but I don't recall too much about it.

I would say that Bobby came into a very good team and he was training and learning from some of the great players and characters at the club. John Bond, Noel Cantwell and Ernie Gregory would have looked after him. Both John Dick and Vic Keeble were a really good pairing up front, so he would have always had something to defend. I don't think John ever missed with his left foot and Vic knew how to head a ball. I think the 101 goals we scored that season is still a record for the club.

Andy on the ball.

I was a lot older than Bobby, so didn't really see much of him and soon after he started playing regularly Ron Greenwood sold me to Chelsea. I hope I set a good example. I was an honest, down to earth pro. I always wanted to be a footballer and I looked after it once I got it, if you know what I mean. Playing in the Eastern Counties league as a 15-year-old helped toughen me up. I used to get knocked about quite a bit and always vowed that when I got a bit stronger I would give some back. It was nothing dirty but I always got stuck in because of how I was kicked about in the Eastern Counties League.

Bobby learned a lot from his youth team days, too, and that experience toughened him up a bit.

Going into the Army also did me a world of good because I was 10 stone when I went in and over 11 stone when I came out, so I had a bigger presence about me.

When I tackled I was always fairly certain I would come away with the ball. Bobby was a strong player, tough in the tackle and keen to learn as much as he could.

I'm so pleased that I played with Bobby because he went on to do so much for West Ham and England and you have to admire somebody like that. I wish I had stayed but Ron Greenwood didn't want me and I've never stayed anywhere that I am not wanted.

All the players and fans from that time always comment on my marking of the great players such as Johnny Haynes and Jimmy Greaves. 'Haynesy' played over here in South Africa at the end of his career and I bumped into him once at Johannesburg airport. He came over to me and joked: 'You're still following me after all these years!'

The final conversation with Andy concluded with his reflections on his time at West Ham. They resonate with the classic West Ham player mentality, the local lad who simply fell in love with everything claret and blue…

West Ham started me off in my life. All my family were Hammers supporters, my father and his brother, so I was brought up in that line. As a schoolboy, I had the chance to sign for other clubs but my father wouldn't let me go anywhere other than West Ham. I felt at home there and it didn't feel like you were going to work every day.

I don't know if I fulfilled all that I should have done but I did my best and had a good time along the way. You can't ask for more than that really.
Andy Malcolm

When sharing the news of Andy's passing with Jimmy Greaves, his old adversary on the field and close friend off it, he was very keen to share some warm and amusing memories of Andy. It is therefore appropriate to share Jimmy's own recollections along with the comments of Andy's team-mates who recall him with such deep fondness.

Unlike the majority of West Ham footballers, Andy was quite a hard man but a good player with it, a very good player. He had this wonderful trick whereby he would grab your shirt and stand on your foot at corners so that you couldn't do anything. We actually became good friends after our careers had ended because he ran a pub in Maldon and I used to pop in there from time to time. I'm saddened by the news but 80 is a good innings and as I stand here in torrential rain walking my dog, Lester, I realise he did the right thing in going to South Africa. Eusebio has also just passed on and he was another that I played against and it is one of those things that time marches on and we all march on with it. All I can say is that it was a privilege to know those guys.
Jimmy Greaves

No one could tackle like he could. He was so thorough and methodical. He also taught me and a few of the lads to drive. He was so patient. He was sharp Andy and had a great laugh and would find the silliest things to laugh about.

When we played Fulham it was always Andy's job to mark Johnny Haynes. Well, Andy would just walk through him and put him on the floor. I remember one time I helped Haynsey up and he moaned; 'It's like being marked by a London Bus!' Andy used to suffer from a bit of gout – It must have been something you got from pulling shirts!

The combative Andy Malcolm.

We were very close friends and it is a sad, sad loss. In 2014, my wife and I had been toying with the idea of visiting him in South Africa as part of my 80th Birthday celebrations.
Ken Brown

Andy had great balance, was never dirty, and always got his foot in where it mattered. He was so very strong and I remember when we played five-a-side I would always want to be in his team. If you were on opposite sides you knew not to dwell too long on the ball, that's for sure.

He had a lovely way about him and off the pitch you could enjoy his company. I have a framed photo of the 57-58 promotion team in my hallway and I look at it every time I put on my coat so I often think about Andy.
Bill Lansdowne

Andy was a really tough tackler and I would back him against anyone. I remember once we were playing a pre-season game and I got hit hard and was concussed on the pitch. When Andy and Ken came over to see how I was I said I was seeing two of everyone. 'Kick the one that moves,' was Andy's response!
Joe Kirkup

Andy was the master of the block tackle.
Eddie Presland

There was a Combination game down at Upton Park between West Ham and Spurs and their inside forward, Tommy Harmer, asked me before the game if Andy Malcolm was playing and I said he was. Anyway, Tommy didn't bother coming out to play! He watched it from the player's pen.

Andy was a first class bloke. He was great mates with Ken Brown.
Terry McDonald

Andy was a great favourite with the West Ham crowd, there is no question about that and he was the best marker in the game at the time. You could stick him on Stanley Matthews and he wouldn't give him a kick.
Vic Keeble

I remember playing for Spurs against West Ham in the 1950s and Bill Nicholson said to me, I want you to stay with Andy Malcolm and don't let him have a kick. Now I'm a striker so I said: 'He should be marking me!' But that just shows how much Bill Nicholson feared Andy.
Dave Dunmore

I liked to run with the ball from deep. I had a bit of pace and loved to score goals. Against Andy I would be flying through the middle, when, suddenly, he would grab my shirt and I would be in the air with my legs still running like some cartoon character!
Harry Obeney

My second and final game for West Ham was up at Blackburn and we got whacked 1-4. I remember Andy Malcolm taking umbrage against one of their strikers and said to Ken Brown: 'If you don't run your studs down his shins I'm going to kick you.' Within five minutes, Ken took out one of their players who limped off.
Mike Beesley

He was a player you simply had to have in your side. You looked for Andy's name on the team sheet even before your own sometimes. Regardless of the opposition you knew he would stop them playing and win every battle. He was a smashing guy and really good with the young players. He would give them his time which meant a lot.
John Cartwright

Andy often worked on his car, an MG Magnet, in the forecourt of the ground. He was a fantastic guy and wore the old style boots which went above the ankle. You could see opposition forwards jumping out of tackles when Andy was around.
Brian Dear

At home in South Africa 2013.

5 – KEN BROWN

Born: Forest Gate, London, February 16, 1934

Position: Centre-half

Games played with Bobby Moore: 275 (1958-67)

Games played for West Ham United: 456 (1953-67)

Honours with Bobby Moore
Hammer of the Year 1959
1964 FA Cup winner
1964 FA Charity Shield (Shared with Liverpool)
1965 European Cup Winners' Cup winner
1966 League Cup finalist

Kenneth Brown played more games with Bobby Moore than any other defender and was voted Hammer of the Year in 1959 – Bobby's first season in the team. He was also the first West Ham United player to win an England cap after Bobby had made his Hammers' debut – against Northern Ireland at Wembley on November 18, 1959. It was Ken's one and only international cap and the memory is sweetened by a 2-1 victory.

Brown is one of West Ham's magnificent seven who managed to win both the FA Cup and European Cup Winners Cup. He is joined in this club by Moore, Jim Standen, Jack Burkett, Ron Boyce, Geoff Hurst and John Sissons.

He initially played schoolboy football in Dagenham with a team called Neville United and signed professional forms for the Hammers on October 16, 1951, aged 17.

The reliable centre-half's great mentor was Dick Walker who, along with Malcolm Allison, wore the Number 5 shirt before Brown made it his own. His first game for the club was against Rotherham United at Millmoor on February 21, 1953, over five years before Moore would be making his debut. According to fellow defender, Jack Burkett, such seniority earned Brown the nickname: 'Grandad.'

Brown quickly established himself in the first team and missed only one game during the promotion season of 1957-58. He was ever-present during West Ham's first full campaign back in the top flight after an absence of 25 years. The general view from his team-mates is that he was as steady as can be and would win most headers. He wouldn't complicate things or dwell on the ball and would despatch it quickly and cleanly. Former team-mate, Eddie Presland, remembers another feature of Brown's game. 'One of the things Bobby would remember about Ken would be how he always ran out before a game to *The Post Horn Gallop* which is a fantastic piece of music. Ken was always the last one out and would sprint so hard across the pitch he almost ended up in the Chicken Run!'

After 16 years at West Ham as a player, Brown joined John Bond at Torquay United under the management of another former team mate, Frank O'Farrell. It was July 1967 and the

Ken and Bobby clearing their lines at Everton.

Ken Brown wins his solitary England cap against Northern Ireland at Wembley in 1959. He is shaking hands with Field Marshal Montgomery.

transfer fee was £4,000. His appearance record at West Ham was 456 games and he was rewarded with a well-deserved testimonial match.

He maintained his links with the Hammers by running the pools promotion for several years after his transfer to the West Country club.

In 1970 he once again joined forces with his lifelong friend, John Bond, this time at AFC Bournemouth. Fellow coach at Dean Court, Trevor Hartley, remembers Ken with fondness: 'He was great for the spirit of the club, a real joker who kept everyone happy. He was the jovial one and you felt like nothing could go wrong at the club if you had Ken there.'

Brown is another former Hammer to win a trophy as a club manager. It came when he was in charge of Norwich City against Sunderland in the 1985 League Cup final at Wembley – an own goal securing both the cup and a lifetime of richly deserved accolade.

Nowadays, Ken still lives in Norwich with his lovely wife, Elaine, and often returns to both the Boleyn Ground and Carrow Road to watch his former teams.

His 80th Birthday celebrations in February 2014 included a mesmerising book of tributes, arranged by his wife, from all those that have admired his contribution to football down the years. These included a prominent message of good luck from Sir Alex Ferguson. However, it was a line from Ron Boyce which caught the eye: 'West Ham failed to win anything for many a year after 1965 and, in my opinion, this was due to not finding a replacement for Ken.' Fitting recognition for a true legend.

Sir Geoff Hurst's description of Ken will also chime loudly with all who know him: 'Browny is a really likeable guy who enjoys life and always has a smile on his face.'

Ken and Elaine renewed their wedding vows in the Caribbean in 2014 and they continue to enjoy travelling as part of their full life.

I am really chuffed to know that as a defender I played more games with Bobby Moore than any other. The reason I played so many games with him was because I didn't have to do anything – Mooro did it all!

I was just a defender, a safety first type of player, but Mooro liked to bring it down and play. He would never just wallop it away. So many times I would run round the back to cover him just in case he didn't control the ball but he never missed it.

As one of the senior players at the club I would like to think a bit of my experience rubbed off on Bobby but he was such an extraordinary talent there wasn't much he didn't possess. His awareness was so much better than everyone else.

Bobby was very quiet about everything, he didn't shout and holler and even when you made a mistake he talked to you calmly and made sure it didn't happen again. I suspect many West Ham fans will recall Preston's second goal in the 1964 FA Cup final. Alex Dawson beat me in the air to put them ahead and you can see Bobby just preparing to resume matters. Not a word of criticism and that is how it always was. For the record, I don't think I get enough credit for setting up Geoff Hurst's goal to make it 2-2!

Walking out at Wembley for that FA Cup final was a magnificent experience. The noise of the crowd hit me like an electric shock and it didn't seem to stop throughout the entire game. It was a tremendous feeling and something I will never forget. I followed Bobby up the steps that day and carried the base of the FA Cup for him.

Ken and Bobby wearing the classic hooped shirt.

One of West Ham's magnificent seven.

Bobby could sometimes be a bit of a loner but you will be hard pressed to find one person who didn't like him. Even after he lifted the World Cup there was no superior air about him. There was no big ego or me, me, me, mentality – far from it.

He used to get so much mail through his fan club that I would help out on occasion by signing his name on photographs. Yes, I hold up my hand. I did forge Bobby Moore's signature but we wanted to ensure every fan got a reply. I became very good at it and you couldn't really tell the difference between my 'Bobby Moore' signature and the great man's actual autograph. I had no idea at the time that some of these would appear on the various auction sites like eBay. Sorry about that!

Most of the players have sold their medals and I couldn't tell you where Bobby's medals are nowadays but a few years back I bought a safe in which to store all my important things. Frustratingly, I've lost the code and can't get in. It's one of those that blanks out once you try a certain number of times – so yes, I've still got my medals but I just can't access them!

I don't have a particular favourite out of the two Wembley finals that I played in. Any final you win is simply fantastic. We had a really good team with the world's best captain and it was great for me because I played my first game for West Ham in 1952, some 12 years before the FA Cup final, so I was just happy to be part of Ron Greenwood's plans.

Back then, West Ham played the Post Horn Gallop as the players came out of the tunnel before a home game. It was such a great piece of inspirational music and really fired you up. Bobby would punch a ball in the air and trot out to warm up but I would love to sprint as hard as I could across the pitch. They should bring back the Post Horn Gallop.

On one occasion all the lads left me to run out first while they all stayed in the tunnel. I went galloping out across the pitch only to look back to see them all laughing at me! There were some cheeky buggers in that team.

Mooro really enjoyed the end of season overseas tours. We went to America a few times and he absolutely loved it because nobody knew him there and he could really relax. He wasn't being pulled this way and that for tickets and autographs and you could see just how much more relaxed he became. He was a different person and could do whatever he wanted without being under the gaze of close public scrutiny.

He was just a great fella. His dress was immaculate whether it was a football strip or a suit. He was neat and tidy on and off the pitch. Ron Greenwood used to say to us: 'Control, pass and run' – and Bobby could do two out of three!

Ken Brown

Another fine landmark – Ken turned 80 on February 16, 2014.

6 – MIKE GRICE
November 3, 1931-August, 2002

Born: Woking, Surrey

Position: Right-wing

Games played with Bobby Moore: 41 (1958-61)

Games played for West Ham United: 150 (1955-61)

West Ham United F.C.
BOLEYN GROUND, UPTON PARK, LONDON

Football League—Division One
WEST HAM UNITED
versus
MANCHESTER UNITED
MONDAY 8th SEPTEMBER 1958

Block D

Row G   Seat No. 32

This portion to be
retained as a   **Price 6/-**
PASS OUT   E. CHAPMAN, *Secretary*

Michael John Grice was the first right-winger Bobby Moore lined up with in the senior team. He began a lineage that would include both Peter Brabrook and Harry Redknapp.

Grice was nine years older than Moore and was signed from Colchester United by manager Ted Fenton in 1956. He was billed as a replacement for the great Harry Hooper who had been sold to Wolverhampton Wanderers against the wishes of the claret and blue faithful.

It was hardly surprising that he endured a torrid reception at the club and it took a long while before he won over the fans. By the time he played with Moore in September 1958 he was part of the much heralded promotion team

Mike scores against Manchester United with Malcolm Musgrove and Bobby Moore in the distance – April 1960.

Taking on the Arsenal defence.

of 1957-58. Indeed, Grice was ever present during that memorable campaign.

Sir Geoff Hurst describes him as: 'A tricky winger, very quick and instrumental in the 1958 promotion team. A quiet fella.'

West Ham scored 101 league goals during the promotion campaign, largely due to the supply from both Grice and his fellow winger on the left flank, Malcolm Musgrove. The prolific strike force of John Dick and Vic Keeble had never had it so good.

Prior to his time at Colchester United Mike had started his football journey with both Lowestoft and Suffolk Boys. Former West Ham team-mates describe him as a quiet, well-dressed man, who had good pace and liked to stay close to the touch-line.

The sudden departure of Fenton in 1961 signalled the end of Mike's time at West Ham. It soon became clear that he was to form no part in the plans of new manager, Ron Greenwood. A brief letter from club secretary, Eddie Chapman, meant Mike's record with the Hammers would stand at: Played 150 games, scored 18 goals. Mike left his house in Caterham Avenue, Ilford, which would soon be occupied by new signing Ian Crawford – someone whom Bobby Moore would visit regularly.

Mike Grice passed away in August 2002 after personal problems resulted in him taking his own life. He was 70.

Mike's former wife, Yvonne, kindly shared the following recollections:

I met Mike when he was playing for Colchester United and I couldn't believe that people played football for a living so I was a little unimpressed by it all.

Mike played for the Army team during his national service but he was a draughtsman by trade and when he came out of the army he worked for a building firm in East Anglia and played part-time for Colchester United under Benny Fenton, Ted's brother.

We met at a local dance and everyone knew he was a footballer but I had no idea. Just like that I was dating a footballer who was signed by West Ham United.

Mike was bought to replace Harry Hooper who was very popular at West Ham and as a consequence Mike was really up against it. He received a tremendous amount of abuse from the fans who didn't take to him initially. There was one guy in particular who gave him a torrid time. He would shout from the Chicken Run: 'I'm here again, Gricey!' It was so daunting and I think it really used to get to him. Mike was not an ebullient character and although he was quite ready with a sense of humour, he was fairly quiet and could be quite deep at times. He was very reserved and wasn't the type to enter a room and introduce himself to everyone.

Mike lived in one of the many boarding houses tied to the club. A lot of West Ham United players were put up in these houses and the landladies were fantastic and so very helpful. Mike stayed with a very nice lady called Mrs Marsh in South Park Drive. She was a mother-like figure and would even clean his shoes. He used to travel back and forth to see me in Great Yarmouth. He drove a Hillman at the time which didn't have a heater so we had to wear great big overcoats to keep warm!

In 1959, a few years after Mike had joined West Ham, we were married and moved into a place in Caterham Avenue, just off Clayhall Avenue in Ilford. It was a very nice house that had been newly acquired by West Ham. Now there were two lovely old boys that worked for the club and they helped with the painting and general repair of all the players' houses. They always had their overalls on and Kenny Brown's wife, Joan, wouldn't let them eat their lunch indoors so they would have to go down to the shed! One of them had no teeth and I used to say to him; 'Len, why haven't you got any teeth?' to which he would reply; 'I'm too handsome so my wife will only let me wear them at weekends.'

Bobby and Tina weren't married when we first met them. Tina was very young, very pretty and very girly. Obviously, they both had to mature quickly. Bobby was a nice guy and had clearly been brought up very well. Mike and Bobby had the same colour hair and Tina and I were watching our blond boys running about during each game.

There were no WAGs at that time and the wives were hardly recognised by the club. Apart from a dinner at the Café Royal to celebrate the promotion in 1958 and a night out to watch West Side Story, I can't think of any other time the wives were included. I used to go to the home games with Jean Musgrove and there would be a little room at the back where we could have a cup of tea.

If Mike was here today he would have been full of admiration for Bobby Moore. We were both very upset that such a great ambassador for football died so young. It seemed as though his world-wide fame didn't make him at all temperamental which is a very fine trait, especially as there are always a lot of hangers-on around stardom. I imagine Bobby didn't suffer fools gladly but he always gave the impression of being a very fine gentleman, indeed.

There were a few events which happened while we were there, which Bobby would have doubtless been privy to. The first involved Noel Dwyer who was one of the goalkeepers at the club. He was an absolute wild one. He had a wonderful wife Jackie and I remember one particular New Year's Eve when we were all out together in a club. Noel got home very, very, late and his wife wouldn't let him in. Anyway in the ensuing row and tussle to get into the house Noel shut his wife's toe in the door and broke it. The next time we saw her she had her foot in plaster and Noel was banished from the family home for a few days.

Mike on the attack with John Dick and Dave Dunmore (far right).

Another character we used to discuss was Malcolm Allison. He was like part of the mafia, actually, and had a distasteful side to him. We much preferred Phil Woosnam, who was a really nice guy. We were very close to John and Yvonne Lyall while we were there. John used to suffer terribly from migraine. Mike and John struck up a very strong friendship. Ken Brown was another favourite of ours and played with Mike during the year they won promotion. Our daughter, Beverly, still has Mike's promotion winners' medal.

The way West Ham ended Mike's time at the club wasn't handled very well. He received a three-line letter out of the blue stating that his services were no longer required. It took him a while to recover from the shock of it all.

I have often thought that while football was Mike's life, in a way it also ruined his life. Mike could never reach the high of playing top-flight football and like so many other footballers he spent the rest of his life trying to replicate it but of course that was impossible. Everything else just felt second rate.

My theory is that if you have plenty of charisma and fine man-management skills, like John Bond and Ken Brown, you can extend your football experience through coaching and management. However, the majority of ex-players don't have those skills and life can become very hard indeed.

It was the demon drink that got Mike in the end and although we had split up in the 1980s we had always stayed in touch and had an amicable friendship. I had re-married and he was with a very nice lady so it was very sad, when in 2002, we heard the news from his brother that he had taken his own life.

Yvonne Symes

The end game.

In typical pose on the wing.

7 – JOHN SMITH
January 4, 1939-1988

Born: Shoreditch, London

Position: Wing-half

Games played with Bobby Moore: 7 (1959-60)

Games played for West Ham United: 130 (1956-60)

John Smith made the Number 6 shirt his own during Bobby Moore's first two seasons at West Ham United. It was only after he had moved to Tottenham Hotspur in 1960 that Moore wore the shirt with such distinction for the next 14 years.

His fellow team mates called him 'Smudge' and describe him as having, 'bellows for lungs,' which helped him win all the cross-country races during training. Smith joined the groundstaff in 1954 and signed professional forms two years later. He clearly impressed during his time at the club and had a reputation for being a skilful player who was tough in the tackle. He gained one England Youth cap and an England Under-23 cap, against France in November 1959.

Moore would have enjoyed John's bubbly, Cockney character and doubtless been impressed by his ability to run forever in training.

Prolific scorer Dave Dunmore joined West Ham as part of John Smith's transfer to White Hart Lane. Unfortunately, John's time at Spurs amounted to no more than 25 games although he was part of the squad which won the League and FA Cup double in 1961.

John Smith (third from the right) with the 1958 promotion winning Hammers.

John was also part of Swindon Town's team that beat Arsenal in the 1969 League Cup final at Wembley Stadium. Later in life, he became a publican but passed away in 1988, aged just 49.

We have the following recollections from his team-mates at West Ham which provide a deeper insight into the type of character Bobby Moore would have known:

I was quite close to John. He used to live in a prefab and was in the youth team just after me with players like Clive Lewis, Terry McDonald, Georgie Fenn and that crowd. He was a very good runner and when we did the cross country runs at Grange Farm, I could never beat him and would always finish second. We had a good rivalry and he would be about 10 yards ahead of me and shout out: 'Why don't you give up you little bugger!'
Joe Kirkup

John Smith was a nice lad who showed a lot of promise. I think he was a reserve for England when he was 17 or 18. He looked like he was going to be a really good player but he went to Tottenham and it never really worked out for him.
Andy Malcolm

In defence with Ernie Gregory against Chelsea.

John ended up managing in Ireland and he ran a social club over there. They absolutely loved him in that village and when he died they held a service over here but buried him in Ireland.
Brian Dear

He was a bubbly character and could run all day and night. His work rate was so impressive.
Ken Brown

John lived in Bethnal Green and when we trained we had to do this bloody long run. They drove us out to a point from where we would have to run back to Grange Farm. It was about a five-mile run. It was a nightmare for me because I was hopeless at that type of running but John had such terrific stamina, the bus would drive him at least another mile further out and he would still get home before us. He wasn't an elegant, athletic type and was a bit of a squat fella.

He must have had bellows for lungs. He played in central midfield and could run up and down all day long. He had an East End comic humour and was a bit of a prankster.
John Cartwright

John loved a game of cards and liked to gamble. He was a bit like Alan Mullery, another very good player. Smithy went to Spurs and we got Dave Dunmore.
Roger Hugo

I signed John when I was manager at Torquay United. He had played for West Ham and Spurs and I got him from Leyton Orient. He was a very accomplished midfielder, he knew the game very well, had quite a bit of skill and was also a good tackler. He was a great competitor and had a good wit about him, which I liked. He was a bubbly Cockney character.
Frank O'Farrell

TED ENDS TWO-YEAR HUNT

Arrived

Departed

WEST HAM'S last-minute deal with Tottenham Hotspur, which took wing-half Johnny Smith to White Hart-lane and brought centre-forward Dave Dunmore to Upton Park, ends a two-year campaign by Hammers' boss, Ted Fenton.

"I first became interested in Dunmore before we bought Vic Keeble from Newcastle the season before last and my interest has never slackened since. I'd say I have made at least half-a-dozen definite inquiries about Dave in that time without any success," said Mr. Fenton yesterday.

Fenton drafts 25-year-old Dunmore straight into his Division One attack against Blackburn at Upton Park on Saturday at centre-forward. Dunmore, whom Spurs bought from York City for £10,000 six years ago, has played 75 first-team games for Tottenham—ten this season without being on the losing side.

First news that Spurs had also handed West Ham £5,000 was incorrect. "I was rather over a barrel," said Mr. Fenton. "Spurs had already turned down £20,000 for Dunmore from Birmingham, and even more from another club. They were not interested in money, only players, and they could afford to wait for them."

If the burly, go-getting Dunmore can transform West Ham's attack as effectively as did Vic Keeble immediately after the latter's signing, then few at Upton Park will worry about the odd thousand or so lost on the deal.

For Dunmore the future could be bright. After years of semi-obscurity at Tottenham he has at last the chance to prove himself.

But what of ex-Hammer John Smith? Smith left West Ham because he declined to play reserve-team football, declaring his intention of going anywhere for a regular first-team place.

And finally the Young England wing-half joins mighty Tottenham where his chances of dislodging either Irish star Danny Blanchflower or Scotland giant Dave Mackay are practically nil.

Some predicted that Tottenham reserve goalkeeper John Hollowbread would be included in the deal, but Ted Fenton said yesterday that West Ham were not making any move now for a goalkeeper.

Newcastle United's reserve, Stewart Mitchell had Hammers keen for a time. "They asked £12,000 for a player who has had nine first-team games this season. They must think I'm soft in the head or something," was Ted's outraged comment.

But Fenton admitted that, had Hammers signed Mitchell, they would have been ready to part with Eire international Dwyer.

"If we'd got Mitchell at a reasonable fee we might well have let Dwyer go for a similar amount," he added.

And with Dunmore's arrival the future must be uncertain for another player—the injury-dogged Vic Keeble who may not regain his place.

Dunmore—six years of semi-obscurity

Keeble – no return

Dwyer – might have gone.

Smith—what of the future?

The transfer of John Smith – a key moment in the rise of Bobby Moore.

He was an excellent player, Smithy. He was always a bit overweight but used to win all the cross country runs. Both he and Harry Hooper loved their running. After our National Service days I remember coming back fitter than ever and Smithy and I left the rest of the team miles behind. He was a great trainer. I preferred the sprints and he was great over the longer distances.

Terry McDonald

John was a very capable ball playing midfielder who thought very highly of Bobby Moore. John had a great Cockney sense of humour. If we went to a restaurant he would leave with the cutlery hanging out of his top pocket. He was a bit stocky which I think put off quite a few managers but his levels of fitness were remarkable. He was a very good manager at Dundalk as well. He only made one mistake and that was signing me!

Willie Penman (played with John at both Swindon Town and Walsall)

Bobby Moore was very lucky in that Smudger went to Tottenham, because he played in his position at the time.

Jack Burkett

I have very good memories of John, or 'Smudge' as we used to call him. We were in the army together down in Aldershot with Terry McDonald. They were very good times together. We were in the Royal Army Medical Corps or 'Rob All My Comrades' as we used to say!

We were playing an A team game on Boxing Day down at Fratton Park, Portsmouth. Now John wasn't a big drinker but he had obviously had a few over Christmas and was a little worse for wear. He said to me: 'I'm not going to head the ball today' and he didn't. He was a very good footballer and didn't get the recognition he deserved because I thought he would go on to play for England. He was skilful, strong in the tackle and was always looking to play the ball from midfield, a lot like Frank Lampard today. But he was stronger than Frank and very robust.

John was the fittest footballer I ever played with in my career but after leaving West Ham he was sadly let down by Spurs. Bill Nicholson said he would go straight into their side at left-half when he signed him but it didn't materialise. Spurs got a bit more out of Danny Blanchflower as well which didn't help Smudge.

He couldn't have played more than 25 games for Spurs before moving on to Coventry City and then Leyton Orient.

After football I ran a pub called the Earl of Beaconsfield near East London cemetery in Canning Town. John came in and asked me what he needed to do to get into the pub game and I helped him out.

A very strange coincidence occurred at the 1980 FA Cup Final between West Ham and Arsenal. I had arranged a pub jolly to Wembley and there were over 100,000 people there and I remember a copper on horseback trying to keep the crowd dispersed. Incredibly, standing next to the horse was Johnny Smith so amongst all those people I just bumped into Smudge. He came back and stayed with me for the night. We had thumped the Arsenal, I was singing in the pub that evening and me old mucker, Smudge, was staying over so the whole day was just fantastic!

Clive Lewis (West Ham Youth Cup finalist)

8 – VIC KEEBLE

Born: Colchester, Essex, June 25, 1930
Position: Centre-forward
Games played with Bobby Moore: 4 (1958-60)
Games played for West Ham United: 80 (1958-60)

Victor Albert William Keeble joined West Ham United in October 1957 for a fee of £10,000. Ted Fenton's pursuit of his signature stands out as one of the greatest transfers in the club's history. Keeble joined with a tremendous pedigree having won the FA Cup with a Jackie Milburn-led Newcastle United in 1955.

While at West Ham, Keeble combined with John Dick to secure promotion to the top flight in 1958, helping the team to score 101 league goals along the way.

'Vic' and 'Jacko' were great mates both on and off the field and stand tall in Hammers' history as one of the greatest-ever strike partnerships. Jacko's wife, Sue, describes them as: 'Twins that were always laughing together and shared a musical love of Doris Day.'

A young Bobby Moore was playing in the Colts at the time of West Ham's promotion to the top flight but would soon be taking the field with them for his debut against Manchester United.

Keeble was almost 11 years Bobby's senior and they played only four games together, before a back injury forced a premature end to Vic's playing days.

Former Hammer John Cartwright describes how keen Vic was to share his experience with the younger players at the club: 'On my debut against Everton up at Goodison Park in 1959,' he recalls, 'Vic came over to me and said: 'Don't worry about anything, you are going to have a good game. Whenever you have the ball, I'll be showing for you and whenever I've got the ball you show for me.' We did that all afternoon and won 1-0, which I think took West Ham to the top of the table.'

It is safe to assume Vic would have had similar words of advice for Bobby Moore on his debut.

Young Moore witnessed Keeble grab a four-goal haul against Blackburn Rovers on October 4, 1958. It was the first time that a Hammer had performed such a feat in the first team since Don Travis scored four goals against Plymouth Argyle during a 7-0 victory on February 16, 1946.

West Ham's scoring machine.

Sadly, Keeble's West Ham career was cut short through injury and he underwent a dramatic career switch when, in November 1960, he joined the advertising team at the *Colchester Express.*

Nowadays, Vic, 84, lives in Earls Colne, Essex and loves sitting out in his garden with a cup of tea and a crossword. He is the only survivor of Newcastle United's great cup teams of the early 1950s and is regularly chauffeured up to St. James' Park as a special guest. Not many can say they played with both Jackie Milburn and Bobby Moore.

It's unbelievable, everybody's effing dead, aren't they? I mean I played in Bobby Moore's debut against Manchester United at Upton Park and we've lost a lot from that line-up. John Bond's gone, Ernie Gregory's gone, Noel Cantwell's gone and Jacko's gone. Poor old Andy Malcolm went recently as well. They'll need him up there! I think it's only me and Ken Brown who are still alive. I may have two false knees but I'm still hanging around!

Young Bob was very popular with the other youngsters at West Ham. I was living with Malcolm Allison in Barkingside for a while and when he lost a lung after suffering from tuberculosis he came back from the convalescence home and we held a big party for him. Malcolm Musgrove, Kenny Brown and Bill Lansdowne all lived close by and left at a decent hour but Bobby and the younger lads wanted to stay up all night drinking and laughing.

Anyway, I was woken up by the lovely lady who owned the house. She asked me to talk to the young lads and to tell them to leave. I spoke to Bobby and told him the situation and he was fine about it, and he got the other lads to go too. I didn't realise it at the time but I was actually throwing a future World Cup winning captain out of my house!

West Ham was quite a bit different from Newcastle when I arrived. It was very cliquey and there were three groups really: The gamblers, who went off to the races; the drinkers, who went up to the West End; and the nice lads, who went home to their wives. I've never had a beer or a cigarette in my life but my old pal, Jacko and I, loved going to the tracks to back the greyhounds and the horses. We'd come back from away games on the train and dash to catch the last couple of races at one of the dog tracks. I used to like the nice stadiums like Walthamstow because they had a bit of class but Jacko would prefer the seedier ones like Romford, Dagenham or Hackney Wick.

There was a big question surrounding Bobby's debut against Manchester United about who was going to play – either Allison or Moore? Malcolm had recovered from a big operation and was back in training. I hadn't seen a lot of Bob because I was quite a bit older and he was playing in the reserves. But Malcolm was pretty much running the club at the time, along with Noel Cantwell and John Bond, so it was a big thing when his pal Noel suggested to Ted Fenton that Bob play instead of Malcolm. I think it affected their relationship for a long time. Anyway, it was a good decision because we won the game even though I didn't score, which was unusual!

Another strong memory I have of Bob was when he was managing Southend United in the 1980s. I was the secretary and general manager at Chelmsford City FC at the time and he brought the reserves along to play. We had a lovely chat and at the time he was running a night club. He invited me and the boys over there one night but it was too late for me and I politely declined.

It was clear to me that young Bob was going to be all right as a player and my only concern was that he lacked a little bit of pace. I played with the great Jackie Milburn in my day and it is great to know that I also played with England's one and only World Cup-winning captain.
Vic Keeble

Vic at home with his memories in 2014.

9 – JOHN DICK
March 19, 1930 – September, 2000

Born: Govan, Glasgow
Position: Inside-left/Forward
Games played with Bobby Moore: 83 (1958-62)
Games played for West Ham United: 351 (1953-62)

John Hart Dick is fondly remembered as one of the most popular characters in the history of West Ham United. He is joint third, along with pre-war winger, Jimmy Ruffell, on the club's all-time goalscorer list, with 166 goals. Only Victor Watson (326) and Geoff Hurst (248) found the net on more occasions. He left a legacy of high achievement and a whole host of colourful stories.

'Jacko', as he was fondly referred to, holds a unique treble in the Bobby Moore story having scored on Bobby's league debut, first FA Cup tie and first League Cup game.

He was also the man to score West Ham's first goal at the Boleyn Ground in the top flight after an absence of 25 years – against then league champions Wolverhampton Wanderers in a 2-0 victory. Little wonder that Jacko often joked about his left leg belonging in a museum!

Dick was one of the most popular players ever to pull on the West Ham United shirt. Despite being 11 years older than Bobby, he took a shine to the young teenager and was always keen to dispense support and advice, something Bobby readily craved. Bobby was a frequent visitor to John's house in Maypole Crescent, Ilford.

Dick began his life in football as a young lad in Glasgow, playing for Maryhill FC. He gained junior international honours with Scotland and after moving south was spotted by West Ham United whilst playing for Crittall Athletic against West Ham's A Team in the Midweek League. At the time John was stationed in Colchester during his National Service.

He signed professional forms on May 12, 1953 before making his debut against Lincoln City at the Boleyn Ground in August of that year. The following season he equalled Bill Robinson's post-war single season goals tally of 26 and improved on this by netting 27 goals during the club's first campaign back in the top flight. An achievement that has only been bettered since by Geoff Hurst, Bryan 'Pop' Robson and Frank McAvennie.

John was the first West Ham United player to win a cap for Scotland. It came in April 1959 against England at Wembley, just one day before Bobby's 18th birthday. Billy

Mooro and Jacko.

Shaking hands with Prime Minister Harold Macmillan before his one and only Scotland cap against England at Wembley in 1959.

Wright, the England captain, was collecting his 100th cap and a British Pathe newsreel has preserved some footage of the game for posterity.

Jacko spent nine years at the club and along with other members of the promotion-winning team – Malcolm Musgrove and Andy Malcolm – just missed out on a well-deserved testimonial year.

John Dick passed away in September 2000 and his wife Sue has proudly preserved his memorabilia and trophies from his West Ham days. We owe her an enormous debt of thanks for her following recollections:

Before Bobby Moore met Tina he would pop round to see John here at our house in Barkingside. Bobby was in the Colts team at the time and John was in the first team but he really liked him. I think John was impressed by the way he played. Bobby was very young and shy at the time and didn't seem to know what to do with himself. Back then he didn't seem to make friends very easily.

John was a very unassuming man, a one-off. He absolutely loved West Ham and knew a good player when he saw one, which is why he had so much time for young Bobby.

John and I actually met at the supporters' club dance in 1953. I was a West Ham fan and had actually sent John a Valentine's Day card before I met him. Frank O'Farrell's wife Anne knew that I liked John and got Frank to introduce us.

Anyway, we started chatting at the bar and the next day we went to the pictures. We saw Laurel and Hardy. It was love at first sight across a crowded room!

Bobby called at our house quite a bit and on one occasion I was bathing our first born baby Jennifer in a mobile bath in the passage way. Bobby commented on how busy I was before going through to see John. Jennifer now tells everyone that Bobby Moore saw her naked in the bath!

When Bobby met Tina they came round for tea one Christmas and I remember my brother's wife running into the kitchen because she didn't want Bobby to see her wearing curlers!

John's great mate at West Ham was Vic Keeble, They were like brothers and did everything together, which usually involved gambling on the dogs. I remember Bobby congratulating John on the various goals he was scoring at the time. Even though John was so much older than Bobby they both loved to talk about football.

John died in 2000 and when I arrived for the funeral at the City of London Cemetery I thought there were two services, because so many people turned up. Rio Ferdinand, Geoff Hurst, John Byrne, Ronnie Boyce and Ken Brown were all there. John had worked with the kids at Hackney Marshes for 25 years and Rio went to Daneford School, so John must have looked after him at some stage. Patsy Holland, who John really liked, was also there.

John Dick's great left foot in action as Bobby Moore and Tony Scott (right) look on in the background.

Afterwards, we went to The Kings Head in Chigwell and I thought John would have loved it because so many of his old playing pals were there. Geoff Hurst was really good that day. He mixed with everyone and really made a positive difference.

I chose 'When I Fall in Love' and 'Unforgettable' for the funeral music because John loved Nat King Cole. He would usually be singing his songs around the house which is something I really miss. Tony Bennett, Andy Williams and Doris Day were his other favourites.

He had a terrific sense of humour. We were the only people to own a Welsh Collie called Angus!
Sue Dick

The following reminiscences from John's former playing colleagues further cement his standing as one of the club's truly great characters:

Jackie wore the Number 10 shirt before me and was a terrific character. He always liked singing Frankie Lane songs whilst banging out a tune on the dressing room door. Not sure what his right foot was for but he had a superb left foot.
Sir Geoff Hurst

The best player for me at West Ham was Jacko. He needed a bit of help because he was all left foot but he would always give you 100%. He wasn't all that in the air but he wasn't too bad. He was a grafter and boy did he know where that goal was! When we used to run out of the tunnel he would always say to me; 'See you at the far post'. There were so many characters at West Ham but he topped them all. He was such a likeable guy, everybody loved Jacko. We would both lose our wages at the dogs no problem and we would go up to Eddie Chapman and ask for a fiver to see us through. Then he would ask all the young lads for a nicker or a deuce at training! When either of us scored a hat-trick Jacko would get the players to sign the matchball and go across the road and sell it to one of the fruit sellers.
Vic Keeble

I remember we would take the train to play up north and we'd get back to Paddington or Kings Cross. Now, John Dick and Vic Keeble were great mates and when the train pulled in John would say to Vic: 'If we hurry with a taxi we'll catch the last two races at Walthamstow.'
Andy Smillie

When Ted Fenton died they had a memorial service in Brentwood. So we went to the Church and after the service Jackie came up to me and said 'Deary, is Ted really dead?' I replied; 'Of course, why?' And Jacko said; 'Because I owed him 40 quid!'

He used to send me up to Eddie Chapman to ask for a tenner on his behalf. Eddie only had petty cash in plastic bags so I would come down and give Jacko loads of small change. He would go straight out to the cinder track and make a mark up against the wall and throw tanners up the wall for money. Jacko used to place his bets with a tiny little man named Lou Baum who used to work with Joe Edwards. They called him the Mighty Atom. He was very smart with a little pork pie hat. Harry Cripps called him up one day and wanted to bet sixpence each way. 'Go away, Harry, I'm trying to take some proper money!' Lou said.

Lou would stand outside the ground on Fridays, holding his bets book with great big writing in it. 'Where's Jacko?' he would ask us all but Jacko would get George Isaacs, the groundsman, to let him out through a different exit!

Jacko was always trying to get money for the dogs. He would sell his season tickets three times over. John would come into the dressing room and use both sides of the door to play the drums and sing all these Spanish sounding songs. He loved singing. Every day he had a new way of getting some extra money. He'd come in selling ties and everything. When we used to get our stamp for some free grub at Cassettari's, Jacko would only buy a cup of tea and get the difference back in cash. 'I'll never earn any money from you footballers!' Phil Cassettari would shout.

Jacko got into coaching and was great with the kids, working in the schools and over at Hackney Marshes.

He had a wicked sense of humour. If he saw some poor old boy hobbling along on sticks he would elbow me in the ribs and say: 'Deary, watch your pockets!'
Brian Dear

Sometimes people would tell him to lay off the dogs for a while and ease back on his gambling but he would say: 'I cannae do it, I cannae do it. I love 'em. I love 'em!' He was one of the great, great, characters at West Ham.
Ken Brown

Jacko was a great bloke. He used to sing in the bath, he was a great singer.
Terry McDonald

My friend Jacko was a very underestimated player. His heart was in the game.
Lawrie Leslie

John was well suited to West Ham because he was a character. The last team I played for was Orsett Athletic and one day Terry McDonald, who has been a life-long friend of mine, suggested that I should get Johnny Dick out of retirement and ask him to play for Orsett. He agreed and it was the last team he ever played for. He was well past his best of course and was limping around like a cripple but he still had all the old deft touches with his left foot and it was a thrill just to be on the same pitch with such a great player.
Clive Lewis

I remember when Ted Fenton was voted Manager of the Month. It happened when my dad, Bill, was the club physio. Ted was presented with a big bottle of scotch. Anyway, it went missing from the dressing room and Ted stormed in and said 'Someone has taken my bottle of scotch and when I find out who it was I'm going to take them into the gym and put the gloves on!' After he walked out, John Dick started dancing around the dressing room shadow boxing!
Rob Jenkins

Treasured memories – John's wife Sue with his Scotland shirt and cap.

10 – MALCOLM MUSGROVE
July 8, 1933 – September 14, 2007

Born: Lynemouth, Northumberland
Position: Left-wing
Games played with Bobby Moore: 110 (1958-62)
Games played for West Ham United: 301 (1954-62)

Malcolm Clarke Musgrove scored on Bobby Moore's debut and is the most prolific goal-scoring winger at West Ham United since Jimmy Ruffell plied his trade in the pre-war era. 'Muzzie's' 89 career goals from the left-wing are unlikely to be bettered. He played over 100 games with Bobby and his 41 goals during that time included a hat-trick against Preston North End on October 22, 1960.

Musgrove joined West Ham United in 1953 having opted for a career in football over rugby. He was top scorer in two seasons and was a vital component in the Hammers' promotion campaign of 1958. He was on the score-sheet with Bobby Moore during the club's first ever League Cup game – a 3-1 home win against Charlton Athletic on September 26, 1960.

Former Hammer and experienced footballing scout, John Cartwright, recalls Muzzie with fondness. 'He was

'Muzzie' takes on Bolton keeper, Hopkinson in January 1960.

a gentleman and a really nice guy. Malcolm was a good player without being an outstanding one. He was quick and combined well with people. I think he had a good career because he was an intelligent player, who got the best out of himself.'

Sir Geoff Hurst is another who recalls Musgrove with high regard: 'A flying winger at West Ham who later got into coaching at the very top level and was with Frank O'Farrell at both Leicester City and Manchester United. A terrific fella.'

Like Andy Malcolm and John Dick before him, Malcolm was another from Bobby Moore's debut line up to be released by the club just prior to his tenth anniversary. His transfer to Leyton Orient for £11,000 denied him the richly deserved recognition of a testimonial game.

After leaving West Ham Malcolm enjoyed layers and layers of coaching experience both at home with Leicester City, Manchester United, Torquay United, Shrewsbury Town, Exeter City and Plymouth Argyle and in the United States with teams from Connecticut and Chicago.

Malcolm Musgrove passed away on September 14, 2007. The following recollections are provided courtesy of Malcolm's wife Jean and their son David.

Even though my dad was eight years older than Bobby Moore he always said it didn't feel like he was playing with a kid and that it felt like he was a mature, experienced pro in that Number 6 shirt.

One lesser known fact about my father was that he was part of the initial England squad of 28 for the 1962 World Cup but missed out when they reduced it to the final 22 which included Bobby Moore, who flew to Chile for his first World Cup. My father never won an England cap largely because he was competing with players like Stanley Matthews and Tom Finney in the 1950s.

There is some BBC film footage of Dad playing with Bobby against Wolverhampton Wanderers in 1960. Bobby wins a tackle and plays Dad in down the wing. He cuts inside and scores. Then Dad sets up Bobby for him to score.

When Dad used to take us to the ground to watch games as a kid we weren't awestruck by Bobby Moore, because to us he was just one of the players. This was in the very late 50s and all his most successful years were still ahead of him.

I remember as kids we would go to the gym in between the dressing rooms and the players' lounge and both Geoff Hurst and Martin Peters would lower the ball for us to head. They had a ball suspended in the air by a piece of wire for the players to head and they would put it in reach of us so we could have some fun.

Even after Dad moved on to Leyton Orient in 1963, the club continued with our season tickets for many years after and mum and I would go and watch all those great games in the 1960s. Peter Brabrook arranged tickets for us, too.

We did have the match ball from the game in which Dad scored a hat-trick – against Preston North End in 1960. It was one of the earliest hat-tricks Bobby witnessed at West Ham. The ball was brought home and put in dad's wardrobe. He

said I could have it when I was five. Sure enough when I was five out it came only to be destroyed over a number of years by myself and my younger brother, Martin. I actually remember Dad bringing home an old goal net to our house in Barkingside, when he was coach at Charlton, and hung it between three fences and the shed at the bottom of the garden so Martin and I could play without losing the ball. We had hours of fun playing one-a-side down the bottom of the garden, but being concrete, the nice new orange Mitre ball didn't stay nice and new for long!

A final word from Jean Musgrove: I think we had the best years at West Ham. We got on well with all the players and went to the weddings of Bobby & Tina and Noel & Maggie Cantwell. We also got on well with Bobby's mum and dad, Doris and Bob. All lovely people together, doing what they enjoyed most.

Malcolm and son David with the hat trick ball against Preston.

11 – BILLY DARE
February 14, 1927 – April 1994

Born: Willesden Green, London

Position: Forward

Games played with Bobby Moore: 1 (1959)

Games played for West Ham United: 119 (1955-59)

Billy's one game with Bobby Moore: March 14, 1959
Burnley (a) L 0-1

Scorer: Connelly

Burnley: McDonald, Cummings, Smith, Seith, Miller, Adamson, Connelly, McIlroy, Pointer, Robson, Harris

West Ham United: Gregory, Bond, Cantwell, Malcolm, Brown, Moore, Grice, Smith, **Dare**, Dick, Musgrove

William 'Billy' Thomas Charles Dare played just one game with Bobby Moore – against Burnley at Turf Moor in March 1959. It marked his penultimate game for West Ham United. He bowed out just one month later with a goal at home against Preston North End. They were his only two games in the top division but his overall West Ham statistics show him having played 119 games and scoring an impressive 49 goals. He was the first Hammer Bobby Moore lined up with who hadn't played in his first team debut. An injured Vic Keeble made way.

Dare was 11 years older than Bobby and had started his football career with amateur side, Hendon, before establishing himself as a prolific striker with Brentford.

He was eventually lured from Griffin Park for £5,000 by Ted Fenton in February 1955. It was a unique event as it was the first transfer which was screened live on television during the BBC's weekly *Sportsview* transmission. It should be noted that only one in four households owned a television at the time and the world was a very different place to the saturation coverage of football we experience today.

Player memories of Dare describe him as honest, hardworking and a very shrewd operator in front of goal, a six-yard box man. Former Hammer, Frank O'Farrell describes Billy as: 'smallish for a centre forward but very clever and a good signing from Brentford. Another likeable character at West Ham, there were so many good lads at that time.'

Much is made of the John Dick and Vic Keeble partnership in securing promotion for West Ham in the spring of 1958 but Billy Dare's 11 league goals in the first 12 games of the season should never be forgotten. He certainly played his part in helping West Ham secure top flight status and it begs the question whether or not Moore, Hurst and Peters, would have stayed at a club in the second tier? Furthermore, would Ron Greenwood have joined the club?

In an era of the fixed maximum wage, Billy was transferred to Yiewsley FC of the Southern League in the summer of 1959. He was 30 years of age. They were the forerunner of today's Hillingdon Borough FC. He was scaling down his football commitments due to a position he held with a coach-building company.

Billy Dare passed away in April 1994, just one year after Bobby Moore. A lasting tribute to the stocky striker came with the following words: '*None who met him could ever dislike him. He was a legend. Loved by all, funny and caring*.'

Billy Dare (right) and John Dick in action versus Blackburn Rovers.

12 – NOEL DWYER
October 30, 1934 – December 27, 1992

Born: Dublin, Republic of Ireland

Position: Goalkeeper

Games played with Bobby Moore: 5 (1959-60)

Games played for West Ham United: 38 (1957-63)

First game with Bobby Moore: April 20, 1959
Manchester City (h) W 5-1

Scorers: West Ham United: Cantwell, Dick (2), Grice (2)
Manchester City: Barlow

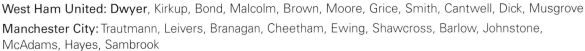

West Ham United: Dwyer, Kirkup, Bond, Malcolm, Brown, Moore, Grice, Smith, Cantwell, Dick, Musgrove

Manchester City: Trautmann, Leivers, Branagan, Cheetham, Ewing, Shawcross, Barlow, Johnstone, McAdams, Hayes, Sambrook

Noel Michael Dwyer was the funny guy at West Ham United and, typical of many Irishmen, liked a drink and had a sparkling sense of humour. Legend maintains that he used to put glue on his gloves before a game.

Manager Ted Fenton signed Dwyer from Wolverhampton Wanderers in December 1958 as a potential replacement for West Ham's veteran goalkeeper, Ernie Gregory. The Dublin- born stopper had been with Wolves since 1953 after he had made the journey across the Irish Sea from his local club, Ormeau.

Noel and his wife, Jackie, moved into Barkingside which housed so many West Ham couples at the time, including Ken and Joan Brown, Malcolm and Jean Musgrove, Bill and Pat Lansdowne, Mike and Yvonne Grice, John and Sue Dick, plus Malcolm and Beth Allison. Bobby and Tina Moore would soon be moving into Clayhall Avenue, too.

Noel gained four of his 14 Republic of Ireland caps whilst at West Ham. They came against Sweden (twice), Chile and West Germany during 1959-60. Noel had the added honour of captaining his country.

Although Dwyer and Moore played together in only five league games, ironically it was a game at White Hart Lane in which Bobby did not play that deserves special mention. The match ended in a 2-2 draw and the Irishman's performance had been masterful. In his autobiography, Moore, watching from the stand, described Noel's performance as 'the best display of goalkeeping I had ever seen.'

There is no small amount of controversy behind the reason for Dwyer leaving the club just 18 months after his arrival. His final game, a 3-5 defeat at home to Newcastle United, was steeped in match fixing allegations. Bookmakers made it public that an inordinate amount of money had been placed on the Magpies just prior to kick-off. Manager Ted Fenton described it as a 'ridiculous

Gloves in hand, ready to go.

allegation' in his autobiography: *At Home with the Hammers*. Noel's family and former playing colleagues dismiss it as pure folly but the fact remains that Dwyer was the only one from that Newcastle game never to play again for West Ham United.

In the summer of 1960, Noel was sold to Swansea Town for £3,000. He had played 38 league and cup games for the Hammers and had clearly made an impression on the young Moore. This was emphatically underlined when, in 1963, West Ham were drawn against the Swans in the fourth round of the FA Cup. Noel returned to Upton Park and despite a fine performance he could not prevent the Hammers prevailing 1-0, courtesy of a goal from Ron Boyce. At the final whistle, Moore jogged 60 yards to shake Dwyer's hand. They had clearly established a rapport which left a positive impression on both men.

One year on, both players came very close to shaking hands again on the biggest stage of all – Wembley Stadium – for the 1964 FA Cup final. Alas, in the semi-final, Dwyer's Swansea had conceded two late goals against Preston North End and missed out.

The last occasion Bobby and Noel saw each other was at a Professional Footballers Association Awards evening after their respective playing days had finished.

When Dwyer finished playing football he became a sales representative for Watts Tyre Company in West Bromwich but his health deteriorated and his final years were

Next to Noel Cantwell in the West Ham blazer. Young Bobby Moore at the back.

defined by illness. It is a sad irony that, just like Bobby, he was diagnosed with bowel cancer.

Noel Dwyer died on December 27, 1992. He was 58 years of age. Two months later Bobby also lost his battle against the same cruel disease.

Noel is survived by his wife, Jackie and their four children, Carol, Joanne, Nicola and Noel junior.

The following recollections are kindly provided by his wife, Jackie, who still lives at the family home in Wolverhampton:

Bobby Moore was only a young boy when we first met him, 17 maybe 18, whereas Noel was 24 so there were quite a few years between them. He was a very charming young man and was really involved at the club. Bobby had an awful lot going for him even at that young age. He had just started dating Tina when we arrived and I used to watch the games with Maggie Cantwell and a few others. Noel slotted in really well and they all seemed to enjoy his company.

Noel and I were already married by the time he joined West Ham, whereas Bobby and Tina had only just started courting so we didn't really socialise a great deal. Bobby loved his football and Tina supported him. They were a quiet couple just starting out on their life's journey together.

I had met Noel at a dance when he was playing for Wolverhampton Wanderers in the 1950s and we had our first child, Carol, when we were at West Ham. It is quite funny because we have three generations of football marriages in our family. Apart from Noel and I, my father, Cuthbert 'Charlie' Phillips played up front for Wolves, Birmingham and Aston Villa. He also won the Home International Championship with Wales in both 1933 and 1934. I still have the dragon table lighter they presented to him. And finally, our daughter Carol, has been married to ex-Huddersfield, Leicester, Birmingham and England international, Frank Worthington for over 20 years. Frank played for 20-odd clubs but don't ask me to name them all!

At West Ham, Malcolm Allison had a big influence on Bobby and a lot of the other players. Noel saw an awful lot of Malcolm over the years and visited him when he was involved with Manchester City.

By the time we went to West Ham, Malcolm had just left the sanatorium in Midhurst after a major operation and wouldn't play again. But he still lived in the area and saw a lot of the players. I remember one day, Malcolm knocked on our door asking for Noel and they went out together. Malcolm had told his wife, Beth, that he was popping out for a loaf of bread but the pair of them didn't return for two days!

Noel was well liked at all the clubs he played for and was definitely one of the lads. West Ham were very good to us and did more for the players than at Wolverhampton.

I recall one funny story that did the rounds when we were at West Ham. After we moved into Barkingside, Vic Keeble loaned us a lawn mower but Noel forgot to return it and, when he came to our house a few months later, he said that he couldn't get into his own garden because the grass was so high! Noel got a lot a lot of stick at the training ground over that one.

Noel was expected to become a top class goalkeeper when he broke into the first team at Wolves. He actually played in five games when they won the old first division in 1957-58 but he dislocated his shoulder at a young age and there were complications, which kept him side-lined for a crucial 18 months which really affected his progress.

He was very unlucky with injuries and his health in general and went on to play out his career at both Plymouth Argyle and Charlton Athletic before retiring from the game in 1966.

Later in life he suffered from a duodenum ulcer before being diagnosed with bowel cancer. He had lots of operations and really went through it. It was shocking really what he had to suffer.

I suspected things were not right during a holiday on the west coast of Ireland. Noel loved swimming and would always say it was as warm as soup on that particular part of the coast even though to me it was freezing. However, on this occasion he said he was too cold to swim and I sensed something wasn't right and he was diagnosed with cancer six weeks later.

In action with Ken Brown.

Quite a few players went to his funeral at the Bushbury Crematoriam in Wolverhampton. Malcolm Allison and Noel Cantwell were there as was Derek Dougan, the Wolves legend, who lived very close to us.

Since Noel died, Swansea City have honoured him, too. In October 2013 the club invited us to a game and they unveiled a plaque in his honour as part of a Wall of Fame they have there. Noel really enjoyed his time at Swansea. The Wolves also have an Old Players Association but that wasn't established when he was alive even though he went back to Molineux to watch a few games.

It was such a shame what happened to Bobby Moore and more recently with the tragic passing of his son Dean who was born on the same day as our son, Noel junior.

If Noel was here today he would say that Bobby Moore was a huge talent with a first-class work ethic and an enthusiasm which deservedly took him to the very top of world football.

Jackie Dwyer

13 – JOE KIRKUP

Born: Hexham, Northumberland, December 17, 1939

Position: Right-back

Games played with Bobby Moore: 154 (1959-66)

Games played for West Ham United: 187 (1958-66)

Honours with Bobby Moore: 1965 European Cup Winners' Cup winner

First game with Bobby Moore: April 20, 1959 Manchester City (h) W 5-1

Scorers: West Ham United: Cantwell, Dick (2), Grice (2) Manchester City: Barlow

West Ham United: Dwyer, **Kirkup**, Bond, Malcolm, Brown, Moore, Grice, Smith, Cantwell, Dick, Musgrove.

Manchester City: Trautmann, Leivers, Branagan, Cheetham, Ewing, Shawcross, Barlow, Johnstone, McAdams, Hayes, Sambrook

Joseph Robert Kirkup's crowning moment at West Ham United came in 1965 as a member of the European Cup Winners Cup team which beat TSV Munich 2-0 at Wembley Stadium. It was also Bobby Moore's finest moment in club football.

Kirkup graduated to the youth side before Moore and played in the 1957 FA Youth Cup final against Manchester United. Moore would have to wait a little longer before his appearance in an FA Youth Cup final – a two-legged defeat against Blackburn Rovers in 1959. Kirkup and Moore were

Joe Kirkup (back row second left), Bobby Moore (back row right) and Johnny Byrne (front row centre) in Billy Wright's England Under-23 team, 1962.

regulars in the reserves during the late 1950s.

Hexham-born Kirkup had already made his first team debut by the time he lined up alongside Moore – against Manchester City on April 20, 1959. In fact Kirkup was making his 10th first team appearance in that game while Moore was pulling on the shirt for only the third occasion. They also played together for England at both Youth and Under-23 level.

Joe is amongst a handful of Hammers to have lined up against Bobby whilst playing for another club – both Chelsea and Southampton, respectively. Perhaps the most memorable instance of this came in a 5-5 draw between West Ham and Chelsea at Stamford Bridge on December 17, 1966 – not a textbook example of defending from either player.

His finest moment. Joe (far right) on the lap of honour following West Ham's European triumph at Wembley Stadium in 1965.

After hanging up his boots, Joe followed his former team-mate, Johnny Byrne, to South Africa. He succeeded him as manager of Durban City during the mid-1970s.

On his return to England Joe became a notable retailer in Surrey with a sports shop in Cranleigh and a newsagents in Ewell.

Joe still has his shirt and medal from West Ham's European triumph and continues to enjoy family life with his wife, Jill, in Ashtead, Surrey having previously lived in France for several years.

Bobby was obviously one hell of a player for West Ham and a great captain but I think he was 10 times the player when he pulled on the England shirt. He must easily be the best England international there has ever been and I cannot understand why he never received a knighthood unless there is something that we lesser mortals do not know about.

He played 108 games for his country, 90 as captain, and I would wager that if you read back through all the match reports you could count his bad games on one hand. The rest of the time he was either man-of-the-match or, at the very least, one of the best players on the pitch. The two Bobby's – Moore and Charlton – were the best players England had and Charlton rightly got his knighthood but I think Mooro outdid Charlton for England and yet he never got knighted. I often wonder if the press or someone at The FA knew something we didn't?

I got to know Bobby really well when we played in West Ham's reserve team together in the late 1950s. After a game on Saturday I would often stay with him at his mum and dad's

Joe in action.

place in Barking. Doris and Bob were lovely people. She was very fastidious, which explains how Bobby got his meticulous ways, too.

When we broke into the first team we drifted apart a little. Obviously you can't all go out in a large unit, so two groups developed. Bobby's set included Ken Brown, John Bond, Peter Brabrook, Budgie Byrne, and Eddie Bovington. Then there was Geoff Hurst, Martin Peters, Jackie Burkett, Ronnie Boyce, John Sissons and myself. So from that time on I didn't really have a great deal to do with Bobby, apart from training and playing together. Furthermore, we both got married in 1962 so once again life took us in different directions.

For someone of his international stature, Bobby was a very quiet and unassuming character. He was just one of the lads. I liken him to George Best who was portrayed in the newspapers in a certain way, the bad boy of football or whatever, but when you met George after a game, as we often did back then, he was just this ordinary little bloke who wouldn't say boo to a goose.

I won three Under-23 caps and was selected to play for Young England against England at Highbury. It took place on the eve of the FA Cup final in 1962. Bobby was also in the Young England side and we both had a good game. It was some time afterwards that Ron Greenwood told me that following the game, the squad was selected for the 1962 World Cup in Chile. Apparently, they wanted to take one of the youngsters along and Ron was at the meeting where a decision was made. He told me it was between me and Bobby and I was narrowly out-voted. Who knows how our respective careers would have panned out if the vote had gone in my favour? Clearly, I don't mean to say I would have done the great things that Bobby did but it could have meant a dramatic change in our respective careers. I did have a lovely photo of Bobby, Budgie and me playing for the England Under-23s but I just can't find it.

It always amazed me how Bobby became so great and yet he couldn't run. All his defending was about interceptions. I'd say the ratio of interceptions to tackles was probably 80/20.

I remember inviting Bobby and all the lads to my wedding in 1962 having checked with Ron that it didn't clash with any pre-season tours. Ron gave me the nod but then arranged a trip to South Africa, so none of the lads could go to my wedding anyway! Ron and I had a falling out over that. Andy Nelson was my best man but he had moved on to Ipswich Town by then.

We were just ordinary lads back then and nothing like the celebrities who pass as footballers nowadays.

I went to Bobby's memorial service at Westminster Abbey in 1993. Bobby Charlton and Jimmy Tarbuck said a few words,

Joe today.

which was quite ironic because Mooro was always regarded as a bit of a softie up north and yet they couldn't speak more highly of him. I think their fans were jealous that he never signed for Manchester United or Liverpool.

I didn't play in West Ham's FA Cup-winning team in 1964 and watched the final in the stand with Martin Peters instead. Bobby was magnificent that day. I played with him in the European Cup Winners' Cup final a year later, though, and he was the best player on the pitch and then, of course, he was at the very centre of England's finest moment in football in 1966. There'll never be another like him.

Joe Kirkup

Back row L-R Kirkup, Lansdowne, Bond, Dwyer, Gregory, Rhodes, Brown, Cantwell, Moore. Front row L-R Wragg, Woosnam, Grice, Keeble, Dick, Musgrove, Malcolm, Obeney.

CHAPTER TWO
1959-60

Bobby Moore's total appearances (July 1959-June 1960): 51 games (0 goals)

Reserves: 18, League Division One: 13, Friendlies: 10, Southern Floodlit Cup: 3, Metropolitan League: 2, London Mid-week League: 2, LFA Cup: 2, Southern Junior Floodlit Cup: 1

Bobby Moore continued to play more matches in the reserve team than he did in the senior side. However, his star was on the rise and, combined with the departure of John Smith to Tottenham Hotspur, the Number 6 shirt would soon become his for the next 14 years.

It was manager Ted Fenton's final full season at West Ham United and his number two - Bill Robinson - had already left the club after deciding to join Hartlepool United in a managerial capacity. Robinson was one of the key contributors to the establishment of the West Ham Youth academy. He helped to develop a teenage Bobby Moore and, subsequently, the academy has seen the development of a wealth of first-class talent, which continues to this day.

The football world started to enter a new, modern era which soon witnessed the abolition of the maximum wage that had placed a £20-per-week limit on a player's earning capacity. Moore's highest wage at West Ham United would eventually be £200-per-week. His first wage had been £6, 15s 0d. (£6.75)

The decade of spiralling transfer fees began in March 1960, when Denis Law joined Manchester City from Huddersfield Town for £55,000. Indeed, West Ham United would themselves set a new British transfer record a couple of years later - signing Johnny Byrne from Crystal Palace for £65,000. Furthermore, the club would finish the decade setting another British record when Martin Peters was sold for £200,000 to Tottenham Hotspur.

In July 1959, Moore began his pre-season on tour in Austria. The 18-year-old formed part of a 16-strong party of senior players', which included experienced pros John Bond, Ken Brown, Noel Cantwell, John Dick, Vic Keeble, Andy Malcolm, Malcolm Musgrove and Phil Woosnam. FC Austria also visited Upton Park as West Ham continued their tradition of staging floodlit friendlies. 22,500 spectators enjoyed a 2-0 victory for the Hammers, with Moore setting up Malcolm Musgrove for one of the goals.

One of the club's final acts of the 1950s was to establish an Old Players' Association. Club Chairman Reg Pratt was the Association's first President while former manager Charlie Paynter was elected as Chairman of the Association. Former players, Jimmy Ruffell, 'Jackie' Morton and Stanley Earle, also formed part of the Committee. It guaranteed the presence of West Ham United legends around the club and cemented the historical links.

18-year-old Bobby Moore.

Malcolm Musgrove was voted Hammer of the Year. He scored 15 goals from the left-wing, which established a new post-war record for that position.

Moore played 13 Division One matches and lined-up, for the first time, with no fewer than 11 Hammers – John Cartwright, Andy Smillie, Brian Rhodes, Harry Obeney, Phil Woosnam, John Lyall, Tony Scott, Dave Dunmore, Eddie Bovington, Ron Brett and Bill Lansdowne.

Here is their story...

14 – JOHN CARTWRIGHT

Born: Brixworth, Northamptonshire, November 5, 1940

Position: Inside-forward

Games played with Bobby Moore: 4 (1959-60)

Games played for West Ham United: 5 (1959-61)

Honours with Bobby Moore: 1959 FA Youth Cup finalist

First game with Bobby Moore (Debut): October 17, 1959 – Everton (a) W 1-0

Scorer: West Ham United: Musgrove

Everton: Dunlop, Parker, Bramwell, King, Jones, Harris B, Harris J, Thomas, Hickson, Collins, Shackleton

West Ham United: Dwyer, Bond, Cantwell, Malcolm, Brown, Moore, Grice, **Cartwright**, Keeble, Smillie, Musgrove

John William Cartwright signed professional forms for West Ham United in November 1957 and played youth team, reserve team and first team football with Bobby Moore. A big highlight was the 1959 FA Youth Cup run which sadly ended with a 1-2 defeat against Blackburn Rovers in the two-legged final. Nevertheless, many consider that youth team to be the best the club has ever produced.

Cartwright first lined-up in the first team with Moore against Everton, a 1-0 victory, in October 1960. It would be another 10 years before Bobby tasted victory again at Goodison Park.

John's style of football suffered under the management of Ted Fenton and he moved on to Crystal Palace in 1961 having played just five games for the club.

Although a very talented player in his day, John remains highly respected as a first-class coach and his CV boasts many fine achievements – the management of the England Youth team, three successful spells in the Middle East and a spell as assistant manager of Arsenal during the mid-1980s. He was greatly influenced by the Brazilian side of 1958 and fellow talent scout and former Hammer, Eddie Presland, still calls John, 'Didi' after the mercurial Brazilian midfielder.

John's book, *Football for the Brave*, is a must read for anyone serious about the art of coaching. There are many who feel that John has not been fully recognised in this country.

Today, John works as a scout with Pat Holland at Arsenal and is a firm believer that anyone who played under Ron Greenwood and John Lyall gained a priceless knowledge of the great game. John shared his memories of Bobby Moore from his Essex home in Great Canfield:

I played with Bobby at West Ham for three or four years but I wasn't close to him. It wasn't because we didn't get on or anything like that, it was more to do with the fact that he broke into the first team while I was still kicking about in the reserves.

John wearing his England Youth cap.

To this day, I cannot believe there has never been a book written about Malcolm Allison's contribution to West Ham United, because he was absolutely fantastic for the club. He is the only reason Bobby and all the rest of us joined in the first place. We didn't go there for West Ham, we went there for Malcolm Allison. I didn't even know where West Ham United Football Club was. I literally had the pen in my hand to sign for Arsenal but chief scout Wally St Pier asked me to come to the club, where I met Malcolm, and that was that. I signed for the Hammers.

Bobby and I started playing in the youth side together and back then we pretty much played a 'W' formation with full-backs, wing-halves, inside-forwards, etc. Then, in 1958, Brazil won the World Cup in Sweden with a different 4-4-2 formation and Malcolm wanted to do things differently. I remember we trained in the car park out at the front of the stadium and if that was busy for whatever reason, we would train on the debris next to the Boleyn Castle. There was a flat scrap of land that we used to play on. Can you imagine the future England captain Bobby Moore and World Cup hat-trick hero Geoff Hurst playing on debris? Unbelievable!

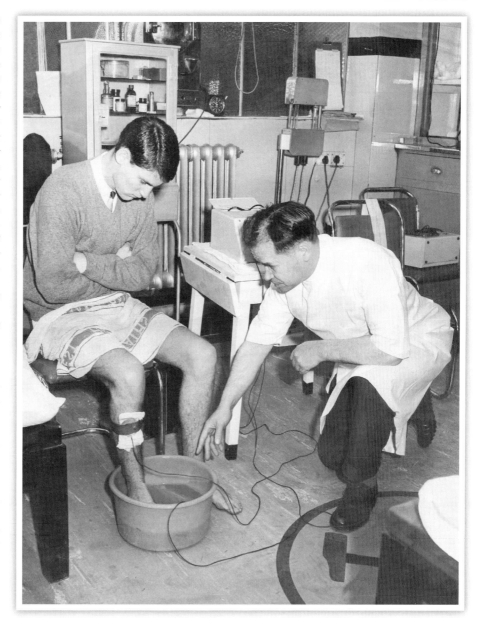

Receiving treatment from club physio, Bill Jenkins.

Malcolm took to Bobby and saw a conversion job in him. West Ham were going on tour to Czechoslovakia, which gave Malcolm his chance to play 4-4-2. One of the players couldn't make it because they were still doing their National Service. It was one of those three players who wore the Number 6 shirt; Bill Lansdowne, Andy Nelson or Malcolm Pyke. So, instead, Malcolm took Bobby, who, until then, had been playing in the reserves as a wing-half and to be fair wasn't pulling up any trees. But neither had Geoff Hurst, to be honest. However, Bobby took to the 4-4-2 formation and that was it, the start of Bobby Moore.

I still say today that good coaches don't look at players in the position they are in. They look at them with enough judgement and courage to try them in other positions and Allison did exactly that with Bobby. A few years back I scouted a boy who was playing left-back for Southampton and gave him an 'A' on my report, which I had never given before. I wrote: 'Arsenal must buy this boy but should play him in left-midfield!' But they didn't buy him because he was playing left-back, a position at Arsenal that was well catered for at the time with Ashley Cole. His name was Gareth Bale.

Who knows what would have happened to Bobby Moore if

Allison hadn't had the courage and know-how to switch him from being a pedestrian wing-half to the position that made him the greatest defender the world has ever seen?

Back then, Bobby was one of many players at West Ham who lived and breathed football. If they weren't playing football, they were in Cassettaris' café talking about football. Cassettaris was the first place I ever learned about mixed hot rice pudding and ice cream! Malcolm introduced it to everyone. It was in there that we started to talk about near-post crossing. Ron Greenwood introduced it but before that we had already been discussing it. I remember the first time we ever tried it in a reserve team match. We put in a short cross and I think Brian Dear got up and netted at the near-post. We were all really excited and were shouting: 'That's what we'd talked about in the café!' Of course, it then became a West Ham trademark.

Bobby, Geoff, Martin and all those boys I played with back then, learned their trade in the streets as young boys. This is what has gone wrong with football in this country. The academics, who have never understood street football, have come in and made the game too complicated. They try and teach football like they teach mathematics and it doesn't work. It is too structured, too organised and too boring. You don't learn it that way. You learn it from doing it, from making mistakes, from appreciating space and getting a good knowledge of where everyone is around you. You did all this automatically on the streets.

If Bobby had been left to play wing-half in the old 'W' formation he would have been roasted every time because, as we all know, he had issues with pace and heading. If it wasn't for Malcolm, Bobby may well have ended up an ordinary midfield player. That is why I think Malcolm needs his picture alongside Bobby. Moore loved Allison.

John Cartwright

'Didi' with one of his coaching books.

15 – ANDY SMILLIE

Born: Ilford, Essex, March 15, 1941

Position: Inside-forward/Midfield

Games played with Bobby Moore: 10 (1959-61)

Games played for West Ham United: 23 (1958-61)

Honours with Bobby Moore: 1959 FA Youth Cup finalist

First game with Bobby Moore (Debut): October 17, 1959 – Everton (a) W 1-0

Scorer: West Ham United: Musgrove

EVERTON FOOTBALL CLUB
GOODISON PARK
LIVERPOOL

OFFICIAL PROGRAMME

FOOTBALL LEAGUE
EVERTON v. WEST HAM
SATURDAY, 17th OCTOBER 1959
KICK-OFF 3 p.m.

Nº 4417   PRICE THREEPENCE

Everton: Dunlop, Parker, Bramwell, King, Jones, Harris B, Harris J, Thomas, Hickson, Collins, Shackleton

West Ham United: Dwyer, Bond, Cantwell, Malcolm, Brown, Moore, Grice, Cartwright, Keeble, **Smillie**, Musgrove.

Andrew 'Andy' Thomas Smillie lined up with Bobby Moore in West Ham United's 1959 FA Youth Cup final against Blackburn Rovers. He was the first player from that youth team to follow Bobby into the senior side, making his debut in a stunning 4-1 victory at White Hart Lane on Boxing Day, 1958. John Smith wore the Number 6 shirt in that game and it would be another 10 months before Smillie and Moore first lined up together in the first team.

Smillie also played in Bobby Moore's first FA Cup tie – a third round 2-2 draw at home to Stoke City in January 1961.

Sir Geoff Hurst recalls playing with Andy in the 1959 Youth Cup final: 'He was a great little player and I was surprised he didn't play at a higher level for longer. He was a very dedicated player.'

Bobby and Andy were two 18-year-olds plying their trade at different ends of the pitch but had known each other

Andy (bottom row, second left) and Bobby (back row far right).

for almost a decade having played against each other in their Barking and Ilford primary school days. Andy played schoolboy football for Ilford, London and Essex before playing with Bobby in the England Youth side and would eventually gain three England Youth caps.

Andy left West Ham in 1961, joining Crystal Palace and then subsequently playing for Scunthorpe United, Southend United, Gillingham and Folkestone.

Andy continues to include work as part of his retirement package and his decision to exchange his boots for batter many years ago has benefited everyone who loves a hearty portion of fish and chips. No trip to Southend is complete without a visit to *Smileys* in Westcliff-on-Sea. Andy is usually there with his hands in cod batter but if he isn't, they'll be wrapped around a golf club improving his seven handicap.

I knew Bobby Moore from the age of nine when we played for our district sides. There was only a month between us in age and he was playing for Barking and I was with Ilford. I also played with him at England Youth level. Even at that age he seemed six feet tall and had this mass of hair which seemed blonder than ever back then.

To get some extra money during the close season, Bobby and I worked together at William Warnes rubber factory in Barking. Bobby's mum Doris was employed there and she would help to get summer jobs for Bobby and his mates. The factory made everything from condoms to rubber tyres. A lot of players worked there – Brian Dear, John Charles, Eddie Bovington, Tony Scott and Harry Cripps.

Before Bobby met Tina we often went to the Ilford Palais together. I didn't live far from the night club – 186 High Road, Ilford – and hosted parties at my house several times a year. We would all be dressed really smart and had so much fun.

The Palais was the place to be back then and Crippsy, Scotty and others would always come back to mine afterwards. I remember one winter evening when Tina and Bobby came along to one of my parties and emptied the wardrobe of all the coats to keep themselves warm.

I played with Bobby at the very start of his career and we went out socially together but a lot of the time you didn't really notice he was there. Obviously, this changed as he got older but back then he was a quiet lad and didn't go out much. Not like Harry Cripps, for example, who was a big character at the time. I suppose another reason for this was that Bobby lived relatively far away in Waverley Gardens, Barking, so it was difficult to get anywhere. I was just a few doors along from the Palais, so it felt like I was at the centre of everything.

West Ham always paid the players on Friday and Bobby, Harry Cripps and I would go up to Cecil Gee in London to buy our suits. We'd have a hot chocolate in a little café near Piccadilly Circus and really enjoy ourselves.

We also had suits made by Phil Segal who worked out of a shop near Blackwall Tunnel in Poplar. I can still see us now, walking out of the shop with our suits slung over our shoulders. We'd have striped blazers, single breasted, double breasted and starched collars with studs in. When we went to the Palais, or the Tottenham Royal, our suits were all the fashion. We all had the tonic mohair, Italian look. We were so smart and really enjoyed ourselves.

Bobby always felt more comfortable around the senior players, in particular Malcolm Allison and Noel Cantwell. I don't mean socially but more in the sense of discussing football and learning from them around the training ground at Grange Farm.

One of the things that really helped to develop Bobby as a player was Hungary's 6-3 defeat of England at Wembley in 1953. The Hungarians played a system which nullified our wingers, Stanley Matthews and Tom Finney. Before that game clubs played a man-for-man marking system all over the pitch and Bobby would often be caught for speed. They would play a ball down the middle for a quick striker to latch onto which was a difficult scenario for Bobby to cope with. However, after the debacle of Hungary, Bobby's role changed because man-for-man marking largely disappeared so the defence tended to have a roaming role. This was perfect for Bobby whose super intelligence and ability to anticipate the play and to mark space made him the best player for that new role.

Given the fact that he was always tackling and intercepting in dangerous areas, it is amazing that he only got sent off once in his career.

They were fantastic times and we really did try to be the best we could be.

Andy Smillie

Always close to his memories.

16 – BRIAN RHODES
October 23, 1937 – July 1993

Born: Marylebone, London

Position: Goalkeeper

Games played with Bobby Moore: 52 (1960-63)

Games played for West Ham United: 66 (1957-63)

First game with Bobby Moore: January 16, 1960
Leeds United (a) L 0-3

Scorers: Leeds United: McCole, Crowe, Meek

Leeds United: Wood, Ashall, Hair, Cush, Charlton, Gibson, Crowe, Revie, McCole, Peyton, Meek

West Ham United: Rhodes, Bond, Cantwell, Malcolm, Brown, Moore, Musgrove, Smith, Keeble, Obeney, Woosnam

Brian William Rhodes' finest hour in a West Ham United shirt came against Arsenal at home on Guy Fawkes Night, 1960. Rhodes, along with a Bobby Moore-marshalled defence, kept a clean sheet in a 6-0 shooting down of The Gunners. Moore would have known him as 'Bruey'.

Rhodes spent 11 years at the club after joining the ground staff in April 1952 and signed professional forms two years later. He was part of the touring squad to America in 1963 which participated in the Challenge Cup. The experience transformed the fortunes of West Ham United. Brian would go on to play 66 league and cup games for West Ham but eventually succumbed to Ron Greenwood's desire for an alternative goalkeeper – first with Lawrie Leslie and then, more permanently, with Jim Standen. Consequently, Brian was reunited with former West Ham manager, Ted Fenton, at Southend United.

Bruey was almost four years older than Moore and was a popular member of the team. On one occasion, he even played up front for the A team.

Sadly, his most enduring legacy at West Ham came when he was driving the car that crashed into a British Rail lorry in London's Clerkenwell, tragically killing his good friend and former West Ham forward, Ron Brett, who was just 25-years-old.

Brian started his life again in Australia, where he had spells as a coach, including a stint with the Australian Olympic team.

Rhodes eventually moved to New Zealand where he re-married and had two children. When John Bond was manager of AFC Bournemouth in the early 1970s he visited Bruey, who was living in Wellington at the time. It was part of a round-the-world tour for the Cherries and Bondy took the opportunity to catch up with his good friend, who he had known since the early 1950s.

Brian Rhodes died from leukaemia in July 1993 five months after Bobby. He was 55-years-old.

The following recollections were kindly provided by Brian's ex-wife, Sylvia, who still resides in Australia and was with Brian during the West Ham years:

Brian never got over the car crash in which Ron Brett died. He was driving and escaped relatively unscathed – just a gash on his forehead. They were very close friends, just like brothers. He was lucky to survive but then had to carry the experience with him throughout the rest of his life. He was never himself again.

Some of the players at West Ham tried to get him out as a distraction and took him to the dog track or horseracing but Brian took to it too much to heart and gambling caused a lot of heartache in his life.

He got on very well with Bobby Moore and we moved into his house in Barkingside after Bobby and Tina got married. We were also very close to Malcolm and Jean Musgrove. Sadly Malcolm has passed on but I still stay in touch with Jean to this day.

We did fly out to America with the club in 1963, which was very exciting. We went out with Bobby and Tina and all the players and their wives most nights and had a fantastic time. I think that experience probably convinced Brian that he needed to start a new life abroad.

Brian's career in football went downhill after he left West Ham and he was looking for a fresh start. He had offers to play in either South Africa or Australia and we decided to emigrate to Australia in the mid-1960s. Initially he had a two-year contract with South Coast United but he didn't want to go back once that was over so we decided to stay. After football he got a job in a steel works.

We didn't have any children and it was sad really because we still loved each other but drifted apart. Brian ended up moving to New Zealand, which is where he stayed until he died from Leukaemia. He had re-married and had two children. The last time we spoke was shortly before he died.

Thwarting Billy Russell of Sheffield United as both Ken Brown and Bobby Moore look on.

He called to tell me that his father had passed away and that was the last I ever heard from him.

One thing I do regret was throwing away all Brian's mementos from his playing days. When we split up I was so cranky I put all his medals and stuff in the garbage. There were lots of photos of him playing and some of him sweeping the terraces at Upton Park and doing all the odd jobs like they all did back then. On reflection I wish I had bundled them all up and sent them to his father who idolised him.

The car crash ruined him really. His heart wasn't in anything anymore and the Brian I knew had gone forever. He just drifted after that.
Brian Rhodes' first wife, Sylvia

Following are a few recollections of Brian from those that knew him at West Ham:

When I joined West Ham, Bruey was one of the first people to welcome me to the club. That says a great deal about the lad because I had been signed to replace him. We trained a lot together after that and he was very dedicated. He was a great lad and I liked him a lot.
Lawrie Leslie

I played against Brian in the Army during our National Service. He was in the Medical Corps and I was a Paramedic in the Para Brigade. I then became his understudy at West Ham
after Ernie Gregory retired. Brian was a really likeable bloke.
Peter Shearing

We went all around the world with John's football career and on one occasion we visited Brian Rhodes in New Zealand. We used to be quite friendly with Brian when we lived in Thorne Road. John came home really shaken up on the night Brian had the car crash in which Ron Brett died. I couldn't calm him down.
Janet Bond

We played a pre-season game against the first team. The ball came over and I went up to head it and Bruey punched me right in the temple and I went down like a sack of potatoes. In those days they just splashed some cold water on your face and told you to get on with it. Nobody really knew how badly I had been injured until I got the ball and started running with it in the wrong direction against my own team-mates! The next thing I knew I was in the dressing room with the doctor looking over me.
John Cartwright

We were playing an A game at Rainham and at half-time Bruey came in and said: 'I don't want to play in goal anymore, I want to play up front.' So he joined me up front and scored a couple of goals!
Roger Hugo

17 – HARRY OBENEY

Born: Bethnal Green, London, March 9, 1938

Position: Forward

Games played with Bobby Moore: 9 (1960-61)

Games played for West Ham United: 27 (1959-61)

First game with Bobby Moore: January 16, 1960
Leeds United (a) L 0-3

Scorers: Leeds United: McCole, Crowe, Meek

Leeds United: Wood, Ashall, Hair, Cush, Charlton, Gibson, Crowe, Revie, McCole, Peyton, Meek

West Ham United: Rhodes, Bond, Cantwell, Malcolm, Brown, Moore, Musgrove, Smith, Keeble, **Obeney**, Woosnam

Henry 'Harry' Richard Obeney was three years older than Bobby Moore and his finest game came in a 4-0 home win against Everton, on February 11, 1961. Harry scored twice that day and the Hammers have never matched nor bettered that result against the Toffees any time since.

Obeney signed professional forms for West Ham United in May 1956 having previously played for amateur side Briggs Sports. He is a member of a very select band of West Ham players who have scored on their first team debut against Bolton Wanderers during a 4-3 win at the Boleyn Ground on March 21, 1959. His record at West Ham would eventually read: Played 27 games, scored 12 goals.

Harry Obeney, Mike Grice and Bobby Moore were the three blond boys at the club in 1956. Obeney had a terrific singing voice and when living in the Dagenham area would often perform in the local pubs.

He played most of his football with Romford FC and was reunited with Bobby Moore on the occasion of Harry's testimonial on October 21, 1970, when Bobby captained West Ham's first team at Romford's Brooklands ground.

Harry is now retired and lives in Poole improving his golf swing.

I first played with Bobby Moore in the A team when I was 18-years-old. The great Dick Walker played in that team, as

Harry in action against Manchester City at the Boleyn Ground on November 7, 1959.

A young topless Bobby Moore watches Harry chase home Malcolm Pyke ahead of John Dick, Joe Kirkup and Bill Lansdowne. Manager, Ted Fenton cheers them on.

did George Fenn and Terry McDonald, two good friends of mine. I then played with Bobby in the reserves along with Martin Peters and Geoff Hurst.

If I've got my football head on, I wouldn't have said back then that Bobby would go on to reach the great heights that he did. As a central defender, it looked like he couldn't jump high enough. Of course, I don't mean it to sound detrimental but he lacked pace and didn't look like a future England World Cup-winning captain.

In the A team, he was coming through with Andy Smillie, Tony Scott, Johnny Cartwright and one or two others. I spent more time with Brian Rhodes, Malcolm Pyke and Terry McDonald, plus I was married at the time so usually went home, which is the reason why I never really saw a lot of Bobby.

We worked in the summer together because, as footballers, our wages were just a little higher than the average working man and were reduced in the close-season so we needed to get a few extra bob from elsewhere. One of the directors at

West Ham arranged jobs for a few of us at an industrial hose company in Barkingside. There was Bobby, Andy Smillie, Tony Scott and myself all doing maintenance work. One particular day, we were given a little petrol truck on which we carried the industrial pipes and Bobby started tearing around on it with Andy and Scotty on the back. They went racing around a corner and drove over a huge industrial rubber pipe, causing several hundred pounds worth of damage. We were all severely reprimanded.

After my time at West Ham I eventually ended up playing for Romford in the Southern League. I played over 400 games for them and was granted a testimonial. I was hoping to get West Ham to put up a team and Ron Greenwood was very good to me.

I was having some back problems whilst I was at Romford and Ron would let me visit Rob Jenkins, West Ham's physio, for treatment on Sundays. Ron came in to Rob's clinic one day and we had a chat and I told him about my testimonial and asked him whether or not it would be possible for West Ham to send along a team.

He obliged, took all the details and arranged for the strongest team to play in the game which took place on October 21, 1970. The West Ham line-up was: Bobby Ferguson, John McDowell, Frank Lampard, Peter Eustace, Tommy Taylor, Bobby Moore, Harry Redknapp, Jimmy Lindsay, Brian Dear, Geoff Hurst and Jimmy Greaves. Both Martin Peters and Les Allen ran the lines! West Ham won the game 2-1 with goals from Lampard and Eustace.

I produced the programme myself and had to arrange all the adverts and printing. We charged 50p to get in and about 4,500 supporters turned up. We were only averaging a couple of thousand at the time. There is a lovely photo of Bobby and me leading out the teams.

Harry Obeney

OLD pals together. Harry Obeney and Bobby Moore, ex-Upton Park team-mates, lead out their sides before the Testimonial at Brooklands last Wednesday.

Hammers help Harry pick-up £500 benefit

ROMFORD skipper Harry Obeney is expecting to pick up in the region of £500 from his testimonial match against West Ham United last week. Under 4,000 fans passed through the Brooklands turnstiles for the occasion, and although Obeney had hoped for 5,000-plus, he was not too disappointed with the response.

Said Harry: "I'd like to thank everyone for making everything go with a swing. I enjoyed myself, and I'm sure everyone else did as well."

Obeney is also organising a testimonial dance at Brooklands Social Club on November 14. Tickets, 7s. 6d. each, can be obtained from the Social Club.

Last Wednesday's match ended in a 2-1 win for West Ham, who fielded a full-strength line-up in the first half.

Frank Lampard gave them the lead after only four minutes, and five minutes later Geoff Hurst neatly laid on a second for Peter Eustace. Hurst, Bobby Moore and Jimmy Greaves were replaced in the second half, when Romford pulled a goal back through Charlie Williams in the 70th minute.

Harry and Bobby lead out West Ham and Romford for Harry's testimonial.

Harry with his testimonial programme.

18 – PHIL WOOSNAM
December 22, 1932 – July 19, 2013

Born: Caersws, Powys, Wales

Position: Inside-right/Midfield

Games played with Bobby Moore: 100 (1960-62)

Games played for West Ham United: 147 (1958-62)

First game with Bobby Moore: January 16, 1960 Leeds United (a) L 0-3

Scorers: Leeds United: McCole, Crowe, Meek

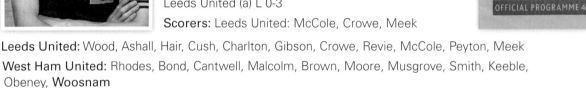

Leeds United: Wood, Ashall, Hair, Cush, Charlton, Gibson, Crowe, Revie, McCole, Peyton, Meek

West Ham United: Rhodes, Bond, Cantwell, Malcolm, Brown, Moore, Musgrove, Smith, Keeble, Obeney, **Woosnam**

Phillip Abraham Woosnam brought a new style of football to West Ham United. That is the verdict of his former team-mates, who still remember Phil with a great deal of respect and fondness. He introduced controlled football, with an emphasis on passing and running with the ball to create more options. He was given the captain's armband following Noel Cantwell's departure to Manchester United and one must wonder how long it would have taken Bobby Moore to become skipper had Phil remained at West Ham? Like John Smith's transfer to Tottenham Hotspur, the sale of Phil Woosnam to Aston Villa was another pivotal moment in the rise of Bobby Moore.

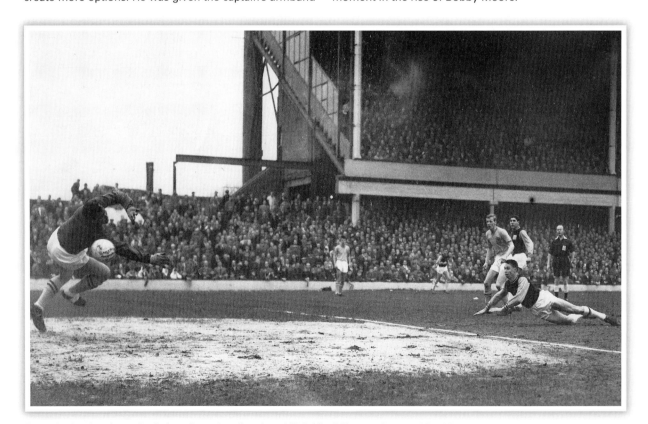

Powering in a header at the Boleyn Ground against Aston Villa's Nigel Sims on January 20, 1961.

Phil with Bobby Moore listening to Ron Greenwood. L-R John Byrne, Joe Kirkup, Phil Woosnam, Eddie Bovington, Bobby Moore, Lawrie Leslie and John Bond.

West Ham paid a club record fee of £30,000 to secure the services of Woosnam from Leyton Orient in November, 1958. His second international cap for Wales was just two weeks away – a 2-2 draw against England at Villa Park. He would eventually play 17 times for his country scoring on three occasions.

Phil's spiky hair earned him the curious nickname 'Brush Bonce' and he is widely regarded as applying both intelligence and method to West Ham's style of play, which helped lay the foundations for the much celebrated, 'Academy of Football' tag which the club has made its own.

Woosnam was another West Ham player to almost break the transfer hoodoo between West Ham and Arsenal. It is now over 100 years since West Ham transferred a player to their north London rivals – Henry Satterthwaite, James Bigden and William Linward all signed for Woolwich Arsenal

in the very early 1900s but no Hammer has made the switch since. However, in 1960 a deal was almost struck between the two clubs which would have taken Woosnam to Highbury and brought both Jimmy Bloomfield and David Herd to Upton Park. History shows this did not happen and Woosnam eventually moved, instead, to Aston Villa in November, 1962 for £27,000.

Phil played 147 games for the Hammers, scoring 27 goals and, after his time at Aston Villa, set off on a football odyssey to America which would revolutionise the status of the game in that country. He was appointed commissioner to the North American Soccer League (NASL) and vice-president of the US Soccer Federation in 1969. Woosnam played an instrumental role in attracting world class players such as Pele, Franz Beckenbauer, George Best and Bobby Moore himself to play in the NASL. The staging of the 1994

World Cup in the USA marks the pinnacle of this contribution.

Phil's considerable commitment to the development of soccer in the United States, where he lived from 1966, is widely chronicled and, as a lasting recognition of his impressive legacy, he is remembered in the country's most important place of all – The National Soccer Hall of Fame at Oneonta, New York where he was inducted on June 14, 1997.

West Ham toured the United States on several occasions throughout the 1960s and Phil would always travel to see Bobby and the team regardless of where they were playing.

Phil Woosnam died in Dunwoody, Georgia on July 19, 2013 after a long battle against prostate cancer. With the help of his lovely wife Ruth, the following recollections were shared:

Phil remembered Bobby Moore as a very, very, nice young man. He didn't have too many specific stories apart from being invited to Bobby and Tina's wedding. He recalled that everyone in the team at that time got along very well and also admired Bobby's playing talents enormously.

He had very fond memories of all the clubs he played for and loved to return to the United Kingdom from time to time even though he spent most of his life in America. One remarkable story came when we returned to Phil's home town of Caersws in mid-Wales. It is a tiny village and when we went to church we were having a chat with a local chap, who delighted in the fact that he lived in none other than Phil Woosnam's house! He proceeded to tell Phil and I about the importance and achievements of Phil Woosnam to the village and football in general. It was such a bizarre moment and it was typical of Phil to listen intently but not divulge who he was and left the man feeling good about the experience. I'll never forget that.

When Phil was playing for Leyton Orient he was actually teaching maths and physics at the same time but had to drop the teaching because it became too much and that is when he joined West Ham United. It was uncanny how he could walk out onto a soccer field, athletics field, or pretty much any arena over here and tell me how many people were in the seats, so easily and so quickly.

Phil did go back to Upton Park in the 1990s and whenever he watched any of his teams on the television – Leyton Orient, West Ham and Aston Villa – he always rooted for them. That was very important to him. One of his prized possessions from his lifetime in football was a framed

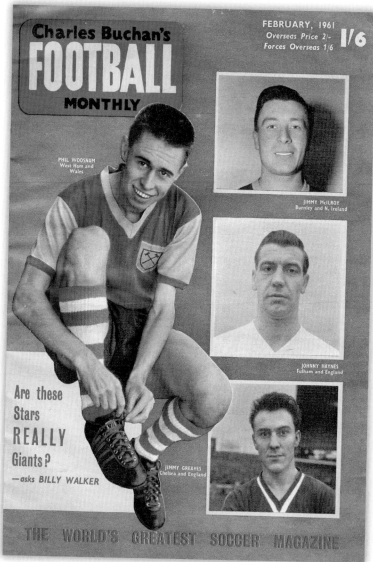

Phil Woosnam on the front cover of Charles Buchan's Football Monthly.

collection of memorabilia from his time at West Ham United, a period when he also represented Wales.

Reading the obituaries in the London Times, Daily Telegraph and the many US papers and magazines, has been wonderful for all of us. Phil will live on in our memories as he really was before his illness. With that fine mind of his, there were still many times when he would amaze us all with memories and stories.

Most importantly, he has been called: 'The father of soccer in North America,' and that would have pleased him tremendously, as it does our family. I'm sorry we don't have any more stories to share but Phil struggled with acute memory issues at the end and we were really overjoyed when he did respond to hearing Bobby Moore's name.

Ruth Woosnam

The following memories are provided by Phil's former playing colleagues at West Ham United:

Phil Woosnam was a great student of the game. He was another one of the senior players at the club with a keen interest in coaching. He was a really good mentor and would help me by explaining how Mooro was developing quicker than me and what I could do to bring on my own game to the same degree.
Sir Geoff Hurst

When I first went to West Ham nobody would hold the ball. Phil Woosnam changed the club a bit and, by that, I mean we played a bit differently. Before Woosie came, I was a target man and they would tend to play the ball straight to me but when Phil arrived he would collect it and come through the middle and lay it off from there. He was a good little player, slowed the play down and seemed to give us more options. Phil was an intelligent man and gave West Ham a new dimension. If he had stayed I think West Ham would have been an even bigger force in the game.
Vic Keeble

For me he was the man who introduced controlled football to West Ham. We previously had the typical 'W' formation with long balls up to Vic Keeble and John Dick and wide players shooting down the wings. Phil introduced more passing and created more space. You see Barcelona doing it now but Phil Woosnam was trying to play that way in the early 1960s.
Harry Obeney

When I was a kid I collected autographs and would write to Phil at West Ham. He would send me signed pictures of all the players. It must have been about 1960. I was a mad collector of autographs and would wait outside hotels, stadiums, car parks the lot. Phil always responded and cemented my love of all things West Ham.
Dave Llewelyn

We used to call him 'Brush Bonce' because he had that short, spiky hair. He was so methodical and would talk about football morning, noon and night. I think he talked about it in his sleep! He would say if you do this, this and this, then I can do this, this and this. He had a lot of influence at the club.
Ken Brown

Phil was very engaging, loved his football and was a very intelligent bloke. He was a good passer of the ball and although he lacked pace he had a lot of guile. He was a real play maker who created a lot of openings for other players.
Peter Shearing

When Phil joined the club I was just breaking into the first team. I was still a kid but was getting more involved in first team training. The year after the team won promotion they brought in Phil because they didn't think I was ready and they needed someone with a bit more experience. From that moment, the only time I got into the first team was when Phil was on international duty with Wales. Phil was a very intelligent player, played with his head and made a big difference to West Ham United. He was very much a part of the footballing legend that the club became. He was one of the key instigators behind wanting to play quality football at West Ham and should never be forgotten as a consequence.
John Cartwright

Phil never forgot his West Ham experience.

19 – JOHN LYALL
February 24, 1940 – April 18, 2006

Born: Ilford, Essex

Position: Left full-back

Games played with Bobby Moore: 32 (1960-63)

Games played for West Ham United: 35 (1960-63)

First game with Bobby Moore (Debut): February 6, 1960 Chelsea (h) W 4-2

Scorers: West Ham United: Bond (3), Dick
Chelsea: Brabrook, Tindall

West Ham United: Dwyer, Kirkup, **Lyall**, Malcolm, Brown, Moore, Scott, Woosnam, Bond, Dick, Musgrove

Chelsea: Matthews, Sillett J, Sillett P, Venables, Mortimore, Anderton, Brabrook, Brooks, Tindall, Greaves, Blunstone

John Angus Lyall is a giant in the history of West Ham United. Although his first team appearances were restricted to 35 games, 32 of them with Bobby Moore, his legendary status at the club is secured by his 15-year tenure as manager between 1974 and 1989, during which he won two FA Cups and a promotion to the top flight.

In the thick of it with Bobby Moore and Cliff Jones of Tottenham Hotspur.

John's playing career was sadly cut short due to a knee injury which never fully repaired throughout the rest of his life. However, he laid a good foundation for his future when qualifying as a coach in both football and cricket.

Lyall played in Bobby's first FA Cup and League Cup games against Stoke City and Charlton Athletic respectively and was on the pitch to witness Bobby's first league goal for West Ham United – during a 5-0 home victory against Wolverhampton Wanderers on December 17, 1960.

John played for Ilford and Essex Boys before joining West Ham. He signed professional forms on May Day 1957 and also gained England Youth recognition in the same year. He was 14 months older than Bobby and graduated to the youth team before him. A particular highlight was making it to the FA Youth Cup final versus Manchester United in 1957.

It is often said that without Ron there would have been no John and it is certainly the case that Greenwood and Lyall did everything together. Along with Bobby Moore, they will represent the very cornerstone of Hammers' history for evermore.

John passed away following a heart attack at his Suffolk home on the evening of April 18, 2006. He was watching Barcelona play AC Milan in the Champions League, two of the teams he most enjoyed watching. Ron Greenwood had pre-deceased him by just two months.

The following recollections are given courtesy of John's wife, Yvonne, who, despite nursing a broken leg, committed both her time and the kind loan of personal photos to help preserve both John and Bobby's memory:

If John was here now he would have spoken for hours about Bobby Moore. He wouldn't have had a bad word for Bobby and would have sung his praises until the cows came home.

John was 17 when I met him and we got married in 1961 when he was playing with Bobby in the first team at West Ham. We met at a bus stop because I was working in the City

John and Bobby together (back row, far right) in West Ham's 1956-57 youth squad.

at the time. The first thing he told me was that he was going to play for England Youth!

John and Bobby had played at youth level together and we went to Bobby and Tina's wedding at St Clement's Church in Park Avenue, Ilford. That was 1962 – I remember it well because John and I were married the year before and I had our son, Murray, in my arms at their wedding.

There was something very special about the people at West Ham back then. Players like Bobby and my John just knew how to treat people. It was passed down from one player to the next but it's not like that today. Patsy Holland used to call John every month right up to the end and David Cross still calls me every April 18, which is the anniversary of John's death. He never misses and I think that type of behaviour was instilled in all the players by people like Bobby Moore and my John. I received so many letters from the players when John died – not just the players he managed but old friends from his playing days, too, like Joe Kirkup.

John had a very high opinion of Bobby Moore. He thought he was a great man as well as a great player. One of John's favourite photos was from the FA Cup final against Fulham. In it Bobby and John are embracing. He loved that photo.

The last time John saw Bobby was at a dinner at The Savoy. It was during the late 1980s and when Bobby saw John he came over and threw his arms around him.
Yvonne Lyall

Further memories of John the player and manager are kindly provided by the following players:

John was a bit of a mentor to me. He joined the club earlier than I did and was a very good, very tough, defender. We used to take the bus together so got to know each other very well. He was a strong character and I believe he would have played for England but injury cut short a very promising career.
Sir Geoff Hurst

The last time I saw John was at a reunion of the Cup teams which took place in a hotel near Canary Wharf in 2005. Bonzo was there so it was a fantastic evening and the thing that sticks in my mind was Tony Gale's compering. He can be so cruel and irreverent but really very funny indeed. Anyway, of the 75 and 80 FA Cup teams Alan Devonshire is probably the player whose appearance has changed the most. He has lost a bit of hair and gained a bit of weight so when Galey and Tony Cottee, the co-host, were introducing the players I was lucky in that Cottee introduced me. Dev wasn't so fortunate. Galey gave him a big introduction: 'One of the club's best ever players and the best I ever played with, please give it up for Alan Devonshire.' Anyway, Dev made his way to the stage through the crowd and as he got there, Galey, with impeccable timing, said to him: 'Excuse me mate, you haven't seen Alan Devonshire?' Well, the whole place erupted with laughter! That was a terrific evening and I'm pleased that John, who was often reluctant to attend reunions, got to see all those players from his most successful time at West Ham United.
Sir Trevor Brooking

John's testimonial with Bobby Moore and John Dick, 1964.

I got on well with John Lyall, another super guy. We were in the London hospital together for a week. He had a big operation and I had a cartilage problem. We had such a laugh and it was the making of us. I went to Bondy's funeral with John Lyall's wife, Yvonne and we've always stayed in touch. No need to change people like Yvonne Lyall and Janet Bond, they're just lovely, lovely people.
Vic Keeble

John was a great friend of mine, a lovely boy. He and Joe Kirkup were good mates. John was a very enthusiastic full-back, a strong boy and I loved him. I recognised that he was a doer and had strong drive. He was one of the youngsters that was doing well so it was a pity when he got injured.
Roger Hugo

I went on a few trips abroad with John when we ran the A Team together. He knew everything there was to know about football and we would talk for hours about the game and the players.
Jim Barrett jnr

I was on the ground staff with John. He smoked like a trooper, even when he was on the touchline. When he had to give up playing through injury, he went on to work in the office with Mrs Moss and Eddie Chapman.
Terry McDonald

John was as hard as nails and had these big thighs like Mooro. Sadly, he had knee trouble from an early age.
Mike Beesley

One day, John asked me if I wanted to get my heels white. I had no idea what it meant but he wanted to try me out on the wide right and I had a lot of success in that position. If you stand on the white line on the wing you can see everything in front of you. There is no danger or anything to worry about from behind and that made a world a difference to me because I was used to playing in the middle up-front with centre halves kicking lumps out of me. John and I thought so much of each other he offered me the number two job at West Ham. I had to turn him down, though, because I wanted to carry on playing. It was one of

the biggest mistakes I ever made in football.
Bobby Gould

John and I coached the kids at Stepney Green school in the 1960s. There was always a bit of banter with the teachers and it was the time of the World Cup so they were speculating on the team Alf Ramsey was going to pick. John and I would say that, as long as he picked the West Ham boys England would be alright.
Bill Lansdowne

It was an education working with John and replacing him with Lou Macari was, in my opinion, one of the worst decisions in the club's history. How do you sack a man like John Lyall?
Mick McGiven

After football, I became a teacher in Stepney for 30 years and retired in 2013. The thing I used in my teaching, which is straight out of the John Lyall book of coaching, was to show the kids how to do things and not just talk to them all the time. Most kids need to see how things work to understand what needs to be done, why things happen, cause and effect, etc.
Joe Durrell

John was my youth team coach and I think I would have gone a lot further if he had been my reserve team coach, too. What an absolute gentleman! He made you feel so welcome and talked so much sense you would run through walls for him. He understood me so well.
Dave Llewelyn

When I played right half in the Colts team, John was left half and we went on to play in the reserve team together. The last time I saw

him was just before he died. I was coming out of the bookies in Colchester having put my bets on as I do every Saturday and John was coming out of Colchester station with his wife. I walked up behind him, put my hand in his back, and said 'Stick 'em up, Trigger!'. Anyway, he turned around and punched me right in the stomach! When he saw it was me, though, we gave each other a big cuddle.
Clive Lewis

...and a final word from physio, Rob Jenkins
John was a very good player, really tough and a bit like an animal on the pitch. I served under him throughout his time as manager and absolutely loved the man.

Family man John pursuing his great passion for angling.

20 – TONY SCOTT

Born: St Neots, Cambridgeshire, April 1, 1941

Position: Right-wing

Games played with Bobby Moore: 85 (1960-65)

Games played for West Ham United: 97 (1959-65)

Honours with Bobby Moore: 1959 FA Youth Cup finalist

First game with Bobby Moore (Debut): February 6, 1960 Chelsea (h) W 4-2

Scorers: West Ham United: Bond (3), Dick
Chelsea: Brabrook, Tindall

West Ham United: Dwyer, Kirkup, Lyall, Malcolm, Brown, Moore, **Scott**, Woosnam, Bond, Dick, Musgrove

Chelsea: Matthews, Sillett J, Sillett P, Venables, Mortimore, Anderton, Brabrook, Brooks, Tindall, Greaves, Blunstone

Anthony James Ernest Scott played in the 1959 FA Youth Cup final with Bobby Moore against Blackburn Rovers and had a reputation for being an outstanding crosser of the ball. He was at West Ham United for nine seasons before joining up with Phil Woosnam at Aston Villa.

Summer work at the William Warnes rubber factory in Barking.

'Scotty' was great friends with Moore, Eddie Bovington and John Cartwright who, as a highly experienced coach, describes Scotty as: 'The best crosser of the ball on the run I have ever seen.'

Tony gained 12 England Youth caps – all alongside Bobby Moore – and, in February 1960, made his first team debut for the Hammers – against Chelsea in a 4-2 victory at the Boleyn Ground. John Bond, the man who would go on to do so much for Tony after their playing careers ended, scored a hat-trick.

Despite an extensive effort to locate Scott, he had been a very important but sadly missing piece of the Bobby Moore jigsaw. It had been a frustrating search littered with dead ends, stretching across three continents. One nugget of humour did illuminate the way. It came from Fred Eyre, who runs the Manchester City Old Boys Association. Scott coached at Manchester City, when his former West Ham team-mate John Bond was manager in the early 1980s. 'They say Scotty found God,' said Fred. 'That was some pass!'

Remarkably, with just a few weeks before this book went to print, Brian Dear found Scotty. He is alive and well and residing in the suburbs of Perth in Western Australia. His high regard for Moore and love of West Ham during that era defined our interview and have not diminished over time. The accompanying photos he kindly shared have not seen the light of day for over 50 years.

Tony started his football journey with Edmonton Schools before joining the West Ham United ground staff.

He signed professional forms in May 1958 and made his league debut two years later. Despite playing almost 100 games for the Hammers, he missed out on the glory of winning both the 1964 FA Cup and 1965 European Cup Winners Cup.

In October 1965, he was transferred to Aston Villa, where he was reunited with his former Hammers team-mate, Phil Woosnam. 'Phil was a great man to play with and loved to talk about football all the time. When he went to America

Scott (7) is congratulated by Moore (6), Malcolm Musgrove and Joe Kirkup after his perfect cross was headed home by John Bond (arms aloft, far right) against Chelsea on February 6, 1960.

he asked me to join him but I was running a butcher's shop in Exeter and had commitments so I didn't go.' Scott later had spells with both Torquay United, AFC Bournemouth and Exeter City.

In the 1980s, Tony emigrated to Australia and initially bought an ice-cream parlour, which he ran for a few years. 'After that I decided to do something I hadn't done for a long time – read! I love to sit around my swimming pool and read autobiographies and anything relating to politics. I still keep in touch with football and watch all the games from England. As a spectacle the Premier League is the best in the world but for our game, the English game, it's a disaster.'

In a remarkable twist of fate, Scotty's neighbour is Roy Goulden – son of the legendary pre-war Hammer, Len Goulden.

Tony lives with his second wife, Sheila. There are five children, all of whom live within 20 minutes of them and they also have 12 grandchildren to keep them busy! 'I go to watch my grandson, Joe, play football,' he says. 'But I get too involved and become the irritating grandfather shouting from the touchline!'

Bobby and I were the same age. In fact, we were born in the same month, just 12 days apart. I played my first England youth match with Bobby, in Luxembourg during 1958. Funnily enough Ron Greenwood was the England Youth coach at the time and we reached the final of the European Youth tournament where we lost 0-1 to Italy. Bobby was

magnificent in those games, he really was. He virtually took that team to the final on his own.

I ended up playing a dozen games for England Youth – all with Bobby.

The following year we played in the FA Youth Cup final. It still rankles with me that we lost to Blackburn Rovers because we were the best youth team in the country at the time. We had some really good players and should have won it, easily. It's weird because the only thing I remember about the game was taking the field for the second half with only 10 men. We were a man short and the referee was asking who was missing. 'Where's Derek?' someone said and it came to light that Woodley was taking a crap!

I then got in to the reserves and eventually the first team. I used to kick about with Bobby Moore, Andy Smillie, John Cartwright, Harry Cripps, Bobby Keetch and Eddie Bovington. Eddie and I were friends for years and used to take the bus to West Ham together. Then I bought a car – a green metallic Sunbeam Talbot – so we drove to training together.

Mooro, Andy and John Lyall were all Ilford boys and often went to the Ilford Palais, whereas the rest of us tended to go to the Tottenham Royal. Later, I moved to Barkingside – across the road from Malcolm and Beth Allison, so I saw a lot more of Bobby.

My ex-wife, Pat, got on very well with Tina so we had some terrific times together. When the club went to America for the second time in 1963, the players were allowed to take their

Tony is seated (bottom right) in front of Bobby Moore in the England Youth line up.

wives and the four of us took a boat trip around Manhattan.

Even though I was born in St Neots, Cambridgeshire, I was only there a few days before returning to Tottenham where I grew up. I actually switched schools and went to Latymer School in Edmonton, a couple of miles down the road, because it was a good school for football. Johnny Haynes went there and that is where Wally St Pier spotted me. He was a great scout and poached five Tottenham boys right from under the nose of Spurs – Eddie Bovington, Jack Burkett, Mickey Brooks, Bobby Keetch and, of course, me. Bill Nicholson must have been sleeping!

After my playing days I worked with John Bond at Manchester City. I did a lot of scouting and, on one occasion, flew over to Perth to check out a few things in Australia. City had just lost 2-3 to Spurs in the 1981 FA Cup final.

It just so happened that Bobby was also in Perth at the time, playing in a couple of exhibition matches. I rang him and we met up. He was with Tina but, if I'm honest, things didn't seem to be very good between them.

The next day we were invited to a party at Ron Tindall's house. Ron was a good coach and Bobby and I had played with him at West Ham. I spent most of the night talking to Bobby and he was still as lovely as ever. I remember Ron

saying that he was finding it very difficult to find any good players in Australia.

It saddens me to see the number of players from our era who have now passed on. They were really good guys who gave a lot to the younger players. They helped me to improve my game and enjoyed doing it.

Bobby should have got into management a lot earlier than he did. Going to Southend United in the 1980s was a no-win situation for him. It was a shame because that club could be a lot bigger than it is but has never quite got there.

Bobby was a nice man. I never saw him rip into other people or put anyone down in a conversation like a lot of the players did back then. He did like a drink which is something people don't like to speak about but Bobby, Budgie, Eddie, Stag, Charlo and me, loved to go out and have a good drink. We were all best pals.

In 1962, I went to Bobby's wedding in Ilford and a year later he came to mine, which took place at St Martin-in-the-Fields, Trafalgar Square. All the current West Ham players came along as well as Noel Cantwell and Malcolm Allison.

Training was great at Grange Farm and, later, at Chadwell Heath. Ron was a really good coach although I felt he could have worked a lot more on our fitness. However, all the theory and mental application was terrific.

My debut was a great time for me and I have a very specific memory of Bobby from that game against Chelsea. I never saw Bobby congratulate people or make a fuss of them if they did something good on the pitch. However, after we had won 4-2, he ran 30 yards to pat me on the back and said: 'Well done!'

John Lyall made his debut in that game as did Terry Venables for Chelsea. John was very good to me and when he became manager of West Ham I used to go back to Upton Park and see him in the early 1980s. He would always have time for me, let me train there and would ensure that I got a good lunch.

John Bond scored a hat-trick on my debut and he did a lot for me in football. He was a good man and it is so sad that all these great men are no longer with us.

I think I could have been a better player at West Ham but nobody really highlighted any weaknesses I had. In my opinion, I could cross the ball well and had a good football brain but I lacked a bit of pace and strength and wasn't very brave, either. At such a young age, I didn't recognise these things in myself

Next to Bobby on his wedding day.

and nobody like Ron, Bobby or anyone else for that matter, ever mentioned anything. So when I was coming up against full-backs, like George Cohen at Fulham, I would try to pass them on the outside and they would beat me easily. I needed someone to tell me my strengths and how to apply them. It would have really improved my play. Ron needed a proper number two really.

I was so disappointed to miss out on the FA Cup and European Cup Winners Cup finals. In November 1963, we were training indoors and Geoff Hurst came in behind me and clipped my heel. My cartilage went and it allowed the young boy John Sissons into the team. I must admit that Sisso was a better player than me and had a great left foot and bags of pace. He should have progressed a lot further than he did.

Bobby and I talked about Sisso's progress a few times. He should have easily picked up a few England caps but for some reason he left all his brilliant play on the training ground.

Even though I didn't play in those cup finals I still felt part of the team and was on the open top coach for the victory parade around the East End which was simply unforgettable.

Because I missed out on the cups, my highlights at West Ham are related to the goals I scored – not many West Ham wingers have scored against Chelsea, Arsenal, Manchester United, Manchester City, Liverpool and Tottenham Hotspur during their time at the club, have they?

The best goal Bobby saw me score was up at Hillsborough in November 1962. Jim Standen was making his debut in that game and we won 3-1. If I had to describe the goal I would take you back to a very famous goal that Pele scored in the 1958 World Cup final against Sweden. He controlled the ball, flicked it over the defender's head and then slotted it home with his right foot. Well, my goal was very similar in technique although I finished it off with my left foot!

Bobby wasn't a Cockney-type, like Eddie Bovington, Brian Dear and me. He was a bit more subdued than us, until, that was, he'd had a few drinks. Then he came out of himself a bit more. Eddie and I used to laugh at him and told him he needed elocution lessons. Physically, Bobby looked sharp but he often got caught out in conversations. He wasn't as good at coming back at someone in the cut and thrust of a mickey-taking conversation. Someone like Brian Dear would never get caught out. He would come back at anyone, lightning fast, if you said something to him but Bobby couldn't do that.

Long after our playing days, I saw Bobby a few times in Australia. On one occasion, I met up with him at his apartment in Sydney and I was so disappointed with what he was doing. He was surrounded by people that were just using his name. 'You have captained England to the World Cup and won trophies with West Ham,' I said. 'But now you're out here playing Soccer Squash?' I was really affected by how people were treating him, or mistreating him, as I saw it. I think everyone let him down. In some respects he didn't help himself either because, business-wise, he just kept his involvement in three or four pubs. Now, would Franz Beckenbauer have behaved in such a way?

I was in Perth when I heard the news that Bobby had died. I had seen him on the television a few times and had thought that he didn't look very well. His passing affected me very deeply. We had so many good times together. Bobby Moore looked like a champion and he was one.

Tony Scott

Following are some recollections from Tony's former team mates:

I played with Scotty in West Ham's youth team. He was a tricky little winger and scored the only goal against Liverpool in my first game up front.

Sir Geoff Hurst

I remember after the 1964 FA Cup final, Scotty came over to me and said he thought I had been our best player. Now, he was very good pals with Mooro so I took this to be a very big compliment. In a strange kind of

Scotty and Mooro in 1963.

way it was endorsed by Ron Greenwood in the dressing room afterwards, when he patted me on the shoulder and said: 'Well done!' He was a very good player, Scotty, and could have easily been part of West Ham's great cup runs of the mid-60s.

John Bond

We were great mates Tony and I. After he finished playing, he went to Manchester City and was looking after the youth team for John Bond. He called me up and said how fantastic it felt to be standing in the centre circle at Maine Road and everything sounded great for him.

Scotty was a bit vain and would always say: 'I love socialising with you, Stag, because I'm better looking than you.' Anyway, he went to Australia in the early 1980s and I hadn't heard from him since. Then, out of the blue, someone called me up and said Scotty was trying to get in touch with me!

Brian Dear

Tony Scott was my best mate at West Ham. Tony, Eddie Bovington and myself were really good pals. We used to go to the Tottenham Royal together because Eddie and Scotty lived over that way.

He was a really good player. Tony would play out on the left wing and would cross the ball with the outside of his right foot. Even to this day he's the best crosser on the run I have ever seen and I have been in football all my life. He was outstanding at that.

The last time I saw him was in the 1980s when we worked together in the Middle East. I helped set him up with a club out in Kuwait and he spent two years over there.

John Cartwright

Scotty loved to gamble. We came back from a reserve team game and played cards all the way home. Scotty was doing his wages and when the coach arrived at Mile End which is where

I needed to get off, he didn't like it. 'Where are you going?' he said. I told him I had to get off. 'You're not going anywhere until we get to the ground,' he replied and we started arguing. 'Why do I want to go to the ground, I live here?' I asked. But he wouldn't have it. 'Keep going driver!' he shouted and by the time we got to the ground, I had won a few more quid off him!
Harry Redknapp

One of the greatest crossers of a ball I've seen. Tony used to play on the left-hand side and whip a cross in with the outside of his right foot, curling away from the keeper.
Eddie Presland

Scotty and John Smith were like blood brothers. John Bond and I had the pair of them playing down at Bournemouth.
Ken Brown

When we first came down from Scotland I had a very difficult time understanding the Cockney girls and I'm sure they had the same difficulty with my accent, too. My father was worried for me because he thought London was a den of iniquity and that I would be exposed to all sorts of bad influences. One day, I bumped in to Tony Scott's wife, Pat, in Barkingside and from what I could make out she was inviting me to a party but under no circumstances was I to bring Lawrie. The husbands were simply not invited. Well, I thought I was being invited to one of those parties where all sorts of wild things happened and I had my father's words ringing in my ears, so I didn't go. A couple of weeks later I met up with Jean Musgrove and she asked me why I hadn't gone to Pat Scott's tupperware party!
Janette Leslie (wife of Lawrie Leslie)

Tony was a good player but was a bit unlucky in that both John Sissons and Peter Brabrook were around at the same time. When Ron Greenwood came to the club he liked Sisso more than Scotty.
Jack Burkett

Tony Scott was great for me at Bournemouth. He set up most of my goals and had this talent of being able to cross the ball with the outside of his right foot from out on the left wing. He said something to me when I was transferred to Manchester United that has always stuck with me. He said: 'Ted, the goals in the top division are the same size as those in our division.'
Ted MacDougall

He was the best crosser of the ball I have ever seen. Left foot or right foot, he was brilliant. I scored so many goals in the youth team and reserves purely on account of his crosses.
Micky Beesley

Bearded Tony Scott with his family in Perth.

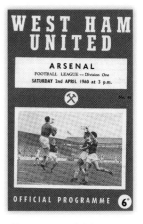

21 – DAVE DUNMORE

Born: Whitehaven, Cumberland, February 8, 1934

Position: Forward

Games played with Bobby Moore: 36 (1960-61)

Games played for West Ham United: 39 (1960-61)

First game with Bobby Moore: April 2, 1960
Arsenal (h) D 0-0

West Ham United: Rhodes, Bond, Cantwell, Malcolm, Brown, Moore, Grice, Woosnam, **Dunmore**, Dick, Musgrove

Arsenal: Kelsey, Magill, McCullough, Charles, Docherty, Groves, Henderson, Herd, Julians, Bloomfield, Haverty

David Gerald Ivor Dunmore joined West Ham United in 1960 from Tottenham Hotspur in an exchange deal which saw John Smith move to White Hart Lane. The transaction was a key development in the rise of Bobby Moore, who would replace Smith in the Number 6 shirt and make it his own for the rest of his time at Upton Park.

Dunmore was seven years older than Moore and was endearingly known as 'Dunmore Rocco' by some of the players, after a popular greyhound of the day. Although he did not stay at West Ham United for very long, his transfer to Leyton Orient was another defining moment in the club's history, with future European Cup Winners Cup hero, Alan Sealey, joining the Hammers as part of the deal.

Dunmore's scoring record at West Ham reads: Played 39 games, scored 18 goals. It is a games-to-goals ratio rarely seen outside of the Bobby Moore era.

One fruitful spell saw him score 10 goals in seven games over a two-month period during the 1960-61 season. Bobby Moore was in the team for every one of those goals, including a hat-trick against Arsenal in an unforgettable 6-0 victory. Little wonder that former team-mate, Ken Brown, exclaimed: 'He could score goals that boy!' when recalling Dunmore's time at West Ham. It was no surprise, therefore, that he went on to become Leyton Orient's leading scorer during their successful promotion campaign to the top flight in 1961-62.

Nowadays, Dave can be found on the golf course in York having spent much of his post-playing career as a sheet metal worker.

Bobby was a one-off. He wasn't a regular in the side when I joined from Tottenham in 1960 but was playing for Young England. You could tell straight away he was going to be something special. A good tackler and a fitness fanatic. There were times when I would go to the dog track with

Dave in action.

Hat-trick hero, Dunmore, during West Ham's 6-0 trouncing of Arsenal, November 1960. Tommy Docherty and John Snedden try to contain him.

some of the players but Bobby would stay behind and do a bit more training.

I tended to go out with players like Brian Rhodes and Ronnie Brett, who were more my age group. Bobby was part of the younger crowd at West Ham but he did like to learn from the senior pros.

We played Manchester United at Old Trafford (April 1960) and it must be one of the youngest teams West Ham has ever selected. Noel Cantwell and I were the oldest players in that team and we were only in our mid-20s. Quite a few of that side were teenagers, like Bobby, Tony Scott, John Cartwright and Derek Woodley. Eddie Bovington was making his debut. I'd scored and we were winning easily at half time but they got the better of us in the second half and ended up winning the game, 5-3.

At the time, Bobby was playing a little bit differently from the usual centre-back role. Back then the centre-halves would give you a hard time, not like nowadays where a striker may as well bring along his slippers. I remember

playing up at Burnden Park against Bolton Wanderers and they had three big lads in their defence – one was called John Higgins – and I could hear them shouting at each other: 'Send him over here, I'll kick him' Bobby was a master craftsman compared to them.

I shall never forget one particular game I played for West Ham. It came against Newcastle United and Bobby was in the line-up. St James' Park was one of my favourite grounds and I had scored on that day as well – we were leading 5-2 with only 10 minutes left. Imagine how we felt when Johnny McGuigan, Jackie Bell and Bobby Mitchell grabbed three quick goals to rob us of victory? It could have been a lot worse as well, because Newcastle hit the post with almost the final kick of the game. It must have been one of the biggest capitulations during Bobby's time at the club.

There's not much else I can say about Bobby Moore. He was a star and that was it.

Dave Dunmore

Dave today with his debut programme versus Blackburn Rovers, March 1960.

22 – EDDIE BOVINGTON

Born: Edmonton, London, April 23, 1941

Position: Wing-half/Midfield

Games played with Bobby Moore: 149 (1960-67)

Games played for West Ham United: 184 (1960-67)

Honours with Bobby Moore: 1959 FA Youth Cup finalist, 1964 FA Cup winner, 1964 Charity Shield (shared with Liverpool), 1966 League Cup finalist

First game with Bobby Moore(Debut): April 18, 1960 Manchester United (a) L 3-5

Scorers: Manchester United: Dawson (2), Charlton (2) Quixall – West Ham United: Dunmore, Cantwell (pen), Scott

Manchester United: Gregg, Foulkes, Carolan, Setters, Cope, Brennan, Giles, Quixall, Dawson, Viollet, Charlton

West Ham United: Rhodes, Kirkup, Cantwell, **Bovington**, Moore, Smillie, Scott, Cartwright, Dunmore, Brett, Musgrove

Edward Ernest Perian Bovington was a member of West Ham United's first-ever FA Cup winning team in 1964 and a one-club man. He was only 11 days younger than Bobby Moore and they shared a close friendship, often rooming together on away trips after that Wembley triumph.

Bovington's inclusion in that fantastic cup run of 1964 came at the expense of Martin Peters who remembers the moment as if it was yesterday: 'I was just a kid when Eddie replaced me after a 2-8 home defeat against Blackburn Rovers on Boxing Day, 1963. He was a couple of years older than me and the team then won up at Blackburn 3-1, a couple of days later. Some might say

Johnny Haynes, Eddie Bovington and Bobby Moore at Fulham.

Eddie and Bobby alongside each other in the youth team.

Ron Greenwood made the right decision by leaving me out! I actually replaced Bobby Moore in the final league game of that season up at Everton, just a week before the Cup final against Preston North End, but Ron dropped me again for the final.'

Bovington and Moore's friendship had its roots in their youth team days of the late 1950s, which culminated in the 1959 FA Youth Cup final against Blackburn Rovers.

Their first senior game together was against Manchester United at Old Trafford in April 1960. Moore had just turned 19 years of age and Bovington would soon be joining him.

Eddie left a fine legacy amongst his team-mates at West Ham and Moore would relate to the wealth of fine comments about him. John Cartwright reflected: 'Eddie and I were good friends and I loved playing in front of him because he was a no-nonsense type of player and got the ball to others quickly and effectively.'

'He was fantastic to me', adds Trevor Hartley. 'He praised me and gave me a lot of encouragement. He liked to tackle and was the hard man at the club. I won the London Challenge Cup with Eddie and think very highly of him.'

Off the pitch, Bovington left a different type of impression

which is aptly summed up by his former playing colleague, Roger Hugo: 'Eddie was so very smart. Bobby Moore, Tony Scott, Jackie Burkett and Eddie Bovington all dressed really sharply.'

Sir Geoff Hurst is another to recall the contribution made by the combative midfielder: 'Eddie was a tough tackling, lively character, who you have to admire for the astonishing work he still does today in the gym. We had a lovely chat at John Bond's funeral and he was telling me how he warms up with a 30 kilometre bike ride. For someone in their 70s it has to be applauded.'

Club physio Rob Jenkins explains how Bovington, Moore and Johnny Byrne were the nucleus of the club's social set at the time: 'The big gathering at any pub, club or social function always included Eddie, Bobby and Budgie.'

Bobby and Eddie always stayed in touch with their great friend 'Budgie Byrne' and would meet up whenever he visited from South Africa.

Eddie played with Bobby on 149 first team occasions before entering the 'rag trade' and running several clothes shops in north-east London.

Nowadays, Eddie lives in Epping and is a fitness fanatic

with a sub three-hour marathon on his life's CV. He is known to enjoy the odd pint and is an ever present at the annual West Ham reunion in Romford, organised by *EX Hammers* Magazine.

I knew Bobby from the age of 16, when we joined the ground staff together. There was Bobby, Andy Smillie, Geoff Hurst, Mickey Brooks, Johnny Cartwright, Tony Scott, Derek Woodley, Mickey Beesley, Harry Cripps and a few others. We played in the 1959 Youth Cup final together and were all just mates enjoying ourselves.

We weren't in awe of each other or anything like that. Bobby wasn't a superstar to us because we were all the same – we all worked at the ground, painting the toilets and sweeping the floor.

Even when he got into the England side in 1962, he was still Bobby Moore, one of the boys. When he was launched into worldwide fame after the 1966 World Cup he didn't become any different. We still met up for a beer and a night out.

We both got married around the same time in 1962 and lived quite close to each other. I was in Clayhall Avenue, near Barkingside, and he was in Glenwood Gardens, about half a mile away. We'd take our wives out most weekends and go for dinner at places like the Moby Dick in Chadwell Heath along with the other lads and their wives.

After we won the FA Cup in 1964, Bobby and Tina booked a holiday in Calella, which is just south of Barcelona and, coincidentally, my wife Pauline and I had also booked a break in the same area only a bit further north. Funnily enough, we both drove there and Bobby left a few days before me. One day, I was in the water having a swim and I looked up and Bobby was standing there next to me. He didn't like it where he and Tina were staying so had driven up to find us. We ended up spending the fortnight together, water ski-ing and just having fun. Once again, it was just old mates enjoying each other's company. No-one was better than anyone else.

Bobby used to shout at me occasionally on the pitch when he thought I wasn't playing well but it didn't really matter and he was usually right anyway! Bobby was lucky in that everyone on the field spoke the same language. It must be impossible nowadays for a captain of the big clubs when they have five or six different languages to overcome.

Bobby's play inspired the best in those around him and he certainly wasn't the type of captain who could deliver a rousing speech or a team-talk to fire you up. I don't mean that disparagingly, it was just the way he was.

Bobby with Tina

Bobby and Eddie on holiday in Spain

Eddie and Bobby playing on Spanish soil

In action against Roger Hunt of Liverpool.

I finished playing in 1969 to enter the rag trade and during the mid-70s I used to drink in a pub called The Spotted Dog in Ivy Chimneys, Epping. They had a Sunday morning football team and were always on at me to get up a side to play them, so I said I would.

On the Friday night before the game, the boys in the pub were quizzing me about who was going to play and I just said I had a few internationals coming along. They didn't believe me, so I just told them: 'Wait and see.'

The game was due to take place on a scrap of land called Stonards Hill in Epping and on the day I went into their dressing room and all the pub boys were changed and ready to play. They were desperate to know the opposition. All of a sudden a few cars pulled up on the other side of the pitch and Bobby Moore appeared with Frank Lampard behind him and Clyde Best following, too.

The irony was that we lost but afterwards we all went back to the Spotted Dog and enjoyed a buffet and a few beers. Those boys have been dining out on that experience ever since.

The last time I was with Bobby was up the West End when Johnny Byrne came over from South Africa. There was Bobby, Johnny, Lou Wade and myself. We had a few drinks in a hotel and went for dinner at a club somewhere. I can't remember the year but that was the last time I saw him. It was a really nice evening.

The whole time I knew him, Bobby was no different to when we first met at 16. He was just one of the boys. People make a lot of the fact that I used to room with him a lot of the time but I don't feel it was anything particularly special – just two mates playing football and rooming together.

Nobody has ever scaled the heights of Bobby Moore and I believe that nobody ever will.

Eddie Bovington

Eddie today with his FA Cup memories.

23 – RON BRETT
September 4, 1937 – August 30, 1962

Born: Stanford Le Hope, Essex

Position: Forward

Games played with Bobby Moore: 6 (1960-61)

Games played for West Ham United: 13 (1960-61)

First game with Bobby Moore: April 18, 1960
Manchester United (a) L 3-5

Scorers: Manchester United: Dawson (2), Charlton (2) Quixall
West Ham United: Dunmore, Cantwell (pen), Scott

Manchester United: Gregg, Foulkes, Carolan, Setters, Cope, Brennan, Giles, Quixall, Dawson, Viollet, Charlton

West Ham United: Rhodes, Kirkup, Cantwell, Bovington, Moore, Smillie, Scott, Cartwright, Dunmore, **Brett**, Musgrove

Ron Alexander Brett died tragically in a car crash on Thursday, August 30, 1962. He was just a few days short of his 25th birthday. His former West Ham United team-mate and great friend, Brian Rhodes, was at the wheel but survived with only cuts and bruises after their car collided with a lorry in London's Clerkenwell.

Brett had previously joined West Ham United from Crystal Palace in the summer of 1959 in exchange for wing-half Malcolm Pyke.

Brett played 13 league games for the Hammers, six of those with Bobby Moore. The highlight of his time at the club came, when scoring in a 2-1 victory over Manchester United at the Boleyn Ground on September 5, 1960.

In 1962, just a few months before the tragedy, Ron had formed part of the transfer deal which had brought Johnny Byrne to Upton Park. Ironically, the two players had opposed each other in a reserve team game on the Saturday before the tragedy. Legend has it that Crystal Palace manager Arthur Rowe was invited to a West Ham reserve team match and asked to choose a player to complete the Byrne deal. He chose a certain Geoff Hurst but West Ham did not want to let him go, so Ron Brett returned to Selhurst Park instead.

Ron's brother and three sisters have all passed on and we extend our gratitude to John Graves, a personal friend of Ron Brett, for the following recollections:

I used to knock around with Ron and we played cricket together for a firm called LATHOL, (London and Thameshaven Oil Wharves Limited). Ron was pretty useful with the bat and usually played at the top end of the order.

We lived about a mile apart in Stanford-Le-Hope and struck up a friendship in our teenage years. He had left Stanford Junior School and later went to a boarding school in Surrey.

Ron played football for Surrey Schoolboys and, as far as I remember, Bobby Charlton kept him out of the

side for England Schoolboys. He was going to play for Sittingbourne but Lawrie Scott signed him for Crystal Palace in the late 1950s.

When I first met Ron he never really liked to drink that much but then he got a taste for it. Like most of the players from that era, Bobby Moore and a few of the others at West Ham liked to wind down with a few beers and Ron would sometimes go up to the West End with them. Ron had a good sense of humour and enjoyed life and was making a good living doing what he enjoyed. He was a good looking guy and had no problem attracting the girls, that's for sure.

Ron Brett

It is with very deep regret that for the second issue in succession our columns record the death of a young ex-West Ham United player. Following the recent sudden death of Peter Chiswick it came as an even greater shock to hear that Ron Brett was killed in an accident last Thursday when his car collided with a lorry in Clerkenwell. At the time of his death Ron was accompanied by Hammers' goalkeeper Brian Rhodes, who was indeed fortunate to escape with cuts, bruises and shock. Ron and Brian were always great friends ; they both came from Southern Essex, and apart from often playing in the same teams at Upton Park also had a joint affinity on the golf course (Ron was also a pretty good golfer).

Ron was born at Stanford-le-Hope ; he played as an amateur for Crystal Palace before signing pro forms for the Glaziers, and established a good reputation with the South London club. He was transferred to the Hammers in the summer of 1959 in exchange for wing-half Malcolm Pyke, and made his League debut for us in the following September at Upton Park against the Spurs. He had seven League games that season and five in 1960-61 before returning to his former club as part of the deal involving the transfer of Johnny Byrne to us last March. His last game for the Palace was against our Reserves in a Combination fixture on the Saturday before his death—with Brian Rhodes among the opposition.

In extending our sincere condolences to Ron's family we would pay tribute to a player who always gave of his very best. A real trier in the team, Ron had that effervescent spirit off the field which endeared him to everyone he came into contact with, and soccer will miss him **very much.**

RON BRETT

The West Ham programme shares the news of the tragedy.

Back row L-R Kirkup, Cantwell, Rhodes, Brett, Moore, Malcolm. Front row L-R Grice, Woosnam, Smillie, Dunmore, Musgrove.

I went to see him play for Crystal Palace against Real Madrid to mark the opening of new floodlights at Selhurst Park. He played on the wing in that game, and given that he was on the same pitch as Puskas, Gento and Di Stefano, it was easily the greatest moment in his short career. I think Madrid won 4-3.

Ron and Brian Rhodes struck up a friendship and would travel into West Ham together. They called Brian 'Bruey,' and he lived on Canvey Island which is about a dozen miles from Stanford-Le-Hope so it made sense for them to make the journey into training together.

I was familiar with the West Ham players because in the late 1950s I used to play for Bata in an annual exhibition game against West Ham United. Bata were based in East Tilbury and was a sports shoe company with its origins in Czechoslovakia.

They had very good facilities and West Ham would bring a full team down for a tour of the factory and a friendly game.

The players were given trainers and boots and enjoyed a dinner and dance afterwards.

It was always a great day and people like Noel Cantwell, Ken Brown, John Bond and Ernie Gregory were so easy to get along with. They were the senior pros at the time and the household names at West Ham. Bobby Moore hadn't yet established himself.

Ron was a good mate, very easy to get along with but he could do some daft things at times which upset a few people. I remember we went to a party in West Mersea and Ron stayed up all night strumming a guitar and singing at the top of his voice. He kept everyone awake that night.

I didn't see much of him during the season but in the summer we would play cricket and a game of seven card brag for a penny a time. Before he died he had been talking about an offer he had received to play in the Southern League even though he had just re-joined Crystal Palace. Sadly, he wouldn't play ever again.

It was a terrible tragedy. Ron and Bruey were driving home in the early hours of the morning. They had been out clubbing. I went with them a couple of times. They must have thought there was no traffic around so went through a red light and got hit by one of the early morning lorries coming out of the Post Office or Smithfield Meat Market. Apparently there wasn't a mark on Ron and you wouldn't have thought there was much wrong with him. Bruey just kept calling his name and couldn't believe he was dead. There was never a great deal written about it in the newspapers.

I've often wondered what happened during those final moments. I remember once when we were driving back from Southend together Ron took a few risks at the wheel. He would take a short cut the wrong way at a roundabout. When you're young you don't care about taking such chances and don't really consider the downside.

I suspect that when he and Bruey were driving that night it would be quite conceivable that they were running the lights because there wasn't much traffic around. Bruey may have been in a rush as well because he was married at the time and was probably out later than he ought to have been. Throw a few beers into the mix and your judgement isn't what it should be. The consequences were so very tragic.
Ron wasn't married but I think he was seeing a local girl at the time called Margaret Hill who went on to marry Stuart Leary the famous Charlton footballer and Kent cricketer. She worked in the Windmill Theatre.

The whole West Ham team went to the funeral at St Margaret's church in Stanford-Le-Hope. It was packed and his three sisters and brother were inconsolable. Ron was living with his mum and sister, June at the time. His father had already passed away. From the church it was about a quarter of a mile to the Stanford Cemetery and everyone followed the coffin in the hearse along Wharf Road to get there.
John Graves

Following are a few player recollections:

I was sitting next to Ron Brett at a Crystal Palace game on the night he had the car crash and died. He had just joined Palace and we were in the stands watching a game. We had a chat and said 'goodbye' and the next thing I heard was that he was dead. Brian Rhodes' car had collided with a truck near Old Street and Ron flew out of the passenger seat and died. I just couldn't believe it. We all went to his funeral.
John Cartwright

On tour in Bermuda with Crystal Palace shortly before his fatal car crash. Ex Hammers John Cartwright and Andy Smillie are also in view just behind Ron as is future Hammer, Alan Stephenson.

I was very good friends with Ronnie Brett and it was a terrible shame when he died in a car crash with Brian Rhodes at the wheel. There was hardly a mark on either of them and Bruey kept shouting; 'Get up Ronnie, get up!' But he had died instantly.
Joe Kirkup

The next day at the training ground the news came through about Ron being killed in a car crash and we all stood there in disbelief. Horrible....Shocking.
Bill Lansdowne

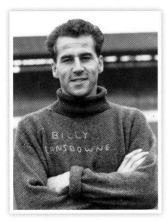

24 – BILL LANSDOWNE

Born: Shoreditch, London, November 9, 1935

Position: Left-half/Midfield

Games played with Bobby Moore: 6 (1960-1962)

Games played for West Ham United: 60 (1960-63)

First game with Bobby Moore: April 23, 1960
Luton Town (a) L 1-3

Scorers: Luton Town: Lansdowne (og), McBride,
Cummins
West Ham United: Dunmore

Luton Town: Baynham, Dunne, Daniel, Morton, Kelly, Pacey, Tracey, Turner, McBride, Groves, Cummins

West Ham United: Rhodes, Bond, Cantwell, Malcolm, **Lansdowne**, Moore, Grice, Cartwright, Dunmore, Smillie, Musgrove

---

William 'Bill' Thomas Michael Lansdowne was both a player and youth team coach at West Ham United. It was his Number 6 shirt that Bobby Moore wore on his debut against Manchester United in September, 1958.

Lansdowne was six years older than Moore and a seasoned professional by the time the young Barking lad graduated to the first team.

He had made his first team debut at home to Lincoln City in April 1956 and his finest season in the claret and blue came during the successful promotion campaign of 1957-58, when he wore the Number 6 shirt on 17 occasions, scoring two goals.

Although he played only six games in the first team with Moore, Bill's coaching role throughout the 1960s and 70s ensured close proximity to the great man. He also had a spell

Bobby wearing Bill's embroidered training jersey.

Bill (right) with Malcolm Allison.

managing Eastbourne United, which was a post held by Ron Greenwood in his very early days as a coach.

Bill continues to enjoy retirement with his wife, Pat, in Barkingside, Essex, the house in which they lived throughout the Bobby Moore era. Their son, Billy junior, also played for the Hammers in the late 1970s.

Most people think that Bobby Moore took Malcolm Allison's place for his debut game against Manchester United but that isn't the case. Yes, of course, Bobby was selected over Malcolm but he hadn't been playing and it was my Number 6 shirt that he wore that evening. I was dropped to make way for Bobby.

I went up to the dressing room where Ted Fenton, the manager, used to pin the team sheet and my name

*In 1957 I was 16 years old . I received a telephone call from my sister's then fiancée **Bill Lansdowne** informing me that he was playing at Oxford on that coming Saturday.*

Bill had been playing for West Ham first team and had been injured; West Ham played him in this Headington United Res (now Oxford Utd) v West Ham A team in the Metropolitan League to get him match fit.

*Bill suggested I went to the game as a young lad of 16 would be playing and in Bill's words "I think he is a bit special" his name **Bobby Moore.** He was 16 also, eight days older than me. He played at No. 5 and Bill Played at No. 6.*

Bobby Moore was a bit chubby and was not the fastest player I had ever seen but Bill was so right, he was a bit special, the longer the game went on the better he became. A sixteen year old playing and holding his own with seasoned pros, he certainly was special.

After the match Bill introduced me to him and I thought he was a smashing lad and very modest.

I met him again years later which was one of the highlights of my life and found him to be a true gentleman.

Mick

Mick Rowles A West Ham Fan of 58 Years

A letter written by Bill's brother-in-law, Michael Rowles.

wasn't on it. Instead there was the name 'Bobby Moore'. That was the start of Bobby Moore and the end of Bill Lansdowne.

I just accepted it and got on with things. I seem to recall doing an interview for radio before the game and they were asking me about Bobby playing instead of me. It was just one of those things. I had taken Frank O'Farrell's place at left-half a few years earlier and now it was my turn to be replaced. I wasn't disappointed because you could see Bobby was going to be some player and he went on to have a million-and-one-fans.

Physically, he was a bit slow but, mentally, he was double quick so one counteracted the other. It's not too bad being replaced by Bobby Moore!

When I trained at West Ham all the players wore woollen roll neck jumpers and the wives and girlfriends would embroider the initials of their man on the front so it was easier to identify. My wife, Pat, embroidered my full name on mine and there is a photo out there somewhere of Bobby Moore wearing my jumper after I had left the club. I would love to see that photo again.

I was a bit older than Bobby and wasn't a drinker, so I didn't go out with him socially. I was more of a family man and liked to get home after training.

My last game for West Ham was in 1962, so we were both set on different paths. I had an initial spell coaching at West Ham and then went down to manage Eastbourne United for a few years, before returning to Upton Park to coach there again.

Eastbourne was a club run on a shoestring and in 1967 Ron Greenwood brought the West Ham first team down to play a game to help the club raise some money. It was a friendly to switch on our new floodlights and Bobby Moore, Geoff Hurst, Martin Peters, plus the whole squad came down and played. The people of Eastbourne absolutely loved seeing all those stars. They were amazed that someone like Bobby – the World Cup captain – would go and play at Eastbourne United but he did it and all credit to that great man. Nothing was beneath him.

Bill Lansdowne

Pat and Bill Lansdowne.

Back row L-R Malcolm, Kirkup, Bond, Rhodes, Brown, Cantwell, Moore. Front row L-R Grice, Woosnam, Cartwright, Dunmore, Dick, Smillie, Musgrove.

They Played With Bobby Moore – The West Ham Years

CHAPTER THREE
1960-61

Bobby Moore's total appearances (July 1960 – June 1961): 49 games (2 goals)

League Division One: 38 (1 goal), England U23s: 4 Friendlies: 3, FA Cup: 2, League Cup: 2 (1 goal)

Bobby Moore was voted Hammer of the Year for what would be the first of four such prestigious awards during his time at West Ham United. He would also finish runner-up on a quartet of occasions, too.

Moore's ascendency through the England ranks also continued as he was made captain of the Under-23s – versus West Germany at White Hart Lane in a 4-1 victory. It was his fourth cap at that level. He played in the annual 'Eve of the FA Cup Final Match' between Young England and England and was also chosen to be part of an FA touring party of both Australia and New Zealand. He would line up with the great Preston North End winger, Tom Finney.

It was a difficult season for West Ham United and the club flirted with relegation, having lost five games in a row during a tense period in March 1961.

An undoubted highlight for Moore came in the home game against Blackpool on September 17, 1960, when he faced the Seasiders' timeless legend, Stanley Matthews. Contemporary press reports confirmed that 19-year-old Moore had acquitted himself very well against the 45-year-old footballing phenomenon.

Moore also scored his first goal for the first team – a volleyed effort against Charlton Athletic during the club's first-ever League Cup tie on September 26, 1960. For good measure, he opened his account in the league, against Wolverhampton Wanderers, a week before Christmas.

Elsewhere, on January 18, 1961 the game changed forever when the professional footballers' salary cap was abolished. Football was destined to change beyond all recognition.

West Ham United manager Ted Fenton published a book titled: *At Home with the Hammers*, but, in March 1961, he had left the club under mysterious circumstances. No reason was given for the end of his 11-year reign and there was no immediate replacement.

On April 11, 1961, Ron Greenwood was appointed as manager-coach, leaving his role as assistant manager to George Swindin at Arsenal. Greenwood had carved out a career as a half-back with Bradford, Chelsea, Fulham and Brentford and had later managed both the England Youth team (from September 1957) and England Under-23s (from 1958). He was, therefore, fully aware of the burgeoning talent of a young Bobby Moore. They would be setting out on a 13-year journey together.

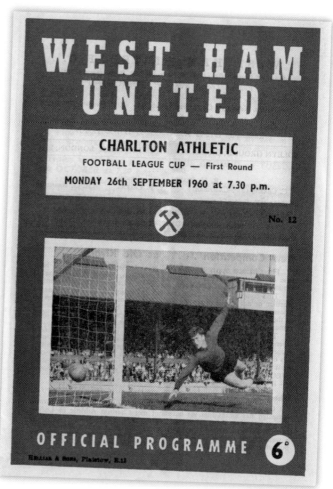

Bobby Moore scored his first goal for West Ham United against Charlton Athletic in September 1960.

By the time the curtain fell on the 1960-61 season, Moore had played with six Hammers in the first team for the very first time – Geoff Hurst, Peter Shearing, Derek Woodley, Mike Beesley, Ron Boyce and Alan Sealey.

The debut of Ron Boyce was of particular interest because, alongside Moore, he was one of half-a-dozen Hammers first selected by Ted Fenton, who would go on to win the FA Cup in 1964 – John Bond, Ken Brown, Eddie Bovington and Geoff Hurst were the others.

Here is their story...

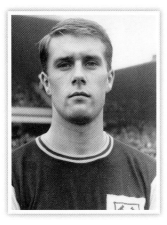

25 – SIR GEOFF HURST

Born: Ashton-under-Lyne, December 8, 1941

Position: Centre-forward

Games played with Bobby Moore: 455 (1960-72)

Games played for West Ham United: 500 (1960-72)

Honours with Bobby Moore: 1959 FA Youth Cup finalist, 1964 FA Cup winner, 1964 FA Charity Shield (Shared with Liverpool), 1965 European Cup Winners Cup winner, 1966 League Cup finalist, 1966 World Cup winner, Hammer of the Year 1966, 1967, 1969

First game with Bobby Moore (Debut): August 29, 1960 Aston Villa (a) L 1-2

Scorers: Aston Villa: Hitchens, Thomson – West Ham United: Dunmore

Aston Villa: Sims, Lynn, Neal, Crowe, Dugdale, Saward, MacEwan, Thomson, Hitchens, Wylie, McParland

West Ham United: Rhodes, Bond, Cantwell, **Hurst**, Brown, Moore, Grice, Woosnam, Dunmore, Smillie, Musgrove

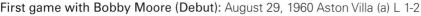

Geoffrey Charles Hurst was a striker to build a dream on. He played in more matches with Bobby Moore than any other player. His contribution to West Ham United Football Club was immense and he remains the post-war leading goalscorer on 246 goals, with only the peerless Victor Watson ahead of him on the club's all-time list with 326 goals.

Geoff also holds the club's post-war record for goals in a single season – his 29 during 1966-67 seems set to be unchallenged for some time to come. Not bad for a player whose first 30 games for West Ham United were in the wing-half position.

Hurst's career statistics deserve the widest possible audience and a huge plaque above the players' tunnel is a fine idea.

League: 411 appearances: 180 goals

FA Cup: 26 appearances: 23 goals

League Cup: 47 appearances: 43 goals (*British record*)

European Cup Winners Cup: 15 appearances: 2 goals

Charity Shield: 1 appearance: 1 goal

England: 49 appearances: 24 goals

World Cup goals: 5 (1966 and 1970)

World Cup final goals: 3 (*World record*)

'Ron Greenwood made Geoff Hurst,' reflects the Lancashire-born marksman. 'The decision to convert me from an average wing-half to a centre-forward is, arguably, one of the greatest coaching decisions in West Ham United's history.'

Geoff played for Chelmsford boys and gained six England Youth caps before earning his full international debut – against West Germany on February 23, 1966. Bobby was captain for that game and was gaining his 36th England cap.

Just a few months later, Geoff would be enjoying both his and the nation's greatest moment on the world's biggest stage – a hat-trick in the World Cup final at Wembley.

Hurst signed professional forms for West Ham United on April 16, 1958, and also played one County Cricket game for Essex. He also captained the West Ham cricket team in their summer matches with local clubs.

He is one of the few players to have lined up with Bobby Moore in the 1950s, 60s and 70s, and played in five major finals with the great man: 1959 Youth Cup, 1964 FA Cup, 1965 European Cup Winners Cup, 1966 League Cup and the small matter of the 1966 World Cup. He also scored four penalties in two days – two for England v France on March 12, 1969 and two for West Ham against Coventry City on March 14, 1969.

Geoff was voted Hammer of the Year on three occasions and remains the only man on the planet to have scored a hat-trick in a World Cup final, a record which is highly coveted by both West Ham and England fans alike. For good measure, going into the 2014-15 campaign, he is the last Hammer to score a winning goal at Anfield – in a 2-1 victory back on September 14, 1963. One year later, on August 15, 1964, he scored the equaliser at Anfield in a 2-2 draw which gave West Ham their one and only share of the Charity Shield.

Bobby Moore lined up in Geoff's testimonial on November 23, 1971. A healthy crowd of 29,250 attended the match, which saw eight goals shared between West Ham United and a European XI which included Eusebio, Jimmy Greaves, Willi Schultz, Dave Mackay, Jimmy Johnstone, Mordechai Spiegler, Uwe Seeler, Ted MacDougall, Rodney Marsh, Mike Docherty, Antonio Simoes, John Jackson and Tommy Gemmell.

A striker to build a dream on.

Parading the FA Cup L-R Ron Boyce, John Sissons, Ken Brown, Geoff Hurst, Bobby Moore and Jack Burkett.

Geoff's football journey took him from West Ham to Stoke City, then West Bromwich Albion and finally, Seattle Sounders. Then he had a spell in management with both Telford United and Chelsea on these shores and with Kuwait SC in the Middle East. He then spent 20 years in the insurance business before retiring in 2002. Since then he has fulfilled the role of ambassador for McDonalds' coaching programme in England. The role is mirrored by Ian Rush in Wales, Pat Jennings in Northern Ireland and, to a lesser extent, Kenny Dalglish in Scotland. He is also an ambassador for Club Wembley and consequently attends every game at the new stadium. He chooses not to undertake too much media work, does the occasional bit of after-dinner speaking and some PR duties. In 1998 he received a Knighthood from the Queen.

Geoff not only gave his time to discuss his recollections of Bobby Moore, in the leafy surroundings of Cheltenham, but he also penned the foreword for the book:

Mooro was the best player I played with, simply because of his skill set, discipline, dedication and composure. He was so committed in everything he did. Every pre-season, the whole squad of players would assemble at Grange Farm and Ernie Gregory would ask us all to lay down flat and raise our legs up in the air. The last man with his legs in the air won a bottle of pop and a bar of chocolate. Inevitably, Mooro would be the last man. His big thighs and strong mind simply refused to quit before anyone else.

He liked a drink but knew when to stop. A year before the 1970 World Cup, Sir Alf Ramsey took England on tour to play Mexico, Uruguay and Brazil. There was no pressure on anyone because the league season was over and a few of the boys viewed it as a holiday. On the flight to Mexico, the attendant was taking everyone's order for drinks and most of the boys were taking lager. When it came to Mooro's turn he said: 'Orange juice, please.' He was clearly taking his responsibility very seriously and was determined to play well

Fully wound-up and unleashing a fierce drive at the Boleyn Ground.

in those friendly games because he was already thinking ahead to the World Cup the following year. He lived his life to be the best he could be on the day.

Nothing seemed to faze him and this was no better evidenced than when he was placed under house arrest in Colombia shortly before the 1970 World Cup. It was just a ludicrous situation when both he and Bobby Charlton were accused of stealing a bracelet at the Tequendama Hotel in Bogota. It was a put-up job and had happened to other people before. To think that the two biggest ambassadors for England could be embroiled in such nonsense is mind-boggling but the world went mad for a while and it took an almighty diplomatic effort to get Bobby out of there. Now, I am no psychologist but the stress and strain both he and the team were put under during that unsavoury episode would, I imagine, have an adverse effect on most people. Instead, Bobby went out against Brazil on the world stage and put in the best performance ever seen from a defender. In my opinion, he played better against Brazil in 1970 than he did against West Germany in 1966 – and he was sensational against the Germans.

People often compare our era with the game and lifestyle of footballers today. I tend to think it is the natural order of

things. What is often forgotten is that during our era we were earning decent money compared to what had gone before.

Jimmy Hill helped to abolish the maximum wage, which had seen great players earing £20-per-week and just £15 in the closed season. Furthermore, most of the time they lived in club-owned houses. You only have to hold Mooro up as an example of how well off we were. He always went to the nice places. He lived in Stradbroke Drive in Chigwell. Incidentally, West Ham chairman, David Sullivan, had a place in the same drive. I foolishly suggested to David that he had a double plot but he called me to order and said it was actually a treble plot! So Mooro lived in a great house, drove a lovely red Jaguar, travelled the world and did everything he wanted to do. Our lifestyle was light years ahead of what had gone before, just like it is light years ahead now compared to our time.

After the World Cup, West Ham gave Bobby the six-year contract he had been after so I asked for, and got, the same.

Bobby's ice-cool composure was another terrific asset which he possessed. I only saw him lose his rag once. It came in a Home International match against Northern Ireland, in Belfast, when Derek Dougan went right through

Refining his talent against Dukla Prague at New York's Randalls Island in 1963.

West Ham United's greatest post-war striker.

him. Mooro lost it completely on the pitch and I can still see the rage on his face in my mind's eye.

It was such a tragedy that Bobby died when he did because he would have been enjoying the fruits of all his success more than ever, now that we are deep into the Premier League era. I am now in my 70s and work about 100 days each year, which gives me the right balance in my life. I suspect Bobby would have been doing something along those lines using his experience, expertise and manner.

If you look back at history and that particular time for West Ham United, it was brilliant. Unusually, there were a lot of senior pros at the club who were interested in coaching at a time when the game was changing rapidly. Malcolm Allison, Noel Cantwell, John Bond, Malcolm Musgrove and others were all taking training sessions on Tuesday and Thursday evenings and applying their ideas and methods on the younger kids that were coming through, like myself and Mooro. Bobby was progressing at a faster pace than I was and it wasn't until Ron Greenwood arrived at the club, and converted me from a wing-half to a centre-forward, that I started to fly. Before then, I was falling behind, largely on account of playing both cricket and football. It was no coincidence that Ron coached three future World Cup

winners at a club which was much smaller than the bigger boys. The club had risen from the wilderness in 1958, won the FA Cup six years later, a European trophy the following year and provided three players for the country's biggest ever achievement in world football. That line of progression is nothing short of sensational. Bobby was at the helm of all that and was the star player in all three cup finals. He was the golden boy during the golden era.

My favourite goal? That would have to be my first in the World Cup final when Bobby put in a free kick and I headed it home at the near post. That goal was hatched in Ron Greenwood's mind, rehearsed at Chadwell Heath and executed at Wembley.

Sir Geoff Hurst

Following are a few memories of Geoff from his team-mates:

One day Ron told me that I was going to play in the reserves and I remember thinking 'West Ham reserves – fantastic!' It was an incredible feeling, like playing for England. We were playing Peterborough United at Upton Park and Ron told me that he was going to play Geoff up front. At the time Geoff had been playing in midfield. It was the very first

time Geoff had been asked to play up front. We were 2-0 up at half time and Geoff had scored both. The rest is history.
Peter Bennett

Geoff and I were good mates and my mum, Doris, always joked that she was going to put a blue plaque outside our council house in Harold Hill saying 'Sir Geoff Hurst slept here!' Geoff's favourite at Cassettaris was double baked jam roll, syrup and custard and he used to eat it boiling hot because he had a false tooth and wore a plate so he didn't feel it. He was terrific to play with. He would say to a defender, 'Through your legs!' and then nutmeg him. He was great, Hursty.
Mickey Beesley

Stuart Morgan and I used to play cricket for the West Ham team and one day there was a game at Clacton-on-Sea but we couldn't get there because we didn't have a car. Anyway, Geoff told us to make our way to Ilford station, where he picked us up and we went to his house for a spot of lunch. His wife Judith made us a lovely meal and then Geoff took us to the game. Now for two young kids from Wales to be shown that level of hospitality by a World Cup superstar was really special.
Dave Llewelyn

When Geoff was breaking into the first team he was lodging with a Mrs Foskett just off Lonsdale Avenue, in Denbigh Road. He would pop round to my house and borrow a fiver off my dad to buy a collar and tie because we were expected to be smart on match days.
Brian Dear

Geoff worked tirelessly for West Ham, a complete workhorse. He made run after run after run and was such a presence, such a willing target for us all. He had two good feet and struck the ball so well. The amount of unselfish running he did in each game was phenomenal. He didn't have the natural talent of Budgie Byrne but his work rate was outstanding.
Trevor Dawkins

I was assistant manager to Geoff at Chelsea. We met on a management course at Bisham Abbey and I did everything for him. I think he liked my enthusiasm because he said that if he ever got a job in management he would take me as his number two. I was playing in Hereford United's reserves at the time, when a call came in from Geoff asking me to join him at Chelsea.
Bobby Gould

Geoff was one of the great centre forwards in England. No one could run off the ball like Geoff. He was big, strong, great with both feet and a wonderful shielder of the ball. You just couldn't get the ball from him once he had put his frame in front of you. A great, great goal-scorer.
Clyde Best

Wherever you kicked the ball on the pitch Hursty would be there.
Tommy Taylor

West Ham United's World Cup legend.

26 – PETER SHEARING

Born: Uxbridge, Middlesex, August 26, 1938
Position: Goalkeeper
Games played with Bobby Moore: 6 (1960)
Games played for West Ham United: 6 (1960)
First game with Bobby Moore (Debut): September 3, 1960 Sheffield Wednesday (a) L 0-1
Scorers: Sheffield Wednesday: Fantham

Sheffield Wednesday: Springett, Johnson, Megson, McAnearney, Swan, Kay, Wilkinson, Craig, Quinn, Fantham, Finney

West Ham United: Shearing, Bond, Cantwell, Malcolm, Brown, Moore, Grice, Woosnam, Dunmore, Dick, Musgrove

Peter Fraser Shearing had a big fan in fellow keeper Ernie Gregory, who was the main impetus behind his signing from Hendon FC in 1960. Peter had just won the Amateur Cup final with Hendon, beating Kingstonian 2-1 at Wembley, and Ernie was suitably impressed to invite him to join West Ham United.

Shearing's route through football had also included Uxbridge and Hayes and he played his first A team game for the Hammers against Crystal Palace at Selhurst Park on January 27, 1960.

Peter's spell at West Ham was brief and his finest moment came when he played with Bobby Moore in the team that beat Manchester United, 2-1, at home on September 5, 1960, courtesy of goals from Ron Brett and Malcolm Musgrove.

He was almost three years older than Moore and played all of his six first team games between the sticks behind him.

Nowadays, Peter is often to be found enjoying his life-time's passion – golf – at the charming course in Whitstable, Kent. He also entertains the locals with his Tommy Cooper cabaret act.

I was only at West Ham for one year and came from the amateur game at Hendon, so I was a bit of an outsider. I hadn't grown up with any of the young lads at the club so I wasn't part of the senior dressing room. Bobby was a few years younger than me and I found him a little stand-offish but there wasn't any strong reason why we should have been really close.

He was the first of his group to play in West Ham's senior team while Geoff Hurst and Martin Peters were playing with me in the reserves. Geoff was a big wing-half at the time.

Peter on his winning home debut v Manchester United, Sept 1960.

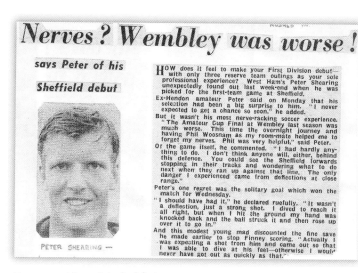

Nerves ? Wembley was worse !

says Peter of his Sheffield debut

HOW does it feel to make your First Division debut— with only three reserve team outings as your sole professional experience? West Ham's Peter Shearing unexpectedly found out last week-end when he was picked for the first-team game at Sheffield.

Ex-Hendon amateur Peter said on Monday that his selection had been a big surprise to him. "I never expected to get a chance so soon," he added.

But it wasn't his most nerve-racking soccer experience. "The Amateur Cup Final at Wembley last season was much worse. This time the overnight journey and having Phil Woosnam as my room-mate helped me to forget my nerves. Phil was very helpful," said Peter.

Of the game itself, he commented. "I had hardly anything to do. I don't think anyone will, either, behind this defence. You could see the Sheffield forwards stopping in their tracks and wondering what to do next when they ran up against that line. The only danger I experienced came from deflections at close range."

Peter's one regret was the solitary goal which won the match for Wednesday.

"I should have had it," he declared ruefully. "It wasn't a deflection, just a strong shot. I dived to reach it all right, but when I hit the ground my hand was knocked back and the ball struck it and then rose up over it to go in."

And this modest young mad discounted the fine save he made earlier to stop Finney scoring. "Actually I was expecting a shot from him and came out so that I was able to dive at his feet—otherwise I would never have got out as quickly as that."

Press report from Peter's debut.

The Hendon amateur in the first team with West Ham United.

I remember in one of my first team games – versus Blackpool – Bobby marked Stanley Matthews out of the game, so there was a growing aura around this young lad who, at such a young age, was starting to make the Number 6 shirt his own and attract the attention of the England selectors.

One day I was called into a first team meeting at the ground and all the players sat on a carpet which had a football pitch painted on it. Bobby Moore, Malcolm Musgrove, John Bond, Andy Malcolm and the others were all sitting around listening to Ted Fenton, the manager who signed me. Ted was very much an advocate of man-to-man marking and the 4-4-2 style of play.

Ted then left the room and much to my surprise two of the players, Noel Cantwell and Phil Woosnam, stood up and said: 'We are not going to play that way, we are going to play 4-2-4.' This just totally surprised me – I was new to the club and any thought of the manager being overruled by the players in that way was something I hadn't ever experienced before.

Bobby would have probably remembered me as the chap who rode a motor scooter to the ground every day. It wasn't any old scooter, it was a Lambretta 175! The club didn't like their players riding motorbikes because of potential accidents, so I would scoot in and hide the bike a few streets away from the ground. I carried a big holdall where I would hide my helmet. It was quite ridiculous really.

I have very fond memories from my time at West Ham United. They gave me my first chance in professional football and if I had been good enough I would have stayed but they soon found me out and moved me on!

Peter Shearing

Peter with the programmes from his six games at West Ham United.

27 – DEREK WOODLEY
March 2, 1942 – January 29, 2002

Born: Isleworth, Middlesex

Position: Right-wing

Games played with Bobby Moore: 10 (1960-62)

Games played for West Ham United: 13 (1960-62)

Honours with Bobby Moore: 1959 FA Youth Cup finalist

First game with Bobby Moore (Debut): September 14, 1960 Manchester United (a) L 1-6

Scorers: Manchester United: Viollet (2), Charlton (2), Scanlon, Quixall (pen) – West Ham United: Brett

Manchester United: Gregg, Foulkes, Brennan, Setters, Cope, Nicholson, Quixall, Giles, Viollet, Charlton, Scanlon

West Ham United: Shearing, Bond, Cantwell, Malcolm, Brown, Moore, **Woodley**, Woosnam, Dunmore, Brett, Musgrove

Derek George Woodley holds the record for the fastest goal ever scored at the old Wembley Stadium. Officially timed at 13 seconds, it came against Wales in 1957 when he was playing for England Schoolboys. Contemporary press reports described the goal as follows: 'Tambling (East Hants) to Sullivan (Edmonton), a back-heeler to Woodley (Heston), a fast, swerving run for goal, finished off with a hard drive just inside the post.' He was known as 'The Fox in the Box' from that moment on.

Woodley's football journey started with Heston Boys and he subsequently played for Middlesex as well as both London and England Schoolboys. He played his first A Team game for the Hammers – versus Brighton and Hove Albion on October 19, 1957 – aged just 15 and signed professional forms on April 16, 1958. He also gained six England Youth caps. He would go on to play 13 first team games with West Ham United, scoring three goals.

Woodley played with Bobby Moore in what many consider to be West Ham United's finest ever youth team. They reached the final of the FA Youth Cup in 1959 but lost, 1-2, to Blackburn Rovers over two-legs.

Former Hammer, Brian Dear, remembers Woodley with fondness: 'One day we were in Eddie's café across from West Ham's ground and Derek was asking us to sub him some money until pay day. We agreed, but only on the condition that he stuffed a whole cheese roll in his mouth and swallowed it. He got his two bob!'

The Fox in the box.

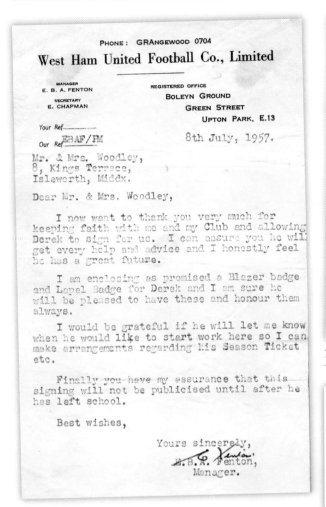

PHONE: GRAngewood 0704

West Ham United Football Co., Limited

MANAGER
E. B. A. FENTON

SECRETARY
E. CHAPMAN

REGISTERED OFFICE
BOLEYN GROUND
GREEN STREET
UPTON PARK, E.13

Your Ref.

Our Ref. EBAF/PM   8th July, 1957.

Mr. & Mrs. Woodley,
8, Kings Terrace,
Isleworth, Middx.

Dear Mr. & Mrs. Woodley,

I now want to thank you very much for
keeping faith with me and my Club and allowing
Derek to sign for us. I can assure you he will
get every help and advice and I honestly feel
he has a great future.

I am enclosing as promised a Blazer badge
and Lapel Badge for Derek and I am sure he
will be pleased to have these and honour them
always.

I would be grateful if he will let me know
when he would like to start work here so I can
make arrangements regarding his Season Ticket
etc.

Finally you have my assurance that this
signing will not be publicised until after he
has left school.

Best wishes,

Yours sincerely,

E.B.A. Fenton,
Manager.

Club letter confirming Derek's signing.

DREAM DEBUT FOR YOUNG WOODLEY

By SAM MILLS
WEST HAM 3, LUTON 1

DREAM debut for young Derek Woodley. This 17-year-old outside-right played his first League game for West Ham yesterday—and hit two of his team's three goals. It was a sensational performance from the former schoolboy international. Both his goals were scored after the interval. But Woodley was in the picture from the start.

In fact after seven minutes he was going for goal when he crashed into goalkeeper Ron Baynham, who had to be carried off on a stretcher.

Baynham returned after seven minutes and a penalty kick was delayed to allow him to get back into position.

Bond crashed the ball against a post and Baynham saved from Woosnam, who shot from the rebound.

From then on West Ham had the upper hand, and Luton can thank their injured goalkeeper for keeping the home team out in the first half.

From the amount of pressure which West Ham had put on they should have had a commanding lead at this point. Woosnam was spraying passes left and right and the Luton defence rarely got a breather.

The second half was only three minutes old when West Ham took the lead. Woodley burst through from a Woosnam pass to loft the ball over Baynham, who had dived at his feet.

Demoralised

Woodley got West Ham's second goal 10 minutes later. He breasted down a centre from Musgrove, beat Kelly and shot. Baynham stopped the ball but could not hold it, and Woodley, running on, netted.

Luton seemed thoroughly demoralised. Occasionally Billy Bingham did dash along the right-wing and once or twice cut into the centre, but the moment the Luton forwards got near the West Ham goal they seemed to get into a tangle.

Keeble got the third goal in the 78th minute and Turner got one for Luton when he netted a centre from right-back Dunne, who had run the whole length of the field.

The best possible start.

With his England Schoolboy cap and shirt.

In terms of Woodley's playing ability, John Cartwright, offers his own assessment: 'I played with Derek in the youth team. He was very quick and we used to play balls inside the full-backs for him to race onto, that was his game. He'd put his head down and away he would go.'

Moore was not playing when 17-year-old Woodley enjoyed a storming debut for West Ham United – scoring twice against Luton Town at home on October 10, 1959 – but Woodley and Moore did line-up together for West Ham's first ever League Cup tie – a 3-1 victory at the Boleyn Ground over Charlton Athletic on September 26, 1960.

In 1961 Woodley's career at West Ham United was affected by the sudden departure of manager, Ted Fenton. He would soon follow Ted to Southend United before playing out the rest of his career with Charlton Athletic and, more prominently with Gillingham.

Derek's other sporting passion was golf. He was also a keen reader and, after his playing career, tried his hand at many things including working as an insurance salesman, cooking in a fish restaurant and being employed as a security guard.

Derek passed away from heart failure, aged 60, in Southend-on-Sea in January 2002. Thanks to his daughter Christine, we have the following recollections:

Bobby Moore was a bit older than my father so he didn't know him as well as other players, such as Andy Smillie.

I didn't even know my dad had played football until I went to senior school. One of the teachers told me that my dad had played for West Ham United with Bobby Moore. I remember saying: 'No he didn't, my dad is a security guard!' He didn't talk about his past very much.

I then discovered that he had scored the quickest-ever goal at Wembley Stadium for England Schoolboys. Officially, it was timed at 13 seconds but it was actually a bit quicker because the timekeeper was so excited he forgot to stop the watch. Someone said it had been filmed but we have never seen any footage.

Dad was always getting into trouble as a young boy. I have very vivid memories of him re-telling childish pranks which usually ended with him having to run away from one belting or another. This is where Dad's athletic talent first surfaced – he discovered he could run!

Dad once had a water fight in a hotel room with Geoff Hurst and Bobby Moore after which they cleaned everything up and went to bed. But they awoke the next morning to find the plaster had fallen off the walls!

The physio at West Ham, Bill Jenkins, had a painful initiation process for new team members. When my dad first arrived at the club he was getting changed and Bill approached him to introduce himself but as my dad extended his arm to shake hands, he smothered his privates with a handful of deep heat ointment – it brought tears to his eyes!

It was Dad's speed down the wing, with the Number 7 shirt on his back that earned him the nickname 'The Fox', for when he was in full flight there weren't many who could catch him. He was still quite fast even in his later years. He had to be, to dodge the plates my mother threw at him!

Dad never talked much about actual games and preferred to share the comical stories from his footballing days. He used to say that he actually dreamt about playing. So much so that he once dozed off on a train and inadvertently kicked the passenger next to him, who turned out to be Jon Pertwee of Dr Who fame!

Another tale he used to share was how he and his England Youth team-mates nearly killed Nobby Stiles by rolling him up – 'Cleopatra-style' – in a carpet. However, the carpet was incredibly long and it got higher and higher until they finally realised Nobby was turning blue. They unrolled him very quickly – it really was a close call. I suspect Bobby Moore would have heard that story from his time playing with Nobby for England.

Dad was a happy-go-lucky type of person and always game for a laugh. He could be brilliant company sometimes but also very quiet at home. He would sit with a book and you wouldn't get two words out of him and then other times he would be the life and soul of the party. He was most comfortable when sporting a pair of shorts.

He suffered from a heart condition and was fitted with a pace maker but it was his heart that took him in the end.

Dad definitely regretted leaving West Ham and said it was the worst mistake of his life.
Christine Woodley

Derek (left) in later life being presented with a framed photo from his England schoolboy days.

28 – MIKE BEESLEY

Born: Epping, Essex, June 10, 1942

Position: Centre forward

Games played with Bobby Moore: 2 (1960-61)

Games played for West Ham United: 2 (1960-61)

Honours with Bobby Moore: 1959 FA Youth Cup finalist

First game with Bobby Moore (Debut): September 24, 1960 Everton (a) L 1-4

Scorers: Everton: Lill, Ring, Vernon (2)
West Ham United: Beesley

Everton: Dunlop, Parker, Jones, Gabriel, Labone, Harris B, Lill, Collins, Harris J, Vernon, Ring

West Ham United: Shearing, Bond, Cantwell, Malcolm, Brown, Moore, Woodley, Woosnam, Dunmore, **Beesley**, Musgrove

Michael Albert Beesley is one of only a few players Bobby Moore saw score on their West Ham United debut. He was 18-years of age and had also lined up with both Moore and Geoff Hurst in the 1959 FA Youth Cup final against Blackburn Rovers. Remarkably, Beesley scored 12 of the 27 goals during that exciting cup campaign.

Mike signed professional forms with West Ham United in early October 1959 having played schoolboy football for West Ham, London and Essex.

He carved out a good reputation for himself by regularly scoring in the reserves. If the team scored more than twice some of the senior pros would ask: 'How many did Beezo get?'

Next to Bobby at a golf shop opening.

Unfortunately, Mike's West Ham career was affected by the departure of manager Ted Fenton and after much soul searching he decided to join Southend United, where he still holds scoring records to this day. Mike had two spells with the Shrimpers as well as a period playing for Peterborough United.

Mike is a fine golfer and an even better property developer. He lives in Thorpe Bay but hurry if you want to see him because he is a serial house-mover!

In September 2013 he attended the 70th birthday celebrations of his former team-mate and lifelong friend, Brian Dear.

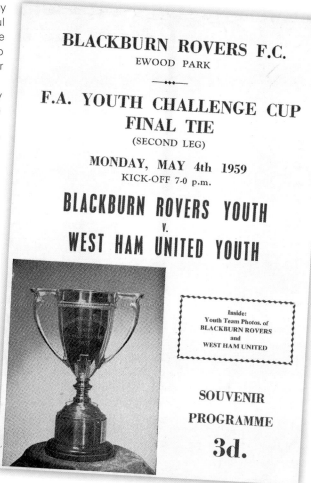

BLACKBURN ROVERS F.C.
EWOOD PARK

F.A. YOUTH CHALLENGE CUP
FINAL TIE
(SECOND LEG)

MONDAY, MAY 4th 1959
KICK-OFF 7-0 p.m.

BLACKBURN ROVERS YOUTH
v.
WEST HAM UNITED YOUTH

Inside:
Youth Team Photos. of
BLACKBURN ROVERS
and
WEST HAM UNITED

SOUVENIR
PROGRAMME
3d.

1959 FA Youth Cup final 2nd leg v Blackburn Rovers.

I remember the moment when I realised just how good Bobby Moore was. It came in 1959, against Aston Villa in the quarter final of the FA Youth cup. That young Villa team were a really good side and although we gained a 1-1 draw, we were under intense pressure for a lot of the game. Now, there was a moment in that tie which has always stuck in my mind and I often reflect upon it. There was a ruck of players right inside our penalty area and all of a sudden Bobby emerged from the chaos with the ball. He calmly ran with it out of the box, looked up and pinged it 30 or 40-yards straight onto my chest and I thought: 'What a player!' It was almost like a rehearsal for England's fourth goal in the World Cup final.

Even at that very early age when I knew and played with Bobby in the youth team, he had an aura about him. There was a presence there. I wasn't part of his main circle of friends because I was a year or so younger than him. I knocked around with Brian Dear, Martin Peters, Geoff Hurst and Jack Burkett. That was my crowd, whereas Bobby would be with Andy Smillie and others who were a bit older than us. I got in Bobby's youth team because they thought I was ready to play with the older lads.

I can remember two things from the Youth Cup final against Blackburn Rovers. The first was the pitch up at Ewood Park which was awful but, at one stage, I was put through with a great pass and had a one-on-one with their keeper Barry Griffiths. If I had scored we would have probably gone on and won the trophy but I tried to chip him and didn't put it high enough and the keeper caught it. Perhaps on that surface I shouldn't have attempted the chip. Griffiths had a good game and saved a penalty from Andy Smillie. In the end they scored a blatant offside goal in extra-time, so it wasn't to be our night.

The second thing I remember was the reaction of Bobby at the final whistle. It was the only time I ever saw Mooro lose his cool. He was absolutely incandescent with rage about the 'offside' goal. He went after the referee and was raging at him. They had to pull him away. He completely lost it. We were all angry because their goal wasn't even close to being on-side and should never have been allowed but Bobby stood out as being angrier than everyone, which was remarkable because he wasn't known for such behaviour.

At the pre-season team photo shoot Bobby always stood at the back to the far left facing the camera. If you look at any photo from his time at West Ham he is always in that same position, top right as you look at the picture. I don't know why but I started standing in the same position at Southend United when I went there after West Ham. You can't go wrong copying an iconic player but that is as close as I got to being as good as him!

After our playing days, Bobby turned up at a few promotional events for me. He came along to open a sports exhibition at the Cliffs Pavilion in Westcliff-on-Sea but the one I remember most was in 1990 when a local businessman in Southend wanted me to invite a celebrity to a golf day at Boyce Hill, Benfleet. Every year he invited someone different and Freddie Trueman and Henry Cooper had previously done it. Initially, he asked for a current Southend United player but I said I could do a bit better than that and asked him what he thought about getting Bobby Moore, Geoff Hurst, Martin Peters and Trevor Brooking involved?

I called them up and they all came down. As you can

'Beezo.'

more accurate! We laughed, shook hands and I never saw him again.

I had just returned from holiday in Austria, when I heard the news that he had passed away. A friend of mine picked me up and said: 'Your mate's died' and when he told me I couldn't believe it. They hadn't reported it in Austria, which I thought was a bit strange. I didn't go to his Memorial Service at Westminster Abbey but I was living in Eastwood, near Southend, at the time and when it was on, I went to the bottom of my garden by a little hut, where I just stood and had a few thoughts for Mooro.

How many people would love to say they played at West Ham United with Bobby Moore? I feel privileged that I was there with him, not just in the first team but in the reserves and youth teams, too.

The way I would describe Mooro would be: 'A class act on the field and a class act off it.'

Mike Beesley

Mike with his debut programme versus Everton.

imagine it dramatically boosted the attendance and grown men were just like little kids around their heroes. They wanted the players to say a few words but Hursty suggested a Q&A session instead because it was easier, so they set up a table and they wanted me to sit on the panel with them because I had also played for West Ham, albeit for just the two games.

One of the questions was: 'Who's the best player you have ever played against?' So Mooro said: 'Pele,' Hursty said: 'Gerd Muller,' Martin chose 'Beckenbauer' and Trevor said: 'Johan Cruyff.' When they handed me the microphone I said: 'Obviously I hadn't played in such exalted company as the others but I remember a left-back at Rochdale called Arthur Smith who was a bit tasty!'

The last time I saw Mooro was up at the Belfry playing golf. It was an event arranged by Adidas and Sir Alex Ferguson was one of the guests. It was the summer before Bobby died and I remember looking at him and thinking he looked well but he had lost a lot of weight. It was funny because he almost took my head off with one of his golf shots. I told him I was lucky it wasn't a football because he would have been

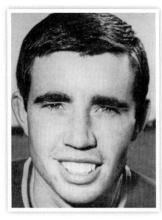

29 – RON BOYCE

Born: East Ham, London, January 6, 1943

Position: Midfield

Games played with Bobby Moore: 301 (1960-72)

Games played for West Ham United: 340 (1960-72)

Honours with Bobby Moore: 1964 Charity Shield (Shared with Liverpool), 1965 European Cup Winners Cup winner, 1966 League Cup finalist

First game with Bobby Moore (Debut): October 22, 1960 Preston North End (h) W 5-2

WEST HAM UNITED
PRESTON NORTH END
FOOTBALL LEAGUE — Division One
SATURDAY 22nd OCTOBER 1960 at 3 p.m.
OFFICIAL PROGRAMME 6

Scorers: West Ham United: Musgrove (3), Bond (pen), Dick – Preston North End: Thompson T (2)

West Ham United: Rhodes, Bond, Lyall, Malcolm, Brown, Moore, Grice, **Boyce**, Dunmore, Dick, Musgrove

Preston North End: Else, Cunningham, O'Neill, Fullam, Singleton, Wylie, Alston, Thompson T, Thompson P, Sneddon, Taylor

---

Ronald William Boyce scored several memorable goals for West Ham United but none more important than the one which resulted in Bobby Moore scaling the 39 steps at Wembley Stadium to lift the FA Cup in 1964.

West Ham fans will recall the moment well. Boyce's headed winner against Preston North End in the dying minutes, when he seemed to appear from a trap-door to head home Peter Brabrook's pin-point cross.

His greatest moment. Boyce scores the winner against Preston North End in the 1964 FA Cup final.

In the semi-final of that famous FA Cup run, Boyce scored twice against Manchester United on a quagmire of a pitch up at Hillsborough. It proved to be the decisive contribution in an unforgettable 3-1 victory. Fellow team-mate, Peter Brabrook, is in no doubt about the colossal contribution Boyce made: 'Ronnie Boyce was absolutely fantastic in the semi-final. He dug in, scored goals and put in an amazing shift. The conditions made it very difficult for me and John Sissons as well as their key ball players – George Best, Denis Law and Bobby Charlton. We all got stuck in the mud but Ron just ploughed on through and dragged West Ham to Wembley. And then he goes on to score the winner in the final from my cross late on! I don't know how I managed to put any power into that cross, I was absolutely gone. My socks were around my ankles and I was running on empty. But I put that cross in for Boycey to score and it was the greatest moment in our careers. '

Scoring against former Hammer Lawrie Leslie of Stoke City in March 1964.

Perhaps more stunning was Ron's unforgettable strike up at Maine Road in 1970, when he returned Joe Corrigan's goal-kick with an unstoppable volley from the half-way line. It was his final goal for the club. Thanks to the power of YouTube we can re-live these moments over and over again.

A lesser-known fact is that Boyce – commonly known as 'Ticker' on account of his tireless work-rate – scored West Ham United's first ever European goal. It came during a 1-0 victory at La Gantoise of Belgium on September 23, 1964. It was his one and only goal in European competition. Bobby Moore was in the team to witness all these memorable, history-making, goals and ultimately lifted silverware as a consequence.

Boyce's footballing journey started with East Ham, London, Essex and England schoolboys. It was a journey which culminated in him becoming one of West Ham United's legendary magnificent seven, having won both the FA Cup and European Cup Winners Cup.

Sir Geoff Hurst joined the club at the same time as Boyce and was keen to share the following comments: 'Ticker was a terrific player and, in my opinion, very underestimated. He could read the game brilliantly, was a good passer of the ball, had a really good engine and was a very important part of our team.'

It is a sentiment echoed by former centre-half Tommy Taylor: 'Ron Boyce was a great footballer who made the game so very simple. Everyone who played with Ron would have him in their team.'

Fellow FA Cup and European Cup Winners Cup winner, Jim Standen, recalls Ron with proud affection: 'Ron was one of my best mates and a charming man as well as a great player. He never said anything bad about anybody and should have played for England. I would have him in my all-time West Ham team and my all-time list of friends.'

When 'Ticker' played his final game for West Ham United – against Leicester City at Filbert Street on December 30, 1972 – Bobby Moore was once again captain of the team. They were the last remaining players from those victorious cup years of 1964 and 1965.

But Moore did not play in Boyce's testimonial game against Manchester United on November 13, 1972, due to an international engagement with England ahead of a World Cup qualifier against Wales.

Perhaps the best tribute to Ticker's playing ability came from Ron Greenwood, who pencilled in the name 'Ron Boyce' ahead of all others on every team sheet during the club's halcyon days of the 1960s. There is a view among Ron's former team-mates that if he hadn't been quite so laid back, he may have earned an England cap. Perhaps more surprising is that he was never afforded the honour of being named Hammer of the Year.

After hanging up his boots in 1972, Boyce was invited back to the club by John Lyall to join the coaching staff. It was the start of a successful union and Ron was on the bench for the

In the thick of it against Leeds United. L-R Jack Charlton, Martin Peters, Geoff Hurst and Boyce.

Wembley Cup finals of 1975 and 1980. He remained at the club, as a scout, until 1995, when almost 40 years of service was brought to a close.

Ironically, in later life, 'Ticker' has had issues with his heart and underwent a quadruple by-pass in 2008. Having been a chain smoker for most of his adult life the habit has finally been dropped. When asked when he last smoked a cigarette, Ron replied with his customary broad smile: 'In the waiting room about ten minutes before I went under the knife!'

Today, Ron runs a farmhouse B&B in East Bergholt, Suffolk, with his wife, Dawn. They celebrated 50 years of marriage in 2014. He still returns to Upton Park, from time to time, as a guest of the club. It was over lunch in Norfolk that Ron gave the following recollections of his former captain:

Bobby Moore is easily the best defender I've ever seen. I think his finest quality was his calmness under pressure. Like all good captains he played his heart out for the team and that is there for everyone to see in West Ham's two Wembley finals of 1964 and 1965. He didn't say much but he could give

you a certain look and you just knew you had done something well or something badly.

Bobby was always available on the pitch for every one of his team-mates. It was so easy to look for him before anyone else and it was Ernie Gregory who took me to one side and suggested that I should take more responsibility on the pitch and look for a pass myself rather than always taking the easy option and laying it off to Bobby.

It is quite an honour for me to have been named man-of-the-match in the 1965 European Cup Winners Cup final because many hold that performance as the best in the club's history. Obviously, I had also scored the winning goal in the FA Cup final the previous season so I like to think that I did my bit for the club. The thing I always remember about my late goal against Preston North End was the amount of time it took for the crowd to respond. It just seemed to take an age. It was just great to give something back to the fans.

It is a shame that so few games from the 1960s were televised because if you could look back at Bobby's 500-odd matches you would see that he was usually the best player on the pitch.

I never mixed with Bobby socially, so most of my memories are from the field of play. He was so commanding with or without the ball and could pick any pass to any player with either foot. He was an expert at forcing opponents into awkward positions where they weren't comfortable. When you think of the quality players West Ham had running through those cup teams, and the fact that each player would show the utmost respect for Bobby as a player and a person, that says it all really.

I didn't get an international cap and never really had any strong ambition to play for England. Jimmy Greaves and Alan Ball wore the Number 8 shirt for the national side and I was a very different type of player to both of them. At West Ham, Ron Greenwood liked me to play a holding midfield role and I felt my one and two-touch play was good and that I read the game well. Of course it would have been nice to have played for my country alongside Bobby, Geoff and Martin but the closest I came was a place on the bench for an England Under-23 match against Turkey. I always say I won half a cap!

It wasn't known at the time but in between the FA Cup and European Cup Winners Cup Bobby was diagnosed with testicular cancer and missed quite a few games.

During our successful European campaign in 1965, he didn't play against Sparta Prague in the second round so Ron Greenwood played me in defence alongside Ken Brown. We did all right at home, winning 2-0 courtesy of a cracking strike from John Bond. Ron then decided to play me in the Number 6 shirt for quite a few games but in one match – against Spurs – I was up against Jimmy Greaves and he tore me apart. I couldn't live with his pace. I was so relieved to see Bobby back in training!

I never roomed with Mooro but I remember we went to America for a six-week tour and I went into his room just before we were leaving to come home and his suitcase was neater and tidier than mine was going out! All his dirty washing was folded, it was as if he had just arrived. The old kit man, Albert Walker, loved him because he never had to do anything to Bobby's kit.

No matter what Bobby had chosen to do with his life, football or otherwise, he would have been the best at it.

I look back on my time at West Ham United with great pride and cherish my shirts and medals. I played for a great team, with a great captain during a great era and I couldn't wish for more.

When I hear the name 'Bobby Moore' I immediately think about all those great memories. Those who played during that era and those who watched it all from the terraces had the best of it.

Ron Boyce

A West Ham United legend.

30 – ALAN SEALEY
April 22, 1942 – February 1996

Born: Hampton, London

Position: Outside-right

Games played with Bobby Moore: 107 (1961-67)

Games played for West Ham United: 128 (1961-67)

Honours with Bobby Moore: 1965 European Cup Winners Cup winner

First game with Bobby Moore: April 8, 1961 Nottingham Forest (a) D 1-1

Scorers: Nottingham Forest: Vowden – West Ham United: Dick

Nottingham Forest: Grummitt, Wealthhall, McDonald, Palmer, McInley, Iley, Cobb, Addison, Vowden, Quigley, Le Flem

West Ham United: Rhodes, Kirkup, Bond, Malcolm, Brown, Moore, Scott, Woosnam, **Sealey**, Dick, Musgrove

Alan William Sealey experienced the brightest high and the darkest low during a career-defining few months at West Ham United. Having scored the club's winning goals in the European Cup Winners Cup final against TSV Munich 1860 – at Wembley Stadium in 1965, he then incurred a career-limiting injury during a pre-season cricket match at Chadwell Heath, when he collided with a bench and broke his leg.

After scoring those two goals, Sealey could not have envisaged that his playing career would take the route of Plymouth Argyle, Romford Borough and Bedford Town, respectively. He eventually retired from playing, aged just 27.

It was not Sealey's first major injury at the club. He sustained a fractured ankle in a match against Bolton Wanderers on November 23, 1963, but, second time around, he never recovered his form after that cruel training ground accident.

Alan joined West Ham United from Leyton Orient in March, 1961, with Hammers striker Dave Dunmore moving to Brisbane Road as part of the deal. Both players would take their place in the folklore of their new clubs – Alan at Wembley in 1965 and, before that, Dave as part of Leyton Orient's 1961-62 side, which won promotion to the top flight.

Sealey was a local lad living in Canning Town. He also holds the distinction of playing at West Ham United's former home – the Memorial Grounds – for local team Memorial Sports FC.

'Sammy,' as he was affectionately known, played 128 games for the Hammers, scoring 26 goals. 107 of these were alongside Bobby Moore. The two men were very good friends and Alan asked Moore to be his best man.

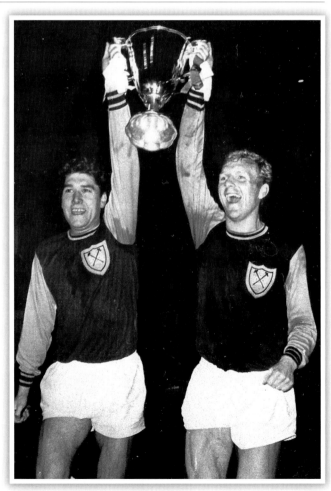

Celebrating West Ham United's highest honour after winning the European Cup Winners Cup in 1965.

Alan (left) and Janice (far right) on their honeymoon in Marbella with Bobby (obscured), Tina and friends.

Bobby and Tina were also in Spain when Alan and his wife Janice, were on their honeymoon in 1965.

The abrupt end to his career resulted in him taking over the family business, which supplied race cards to the bookmaking industry.

Alan's nephew, Les, would also play for West Ham United during the 1990s but sadly an all too common family trait of heart failure would claim them both at an early age. Alan's father, Billy, had also died from the same condition.

Sammy died suddenly from a heart-attack in February 1996, aged just 53. Two years earlier, he had returned to West Ham along with the famous cup teams of 1964 and 1965, to pay his respects to Bobby Moore before a memorial match to honour the club's greatest-ever player. He is survived by his second wife, Barbara and their son, Anthony.

Alan Sealey remains the only Hammer to have scored the winning goals in a major European final. Following are the recollections of his first wife Janice to whom we extend an enormous thank you for sharing her memories and photos. She is also another from the Bobby Moore era, who loves to keep in touch with people from that time. These include both Lucy Greenwood and Yvonne Lyall, the respective wives of Ron and John:

There was a Bobby Moore connection with my family long before Alan joined West Ham. My grandfather, Obed Gilbert, *was the treasurer at Barking Football Club. They called him 'Sid' and one day he was standing next to Bobby Moore's father, Bob senior. Bob was over there watching his son but he asked my grandfather what he thought about young Bobby. My grandfather looked at Bobby playing for a little while and replied: 'You must take him to West Ham.'*

Bobby called Alan either 'Sammy' or 'The Epilogue' because he was always the last one coming out of the tunnel. They were both extremely laid back characters and very easy going.

Alan and I were very close to Bobby and Tina and we even met up on our honeymoon in Marbella. The Cantwells were also there as was Denis Law and his wife. As we arrived at the hotel, Frank Sinatra had just left. It was just a coincidence that we all ended up there but it was the popular place to go at the time.

Alan and I were supposed to get married in June 1965 but West Ham were going to America on tour so we had to bring forward our wedding to May 16. This was just three days before the European Cup Winners Cup final. Alan wanted Bobby to be his best man but he was on international duty so Johnny Byrne did the honours instead. We were all very friendly together so, yes, it was sad that Bobby couldn't make it but we all loved Budgie and he did a great job.

I met Alan in 1961, the year he joined West Ham. I was 17 and we met in a pub in Dagenham called the Hind's Head. A

In his cricketing whites with L-R Jim Standen, Ron Boyce and Brian Dear.

lot of West Ham and Chelsea players went to that pub. Terry Venables and Ken Shellito often went in there while Bobby Moore tended to go to Ilford Palais at the time.

Alan and Bobby hit it off immediately at West Ham and then Tina and I became best friends. We did everything together. We looked after their children and Tina and I would go away on holiday, when Bobby and Alan were away with the club. We usually went to Spain because Bobby and Tina had a house in Marbella.

We went to their wedding and, in fact, Alan went with Tina to pick up her bride's dress. It was 1962 and not all the players had a car at that time so Alan drove her to the shop in his Ford Anglia.

Alan, Bobby and most of the West Ham players were so very smart. They had their shirts tailor made and got them washed in the Chinese laundry near the ground.

There were quite a few great jokers at West Ham and Alan and Bobby were always up to mischief. There was a very popular television programme called Candid Camera which performed practical jokes on people and secretly filmed everything. Alan and Bobby would play similar pranks on the general public just for a laugh.

I think one of the things Bobby liked most about Alan was his fun character. For some reason they loved to wind up the old boot man at West Ham, George Isaacs. It was all good fun of course and George was a lovely man and took it in all in the right spirit. He made us a little table for our wedding day. I still have it in my conservatory. George died in 1987 in Oldchurch hospital, which is a time I remember well because my dad was in the same ward. Ron Boyce used to visit George right up until the very end.

Throughout the 60s, we were socialising with well-known footballers and celebrities but I didn't take much notice because it was our lifestyle at the time. When I was young I had been the Dagenham carnival queen and got used to being in the spotlight and having lots of people around me.

Alan wasn't the type to brag about his two goals in the European final. He didn't say much about them at all. He was too easy going for that. We were already having the time of our lives and those few days when we got married and won the European Cup Winners Cup at Wembley topped it all, especially because he had missed out on the FA Cup final the previous year. He had fractured his ankle but could have played and it was purely Ron Greenwood's decision not to

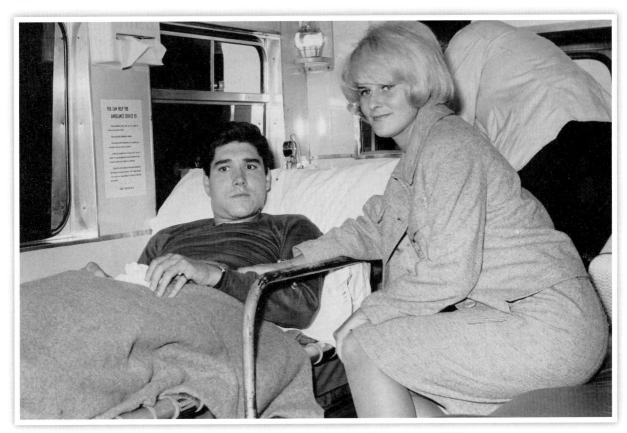

Leaving King George V Hospital in Ilford with Janice after his freak cricket accident in August 1965.

include him. Ron once said to me: 'You ladies are the only chance we have of keeping these boys' feet on the ground, so please try and make sure you do it.'

Then Alan's whole world fell apart when he sustained that cricketing injury a few months later. He took that very badly. It was the end of him as a player but we didn't know that at the time. Bobby and the players were ever so good and visited him all the time in Oldchurch hospital and afterwards when he came home.

It was such a pity because Alan also loved his cricket. He played for the Essex seconds and a few people told me he was a good batsman. He certainly enjoyed playing the game and it was such a tragedy that something he loved so much ironically cut short his career in football. It was so hard for him to cope with reaching the heights in football that he did and then have everything brought to a premature end. It obviously impacted on our marriage and we were divorced in 1972.

I had been living in Ibiza for a long time when I heard the news that Alan had passed away. Coincidentally, my partner at the time had also just passed away so I would have been a comparatively young widow whatever the route I had taken. Alan died of a heart attack, the same way his father had passed away. His father, Billy, dropped dead opposite the West Ham ground. He had just been to the surgery complaining about feeling unwell and the doctor gave him a

letter to go to the hospital but on the way home he collapsed and died. John Bond had seen it happen and called me up. It was typical of how close we all were that we had each others phone numbers.

Alan took over his father's business, which provided betting shops with the race cards each day. It was a big concern and well before the days of computers so they worked through the night to produce the lists of horses, which the bookmakers hung in their shops for the punters.

There was such a great camaraderie among us all at West Ham. We were always out doing something together and took our holidays at the same time. Whether we were in the local pub or the Moby Dick restaurant eating a meal, I just remember laughing most of the time. It was just a pity that it all ended so soon.
Janice Sealey

Alan's former team-mates also provided the following recollections:

Everyone loved Sammy. I was there when he had the accident playing cricket. He broke his leg and his foot was hanging limp. It was snapped like I've never seen before or since and when he came back he ran with a limp. It finished him.
Harry Redknapp

I was involved in Alan's first goal at Wembley. I went up for a free kick which was taken by Bobby Moore. He knocked it into the box and I got on the end of it but someone whacked me and I fell over. Fortunately, Alan knocked it in. It wasn't spectacular but one of the most beautiful sights I saw as a West Ham player.
Martin Peters

Sammy was the life and soul of the party, a typical East End lad. I think his father was a bookie and Sammy had a similar gift of the gab, a cheerful Charlie Chester type. It was sad when his career was ruined after he fell over the training bench at Chadwell Heath.
Joe Kirkup

I remember a game against Manchester City at the end of the 1966-67 season. It formed part of Sammy's comeback after breaking his leg the previous year. I was quite close to him and we had played together in the reserves. We both scored against Leicester's Peter Shilton in one reserve game. I played in that Manchester City game and I remember he wasn't fit. He was still limping and it felt as though we only had 10 men. He never recovered, which was a real shame because he was good for West Ham. Alan was a very jovial person and got on well with people like Brian Dear. From that game, Sealey, Doug Eadie, and Dave Bickles never played for West Ham again.
Trevor Hartley

He was a good cricketer and the story goes that he was playing for Essex' Second XI at Green and Silley Weir's ground near Wanstead. He was batting number three or four but needed to go to the toilet so said to some young lad that if a wicket fell he should go in if he wasn't back in time. Sure enough a wicket fell and the young boy took Sealey's place in the order – his name was Keith Fletcher, who went on to captain Essex and England!
Terry McDonald

I knew Alan well because we played for West Ham schoolboys together. It is quite an irony that he couldn't get in that schoolboys team because of me and yet he sort of replaced me at West Ham and went on to become a legend at the club.

He wasn't a centre forward as such and used to get a round of applause if he headed the ball!

Sammy and I went to a holiday camp together in Lowestoft. There were about eight of us including Brian Dear, Martin Peters, Geoff Hurst, Roger Hugo, Ronnie Boyce and a boy called Johnny Ford, who was my best mate and played senior amateur football. The camp organised a football competition on a scrap of land and we entered. We were only about 17-years-old and nobody at the camp knew who we were. There was a team there called Gorleston Town and they had never been beaten. We ended up thrashing them 9-0!

It was weird because Ron Greenwood would say to me: 'I wish I could get Alan Sealey to shoot as often as you do.' But he still wouldn't put me in ahead of him! Of course, Ron's decision reaped the biggest reward of all so I take my hat off to him. Ron always said: 'Pass it fast along the grass.' They should have that in big letters at West Ham United.
Mike Beesley

When I was an apprentice, Sammy used to pick me up in his Ford Anglia in the morning and take me to the training ground. He'd drop me off afterwards because we lived just round the corner from each other in Canning Town.
Frank Lampard

Alan sang at my wedding, which took place on the day of the 1966 World Cup final. Sammy had a stutter but he had a fantastic singing voice. He got up and belted out Tony Bennett's San Francisco. He was brilliant!
Dennis Burnett

With another Wembley hero, Alan Taylor, in 1994.

Ron Greenwood – The beginning of something special.

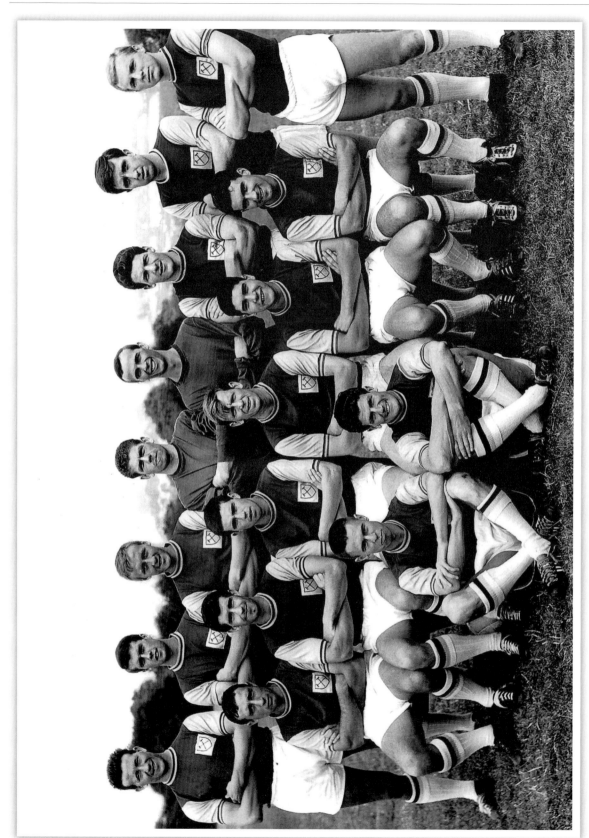

Back row L-R Brown, Hurst, Kirkup, Leslie, Rhodes, Lyall, Bond, Moore. Middle Row L-R Malcolm, Brett, Boyce, Dick, Sealey, Crawford. Front Row L-R Woosnam, Musgrove.

They Played With Bobby Moore – The West Ham Years

CHAPTER FOUR
1961-62

Bobby Moore's total appearances (July 1961-June 1962): 61 games (3 goals)

League Division One: 41 (3 goals), Friendlies: 8, England: 5, England U23: 4, League Cup: 2, FA Cup: 1

Bobby Moore captained West Ham United for the very first time – against Cardiff City on April 20, 1962. He was given the responsibility after Ron Greenwood dropped club captain Phil Woosnam following a 0-3 defeat up at Everton in the previous game. For the visit of the Bluebirds, Martin Peters made his debut and record signing, Johnny Byrne, scored his first goal for the club in a 4-1 victory.

Two other events defined Moore's season. The first came on June 30, 1962, when he married Christina Elizabeth Dean at the Church of St Clemence, Ilford. Former team-mate and lifelong friend, Noel Cantwell, was Moore's Best Man. Mike Sarne and Wendy Richard had the number one UK hit at the time with *Come Outside*. It was also the year of Nut Rocker by B. Bumble and the Stingers, and I Can't Stop Loving You by Ray Charles.

The second landmark was Moore's inclusion in England's World Cup squad for the 1962 tournament in Chile. He would make the first of 108 appearances for his country, against Peru in a pre-tournament friendly in the capital, Lima. England won 4-0 and Moore would go on to play in every one of England's four World Cup matches, before losing to eventual winners Brazil in the quarter finals.

One noteworthy blight on an otherwise encouraging season came when Moore was sent off for the one and only time in his career – against Manchester City following a tackle on David Wagstaffe on November 4, 1961.

In the Upton Park dug-out, Ron Greenwood set out on his first full season with West Ham United and made his first foray into the transfer market – buying Lawrie Leslie from Airdrieonians for £14,000 and Johnny Byrne from Crystal Palace for a then British record, £65,000. Leslie won

The rising star

Hammer of the Year at the end of the 1961-62 season and 'Budgie' was destined to be part of the club's first ever FA Cup winning team in 1964.

A quintet of other players also lined-up with Moore in the first team for the very first time. They were Ian Crawford, Ron Tindall, Martin Peters, Jack Burkett and Alan Dickie.

Here is their story…

31 – LAWRIE LESLIE

Born: Edinburgh, March 17, 1935

Position: Goalkeeper

Games played with Bobby Moore: 59 (1961-1963)

Games played for West Ham United: 61 (1961-63)

Honours with Bobby Moore: 1962 Hammer of the Year

First game with Bobby Moore (Debut): August 19, 1961 Manchester United (h) D 1-1

Scorers: West Ham United: Dick
Manchester United: Stiles

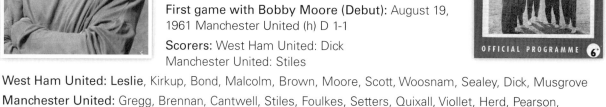

West Ham United: Leslie, Kirkup, Bond, Malcolm, Brown, Moore, Scott, Woosnam, Sealey, Dick, Musgrove

Manchester United: Gregg, Brennan, Cantwell, Stiles, Foulkes, Setters, Quixall, Viollet, Herd, Pearson, Charlton

---

Lawrence Grant Leslie found a place in the hearts of all West Ham United fans with his own particular brand of fearless goalkeeping. In 1962 he was voted Hammer of the Year at the end of his first season at the club. Bobby Moore and John Dick were runners-up.

Ron Greenwood signed Leslie from Airdrieonians for £14,000 in the summer of 1961. He quickly became the regular first choice keeper ahead of Brian Rhodes but brave hearts usually suffer the heaviest blows and Leslie took more than his fair share of injuries – eventually being replaced by Jim Standen

In action with Moore against Burnley on October 14, 1961.

With his Hammer of the Year trophy. Wife Janette, John Dick and Bobby Moore look on.

– before moving on to Stoke City for an identical transfer fee in October 1963.

Despite a relatively short stay at Upton Park, Leslie is fondly remembered by all who played with him. Brian Dear leads the plaudits: 'I remember running through Epping Forest with Lawrie and he had this great big scar on his leg. I asked him how he'd got it and he said he'd cut himself shaving!'

Ken Brown recalls a similar memory: 'There was an event at the East Ham town hall and Lawrie had his arm in a sling so I asked him how it was. 'It's only a break' he said!'

Joe Kirkup highlights Leslie's courage: 'He was the bravest guy I've ever seen. He would not only go in where nobody else would but he would fly in head first. Phenomenal courage.'

Leslie played 59 games with a young Bobby Moore who, aged 21, must have looked on in wonder when Lawrie played outfield at home to Arsenal following a hand injury, which saw John Lyall replace him in goal. Leslie's antics on the right wing galvanised a struggling West Ham to secure a point from a 1-3 deficit. In typical wry fashion Lawrie smiles at the memory: 'I showed my great mate, Jackie Dick, a trick or two that day!'

Lawrie still lives in Bexley, Kent, with his wife Janette and, despite suffering with his health, enjoys a comfortable life

Playing outfield against Arsenal in April, 1962.

surrounded by those who love him dearly and, of course, his Scotland caps plus Hammer of the Year trophy.

Both Lawrie and Janette Leslie were so very generous with their time and memories in helping with the following recollections:

I miss the football and I find it difficult to recognise people I used to know. It takes a bit of getting used to. Bobby's attitude towards the game was great. He loved his football and he really was as good as he is said to be. He was a class player. He learned it all at West Ham United, where he picked everything up off others, like Malcolm Allison and Noel Cantwell. He seemed to rise to the top so quickly.

Early on, I couldn't see that he was a special talent. Bobby just seemed to be another player. Then later on, he seemed to gain grandeur and, from that point, he simply flew. He was so determined to succeed. You look at the old photos and Bobby is never too far away from the play. You always had a chance with him in your team.

We are thankful to Lawrie's wife, Janette, for her pin sharp memory and following recollections:

Lawrie was six years older than Bobby so we were not in the same social circle. At the time, we had a family but Bobby didn't and that made a big difference in terms of spending time together, socially.

The illness Lawrie suffers from was caused by an accident he had when he was younger. His leg was smashed in seven places, his hip was broken and his face was scarred when he got knocked down by a truck. He had to have so many blood transfusions at a time when the impurities in the blood weren't screened. He was in plaster up to his waist and he kept getting infections. So, over the years it has affected his liver. They said that if he had been a drinker he would not have survived. He wasn't paid enough to drink on a regular basis, thank God! His memory has also begun to fade but we'll get through it.

At West Ham, the players' agent, Jack Turner, wanted Lawrie to run the sports shop across from the ground in Green Street before it became Bobby Moore's shop. Lawrie had just been made Hammer of the Year and Jack thought it would be a good promotional idea for him to run it. It was a pity because Lawrie then broke his leg and we had two kids at the time and it just wasn't feasible to get involved so Bobby took it over and did really well with it.

The last time I think we saw Bobby and Tina in person was at a charity game at Dagenham in the early 1970s. Tina was sitting on the bonnet of Bobby's red Jaguar. Our daughter, Jennifer and their son Dean were about the same age and they were charging around in the stand so Tina and I tried to settle them both in the back room and we had a nice chat. I really felt for Tina when, in 2011, I heard the news of their son Dean's sad passing.

I always say how disappointed I was that West Ham didn't give Bobby a job. He should have been taken into the board room and asked what he would like to do for West Ham United. Obviously, this wouldn't have meant the manager's job but the knowledge and experience that man had would have been invaluable to the kids at the club.

What annoys me more than anything else is that they have used his name relentlessly ever since and yet they wouldn't give the poor fellow a job. Instead, Bobby had to jump around all over the world taking things for a few months here and six months there. When you have got a young family it is very hard to keep doing that especially with their schooling and it must have taken its toll. It wasn't right.

We'll leave the last word with Lawrie who commented on a raft of black and white press photos from his playing days. One after the other he looked at every player that he had lined up with at West Ham and the response was heartfelt: *'I can remember how they move, but I can't remember their names... but I know that's Bobby.'*

Lawrie & Janette Leslie

Lawrie with his pride and joy – the 1962 Hammer of the Year trophy.

32 – IAN CRAWFORD
July 14, 1934 – November 30, 2007

Born: Edinburgh

Position: Right/left wing

Games played with Bobby Moore: 26 (1961-62)

Games played for West Ham United: 26 (1961-62)

First game with Bobby Moore (Debut): September 9, 1961 Aston Villa (a) W 4-2

Scorers: West Ham United: Dick (2), Scott, Sealey
Aston Villa: Crowe, McParland

West Ham United: Leslie, Kirkup, Bond, Hurst, Brown, Moore, Scott, Woosnam, Sealey, Dick, **Crawford**

Aston Villa: Sidebottom, Neal, Lee, Crowe, Dugdale, Deakin, MacEwan, Baker, McParland, O'Neill, Burrows

---

John 'Ian' Crawford had secured legendary status at Heart of Midlothian prior to his transfer to West Ham United for £7,000 in 1961. His two goals against Celtic in the 1956 Scottish Cup final helped Hearts to win their first trophy in 50 years. He had also gained two Scottish League championship winners' medals and Scotland Under-23 honours.

Ron Greenwood with his two Scots, Leslie and Crawford.

Crawford was almost seven years older than Bobby Moore but he and his wife, Helen, struck up an immediate friendship with Bobby and Tina. Both players would often share lunch together after training and he was something of a lucky talisman for West Ham, scoring in five different games and winning on each occasion. He left the club after just two years but did appear 26 times with Moore.

Fellow Scot, Lawrie Leslie remembers Ian from their days living north of the border: 'We knew Ian up in Edinburgh before we joined up at West Ham. We would see him in the Edinburgh Palais sometimes. He knew Bobby well and would often have lunch with him after training. Like Bobby, Ian was always very dapper at West Ham.'

Ian was transferred to Scunthorpe United in March 1963 before playing as a left-back for Peterborough United. In 1970, he joined the back room staff at league champions Everton and spent the rest of his life in various coaching capacities. He always maintained that the influence of Ron Greenwood had been pivotal in his pursuit of a coaching career.

In November 2007, Ian Crawford passed away suddenly from pneumonia, aged 73.

We extend our gratitude to his former wife, Helen, for sharing her memories of both Ian and Bobby:

When we moved down from Edinburgh to London in 1961, Bobby and Tina became our best friends. We clicked with them right away. At that time they weren't married so we used to socialise a lot together.

Ian Crawford in typical pose.

I thought Bobby was a super person and the four of us had so much in common. We all went and saw Ella Fitzgerald at the London Palladium, which was a fantastic evening. It was a real treat to see such an amazing singer and someone whose music we all loved.

We used to go to the Talk of the Town in Leicester Square to see performers such as Matt Monro and Shirley Bassey. All the greats appeared there – Tom Jones, Dusty Springfield and Frank Sinatra. They really were very special times indeed.

Bobby had such a lovely nature and was so easy to get on with. They were lovely with our kids. I remember they found a tortoise in their garden one day but they didn't have any children at the time. We had two boys and didn't live too far from them so they brought it round for them to keep. We called it 'Tibo' after Tina and Bobby.

Ian played for Peterborough United later in his career and there was a lovely photograph of his testimonial in the Peterborough Evening Telegraph. Bobby came to play in it along with Johnny Haynes, Terry Venables, Geoff Hurst, Martin

Two goal Crawford halts Plymouth

WEST HAM 3, PLYMOUTH 2

AN 83rd minute match-winner by Scot Ian Crawford rescued West Ham from humiliation and a fixture pile-up in the first round of the Football League Cup at Upton Park on Monday.

The goal — hammered in from close range following a left wing cross from roaming Tony Scott — ended Plymouth's brave bid for glory.

And it saved West Ham from a replay date at Plymouth just two days later.

Hammers can count themselves lucky to have won. They very nearly came croppers against a Plymouth side that countered its obvious lack of skills with a tremendous fighting spirit.

West Ham were flattered by their 30th minute lead. Ian Crawford netted with a snorting drive after receiving from live-wire Alan Sealey.

Ken Maloy, one-time Ilford winger, equalised ten minutes later. He shot high into the net after a brilliant diving save by Brian Rhodes.

There was a complete lack of urgency about West Ham's work. Phil Woosnam added a touch of class to proceedings when he fired a 25-yard drive high into the net following neat pattern-weaving by Moore and Sealey in the 63rd minute.

Plymouth drew level two minutes later when right-half John Williams netted during a goalmouth scramble.

Near-panic was noticeable in the West Ham ranks now. Sealey had a rocket shot pushed out, Dick was just wide with a header and Scott and Woosnam went close before Crawford scored the winner.

Football League Cup Win

Last Monday's Football League Cup First Round tie against Plymouth Argyle at Upton Park did not prove easy for the Hammers. Indeed we must truly admit that to some extent we could consider ourselves somewhat fortunate to be on the winning end of a 3—2 score against a Second Division side which showed plenty of good football.

There were periods when the opposing attack had our defence in a tangle and Brian Rhodes was called upon to make several good saves. But in addition the Pilgrims had bad luck not to score more than twice, and a drive from the right-wing would have made the score 1—0 in Argyle's favour had it been a couple of inches lower instead of bouncing off the bar. We also had to thank Joe Kirkup for blunting the power of dangerous left-winger Ken Maloy, although the ex-Ilford amateur managed to elude Joe's attentions in the 40th minute to net an equaliser from the edge of the penalty-box.

Our own left-winger—Ian Crawford—also distinguished himself by netting his first two goals for our senior side. He ran on to Alan Sealey's pass in the 32nd minute to put us ahead, and then got the winner seven minutes from time with an opportunist effort as the ball ran loose in the goalmouth when it seemed quite likely that the tally would remain 2—2 until the final whistle.

Prior to this Phil Woosnam had scored with a 20-yard drive from Alan Sealey's pass in the 65th minute, though several critics were inclined to fault goalkeeper Maclaren on that occasion (despite the visiting custodian giving a good all-round performance) ; and it was a goalmouth scramble that ended with John Williams toe-ending the ball into our net three minutes after Phil's goal for the equaliser.

Nevertheless, all in all, it was an interesting 90 minutes for the 12,170 spectators, and there was some spirited " cup tie shouting "

Two goals by Crawford save Hammers

By KEN JONES

W. Ham 3, Plymouth A. 2

IAN CRAWFORD, £7,000 close-season signing from Hearts, spared West Ham blushes and a long-train trip for a replay, when he put them into the second round of the League Cup last night.

In front of a flop crowd of little more than 12,000,

that once again proved the futility of this competition, West Ham never looked like getting a grip on Second Division Plymouth.

And it was left to Crawford, who could not get a first-team game until last Saturday, to show the Hammers the way to goal.

Crawford cracked home a goal in the thirtieth minute, then popped up to grab his second—the winner — seven minutes from time.

Equaliser

Ken Maloy, Argyle's Ilford-born left winger, hit a great equaliser in the thirty-eighth minute.

Right half Johnny Wil-liams equalised again in the second half, after Phil Woosnam had made it 2—1 to the Hammers.

Plymouth had a great let-off just after half-time, when Dave McLellan nearly punched the ball into his own net from a left wing cross.

Early press plaudits for new signing Crawford.

Peters and many others. The photograph shows Ian sitting on the ball with Bobby and all the other players surrounding him.

The last time I saw Bobby was when he came to Robbie Cantwell's funeral. Robert was the son of Noel and Maggie and he had died tragically in a road accident. Obviously, it was such a sad occasion but Bobby was so very supportive of the Cantwell family that day.

When we heard that Bobby Moore had died it was like a wound. We had heard he wasn't well and when he came to Robbie Cantwell's funeral he gave me his customary big hug but I noticed then he had lost a lot of weight. He had always been chunky with those nice big thighs so it was sad to see him like that. I think Ian was coaching in Norway at the time so he couldn't be there.

I was very affected when the postage stamp of Bobby Moore came out a few years ago. I thought it was absolutely marvellous because he was so special, so lovable and someone who would do anything for anyone. He just didn't know how to say no. A big smile appeared and you just knew he was going to help in any way he could.

Ian was ever so fit and as healthy as anything but in 2007 he died overnight from viral pneumonia. He was out and about in the morning but was dead 12 hours later. It was a tremendous shock to everyone. Several people made the trip from Edinburgh to Peterborough to show their respects at his funeral and there were so many lovely comments on various websites and message boards.

Our memories with Bobby and Tina during our time at West Ham are so very special and I wouldn't swap them for anything.

Helen Crawford

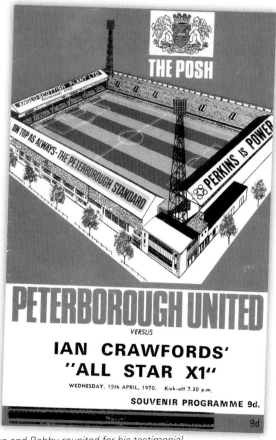

Ian and Bobby reunited for his testimonial.

33 – RON TINDALL
September 23, 1935 – September 9, 2012

Born: Streatham, London

Position: Forward

Games played with Bobby Moore: 14 (1961-62)

Games played for West Ham United: 14 (1961-62)

First game with Bobby Moore (Debut): November 25, 1961 Everton (h) W 3-1

Scorers: West Ham United: Dick (2) Crawford Everton: Vernon

West Ham United: Leslie, Kirkup, Bond, Hurst, Brown, Moore, Crawford, Woosnam, **Tindall**, Dick, Musgrove

Everton: Dunlop, Parker, Thomson, Gabriel, Labone, Harris, Bingham, Collins, Young, Vernon, Fell

---

Ronald Albert Ernest Tindall joined West Ham United from Chelsea on November 2, 1961. It was a transfer deal, which saw Hammers' legend Andy Malcolm head in the other direction to the Blues.

Tindall had partnered Jimmy Greaves at Stamford Bridge and their combined single season goals tally of 59 (16 for Tindall and 43 for Greaves) remains a club record.

Greaves recalls that when he made his first team debut for Chelsea at Tottenham Hotspur on August 24, 1957, he gained a lot of confidence from looking around the changing room and seeing players like Ron Tindall and Peter Brabrook: 'Ron was easily the most intelligent player in the Chelsea team. He was well-read and well-informed across a great many subjects but was quiet and unassuming with it.'

Tindall's spell at West Ham United lasted just under one year, at which point he was then transferred to Reading on October 9, 1962. His cricketing commitments with Surrey were not as well accommodated at West Ham as they had been at Chelsea.

Sir Geoff Hurst recalls a particular feature of Ron's game: 'He was a great header of the ball and could score goals from the edge of the box with his head. He was absolutely terrific and a really nice man.'

Ex-Hammer Roger Hugo remembers Ron well: 'I used to meet Ronnie Tindall on the train. He lived in Guildford and we would travel up every day which must have been hard

Andy Malcolm, Ron Greenwood, Tommy Docherty and Ron Tindall on transfer day, November 1961.

for him. He was a bright guy and a great cricketer. He was doing better at Surrey than he was at West Ham.'

'Gentleman Ron' was one of quite a few duel sportsmen during the Bobby Moore era. He was a fine all-rounder for Surrey CCC and scored 5546 runs in first class matches. His contemporaries argue that he was stronger with the bat than the boot.

Tindall had a flying start at West Ham, scoring twice at Arsenal in a 2-2 draw on December 2, 1961. It was a feat which had only been achieved by a Hammer at Highbury once before in the club's history to that point - by John Dick - who bagged a brace at the Gunners in 1958-59. Of the 14 games Tindall played with Moore, that was undoubtedly his biggest highlight.

After seeing out his career as player, coach and manager of Portsmouth, Tindall emigrated Down Under in 1977 where he helped to establish the coaching foundation of Western Australia. He wrote several books on the art of coaching and was later awarded the Order of Australia medal for services to sport.

It is important to note that both Ron Tindall and Phil Woosnam – very good friends at West Ham – went on to develop football in their adopted countries, Australia and USA, respectively.

Ron Tindall died in September 2012, aged 76. His wife Anne, who still resides in the family home in Australia, kindly took the time to share the following recollections:

In action for Surrey.

Ron was very happy at West Ham United because he was playing with some great players and he felt very privileged to be amongst them. He was a very humble man and looked up to them all because they were a formidable bunch of players, and men. Many of them did great things both as players and managers. He thought Bobby was the greatest footballer in his position.

Ronnie revelled in the teachings of Ron Greenwood after the somewhat lack of coaching practised at Stamford Bridge, although he had been very happy at Chelsea, too.

In November 1961 Ron's life changed. Greenwood took the West Ham professionals to Lilleshall for a week's training away from London. It was here that he spotted something in my Ron that would potentially make a good coach. He talked to him about taking the Level 1 coaching badge but because the exams always took place in the summer months Ron explained that he was always playing cricket so he would find it impossible to sit for the badge.

Greenwood asked him if he was serious about wanting to do it and he replied: 'Yes.' So Greenwood said: 'OK, we'll do it this week!' It was arranged, and he had to coach his team-mates with very little warning and he came home with his Level 1 badge.

It turned out to be the best qualification Ron could have had. It was the first of many and was the start to his new career in coaching. His first coaching role was at Portsmouth, where he graduated to the manager's role.

We then moved to Western Australia where, as the State Director of Coaching, he literally introduced soccer to the entire state of Western Australia. His job was to coach coaches, which is something he eventually did across all the states of Australia. One of his proudest moments came when he went to Russia in 1985 with the Australian Under-23 team. Jimmy Shoulder was the coach.

Returning to Ron's time at West Ham, he loved the training sessions put on by Ron Greenwood. He also revelled in the football conversations which took place in Cassettari's cafe after training. These often went on for hours with Phil Woosnam instrumental in analysing and strategising the game.

Ron and Phil forged a very good friendship. Like Ron, Phil was a great thinker of the game and many an idea was tossed around over a cup of tea and a sandwich. When Ron left West Ham, Phil wrote him a very nice letter of encouragement, which I still have today.

It was an exciting time at Upton Park and Ron was sad to leave but he always stayed in touch with Bobby Moore. In 1982 Ronnie wrote a soccer coaching book titled: 'Soccer Fundamentals' and

Bobby kindly wrote a very good foreword.

In 1995, West Ham United visited Perth as part of the first leg of their Centenary Season tour of Australia. In the programme for the game, Ron is quoted as saying: 'At West Ham I learned to recognise Bobby Moore as a colossus in the game.'

The last time we saw Bobby was when he and Tina visited us in Western Australia. They stayed for dinner and the football discussions continued long into the night!

Ron was devastated when he heard of Bobby's death, he just could not believe it. We were so far away and didn't know of his illness so it came as a tremendous shock which affected us both for some time afterwards.

Anne Tindall

Ron Tindall with wife Anne in 2008. Ron was awarded the Order of Australia and voted Western Australia's Citizen of the Year for Services to Sport.

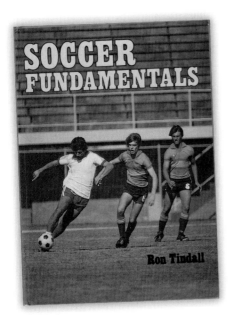

Ron's book on the art of coaching.

34 – JOHNNY BYRNE
May 13, 1939 – October 27, 1999

Born: West Horsley, Surrey

Position: Forward

Games played with Bobby Moore: 177 (1962-67)

Games played for West ham United: 206 (1962-67)

Honours with Bobby Moore: 1964 Hammer of the Year, 1964 FA Cup winner, 1964 Charity Shield (Shared with Liverpool), 1966 League Cup finalist

First game with Bobby Moore (Debut): March 17, 1962 Sheffield Wednesday (a) D 0-0

Sheffield Wednesday: Springett, Johnson, Megson, Hardy, Swan, Kay, Finney, Dobson, Young, Fantham, Holliday

West Ham United: Leslie, Kirkup, Bond, Hurst, Brown, Moore, Sealey, Woosnam, **Byrne**, Tindall, Musgrove

---

John Joseph Byrne is considered by many to be the most technically gifted player in West Ham United's history. He played with Bobby Moore at both club and international level before an unfortunate injury prevented him from adding a European Cup Winners Cup medal to his 1964 FA Cup winners success. Known as 'Budgie' on account of his non-stop chattering, he built a strong and lasting friendship with Moore, which spanned three decades.

Byrne had worked his way through the Crystal Palace junior sides before breaking into their first team. He gained his first full England cap whilst playing for Palace in the third tier of English football and is one of only five post-war players to have achieved this.[1]

Budgie signed for West Ham United in March 1962 for a club-record transfer fee of £65,000. It was Ron Greenwood's first marquee signing and was soon followed by two other key players in both Peter Brabrook and Jim Standen. Signing Budgie was a statement of intent and, after a slow start in front of goal he transformed the fortunes of the club for evermore.

Those fans who saw him play have neither forgotten the thrills, nor his irrepressible character. The history books will feed future generations of West Ham fans the details of his all too brief spell at the club. Being voted Hammer of the Year – ahead of Bobby – at the end of the landmark 1963-64 campaign, in which West Ham won the FA Cup for the very first time in its history, underlines his standing in the hearts and minds of the claret and blue faithful.

On February 15, 1967, Budgie's career at West Ham came to an end. He returned to Crystal Palace, bringing to a close almost five years of unforgettable excellence at Upton Park. His record is highly impressive, having played 206 games and scored 108 goals. He also won nine England caps whilst a Hammer.

Byrne followed his second spell at Selhurst Park with a season at Fulham. He then emigrated to South Africa, where he played and managed both Durban City and Hellenic. Bobby Moore joined him for a couple of spells and played in 17 matches, remaining unbeaten throughout.

In October 1999, the great Budgie Byrne died suddenly following a heart attack in Cape Town.

Sincere thanks are extended to Budgie's wife, Margaret, who still resides in Muizenberg, the beach-side suburb of Cape Town. She kindly shared the following memories of the great Budgie Byrne:

We were very good friends with Bobby and Tina as well as Eddie Bovington and his wife, Pauline. We used to go out a lot together to various clubs and restaurants. Budgie invited Bobby to South Africa to play in quite a few games in the early 1970s. He ended up visiting twice and they had an absolute ball together. They just picked up from where they had left off at West Ham. Their friendship lasted a lifetime.

Budgie and Bobby played together for West Ham United and both England Under-23s and the full international team. They spent so much time together both on and off the pitch.

I was two years older than Budgie. He was just 17 when we got married. I was living in Ockham and he lived five minutes away in West Horsley. We met at a dance together and ended up being married for 42 years.

He was very much a man's man and loved to drink and gamble. He was always at the dog track or watching the

---

1. The others were: **Tommy Lawton**, *four caps while playing for Notts County in 1947-48*, **Reg Matthews**, *five caps while playing for Coventry City in 1955-56*, **Peter Taylor**, *four caps while playing for Crystal Palace in 1975-76 and* **Steve Bull**, *two caps while playing for Wolverhampton Wanderers in 1988-89.*

horses. It was a wonder really that Ron Greenwood loved him so much because he did all those things about which the manager took a dim view.

In fact, Ron wanted Budgie to stay on at West Ham before he returned to Crystal Palace. He asked him to be his right-hand man and wanted to help him develop as a coach. Budgie turned it down because being number two to anybody wasn't his style. He always wanted to be number one.

I went to most home games at West Ham to watch him play and it was wonderful to see just how much the crowd adored him. Being at Wembley in 1964 and seeing his great mate, Bobby, lifting the FA Cup was just perfect. There are some lovely photos of Budgie and Bobby on a lap of honour with the trophy.

Budgie and I had four children together – Kevin, David, Mark and our youngest, Karen. Thank god for Karen because I think we would have had an entire football team while trying for a girl! There were 11 babies born after the FA Cup and the newspapers took a photo of all the players holding their babies at the ground. Budgie took along Karen, who was born in that year. Tina and Bobby had just had Roberta so all the wives had a lot in common. We lived in Sandhurst Drive, Ilford, which was close to quite a few of the players. We had many parties at our house and Bobby and Tina would be there every time. Kenny Lynch came a few times and he another whom Budgie liked a lot.

The great Budgie Byrne at Chadwell Heath in 1962.

Budgie was set back a long way when he had his cartilage removed. He ended up missing out on the European final at Wembley in 1965. He also made it into England's final 28 for the 1966 World Cup but missed out on that, too. He never really recaptured his form.

He was particularly disappointed to miss out on the Cup Winners Cup final because he had played in every previous round of that European campaign. They didn't give him a medal. Ironically, I donated all of John's medals, shirts and caps to the club when they opened the museum. I kept four of his England caps – one for each of our children – but gave everything else to the club.

John was devastated when Bobby passed away. He really was affected by it and flew to England to be part of a memorial evening at Upton Park. He came back full of stories about everyone and I think it helped him get over the pain of losing someone he really did love. Nobody ever said anything bad about Bobby Moore. He was the perfect gentleman. I'm sure they got up to some tricks when they were together but they just loved each other's company.

When Budgie died in 1999 we had a church service for him over here in South Africa but I flew over to England with his ashes, which he wanted buried under the pitch at West Ham. They are buried in a box behind the goal next to the Bobby Moore stand.

I must say West Ham did us very proud. The chairman,

Walking out behind Moore at Wembley in 1964.

Terry Brown, sent us 40 tickets for the match. We went to a church service first which was packed with people. Harry Redknapp, Frank Lampard, Ken Brown and Brian Dear were there and Geoff Hurst delivered a lovely eulogy. This was followed by lunch and then back to the ground to watch the match. After the game there was a ceremony on the pitch during which we buried Budgie's ashes behind the goal. There was no better place for him.

Even now I have people coming up to me and telling me things that Budgie had once said or done. He loved the bars and restaurants out here and would take centre stage regaling people with stories from his time in football. I used to like to call him 'Johnny' but nobody knew him by his real name over here so I had to start calling him 'Budgie' so that people knew who I was talking about!

We had a fantastic five years at West Ham. It was just too good to be true. Budgie always said it was the best time he ever had in football. I kept paper clippings and photos of everything Budgie did from the moment he joined Crystal Palace right up to when he died. There are about 15 large folders with everything filed away neatly. It tells the story of his life.

I miss his chirpiness and the fact that he was always doing something here, there and everywhere. He would take me with him whenever he could so it has taken a bit of getting used to not having him around.

Margaret Byrne

Stories about Budgie could fill an entire book but following are a selected few from his team-mates:

Budgie was one of the great players. He lacked a bit of discipline but was a truly great character. I enjoyed a lot of great times with him both on and off the pitch. We had a terrific four year spell between 1962 and 1966 when we scored about 250 goals between us.

Sir Geoff Hurst

Budgie was a great player but he was even better company off the pitch. He was a good friend at the time and we had a lot of fun together. Ron Greenwood loved him and he let him get away with everything.

Eddie Bovington

The last time West Ham won up at Anfield was in 1963 and I remember the match well because of something that happened at the end of the game. We were winning 2-1 and had a corner. Budgie, Mooro and Hursty came over to me and said 'Braaders, do the corner, do the corner'. Now, I used to waste time by kicking the back of my leg when taking a corner but this was on a whole different level, in front of almost 50,000 Liverpool fans all baying for blood. I ran up to take the corner and kicked my leg and fell forward in a heap without even touching the ball. Mooro, Hursty and Budgie all came over and helped give the impression I was genuinely injured. When Ron found out I was playacting he went completely mad! Once the game resumed the ref blew his whistle and West Ham have never won there since. Budgie was one of the big characters in the dressing room. Both he and I were the

chatty ones before a game but I was the funnier one!
Peter Brabrook

Bobby, Budgie and Eddie Bovington were great mates and it is well known that West Ham lost 2-8 to Blackburn Rovers at home on Boxing Day, 1963. Ron Greenwood thought the sun shone out of Johnny Byrne's backside. Budgie was a great player and had a lot of power and influence over Ron. It is only my opinion, but I believe John had a word with Ron about dropping Martin Peters and replacing him with Eddie Bovington. After that game Martin went to Ron and said: I'm not complaining about being dropped but I'm sure I wasn't the only one who had a bad game in our 2-8 defeat. The record books show that Martin never regained his place in that FA Cup run and Eddie has his place in history.
Brian Dear

Budgie was one of the best players I ever played with. Oh man, he could make the ball talk! His lifestyle let him down in terms of his football progression but he certainly had a lot of fun along the way.

I played for him out in South Africa. I was about 38 years old and he called me up and said he needed me to play in a cup game for a side he was managing – the Greek-owned team, Hellenic. He talked me into it and we got to the semi-final and lost to Orlando Pirates or Kaiser Chiefs. We were always bumping into each other around Cape Town and I went to visit him in hospital after his first heart attack.

Enjoying the FA Cup victory parade.

I miss him terribly. In fact I think the whole of Cape Town misses him terribly!

Budgie would have made a fantastic manager for West Ham, Oh man, he would have been absolutely brilliant if he had been given the chance! Sadly, his behaviour often prevented anyone from employing him.

Budgie owned a few greyhounds when he was at West Ham. He and Hursty had one called Bridges Cheer which won at Dagenham. We all went to see it. Budgie had a couple of others called Find the Ball and On the Ball. It was great at the dogs back then. They played Find the Lady outside with the card sharks and the whole place had a great atmosphere.

I think Budgie had some involvement in bringing about the

replacement of Martin Peters with Eddie Bovington after we had lost 2-8 at home to Blackburn Rovers. Budgie felt we were lacking a bit of bite in the middle of the park. We needed someone to win the ball and get stuck in but this had never been Ron's style of play. He always preferred entertaining, one-touch football but I think Budgie talked him round and Eddie got his chance. Amazingly, we then went up to Blackburn for the return two days later and won 3-1 and continued on a fantastic run which culminated in winning the FA Cup.
John Sissons

He was a little bit special and as good as I saw at holding the ball up and bringing the wingers into play. He was the master

Something for the fans.

at getting players into the game. I was out in South Africa with Budgie for two years. He managed Durban City and I played for a team called Durban United. We used the same pitch so I saw him every day. He had Johnny Haynes playing for him. We had our lunch together every day. Well, it was lunch for me but Budgie and Haynsey used it as a platform to drink all day!

I remember one time Budgie was being chased by the police in Cape Town and he had smashed into about six cars before writing off his own car. He managed to get out and started running up a hill to get to his home. The police actually fired some shots and Budgie thought he was going to die, either from a bullet or a heart attack!

He was a massive character and every Saturday night four of us would eat at our favourite French restaurant in Durban. There was me, Budgie, Johnny Haynes and Frank McLintock. We never missed a meal and had the time of our lives. I don't think Budgie was sober the whole time he was in South Africa!

Trevor Dawkins

We were good buddies and it was great news when Ron Greenwood paired me with Budgie as room-mates. I was never certain of my place under Ron but he had just bought Budgie from Crystal Palace and was obviously going to play him. If I was rooming with him it meant Ron was going to play me as well. Before that I was always on my nerve ends and would have to check the team sheet every Friday.

It wouldn't have surprised me if I wasn't on the team-sheet because I never felt I was a good enough player for Ron. He was such a perfectionist. He used to flinch if I tackled someone, he didn't like that. He wanted football to be played neat and tidy, with little passing triangles moving up the pitch. I think Ron thought I would be a calming influence on Budgie but, blow me, I had no chance! Budge was such a busy person, always playing tricks on people. It was hopeless trying to rein him in. He used to do little things like putting knots in people's ties if he was in their room. Ron absolutely idolised him, which was just as well given his behaviour. I don't think he would have lasted at the club otherwise.

Ken Brown

I'm sure he must have talked in his sleep!
Jack Burkett

I remember when Budgie came over from South Africa and was out with my John and Eddie Bovington. Budgie was getting a bit nervous because they kept saying they were going to come out to South Africa to see him. Now, Eddie has always had swarthy skin and Budgie didn't want to say they couldn't come because of their skin colour! In the end I said I would go and John and Eddie could be my servants! I've got this old bit of brown paper at home which Budgie wrote a message on for John. It reads: 'Charlo, when Nelson Mandela is released you can come out and have a drink with me – Budgie 29.1.1990.'
Carol Charles

After my time at West Ham and Brentford, I spent a year at Fulham. There were still some players there who remembered Budgie from his brief time at the club. One of the stories described how one day he was training on the pitch and kept holding his side as he ran. It transpired that he had won a lot of money at the track but because he owed so many people he didn't want to leave the cash in the dressing room. Instead he tucked it in inside his tracksuit and held on to it throughout the training session.
Roger Cross

I liked Budge and he liked me. I remember he played centre-back for Crystal Palace reserves in the late 1960s and ended up marking me. He was the best instinctive player I ever saw.
Trevor Hartley

Budgie used to drive me to training. He'd pick me up at Peckham Rye and we would be late every day. Budge liked to stop for a bacon sandwich at Cassettaris on the way! Ron Greenwood advised me to take the Underground in the end.

Budgie and I were out in South Africa at the same time and had some good laughs. He and Johnny Haynes were at Durban City together. Can you imagine the times we had?
Roger Hugo

I played with him for England Youth out in Hungary in 1956. He'd just signed for Palace at the time and I couldn't believe he was married at just 17.
Terry McDonald

My father, Bill, who was the club physio until his death in 1966, absolutely loved Budgie. He told me a story about how he, Budgie and Mooro were in the States together in 1963. The three of them got drunk and apparently my father said something to Budgie which he didn't like so he started to chase my dad around the streets of New York, causing him to slip over and smash his head on the pavement. Budgie sobered up on the spot when he saw how my dad's head was completely split open. 'Just get me home to Connie,' my dad said, which was a reference to my mother. 'She'll stitch me up.' As Bobby and Budgie lifted him into a yellow taxi he turned to them both and said: 'If I die Budgie, always remember, you're to blame!'
Rob Jenkins

1964 FA Cup Winners medal.

Lifelong friends.

35 – MARTIN PETERS

Born: Plaistow, London, November 8, 1943

Position: Midfielder

Games played with Bobby Moore: 327 (1962-70)

Games played for West Ham United: 364 (1962-70)

Honours with Bobby Moore: 1965 Hammer of the Year, 1965 European Cup Winners Cup winner, 1966 League Cup finalist, 1966 World Cup winner

First game with Bobby Moore (Debut): April 20, 1962 Cardiff City (h) W 4-1

Scorers: West Ham United: Baker (og), Sealey, Crawford, Byrne – Cardiff City: Pickerell

West Ham United: Leslie, Kirkup, Lyall, **Peters**, Lansdowne, Moore, Scott, Byrne, Sealey, Dick, Crawford

Cardiff City: John, Stitfall, Milne, Baker, Rankmore, Hole, McCarthy, King, Charles, Durban, Pickerell

Martin Stanford Peters was the most complete player out of the Moore, Hurst, Peters triumvirate. He could play in defence, score goals, had two great feet and was a very tough player indeed. This last aspect of his game is perhaps the least recognised but Clyde Best's description of him as a 'Smart Assassin' is difficult to refute.

Peters signed for West Ham United as an apprentice professional in May 1959 and turned full professional in November 1960, just two days after his 17th birthday. His formative years as a player had taken him along the Dagenham, Essex and England schoolboys line. He promoted himself as a future England international when, on his England Under-23 debut in November 1962, he scored twice in a 6-1 rout of Belgium. The game was also televised, which broadened the reach of his reputation. He had also previously gained three England Youth caps.

Martin missed out on Moore's first club trophy when Ron Greenwood left him out of the victorious 1964 FA Cup campaign. He was the only player to be dropped after a club record 2-8 league defeat at home to Blackburn Rovers on Boxing Day 1963. Martin is philosophical about the experience: 'I don't think I was the only player to blame for the Blackburn defeat.'

But the next two years were to bring both European and World achievement which has never since been matched, while Peters was also voted the Hammer of the Year after the successful 1964-65 campaign.

The master craftsmen.

Remarkably, Martin did not gain his first full England cap – against Yugoslavia at Wembley Stadium – until May 4, 1966, just a couple of months prior to the biggest football achievement of his life – a World Cup winners medal.

'The Champions' statue opposite The Boleyn pub on Barking Road is a lasting tribute to his success story. He also won two League Cup winners medals and a UEFA Cup winners medal after his record £200,000 transfer to Tottenham Hotspur in March 1970, which saw Jimmy Greaves move the other way.

Martin still lives in Shenfield, Essex with his wife Kathy and enjoys working in the hospitality lounges at both West Ham United and Tottenham Hotspur. He still likes a round of golf with his friends and, in September 2013, attended the 70th birthday celebrations of his former West Ham team-mate, Brian Dear. No West Ham midfielder played more games with Bobby Moore than Martin Peters and he took the time to share a pleasant afternoon discussing his former club and country team-mate:

With Mooro and Charlo aganst Manchester City's Francis Lee in November 1968.

There has never been a better defender in the game and I thought that Bobby was also a first-class captain, a natural leader of men.

I joined West Ham United in 1959 and was paid £5-per-week. I gave my parents £2 and kept £3 for myself. It was three years before I played in the first team and Bobby Moore was made captain on my debut at home to Cardiff City in April 1962. We ran out 4-1 winners and it was the start of five games in ten days which will never happen again. In fact the first three games were played over three days!

After victory over Cardiff City, we then drew 3-3 against Arsenal the next day at Upton Park. Lawrie Leslie ended up playing outfield in that game and John Lyall went in goal. Then, remarkably, I took over in goal from Brian Rhodes in my third game, this time at Ninian Park, Cardiff on Easter Monday, so it was quite a baptism of fire for me.

It was fantastic playing with Bobby because I was one of the youngest in the team and I relied on him to help me as much as he could. He assisted me so much in my early days at West Ham.

Bobby played behind me because I started in midfield, wearing the Number 4 shirt. He would play the ball in to me and I would give it back to him. He would then pick out Budgie Byrne or Geoff Hurst up front. Bobby was very quiet and we helped each other out in every match.

I wasn't part of Bob's social set really and tended to spend my time with Geoff Hurst and Ron Boyce. However, given what we both achieved in our football careers we obviously attended many, many functions together. If we had been out at an event together somewhere we would usually sit down and have a chat over a sandwich.

We did appear in an advert together during the 1960s. It was to promote local pubs up and down the country and I don't think there has been an advert like that since. It was funny because I was in the advert the whole time with Bobby but did not get a single mention!

I went along to the pubs Bobby ran and played in various charity golf events with him and can distinctly remember us both being on holiday in Menorca together while we were at West Ham.

In training, he wanted to practice different things. He loved passing and running and Ron Greenwood was always setting up situations for him to demonstrate to the team. Both Bobby and Budgie were usually used as an example to the rest of the players because they could put the ball anywhere they wanted.

Ron saw me as a very versatile player and, on those few occasions when Bobby wasn't playing, I usually wore the Number 6 shirt. Furthermore Sir Alf Ramsey famously said that I was 10 years ahead of my time but I still couldn't fill Bobby's boots!

Right at the end of his life I sometimes saw Bobby over at West Ham when he was working for the radio and I was working in the lounges. We would always take the time out to have a chat together.

I went to Westminster Abbey for his funeral service in 1993. I was really choked and cried. He was only 51. No footballer has ever received a send-off like that. It was like saying goodbye to a king. I also went to the private service in Putney Vale.

Playing with Bobby for club and country is something I am immensely proud of and we were lucky enough to achieve something that is worth looking back upon. Bobby Moore truly was a fantastic footballer and a wonderful man. I really miss him.

The biggest three names in the history of English football – Moore, Hurst and Peters, or should I say – Peters, Moore and Hurst!

Martin Peters

There is a wealth of respect and admiration for Martin's footballing talents from former playing colleagues:

Ron Greenwood said that if Martin had played on the Continent he would have been a sensation given the technique and style of play he possessed. I think he was underestimated and under-valued by the club. Even when he went to Norwich City at the very end of his long career, he was still one of

In control.

the best players ever to play for them. People often forget the four goals he scored for Tottenham Hotspur at Old Trafford in 1972 which was absolutely sensational! Ron Greenwood could talk to Alf Ramsey about Martin until the cows came home. Alf didn't make too many errors of judgement but his belief that Peters wasn't a great header of the ball was a very bad assessment, indeed. Martin was the best header of the ball at both West Ham and England.
Sir Geoff Hurst

The second best player in the country behind George Best.
Joe Kirkup

Despite all the recognition Martin has received, he is still seriously underrated.
Pat Holland

Pure class and an absolute gentleman.
Jim Standen

Ron Greenwood introduced something at West Ham that I still don't see happening in today's game. The class nowadays is fantastic and the skills of today's players are brilliant, but what I still don't see is any real quality of movement. It hasn't got to be a great, big, long run but, instead, a little run which is highly effective. One movement that Ron Greenwood instilled in West Ham players – and in Martin Peters specifically – was a little looping run around the back of the defence to support the winger. You see it all the time with an overlapping full-back but never from a midfielder. Martin used to do a little loop round to support John Sissons or whoever was out there on the left-wing. That is how they beat the full-backs and got into the danger area. It is a move that is very difficult to mark. Gianfranco Zola did it a lot at Chelsea but pundits and commentators rarely mentioned it. Martin Peters had it off to a tee and created attack after attack and that is one of a few brilliant nuggets of advice Ron made us practise at West Ham.
Peter Bennett

The thing about Peters is that he was the most all-round player out of the three World Cup stars. He could play centre half, score goals up front, had two great feet and could really look after himself. When we played against Leeds United he just didn't give or take any quarter and was one of those that would break your

legs sooner than look at you. He was very hard and West Ham didn't have many hard men. Eddie Bovington could kick a bit, but Peters was a tough, tough player.
Jimmy Lindsay

He was such a fantastic header of the ball. He timed his runs so well and the power he generated was so good.
John Sissons

Martin was a big part of the evolution of West Ham United. He could play anywhere and had tremendous all-round ability. When the wingers started whipping in the ball low, Martin was one of the best near-post executioners at the club and for the country.
Trevor Dawkins

The highest achievement.

36 – ALAN DICKIE

Born: London, January 30, 1944

Position: Goalkeeper

Games played with Bobby Moore: 12 (1962-65)

Games played for West Ham United: 15 (1962-65)

First game with Bobby Moore (Debut): April 28, 1962
Bolton Wanderers (a) L 0-1

Scorer: Bolton Wanderers: Holden

Bolton Wanderers: Hopkinson, Hartle, Farrimond, Hatton, Edwards, Rimmer, Holden, Hill, Davies, McGarry, Pilkington

West Ham United: Dickie, Kirkup, Lyall, Peters, Lansdowne, Moore, Scott, Byrne, Sealey, Dick, Crawford

Alan Leonard Dickie is one of only two goalkeepers in West Ham United's history to have lined up with Bobby Moore in a European match. It came at the Boleyn Ground against La Gantoise of Belgium, in a 1-1 draw, on October 7, 1964. He travelled to most of the European games as first team reserve to Jim Standen and appears in the famous dressing room photograph after the Wembley triumph against TSV Munich 1860 the following May.

Dickie joined the ground-staff on July 29, 1960 and became a full professional on January 30, 1962. Later that year, he was only 18-years-old when he lined up with Bobby Moore to make his first team debut at Bolton Wanderers. It was Moore's penultimate club game before flying off to the World Cup finals in Chile where he would make his international debut – a friendly against Peru, on May 20, 1962.

Alan (bottom left) with fellow Hammers, Brown, Moore, Bovington, Sissons, Sealey, Standen, Hurst, Byrne, Burkett, Boyce, Kirkup, Dear and Peters.

Posing for the camera outside the ground while Brian Dear sweeps and John Lyall shovels.

After only 15 games with the Hammers, Dickie was transferred to Coventry City on March 9, 1967. He was soon moved on by Sky Blues boss and former Hammer Noel Cantwell. He ended his playing days at Aldershot Town before entering the police force in 1969 aged just 25. As a police constable he was stationed at Bexleyheath and, from 1982, was seconded to the Coroner for the Southern District of London, based in Queen Mary Hospital, Sidcup, Kent. He is one of four Hammers to join the police force from the Bobby Moore era. Colin Mackleworth, Bill Kitchener and John Dryden are the other three who, interestingly, formed part of the successful 1963 FA Youth Cup winning team.

Alan played 'veterans' football during his 50s, cricket until his late 60s and continues to be a member of Shooters Hill Golf Club. His hobbies include music from the 1920s, 30s and 40s. Fats Waller, Jack Smith, Hoagy Carmichael and Dick Haymes are particular favourites.

Alan lives with his wife, Anna, who is the cousin of a Swedish Countess and a descendent of the world famous Rudbeck family which dates back to the 14th century. The family are noted for their pioneering work on the lymphatic system, the naming of the resplendent Rudbeckia flower and the discovery of the lungfish in Gambia!

I was playing in West Ham United's junior side, aged 14, when I first saw Bobby Moore play. Sometimes, after we had played a match, I would go to the player's pen next to the tunnel and watch the first team play. Bobby was 17 at the time and was already playing senior football. I had no idea that I would be playing with him just a few years later.

I have never forgotten something Bobby Moore told me on my debut. We were playing up at Bolton Wanderers and the game had been switched to an evening match which, back then, was unheard of. There had been an outbreak of small-pox and the late kick-off had kept thousands away from the game. Normally, there would have been around 30,000 watching, but only 17,000 turned up.

We took the train up to Burnden Park and I was feeling a little apprehensive. I was only 18 but that season I had played for West Ham Colts, the A team, the reserves and was now on the verge of my first team debut. It was completely unexpected and largely based on circumstances rather than ability because our first choice keeper, Lawrie Leslie, had sprained his hand and his stand-in, Brian Rhodes, had dislocated his shoulder. I was the third keeper to play for West Ham in as many games.

Bobby must have noticed my nervousness because he came over to me in the dressing room before the game and said: 'Al, once you cross that white line you are as good as anybody else, especially that little fella in the other goal.' At the time Eddie Hopkinson was the Bolton keeper and he had played for England quite a few times. 'You are the equal of everyone on that pitch,' Bobby said. That has always stayed with me. It was such mature advice for someone who was only 21 and, at the time, hadn't won any cups or played for England. At the end of the game Eddie Hopkinson came over to me and said: 'Well played, son.' I was six feet three inches tall and a bag of bones so it was a great thrill when an England goalkeeper shook my hand.

The other thing I remember about that Bolton match happened in the dressing room afterwards. They asked both sets of players to sign the match ball before raffling it to raise some money for the supporters club. The person taking the ball round to be signed was none other than Nat Lofthouse. One of the highlights of my life is the moment when Nat Lofthouse – The Lion of Vienna – asked me for my autograph!

I bought my first set of golf clubs from Bobby Moore. I paid him five pounds and he must have had a great slice because the driver looked as though it had been flattened in a vice!

Bobby was always a smart fella. I would turn up for training in a jumper knitted by my mum, Rosa, but Bobby would be there wearing a smart polo neck top. A lot of the lads went out for a drink after a game or after training but I have always lived south of the river so usually went straight home.

Back then I lived in Abbey Wood and took the 177 Bus to Woolwich, walked under the subway and then took the 101 bus to East Ham Town Hall before walking to Green Street. Sometimes I took the number 15 if there was one. After training at Chadwell Heath, Bobby would sometimes give me a lift back to the Town Hall because he usually dropped in to see Jack Turner at the ground. He was driving a dark maroon 375 Ford Consul with a column change and bench seat.

I cannot remember the exact occasion I last saw Bobby but it would have been at Upton Park in the 1980s He always had time for a chat and was genuinely interested in my life and family. Ironically, I played with him at the Boleyn Ground about eight years after I had left the club. Ron Greenwood sent me a letter asking me to play in Wally St Piers' testimonial. I played 45 minutes behind Bobby Moore for the 1964 FA Cup final team against the 1975 FA Cup final team, and the game finished finished 0-0. We had a chat and a drink afterwards.

Booby Moore was the type of person to look up to, not only because of what he achieved but because of who he was and how he conducted himself. Not only was he the man of the match in every game but he had time for everyone on a human level.

You will never find a footballer who didn't like Bobby Moore.
Alan Dickie

Alan with his debut programme.

37 – JACK BURKETT

Born: Edmonton, London. August 21, 1942

Position: Left full back

Games played with Bobby Moore: 161 (1962-67)

Games played for West Ham United: 185 (1962-67)

Honours with Bobby Moore: 1959 FA Youth Cup finalist, 1964 FA Cup winner, 1964 Charity Shield (Shared with Liverpool), 1965 European Cup Winners Cup winner, 1966 League Cup finalist

First game with Bobby Moore (Debut): April 30 1962 Fulham (h) W 4-2

Scorers: West Ham United: Dick (2) Crawford (2) – Fulham: Langley (pen), Henderson

West Ham United: Dickie, Kirkup, Burkett, Peters, Lansdowne, Moore, Scott, Byrne, Sealey, Dick, Crawford

Fulham: Macedo, Cohen, Langley, Mullery, Dodgin, Lowe, Leggat, Henderson, Cook, Haynes, O'Connell

---

J ack William Burkett is one of the magnificent seven in West Ham United's history, having won both the FA Cup and European Cup Winners Cup. Bobby Moore captained both those victorious teams at Wembley Stadium in 1964 and 1965.

Burkett played schoolboy soccer for Tottenham Hotspur but signed professional forms for the Hammers in October 1959. He played alongside Moore at left-back throughout his entire career at West Ham United.

Burkett and Moore first played together in the late 1950s in Bill Robinson's youth team. The highlight came when reaching the 1959 FA Youth Cup final against Blackburn Rovers, which was lost, 1-2, over two legs. Burkett impressed manager Ted Fenton but it was Ron Greenwood who gave him his first team debut on April 30, 1962. Burkett followed both Noel Cantwell and John Lyall into the left-back position and made it his own throughout the golden era at West Ham United. He also played for the England Youth team alongside Moore.

Edmonton-born Burkett headed further south when he was transferred to Charlton Athletic for £10,000 before the start of the 1967-68 season, bringing to a close some nine years with the Hammers. He wore the claret and blue on 185 occasions.

The players' view of Jack Burkett always refers to him as being smartly dressed and 'Mr Steady' on the pitch. He never panicked, had an educated left foot, made quick overlapping

Burkett, Moore and Brabrook during the FA Cup celebrations at Wembley.

runs and possessed a terrific sliding tackle. Moore would have witnessed all this which is why he appointed Jack as youth team coach at Southend United in the early 1980s.

Sir Geoff Hurst remembers the back problems suffered by the dependable left-back: 'Jack had a good left foot and was a fine player. Sadly, a recurring back problem meant that he spent most of his time in the swimming pool at West Ham. It probably made him less mobile than he otherwise would have been.'

Jack still resides in Southend-on-Sea with his lovely wife, Anne. In 2009 he published his autobiography, 'West Ham in the Sixties – The Jack Burkett Story.'

In 2013, Jack decided to sell both his FA Cup and European Cup Winners cup shirts and medals. A premium price of £40,000 was paid for the 'priceless' collection.

Playing European football.

I don't regard Bobby Moore as an idol or an icon like the rest of the world because I played with him. I was in defence with him throughout my time at West Ham and was one of the nearest players to him on the pitch. An icon to me was someone like Elvis Presley because there was the mystique of not knowing him but how could Bobby be my idol when I was eating sandwiches with him at Harry Cripps' house every week?

Bobby was the same towards me, from July 1, 1958, when I joined West Ham United, as he was for the rest of the time I knew him.

When I joined the ground staff in 1958, Bobby had been there for a year or so and was already training with the first team at Grange Farm while I had to stay at the ground doing chores. I had to dig up the pitch from penalty area to penalty area so that George Isaacs, the groundsman, could plant the grass seeds for the new season.

The best job was clearing out the rubbish from under the wooden slats in the Chicken Run. There was a peanut seller at the home games called Bill Larkin, and he used to throw the change back to the punters which would sometimes fall beneath the slats so we would collect a nice few bob for our effort. There were rats under there and all sorts.

One day when I was on the ground staff with Mike Beesley, a good striker at the club, we pulled the short straw and had to paint the toilets in the old Chicken Run. The whole place reeked of urine and we had to hold our breath, race in, put a coat of black paint on the splash back, and run out again. Try explaining that to the players nowadays!

Even though Bobby trained with the first team he would still come back sometimes and help us work on the ground which is another reason why everyone respected him and viewed him as one of us.

Bobby's mum, Doris, worked in William Warne's rubber factory in Barking and she got summer jobs for a lot of the

On defensive duty.

youth players there. Bobby, Harry Cripps, Tony Scott, Eddie Bovington and quite a few others all worked there. Harry, who we used to call 'Bulky', fell through the roof one day but landed on a load of rubber tyres. He could easily have been paralysed.

We got paid more at Warnes than we did at West Ham. By the time we had finished the work we were completely filthy and usually went back to Bobby's mum's house but she never complained and was really good to us.

Bobby helped to make me a better player because if an opponent got by me – and I was quite quick – he would still be there to clear our lines. One of the main strengths at West Ham was that we all worked hard for each other. You can't win the trophies we did without running through walls for each other.

I got changed next to Bobby in the dressing room. He didn't talk much about football and just went about his business like the rest of us. I would put my shorts on last because he did.

We should have won the FA Cup a year earlier in 1963. We got to the sixth round but eventually went out to Liverpool up at Anfield, losing 0-1. Bobby was very angry at the decision to allow the winning goal because he was ushering the ball out for a goal kick but Jimmy Melia scooped the ball from him and knocked it across for Roger Hunt to score. Bobby was in no doubt the ball had gone out and he was a very honest player. Jim Standen never moved because he thought it had gone for a goal kick. I believe we would have beaten Liverpool in the replay.

One of the great games I was involved in with Bobby was the FA Cup semi-final in 1964 against Manchester United at Hillsborough. It was pouring down with rain but our fans had their banners up and were singing their hearts out. They were drenched to the skin but as happy as anything. I remember some of the players saying we must win for those fans, we just had to do it for them.

It was probably the second best West Ham performance in our lifetime behind the TSV Munich game at Wembley a year later. The conditions at Hillsborough were really bad and some of the pitch was completely under water. We were told it was going to be called off but they got pitch forks out and managed to get it underway. We played much better than United and deserved to win.

I got to know Bobby a lot more when I worked with him at Southend United in the early 1980s. He confided in me a bit more. He was manager and I was appointed youth team coach with Harry Cripps as first team coach. Not many people got really close to Bobby but he was like a brother to me for a while at Southend. He lived next door to my son in Blenheim and I picked him up each morning because he had received a driving ban. I felt sorry for him because Southend didn't have any money to buy new players so he was managing in a strait jacket really.

West Ham completely screwed Bobby Moore by totally ignoring him after he left the club. When you see ex-players like Gary Neville having that ambassadorial role for Manchester United it brings it home to you. He couldn't have

laced Bobby's boots. These are the things you look at and they leave a bad taste in the mouth.

In today's market you could start at £200 million for Bobby and that would be a low estimate. We will not see an England captain lift the World Cup again in our lifetime and for a very long time after that. They have cheapened the honour of wearing the England shirt and I can't see the pride ever coming back.

I look at Bobby and if he had been a cleaner in Buckingham Palace he wouldn't have needed a broom. If he had been a soldier in the war he would have gone through the trenches and emerged spotless.

Bobby's brain was like a time machine. He was like Dr Who. His brain could take him to see something before it happened and it made him the world class player he became. Not bad for a slow wing-half from Barking!

One of West Ham United's magnificent seven.

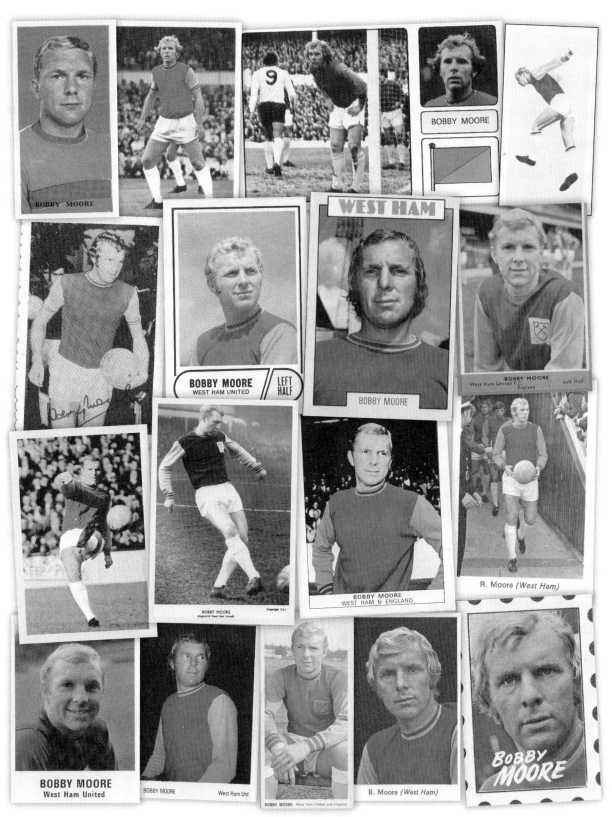

Let the Bobby Moore trade card era commence!

Back row L-R Lyall, Brown, Bond, Leslie, Lansdowne, Peters, Moore. Middle Row L-R Scott, Woosnam, Musgrove, Byrne, Crawford, Dick. Front Row L-R Bovington, Sealey, Kirkup, Boyce.

CHAPTER FIVE
1962-63

Bobby Moore's total appearances (July 1962-June 1963): 71 games (5 goals)

League Division One: 41 (3 goals), England: 9, American Tour: 8, Friendlies: 5 (1 goal), FA Cup: 5, Reserves: 2 (1 goal), League Cup: 1

Bobby Moore became West Ham United's club captain in November 1962, following the departure of Phil Woosnam to Aston Villa. Moore held the responsibility with distinction throughout the following 12 years, until his own time at the club came to an end.

The great freeze which gripped the country decimated the football schedule between December 22 and February 4. In order to sustain fitness levels the club used the Forest Gate Roller Rink to play indoor 11-a-side.

Ron Greenwood signed both Peter Brabrook from Chelsea for £35,000 and Jim Standen from Luton Town for £7,000. Combined with John Sissons, who made his debut in May 1963, the club's famous FA Cup team of 1964 were now firmly installed at the club.

Two landmark events occurred during the season which laid the foundation for West Ham United's future success. The Under-17s won the FA Youth Cup for the first time in the club's history, beating Liverpool 6-5 on aggregate, while the first team won the American International Soccer League during the summer of 1963, beating Gornik of Poland in the final over two legs. The wheels of success at West Ham United had started to turn and Geoff Hurst's tally of nine tournament goals in America was a portent of things to come.

For the record, the Hammers returned to the United States in August to play in the American Challenge Cup but lost 1-2 against Dukla Prague, a team which boasted six of Czechoslovakia's players, who had been defeated by Brazil in the 1962 World Cup final. Their captain Josef Masopust bullishly declared afterwards: 'I predict West Ham United will be a world-class team within two years.'

A significant footnote to the American experience came when Bobby Moore won the Eisenhower Trophy, which was awarded to the Most Valuable Player of the tournament. Recognition of his talents was becoming a frequent occurrence. He had been voted Hammer of the Year for the second time in three years and 500 guests attended the awards ceremony and dance at East Ham Town Hall.

On May 29, 1963, Moore captained England for the very first time. He was winning his 12th cap and took over the responsibility from Blackpool's Jimmy Armfield. Moore led his country to victory over Czechoslovakia in Bratislava,

BOBBY MOORE (West Ham)

The first trade card, issued by Quaker Oats for the 1962 Chile World Cup.

4-2. It was the first of 90 occasions on which he would captain his country.

The season saw the following Hammers make their debuts with Moore in the first team - Brian Dear, Peter Brabrook, Jim Standen, John Charles, Martin Britt and John Sissons.

Here is their story...

38 – BRIAN DEAR

Born: West Ham, London, September 18, 1943

Position: Forward

Games played with Bobby Moore: 81 (1962-70)

Games played for West ham United: 85 (1962-70)

Honours with Bobby Moore: 1965 European Cup Winners Cup winner, 1966 League Cup finalist

First game with Bobby Moore (Debut): August 29, 1962 Wolverhampton Wanderers (a) D 0-0

Wolverhampton Wanderers: Davies, Showell, Thomson, Goodwin, Woodfield, Flowers, Wharton, Crowe, Farmer, Murray, Hinton

West Ham United: Leslie, Kirkup, Burkett, Peters, Brown, Moore, **Dear**, Woosnam, Sealey, Byrne, Crawford

Brian Charles Dear was West Ham United's leading goalscorer in their successful European Cup Winners Cup campaign of 1964-65. His three goals against Lausanne over the two-legged quarter-final and another strike against Real Zaragoza in the semi-final, made an immeasurable contribution to West Ham's only major European success. Bobby Moore ensured his good pal took centre stage in the final.

'Stag' as he is more commonly known, was two years younger than Moore and made a big name for himself when setting a new record in the world of football by scoring the quickest ever five goals in a match - 20 minutes either side of half time, during a home encounter with West Bromwich Albion on April 16, 1965.

A lesser known fact is that Dear scored more goals against former England goalkeeping legend Peter Shilton than any

Following Bobby Moore out at Wembley in 1965.

Stag scores against Peter Shilton of Leicester City at Filbert Street in 1968.

other player. His tally of eight could, in fact, have been more, but for the Foxes' relegation in 1969.

Dear was involved in the infamous 'Blackpool affair' in 1970 when he and Moore, Jimmy Greaves, Clyde Best and club physio Rob Jenkins were caught having a drink late at night in former boxer Brian London's 007 nightclub. A dim view was taken by manager Ron Greenwood and Dear never played again for West Ham United.

Stag's post-playing career included a spell as a publican in Southend-on-Sea and, even in his retirement, he occasionally helped out in the cockle sheds in Leigh-on-Sea. He now performs an ambassadorial role for Southend United. He is also a frequent visitor to Upton Park and is often seen regaling the claret and blue faithful in the hospitality lounges. Long may it continue!

Stag tirelessly champions the cause of the Bobby Moore Fund, which was set up by Stephanie Moore following Bobby's untimely death in 1993.

Brian's 70th Birthday celebrations at The Roslin Hotel, Southend-on-Sea, in September 2013 were attended by former Hammers Martin Peters, Frank Lampard, Roger

Hugo, Mike Beesley, Eddie Bovington, Terry McDonald, Jack Burkett, Ken Brown, Ron Boyce and Roger Cross.

Stag still lives in Southend-on-Sea with his wife, Jan, and has been enormously helpful with his time and colourful stories about West Ham in the Bobby Moore era. His photos have also added a priceless visual feast.

The following recollections were shared during several visits to Andy Smillie's fish and chip café in Westcliff-on-Sea:

One of my biggest memories of Bobby came before the European Cup Winners Cup final in 1965. He came up to me in the dressing room and asked me if I was alright. He knew I'd had a bit of a run-in with Ron Greenwood earlier that day. The background to it all was that I'd suffered a reaction to some injections I'd had for a trip to New York. In the photos from the final I am wearing a plaster on my neck.

Earlier in the afternoon, before the final, Ron called me up to his room at the Hendon Hall Hotel, where we were staying. Bill Jenkins, the lovely old physio, was also there. Now, I had a bit of a temper that would flare up if things weren't going right for me so when Ron started saying how

Looking on as Jimmy Tarbuck introduces Bobby Moore to the Mayor of Margate in 1969. John Charles, Frank Lampard and Tommy Steele are also present.

worried he was about the reaction and that he might bring in Peter Brabrook, I lost it completely. I told him I would break his effing neck if he didn't play me!

Back in the dressing room before the game, Bobby came over to me for a chat. He could see that I was still upset and he said a few things which made me feel better. I remarked that it must feel like a home game for him playing at Wembley Stadium? And he said something for which I am eternally grateful. He turned to me and smiled: 'Walk out behind me tonight, Stag. That way, you'll be in all the pictures and you'll never forget it.'

When Ron Greenwood first joined West Ham he set up training sessions whereby we would all practice a particular skill such as volleying or one-touch passing. He would make us practise over and over again. Sometimes Greenwood would get involved himself and try to volley the ball but he wasn't skilful enough to demonstrate his point. Bobby would often step up and do it first time and then wipe his boot on the back of his own leg as if to say: 'Perfection once again!'

Bobby had such a meteoric rise for England. One minute he was playing in West Ham's Youth team and the next minute he was going to Chile for the 1962 World Cup. After a dozen games he was made captain of his country ahead of all those great players such as Johnny Haynes, Jimmy

Armfield and Bobby Charlton. It is quite staggering really but fully deserved.

West Ham had the best passers and crossers of the ball. Bobby Moore could ping a ball 20 or 30-yards to feet all day long. Tony Scott was an incredible crosser of the ball and Budgie was absolutely superb at finding the wingers. Sisso, Brabrook, Trevor Dawkins and Harry Redknapp were right up there, too. Players like Geoff Hurst had the best supply any forward could wish for.

Bobby had a terrific sense of humour and once in the late 1960s, when West Ham signed Peter Eustace, Ron Greenwood was telling us all about him. 'He comes from the countryside near Sheffield – a place called Stocksbridge – and goes hunting and fishing.' On hearing this Bobby turned round to Ron and said: 'We need a midfielder not a gamekeeper!'

I remember standing in a bar having a drink with Bobby and after we'd had a few he said to me: 'Stag, you've seen that film 'Escape To Victory', haven't you?'

'Yes, Bob,' I replied.

'Well, what a great film,' he continued. 'I didn't have much of a talking part but do you remember the cross for Pele's volleyed goal? One take!' Then he turned to the barmaid and nonchalantly said: 'Another Gin and Tonic, please.'

The Blackpool affair was a storm in a tea cup but it ended my time at West Ham. There is a photo of me and Jimmy Greaves leaving the ground after a disciplinary meeting and in it I am wearing Bobby's coat. The 0-4 defeat didn't help matters and the press got hold of it and that was that. I never played again.

Bobby's total number of games for West Ham United must be nudging 1000 matches if you include everything. He played in so many charity matches and testimonials and there is one friendly which springs to mind. In 1969, we played for a Jimmy Tarbuck XI against a Mayor of Margate XI. Both Tarbuck and Tommy Steele were performing the summer season at the Winter Gardens in Margate. One evening 'Tarby' and the Mayor were arguing over who could pick the strongest team and ended up agreeing to play a friendly. The next day Tarbuck was on the blower to Mooro asking if Ron Greenwood would allow a few of the players to come down and play? West Ham had just played Arsenal on August Bank on Holiday Monday and were due to play Nottingham Forest the following Saturday. Neverthless, Bobby brought me, Charlo and Lampard down to play. There were five or six thousand holidaymakers watching the game. In the first half there was a big row during the match because we were awarded a penalty and Tommy Steele was squaring up to take it but Tarby snuck up behind him and took it instead. Tommy went mad!

In the 1980s I ran a pub called The Hope, in Southend-on-Sea, and Bobby stayed with me while he was manager at Southend United. He was looking for a place in the area at the time.

We had a lot of fun down there and I remember Bobby appearing on BBC's Breakfast Time show with Selina Scott. He played a game of mud ball on Southend beach!

On another occasion Bobby was involved with the Motor Show at Earls Court and we were invited up to Brands Hatch to drive a few fast cars. It was a fantastic day and afterwards we went out for a drink with the organisers. Now, Bobby had given his word to ex-Hammer Malcolm Pyke that he would officially open up his new pub in Dartford but we were enjoying ourselves so much we left it really late to get down there. When we eventually arrived it was late and there was an enormous crowd outside who were clearly getting a little bit agitated. Pykey has always had a stutter and when he saw Bobby I remember his first response started with: 'B-B-Bobby, F-F-For FU, FU, FU.' You can probably guess the rest!

There was also the time when Bobby lost his driver's licence. He had driven up to Peterborough for the opening of Noel Cantwell's club. On the way back he was stopped in Biggleswade and failed a breathalyser test. He was banned from driving for one year.

Stag the publican with Bobby Moore...

The Bobby Moore fund raiser with Terry Creasey and Stephanie Moore

And big-hearted Stag at Ernie Gregory's funeral in 2012, with Tony Carr (left) and co-chairman David Gold.

I had been through a similar experience but had appealed my ban and managed to get the judgement overturned so I was urging Bobby to lodge an appeal, which he did. He asked me to accompany him to the magistrates in Biggleswade and I drove him up there. I remember the experience very clearly and can still picture Bobby standing in court, his hands behind his back with his fingers crossed! The judge referred to him as 'Robert Frederick Moore' and for some reason dropped the 'Chelsea' part of his name. Bobby's defence mentioned his charity work and how necessary it was for him to have his licence to fulfil his commitments and they returned it there and then.

It was while Bobby was at Southend United that I first met Stephanie his second wife. It was 1983 and Bobby introduced her to me and my wife, Jan. We all went out for dinner together and got on really well. It was always funny when we went to a restaurant because my wife's maiden name is 'Moore' so after Bobby and Stephanie were married there were three Moores and me! Stephanie was living in Heathrow at the time so it was a bit far for them to meet and they ended up sharing a place together in Chelsea. It was always great to have Bobby close by. He never lost that special aura.

I was so worried for him when it was clear that his illness wasn't improving. He never once complained. He was so brave. It was the worst day of my life when he died.

Brian Dear

Brian Dear is such a colourful character from West Ham United's illustrious past it seemed fitting to glean a view of the man from his former playing colleagues. The response was overwhelming:

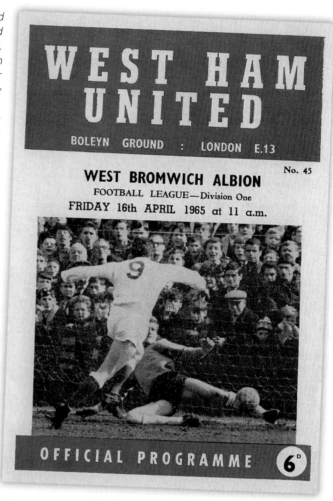

Programme from Brian Dear's record breaking five goals in 20 minutes.

He was a real live wire at the club and created a good atmosphere in the dressing room. A very good left foot.
Sir Geoff Hurst

I played against Stag for Dagenham schoolboys against East Ham schoolboys. He was a good striker.
Martin Peters

Charlo and Brian spent a lot of time together and were really great mates. When Charlo finished football and ran a chain of fruit stalls, Stag would always pop over to see him. He is an amazing man and has always got an entertaining story. My John wasn't a great talker but Brian is and he keeps all the memories alive and keeps people in touch with each other. We all love Brian.
Carol Charles (wife of John Charles)

I used to have some fun with Stag. I would put a broom handle up my arm and smack him around the neck in training!
Andy Malcolm

Stag came to my wedding. He was a good singer and could belt out 'Hello Dolly' really well. He and Alan Sealey had their own cabaret act which was fantastic.
Dennis Burnett

I was playing in a reserve team game at Home Park, Plymouth and Stag was in the side. There were only a couple of thousand people there and it was a lovely sunny day and people were sitting on the terraces watching the game rather than standing. Anyway, there were these two blokes giving Stag a lot of stick and they just kept going on and on at him. After a while, Stag came over to me and said he was going to switch with me and play out on the right. He was the senior pro so I was happy to follow his instructions. All of a sudden the ball went into the crowd and Stag jumped over the barrier to get it. He smacked one of the geezers on the chin and jumped back out again!
John Ayris

Brian used to give everyone a nickname. I used to wear one

of those pilot jackets with the fur round the trim and Stag called me 'Wingco' as in Wing Commander. He called me 'Milk bottle' as well. I thought Stag was a very good striker and a good finisher. He has never got the recognition he deserves because of the Moore, Hurst and Peters legacy.
Trevor Hartley

I should have been a bit more like Brian Dear. He was a bit cocky and had confidence in his own ability and everything else that he did. I never thought I was good enough and because I was the youngster in the team I never really grew up.
John Sissons

Stag had a wicked sense of humour. After Bobby Moore was awarded the O.B.E, Stag nicknamed him 'One Boiled Egg' because he'd had a testicle removed!
Alan Stephenson

The groundsman at West Ham was a chap called George Isaacs and he always wore a hat. It was never off him until one day the wind blew it off and Stag shouted out 'It's off!' and all the players ran out to take a look at his bald head.
Mickey Beesley

If ever anyone was arguing, Ernie Gregory used to say 'Just put the gloves on and sort it out that way'. One day they did just that and Stag had a fight with one of the players in the gym.
Peter Bennett

Stag had a tremendous left foot and could sniff out the goals. He probably didn't score two goals with his right foot but used to work an opening for his left foot which had a lot of power in it. He had a lot of success doing that. Stag has got a heart of gold.
Trevor Dawkins

Brian let me use his house when I got married. It all happened very quickly and we needed a place for the reception and Stag said: 'You can use my house,' which was a really nice gesture. He wasn't a great athlete but he always scored goals.
Jimmy Lindsay

'Stag' – West Ham's leading goalscorer during the successful 1965 European campaign.

Stag, like me, played for East Ham Boys. He was a bit younger than me but we had the same manager. Joe Langley was his name but we called him 'Carbunkle' because he had a big carbuncle on his neck. He was a little fat fella. I mean Carbunkle not Stag!
Peter Brabrook

39 – PETER BRABROOK

Born: Greenwich, London, November 8, 1937

Position: Right-wing

Games played with Bobby Moore: 167 (1962-67)

Games played for West ham United: 215 (1962-67)

Honours with Bobby Moore: 1964 FA Cup winner 1964 Charity Shield (Shared with Liverpool), 1966 League Cup runner-up

First game with Bobby Moore (Debut): October 22, 1962 Burnley (h) D 1-1

Scorers: West Ham United: Hurst – Burnley: Robson

West Ham United: Leslie, Bond, Burkett, Peters, Brown, Moore, **Brabrook**, Woosnam, Byrne, Hurst, Musgrove

Burnley: Blacklaw, Angus, Elder, Adamson, Talbut, Miller, Connelly, Lochhead, Towers, Robson, Harris

Peter Brabrook's crowning glory at West Ham United was winning the FA Cup Final in 1964. He is immensely proud of the achievement and his framed shirt and medal are a daily joy. He sent over the cross for Ronnie Boyce to head home the winning goal against Preston North End to secure a 3-2 victory in the final minutes.

Brabrook joined West Ham with a big reputation. He was part of Chelsea's League Championship winning side of 1954-55 and had already gained three caps for England.

He played in the 1958 World Cup in Sweden and was on the opposite wing to Preston North End's legendary Tom Finney. This was four years before Bobby Moore made his England debut against Peru in the 1962 World Cup in Chile.

Brabrook and Moore's football journey might have been somewhat different if there had been any substance to contemporary newspaper speculation regarding Brabrook's transfer to West Ham in 1962. It was mooted in the press that either Bobby Moore or Geoff Hurst would form part of the deal to bring Brabrook from Stamford Bridge to Upton Park. Thankfully, the press got it wrong.

It is an expensive irony that West Ham could have signed Brabrook some nine years earlier but dithered badly, allowing Chelsea to swoop and sign him. The

Training with Moore at West Ham stadium before the 1964 FA Cup final.

Hammers did eventually get their man but at a cost of £35,000. Thank god they did!

Brabrook eventually signed on the dotted line on Friday, October 19, 1962. His schoolboy days had seen him play for East Ham, Essex and London before signing for Chelsea over Easter 1953. He played in 250 league games for the Blues, scoring 47 goals.

Peter's happy-go-lucky attitude made him popular at West Ham and he was a big part of Bobby Moore's social crowd. His experience with Jimmy Greaves at Chelsea bolstered his reputation as a dangerous winger blessed with pace and two good feet. Greaves remembers Brabrook fondly: 'I used to room with Peter at Chelsea and he was the first player I knew to own a car. It was a light blue Vauxhall Victor and he often gave me a lift. Peter knew how to bring out the best in me. He was a tricky winger, very direct, and he knew that I liked to receive the ball early which is why he set up so many of my goals at Chelsea. We were good friends.'

Former team mate and experienced coach Trevor Hartley still recalls one particular moment involving Brabrook: 'He was the only player I've ever seen running down the wing, jumping over the ball and flicking it over his head and carrying on running with it. He did it in a match I was watching with a few of the lads in the players' pen and we all looked at each other and said: 'Did he really do that?'

Brabrook was part of the last West Ham team to beat Liverpool at Anfield. It happened on September 14, 1963 and his own antics in the closing minutes of that game have become the stuff of legend and widely shared by the goal scorers on that memorable day, Geoff Hurst and Martin Peters. Sir Geoff takes up the story: 'There wasn't much time left on the clock and we had a corner. Peter had this trick of going to kick the ball but, instead, kicked the back of his leg and fell over. That is exactly what he did. He just fell over and rolled around until our physio, Bill Jenkins, tended to him. By the time the game was restarted the whistle was blown!'

Behind Moore, Brown and Byrne at Wembley.

'Peter is a very funny guy,' continues, Sir Geoff. 'He had this habit of messing up his words. For instance, instead of saying 'relations' or 'relatives' he would say 'relatations!' His shoulder popped out once and he said it was 'discolated!'.

The comical side of Brabrook is also remembered by Tommy Taylor: 'When I was at Orient there was Peter Brabrook on one wing and Mark Lazarus on the other. I was only 16 at the time and they used to make me cry with laughter. Braaders had so many tricks he was a joy to watch. He used to feign injury at the end of the game and ask the ref how long there was left to play. 'One minute,' came the repsonse and Peter would say: 'That's good I'll be up in a minute!'

Peter was transferred to Leyton Orient prior to the 1968-69 season, having played 215 games and scored 43 goals in the claret and blue. He had already entered the meat trade as a butcher, which he continued throughout the 1970s.

Peter continues his association with West Ham United in a scouting capacity. Harry Redknapp brought him back to the club in 1996 and he had an influential role in the development of players such as Joe Cole, Rio Ferdinand, Frank Lampard and Michael Carrick. In fact Joe Cole generously funded a knee replacement for Peter. Sadly, money denied West Ham fans another era of success as each talent Peter brought through won trophies at other clubs.

It was at his home in Laindon Hills, Basildon that Peter kindly shared the following recollections of Bobby Moore:

With Moore on the hallowed Wembley turf.

One of my favourite memories of Bobby Moore came when we used to travel back on the train from away games up at places like Manchester or Newcastle. We would take the coach to the station and then get on the old Pullman train into Kings Cross or Euston. At the time there were two groups at West Ham. I was in one group with Bobby, John Bond, Ken Brown, Jim Standen, Budgie Byrne and Eddie Bovington. In the other group, Geoff Hurst, Martin Peters, John Sissons, Jackie Burkett, Ronnie Boyce and Joe Kirkup tended to stay together. They were the non-drinkers. Not only did they not drink but they didn't buy any either!

The train would pull in and Bobby was always near the front waiting to see the train guard who usually had his window down. We had a whole carriage to ourselves and the guard would shout: 'Bobby, Bobby, you're in that one,' and Bobby would wave his thanks and off we would all go. We'd get in the carriage, walk down the gangway and as we sat down there was an obstruction under the table – Bobby always arranged several cases of lager to be put there by the guard.

When we got into London we would often go to a club owned by an old boy called 'Sulky' who would sometimes go to the games with us. We would ask who was going on for a drink at his club and it was always the same crowd. Then we would ask Bobby if he was going and he would give us the same answer every time: 'No, I've got a few calls.' No more information than that. Then, later in the evening, when we were all having a good beer in the club, the door would open and in would walk Mooro. He never missed!

To be fair, Bobby was a bit of a quiet, secret person. You never knew where he went, what he was doing and who he was with because he didn't tell you but he was always there at the end.

We went out everywhere together, The Black Lion in Plaistow and, if the wives came out with us, we had a spell when we would go to The Moby Dick at Chadwell Heath. Tina and Bobby, me and my wife, Doreen, Hursty and Judith, we would all go. There was a bloke there we called 'Gateau Dick'

because he was always pushing dessert down us after the meal!

Bobby's presence on the pitch was enormous. He was on the left side of defence so would naturally build the play through Boycey and Sisso or up to Budgie and Geoff. I was on the right wing so he didn't find me as much and I usually got the ball from someone else. The best part of Mooro's play was his reading of the game. No one has ever read it as well as him and they never will.

I used to play against him when I was at Chelsea and I would try to take him on one-on-one but couldn't beat him. Now, I was light years faster than Bobby and he couldn't catch me if I was running backwards but he used to close me down in such a way that he stopped me getting by him.

My greatest game with Bobby was the 1964 FA Cup final. Bringing the cup home to all those West Ham fans is something I will never forget. I thought it was a great team performance and all the players did what was asked of them. I don't think we will ever see a team like those cup teams of 1964 and 1965 assembled at West Ham ever again. We had three future World Cup winners and eight internationals in total, plus the future England manager coaching us.

Obviously, it was a particular highlight for me to put in the cross for Boyce's winning goal. I can't imagine it is a nice feeling to lose a cup final at Wembley but thankfully all the West Ham boys I played with never had to experience it! That game is on a par with winning my first England cap in the 1958 World Cup tournament in Sweden when I played on the opposite wing to Tom Finney.

Bobby didn't say a great deal in the dressing room but when he did it always made sense. In the six years I was at West Ham, Ron Greenwood generally did all the talking and Mooro wasn't the type to interrupt but he might have a quiet word with one or two of the players. His presence alone was enough. I don't ever remember Ron once saying: 'What do you think Bobby?'

Bobby would put his shorts on last and I think it was because he didn't want to crease them. He would have one neat crease in his shorts and it was still there after the game, he was that good!

There was a fella called Phil at West Ham, who ran the player's bar in a little room next to the gym inside the ground. One day he started up a syndicate to play the football pools with Littlewoods. There was me, Bobby, Browny, Jim Standen, Bondy, and Budgie. We each chipped in a pound or so and picked the same numbers every week. After the game we would check our numbers and this went on for a year or so. Phil filled everything in and we would pay him. We never had one win the whole time we did it and eventually it broke up. I don't think we were that good at keeping up with the payments to Phil! A short while later our numbers came up and we missed out on a fortune. It made Phil so ill he had to leave the club. It finished him.

The first time we went to New York on tour was in 1963 and the flight took 14 hours. We went from Heathrow to Scotland and then on to New York. When the coach finally got us to the hotel we were shattered. Mooro asked Ken Brown to take his luggage up to his room because he had a few people to see! None of us had ever been to New York before, let alone knowing someone there, but that was Bobby, he always knew someone, somewhere. We didn't see him for two days but he played in all the games and we ended up winning the tournament. I think that was the first time we wore the blue strip with the claret hoops.

It was on that trip that I first noticed how tidy he was. I was in his room and he had his hankie folded neatly on the bedside table and on it would be his watch. In line with the watch would be his ring and then his cufflinks. His room was immaculate for the whole trip whereas mine was like a khazi about five minutes after arriving!

His knowledge of players was very good. If ever we talked football when we were out everyone listened when Bobby was giving his opinion. He talked like a manager talks and very rarely, if at all, did he ever bad mouth a player and say they were poor or rubbish.

Everybody loved Bobby Moore. You only have to say his name and the first words to come out of everyone's mouth are: 'What a lovely fella.' Even after I left West Ham I liked to return to see all the boys. I was running a butcher's shop at the time and brought them each a turkey every year.

They were fantastic times, the best in West Ham United's history, with not only great players but really nice guys. We were very lucky indeed.

Peter Branbrook

In 2014, only 30 Hammers had won an FA Cup winners medal.

40 – JIM STANDEN

Born: Edmonton, May 30, 1935

Position: Goalkeeper

Games played with Bobby Moore: 205 (1962-68)

Games played for West ham United: 236 (1962-68)

Honours with Bobby Moore: 1964 FA Cup Winner
1964 Charity Shield (shared with Liverpool),
1965 European Cup Winners Cup winner,
1966 League Cup finalist

First game with Bobby Moore (Debut): November 24, 1962 Sheffield Wednesday (a) W 3-1

Scorers: Sheffield Wednesday Fantham – West Ham United: Brabrook, Peters (pen), Scott

Sheffield Wednesday: Springett, Johnson, Birks, MeAnearney, Swan, Kay, Finney, Wilkinson, Layne, Fantham, Holliday

West Ham United: Standen, Kirkup, Burkett, Peters, Brown, Moore, Brabrook, Boyce, Sealey, Hurst, Scott

James Alfred Standen is one of West Ham United's magnificent seven, having won both the FA Cup in 1964 and the European Cup Winners Cup a year later. It was a lofty return on Ron Greenwood's £7,000 investment when buying him from Luton Town in 1962.

For good measure, Jim also won the County Cricket Championship with Worcestershire in 1964, topping the bowling averages along the way. Remarkably, such a feat from a 'double sportsman' was not placed on the radar of BBC's Sports Personality of the Year, which went to Olympic athlete Mary Rand for her Tokyo achievements.

It is disappointing that Jim's unique achievement has never really been properly recognised. The hysteria which exists today around the cult of the sporting individual did not exist back then, largely due to the absence of any saturation television coverage. As a consequence, Jim has had to settle for being the subject of sports quizzes throughout every pub in the land!

1964 was the first time West Ham United had won the FA Cup in its 69-year history and, similarly, Worcestershire had not won the County Championship in its 99-year existence. Clearly, all successful clubs must wait for the right man.

Jim's cricket and football duties often clashed and, on one occasion, he played cricket for Worcestershire during the day and football for the Hammers in the evening.

Sir Geoff Hurst recalls Jim fondly: 'He was the best keeper I played with at West Ham. He could eat and drink anything he wanted and not put on an ounce of weight.'

Ron Boyce echoes this view and remarks: 'Jim had the perfect build for a keeper and is a wonderful man. We got on very well and I wish he didn't live on the other side of the globe!'

Ken Brown smiled wryly when commenting on Jim: 'I don't think I ever saw him dive! He was brilliant at ensuring his body was right behind the ball. I used to say to him: 'Don't you ever dive?' But he would just reply: 'I don't need to, my positional sense is that good!''

Jim and his wife Lisa were known by some of the players as 'Sonny and Cher' and struck up a good friendship with Bobby and Tina.

It was a reluctant Jim Standen who left West Ham United in the summer of 1967 when he was transferred to Detroit Cougars. He later returned to these shores and had spells with both Millwall and Portsmouth. After hanging up his gloves, the likeable extrovert opened up two sports shops in Camberley, Surrey.

A coaching opportunity in Fresno, California, tempted Jim away from England and he still remains on the west coast of America today.

Jim and Lisa are approaching 60 years of marriage. In May 2005, *EX Hammers* Magazine flew him back to the UK for a reunion of those glorious West Ham cup winning teams of 1964 and 1965. He took the time to combine the trip with a visit to Worcestershire to visit a few of his old cricketing pals.

The rigours of a long sporting career have taken their toll on Jim, who has had both his knees and hips replaced. He loves to stay in touch with both cricket and football on these shores and was keen to share his recollections of Bobby Moore from the heat of Fresno, California:

Bobby Moore was one of the nicest people I have ever met. He was so dedicated. I couldn't help but be impressed by the man. We got on well and our wives, Lisa and Tina, were also very close and went out socially a lot of the time. They were a real couple of glamour girls. There was always a crowd around Bobby but perhaps not always the greatest crowd.

Being introduced to the Earl of Harewood (President of The FA) by Bobby Moore.

He may have got mixed up with one or two undesirables but the man himself was first class.

He would always ensure Lisa and I were invited to any parties at his house or any other big events. We got to meet the Beatles through Bobby.

Bobby had quite a dry sense of humour. After we had won the FA Cup and European Cup Winners Cup I commented that I had £4,000 in the bank. 'Do you think that's a lot of money then, Jim?' he responded with that smile in his eyes.

Ron Greenwood bought me from Luton Town for £7,000. Geoff Hurst urged Ron to buy me and he did. I replaced Lawrie Leslie, who was a real character but injury-prone. He would think nothing of diving on concrete or into the posts, anything to keep the ball out. Ernie Gregory coached me at West Ham and was one of the nicest guys I ever met in football. He was the first to train me in a sand pit.

When I arrived in 1962, Bobby's star was on the rise. He had played in Chile during the World Cup that summer and things were starting to move for both him and West Ham

United. I was the first goalkeeper at West Ham to wear the Number 1 on the back of his shirt.

As soon as I arrived at the club, I realised I had joined a proper footballing team. There were so many good players at the time and such a rich vein of talent coming through the youth squad. Bobby was the perfect person to lead that talent. It was incredible how committed everyone was to playing good football. We would get the team list on Friday and all make our way over to Cassettari's café to discuss the game. John Bond was terrific and knew so much about the opposition. I can still hear him now: 'He likes to cut in from the wing and get his shot away early so be on your guard, Jim.' By the time I lined up to play I felt I knew how the game was going to pan out.

Bobby was just that cut above the rest of us in everything he did. He was our master and our friend and we all admired him so much. I was a little bit different than the rest of the team because I played all my games between the sticks, right behind Bobby. He always wanted the ball and, sometimes,

Punching clear against Olympiakos under the watchful gaze of Moore, December 1965.

when I was looking for a quick release up front to either Geoff Hurst or Johnny Byrne, Bob would be shouting: 'Give it to me!' He got me into trouble on a couple of occasions like that – once against Bolton Wanderers – when he lost the ball and I had to get my head kicked in cleaning up his mess! But most of the time he would sweep the ball into space and play the perfect pass to feet.

At the end of my first season with West Ham, I finished runner-up to Bobby for the 1963 Hammer of the Year award. I think I missed out by a handful of votes.

Bobby wasn't a bad cricketer but football was definitely his game. He wasn't county standard or anything like that and Geoff Hurst was a better cricketer than Bobby. West Ham played cricket against Ilford every summer and, one year, Bobby and I put on over 100 runs together. It was such good fun and we used to attract big crowds.

I wish I had got an England cap with Bobby. I was always behind Ron Springett and Gordon Banks but I believe I missed out because of my cricket commitments. After the final game of the season with West Ham I was in the nets with Worcestershire the next day. Similarly, I went straight back to

West Ham once the cricket season was over. Ironically, my football commitments cost me an England cricket cap. I was invited to join the England cricket team on a tour of South Africa but Ron Greenwood called me up and said: 'Jim, if you go on tour, I will have no choice but to buy a new keeper.' So I didn't go. Ironically, the first game that season we lost 0-3 to West Bromwich Albion and we laughed that I should have gone on tour!

I think I left West Ham prematurely. With the greatest respect to Bobby Ferguson, his transfer to West Ham from Kilmarnock wasn't a great buy. If I could have stuck it out in the reserves for a while I am certain I would have got back into the first team but I was offered a good deal to play in America for Detroit Cougars. However, their season didn't start until December and I remember Ron Greenwood coming around to my house and asking me to play a few more games in the first team. He brought me back for three games – Walsall in the League Cup which we won 5-1, Sunderland in the league which we also won 5-1 and a 1-2 home defeat to Wolves.

I was only 33 and felt I had a good five years left in me. I was so angry and annoyed to be playing in the reserves at West Ham. I wasn't the best goalkeeper in the country at the time but I was certainly among the top three or four. I wasn't happy that my career should be going in such a direction after the Wembley successes just a few years before.

After my playing days, I opened up a couple of sports shops in Camberley, Surrey – Jim Standen Sports. Both Bobby and Geoff came down and opened each shop. We had about 2,000 people turn up for one of the openings.

I bought one of those shops from Keith Moon, the ill-fated drummer from The Who. It was a flat which I converted into a shop. Keith had filled it with giant snakes and all sorts. He was a crazy character and visited me in Chertsey a couple of times. He arrived in a huge chauffeur-driven Rolls Royce with a few birds in the back!

I had those shops for three years before selling up and moving to the United States. I loved the climate and was offered a coaching role at Fresno State University so Lisa and our three kids sold up and emigrated to the west coast. It was a hasty decision but not one we regret. I also sold my European Cup Winners Cup medal in 1994 to raise some money for a real estate deal.

The last time I spoke to Bobby was when he was in Hong Kong coaching Eastern Athletic in the early 1980s. I had been coaching a terrific goalkeeper called Kirk Shermer at Fresno State University and I called up Bob to see if he needed a keeper. 'Yes, I do, Jim,' he said. 'Bring Kirk over, we'll arrange the air fares because I want him.' That was the last I heard because Bobby left Hong Kong soon after.

I was in the States at the time of Bobby's illness. It was so upsetting to see the photographs of him and,

Runner-up to Bobby Moore for the 1963 Hammer of the Year.

Back in the East End in 2005 with L-R Joe Kirkup, superfan Terry Connelly, Jim and author Tim Crane.

in a sense, I am pleased that I didn't see him in person at that time because I admired him so much and it would have been too much to see him suffering like that.

I remember when he had testicular cancer at West Ham in the mid-1960s. 'Cancer' has always been a dreadful word but back then it was like a death sentence. Some of us thought we might not ever see him again. To make the recovery he did and to come back to win a European trophy and the World Cup will never get the recognition it deserves. I look back on him as the immaculate, imposing figure we all knew and loved. A hero for man and boy.

Jim Standen

41 – JOHN CHARLES
September 20, 1944 – August 17, 2002

Born: Canning Town, London

Position: Left-back

Games played with Bobby Moore: 133 (1963-70)

Games played for West Ham United: 142 (1963-70)

First game with Bobby Moore (Debut): May 4, 1963 Blackburn Rovers (h) L 0-1

Scorer: Blackburn Rovers: Pickering

West Ham United: Leslie, Kirkup, Lyall, Peters, Moore, **Charles**, Scott, Boyce, Britt, Sissons, Brabrook

Blackburn Rovers: Else, Bray, Newton, Clayton, Woods, England, Douglas, McEvoy, Pickering, Byrom, Harrison

John William Charles wore the Number 6 shirt on his debut for West Ham United. Bobby Moore wore the Number 5 jersey that day for the visit of Blackburn Rovers and, to underline the unusual spectacle, played up front in the second half. It was also the first line up which didn't include a single player from Moore's own first team bow almost five years earlier.

Ron Greenwood had given debuts to the other two youth players who had formed part of the England squad which had won the International Youth Tournament in 1963 – John Sissons and Martin Britt.

'Charlo' had risen through the ranks of West Ham, Essex and London Boys before signing professional forms for his local club, in April 1962. His first great honour was to captain the West Ham team which successfully overcame Liverpool 6-5 on aggregate in the 1963 FA Youth Cup final. He also gained five England Youth caps. He would eventually go on to play alongside Bobby Moore in 133 first team matches before leaving the game to run a chain of fruit stalls.

Charlo is described by his contemporaries as being very competitive, very feisty but usually sporting a big smile. Clyde Best showed particular gratitude to Charlo for the help he had given to him while at West Ham. 'No trip to London would be complete without a visit to Charlo's wife, Carol and sister, Rita. They are family to me.'

Through Charlo West Ham United pioneered the breaking of the colour code in the 1960s. His brother Clive would follow him into West Ham United's defence while both Ade Coker and Clyde Best established themselves at the other end of the pitch.

The warmth of Charlo and his family is summed up by former playing colleague, Alan Dickie: 'I joined the ground staff at the same time as Charlo, Brian Dear, Dave Bickles and a lad named John Starkey. After we had finished all our chores for the day we would go back to Charlo's house

in East Ham and his mum Jesse would make us all egg and chips.'

Charlo left West Ham United in the summer of 1970 and took over the family green grocery business. Former Hammer, Lawrie Leslie, worked for him for a while.

Later in life John struggled against depression and addiction. In 2001 he was diagnosed with cancer and died on August 17, 2002 aged 57. His memory is kept alive by his devoted family and we thank Carol Charles for sharing the following recollections from her home on Canvey Island:

If John was here today he would say Bobby Moore was a thorough gentleman, immaculate in every way and a fantastic footballer.

He and Bobby used to drink in The Retreat at Chigwell when Johnny and Connie Driver ran it. John was also close to Brian Dear, Dave Bickles and John Cushley.

The footballers in John and Bobby's day were nice men. They weren't flash, they were just ordinary fellas doing their day's work as best they could before going out to enjoy themselves.

Sometimes I would come home to our house at 60 Birkbeck Road, Newbury Park, having been working on the fruit stall in Gravesend, and John would be chatting and listening to music over a few beers with Bobby Moore, Brian Dear and Eddie Bovington. They were ordinary fellas doing the things ordinary people did.

John and I got married in the summer of 1963, not long after he had captained West Ham's youth side to victory over Liverpool. I was 21 but he was only 18 so his mum had to sign her permission for him to get married, bless him.

During John's early days at West Ham, Ron Greenwood decided not to take him on a club tour of America because of the colour bar and Civil Rights campaign which was flaring up at the time. Ron was very sensitive about the situation and he visited John's mum to explain to her why he felt it best that John shouldn't go.

Captain of the 1963 FA Youth Cup winning team with L-R Harry Redknapp, Colin Mackleworth, Dennis Burnett, Bill Kitchener and four-goal sensation, Martin Britt.

John did join the team for a tour of America in 1969. At the time I was pregnant with our second child, Lesley and gave birth at our home.

John was in America for six weeks so couldn't be at the birth but it was really amazing because he called up just after she was born at 4.30 in the morning. It was late evening over there and I was so happy that he was the first to know and could hear her crying. Bobby and Tina came and visited me. Bobby was flying out the next day and took photos of Lesley with both me and Keith, our first born. Bobby had a Polaroid instamatic so they developed on the spot and he took them out to John. It was typical of his thoughtfulness.

One time we went with Bobby and Tina and Brian and Jan Dear to Johnny Speight's house. He wrote: 'Til Death us Do Part' with Alf Garnett which was very popular at the time. What a lovely house he had! It was like an old Church.

I remember Johnny Speight was annoyed because we had got lost and arrived late. It was a terrific night and he had magicians and jugglers there. We had a really good laugh together. We would often go to Bobby and Tina's house in Chigwell for birthday parties and to socialise.

One story I simply must tell involves all the wives of the West Ham players from that time. We used to meet in a little motel down the Romford Road when we were waiting for the boys to come back from a game. We would be drinking and gossiping. On one occasion, they had just returned from a tour abroad and John had bought me a beautiful ring with a cluster of diamonds which sparkled different colours in the sun.

The next time the girls met up in the hotel I had my ring on and I was making sure it was visible because I was really chuffed to be wearing it. All of a sudden I noticed that Jan Dear was wearing the same ring and so was Tina Moore and Lisa Standen. The cheeky buggers had bought a job lot from some bloke at the airport!

There was a lovely man at West Ham called Stan Botham and he used to take photos of all the matches. He usually left copies of them in the dressing room. There were lots of photos of John and Bobby which I collected and arranged in two big albums. They were really special but one day I loaned them to a staunch West Ham supporter Tony Hutchinson who I worked for on a fruit stall in Barkingside. We were so unlucky because we left them locked up on the stall for a night but a fire destroyed everything.

John struggled with his health in later life and we moved to Spain for a while where he showed real improvement. Sadly, it didn't last and depression took hold again and he was in and out of hospital.

What disappoints me is that when John came out of hospital on one occasion, his great mate Brian Dear took him to a game at West Ham and John wanted to talk to Joe Cole but Joe didn't want to know and told him to talk to his father who was his agent. Now, John, Bobby, Stag and Eddie weren't like that in their day. In fact they were the exact opposite and even now both Stag and Eddie have time for everyone. We all had open houses and would drop in to see each other regularly.

The thing I miss most about John is his banter. He was a very, very funny man. Things just came to him in an instant. I remember he was talking to a couple of blokes and just like that said: 'I've got to go home now, I'm going to a fancy dress party.' I was standing there thinking: 'Here we go.' So they asked him what he was going as and he said 'Carol's going to stick a piece of string up my arse and I'm going as a conker!'

They were great days at West Ham. I just remember laughing all the time. I went out one night with John Charles and John Charles! I had my John on one arm and the Welsh John Charles on the other.
Carol Charles

Following are some player recollections of Charlo:

Charlo and I used to get a lift with Bill Jenkins, the club physio. He lived at 49 Benson Avenue and would sit in a big armchair with quarts of cider down the side. He drove a big white Zephyr Zodiac and revved it up and drove like a mad man. It was a big powerful car and he was a big powerful man. Bill was a real man's man and when he died after the World Cup in '66 Ron Greenwood cried his eyes out over at Chadwell Heath. Like me, Charlo loved him but it didn't stop him burning us with some of the equipment he had in his clinic! Bill burnt everyone at West Ham. Tony Scott, Eddie Bovington, they've all got scars on their legs from Bill's treatment. He wouldn't say no to anyone that needed help and treated loads of people at his house. They'd be sitting on his stairs, waiting in the bedroom or sitting in the living room and he would be tending to them all. Charlo and I were gutted when he died, it was so sudden.
Brian Dear

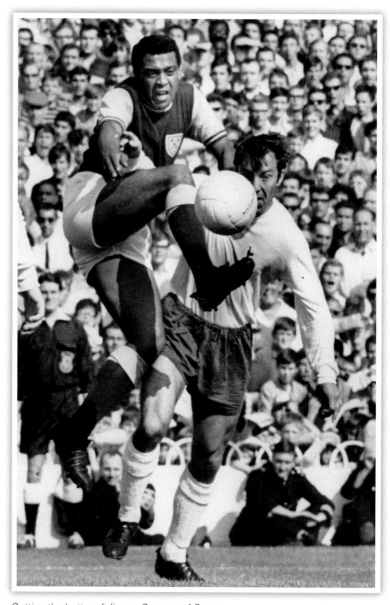
Getting the better of Jimmy Greaves of Spurs.

John captained our youth side and was very competitive, very feisty. He would take no prisoners and was a very good footballer.
Trevor Dawkins

When John finished playing he used to come into a pub I managed called The Britannia in Plaistow. Charlo had a good sense of humour and he told a story about when he was trying to get back into the team and how he was going to get right up Greenwood's arse to accompolish this. The punchline was: 'When I went to Ron's office, Lampard was already up there!'
Frank Lampard

I loved Charlo because he had this beautiful big smile on his face. A great lad with a terrific personality.
Peter Eustace

I admired John for many reasons. He was the captain of our youth team in 1963 and he was a good captain, very considerate and very personable. One of my greatest recollections of John came many years ago when I went back to West Ham to watch a game. I had arranged to meet his brother Clive outside the main entrance where all the autograph collectors congregate and out the corner of my eye I caught sight of John. It was fantastic to see him, with his big smile and we hugged each other and had a chat. It was a very special encounter.
Bobby Howe

My dad always respected John Charles because they both had to overcome a different type of racism. My dad came from a sectarian area in Glasgow where there was a lot of hatred and bigotry so he sympathised with John.
David Eadie (son of Doug Eadie)

I remember we were playing in Wales and had travelled up to the hotel the night before. We had our dinner and were sitting around relaxing when this fella came in who had clearly been drinking. He was asking who we all were and where we were from. We were trying to brush him off politely but he was undeterred and turned to Charlo: 'Where are you from?' he asked. 'London' replied Charlo. But the guy shook his head and repeated: 'No, where are you from originally?' Likewise, Charlo just repeated 'London.' Well, this chap wasn't being put off and came back again: 'No, I'm asking about where you are from originally?' To this

Charlo stood up and said: 'London! It was a bloody hot day when I was born!'
Ken Brown

John helped me a lot with my game and was a great battler. I stayed at his mum's house and was great mates with his brother, Clive. Charlo is the one I will always be indebted to.
Clyde Best

Charlo on his fruit stall in the early 1970s.

42 – MARTIN BRITT

Born: Leigh-on-Sea, Essex, January 17, 1946

Position: Forward

Games played with Bobby Moore: 23 (1963-66)

Games played for West Ham United: 26 (1963-66)

First game with Bobby Moore (Debut): May 4, 1963
Blackburn Rovers (h) L 0-1

Scorer: Blackburn Rovers: Pickering

West Ham United: Leslie, Kirkup, Lyall, Peters, Moore, Charles, Scott, Boyce, **Britt**, Sissons, Brabrook

Blackburn Rovers: Else, Bray, Newton, Clayton, Woods, England, Douglas, McEvoy, Pickering, Byrom, Harrison

Martin Charles Britt is a member of a very select band of West Ham United players who have scored a winning goal at Old Trafford. Bobby Moore only witnessed it twice in his West Ham career – Martin Britt in 1963-64 and before that John Dick in 1961-62.

Martin catapulted himself into the West Ham consciousness with an unforgettable four-goal haul against Liverpool in the 1963 FA Youth Cup final. Ron Greenwood commented that the 6-5 aggregate victory was one of the most exciting matches he ever saw.

Former playing colleague Trevor Dawkins recalls how the crosses from both Harry Redknapp and John Sissons were given the treatment they deserved by 'Britto.'

Britt played schoolboy football for both Essex and London before chief scout, Wally St Pier, brought him to West Ham United.

He was almost five years younger than Moore and played in 23 matches with him. He also won three England Youth caps. Sadly, Britt's career was cut short due to a knee ligament injury and a £25,000 transfer to Blackburn Rovers in 1965 caused a major dispute between the two clubs. Blackburn claimed West Ham had not made them aware of the injury. He was 21 years old.

After a successful post-playing career in the textile trade, Martin is now retired and continues to live in his native Leigh-on-Sea, with his wife, Christine.

Right from the very start of my experience at West Ham United, Bobby played a part. Before I signed I was invited by scout Wally St Pier and then manager Ted Fenton to participate in evening training sessions which took place every Tuesday and Thursday. This was 1961 and I was only 15 years of age.

I took the train from my parents' home in Leigh-on-Sea, up to Barking and then on to Upton Park by tube. Bobby

was usually there and because he knew I was going back to Barking he would always go out of his way to give me a lift.

If I remember rightly he had a maroon Ford Consul. Bobby became the most familiar player I knew there and he was just on the cusp of becoming famous and going to Chile for the 1962 World Cup.

The moment we all dream about – Martin in the dressing room before his debut against Blackburn Rovers, 1963.

I loved his sense of humour which was dry and sarcastic but lots of people didn't like it or rather they failed to appreciate it. They wrongly confused it with arrogance but I really liked it because I have a similar type of humour.

I remember one time when the opposition coach pulled into the ground and Bobby went and met them all and shook their hands as if to say: 'Welcome to my club.' It was beautiful to watch and typical of the wonderful sense of humour he possessed. I couldn't help but laugh but if you didn't know him you might have thought: 'Cocky sod!' That would have been missing the point completely.

I signed for West Ham when I was 15 and under Ron Greenwood the club was at the forefront of modern football. I used to think a lot about the game and was, dare I say it, quite an intelligent target man so when people like Ron and Bobby were talking about timing and positioning it really hit home.

The aerial threat of Martin Britt in the FA youth Cup final against Liverpool. Team-mates Redknapp, Bennett and Sissons are also in view.

People often talk about the four goals I scored in the 1963 FA Youth Cup final against Liverpool and the odd voice will say the key passes in that game from Harry Redknapp, Bobby Howe and Bill Kitchener, made the goals easy for me. But, I would add that while they were first class crosses I like to think my timing and positioning ensured they got the right end result.

That is what I was good at. Ron saw it in me, too. I wasn't any good at all the tricks and flicks but he told me not to underestimate the skill set I had. He said the fact I could take a 50-yard ball and lay it off to a player a few feet away demonstrated real ability.

That was something I learned from Bobby because one of the things I picked up in training and playing with him was that he was such a good passer of the ball.

As we all know, Bobby had fantastic vision. If he played the ball up short to you, then you would know that you had a defender up your backside and by going to meet the ball that then allowed you to gain that extra yard. Conversely, if Bobby fired the ball in hard to you, then you knew that you had time and space to control the ball and turn with it. His passing ability was phenomenal.

Many times he would play the ball into me from distance and it would stop dead in front of me. Now that is real ability. For him to hit a 40 or 50-yard ball that I didn't need to control because it had stopped in front of me was world class. He not only found me with the pass but he controlled the ball for me as well.

I was fortunate enough to score the only goal in a game up at Old Trafford in October 1963, but I remember the occasion for different reasons. In the dressing room at half time John Bond was shaking his head and Ron asked him what was wrong. 'It's Bobby Charlton,' he said. 'Every time he gets the ball, I know he is going to jog up to me, wind up his left foot and make that pass but I can't stop it. He does me every time.' Ron replied: 'Look, John, don't get upset because if you know what a player is going to do and you still can't stop them, that is world class.'

This could easily be applied to Mooro. Opposition players knew he couldn't run, couldn't jump, and was a little bow-legged but they still couldn't get past him. Absolute world class!

An interesting footnote to that game up at Old Trafford came after I left football and entered the world of textiles. I used to have a lot of meetings in the north and was often invited by clients to watch Manchester United. Now, a lot of the old guard up there used to say it was during that time in the early 60s when people recognised Bobby Moore to be a great player and not just a flash East End boy who wore tight shorts!

Later on in life, I had another encounter with Bobby that I will never forget. In fact I get quite choked when I recall it. In 1989, my wife, Christine, was working at a new hospice which had just opened in Westcliff-on-Sea. A priest, who was involved with the project said to Christine that they needed to act fast to buy the property next door. They needed ideas to raise a lot of money, quickly.

Martin Britt (circled) in the England Youth team with fellow Hammers, Brian Dear, John Charles and John Sissons.

Well, at the time I had just attended a golf tournament at Wentworth for the textile industry so I suggested that we should try to arrange a Charity Golf Day in Leigh-on-Sea. I had just joined the local golf club and they were fantastic, agreeing to close the course on Wednesday for us to use to raise money for the hospice.

We needed to get a couple of stars along to help with publicity, sponsorship and turnout so I called up Bobby, Martin Peters and Geoff Hurst and asked them if they would come down and be the celebrities for the day. Thankfully, they all agreed.

We managed to get the local radio and newspapers involved and my daughter, Hannah, produced a brochure which helped to raise a lot of money for the cause. We had no problem selling out the golf day and the whole place was going to be choc-a-bloc. On the Monday before the event, Bobby called me up and said that he couldn't make it!

Naturally, I told him not to worry and that Geoff and Martin were still coming and that we would be all right. It wasn't his fault, he had a commitment at Wembley Stadium and a game needed to be replayed on the day of the charity event. It was just terribly bad luck.

At the time Bobby was getting some bad press in Southend and people were asking me if he was an alcoholic or a crook or whatever other nonsense they could dream up and I just said: 'That's not the man I know.'

On the day, the place was mobbed, Geoff and Martin turned up and I can remember getting back to the club house at about 3 o'clock and who should walk in but Mooro?

He had driven all the way from Wembley Stadium and said: 'I couldn't let you down.' He spent an hour signing autographs before getting back into his car and driving back up to Wembley for the game itself. The man was incredible and just a few years later he died. What I am trying to explain

is that all those people were saying horrible things about him but he was just magnificent. In fact, we have run the charity event every year since.

Martin Britt

'Britto' with the match ball from the 1963 FA Youth Cup final.

43 – JOHN SISSONS

Born: Hayes, Middlesex, September 30, 1945

Position: Left-wing

Games played with Bobby Moore: 236 (1963-70)

Games played for West Ham United: 266 (1963-70)

Honours with Bobby Moore: 1964 Charity Shield (Shared with Liverpool), 1965 European Cup Winners Cup winner, 1966 League Cup finalist

First game with Bobby Moore (Debut): May 4, 1963 Blackburn Rovers (h) L 0-1

Scorer: Blackburn Rovers: Pickering

WEST HAM UNITED

BLACKBURN ROVERS
FOOTBALL LEAGUE—Division One
SATURDAY 4th MAY 1963 at 3 p.m.

OFFICIAL PROGRAMME 6°

West Ham United: Leslie, Kirkup, Lyall, Peters, Moore, Charles, Scott, Boyce, Britt, **Sissons**, Brabrook

Blackburn Rovers: Else, Bray, Newton, Clayton, Woods, England, Douglas, McEvoy, Pickering, Byrom, Harrison

John Lesley Sissons is one of the magnificent seven in West Ham United's history having won both the FA Cup and European Cup Winners Cup.

Sissons' medal tally at West Ham is highly impressive, having won the FA Youth Cup in 1963, FA Cup in 1964, European Cup Winners Cup in 1965 and a runners-up medal in the 1966 League Cup. He also won two European Youth tournaments with England in both 1963 and 64.

For many years he was the youngest player ever to score in an FA Cup final, having equalised against Preston North End in 1964. It was a record that stood until Norman Whiteside scored for Manchester United in the 1983 final against Brighton and Hove Albion. Somewhat mischievously, John shakes his head when acknowledging the fact; 'Norman had to wait for a replay to score his!'

John played for both Middlesex and England Schoolboys as well as England Under-23s. It is a travesty that he never gained a full England cap but he played 12 times for England Youth.

Bobby Moore was training at Grange Farm when a 15-year-old Sissons was putting John Bond through his paces. 'Who the effing hell you got here?' Bondy enquired of manager, Ted Fenton. 'Get him in the first team!'

West Ham's signing of John Sissons is a story that would have doubtless caused much amusement between Bobby Moore and the players at Upton Park.

Legend has it that Charlie Faulkner, part of Wally St Pier's scouting team, went to the Sissons' household to get his signature. However, he was told by John's mother, Emily, that her son would not be signing for anyone unless Charlie mowed her lawn! Thankfully, Charlie performed the task and on July 29, 1961, West Ham signed the most decorated left-winger in the club's history. He was a worthy replacement for the prolific goalscoring talents of Malcolm Musgrove.

One of Sisso's finest moments in the claret and blue came when scoring a hat-trick during the dismantling of Don Revie's

Mooro congratulates 'Sisso' on his FA Cup final equaliser.

Leeds United, 7-0, in a League Cup encounter in November 1966.

Sir Geoff Hurst recalled John with fondness 'We were neighbours in Hornchurch for many years and, as a youngster, John was a very good player and a dedicated trainer. I was surprised, given all his attributes, and his goal in the 1964 FA Cup final, that he didn't go on to do as well as I thought he should have done. He seemed a dead cert to get an England cap but it just didn't happen for him.'

John left West Ham in early August 1970 and signed for Sheffield Wednesday. It brought to a close nine trophy-laden years at the club.

John continues to reside in South Africa where he has been for almost 40 years. He recently moved to Langebaan on the Western Cape.

Sisso's love of golf, which he plays with his wife, Sandy, remains a keenly pursued passion. He is officially retired but does raise a bit of 'pocket money' buying and selling the odd car. His hobbies include cycling, gardening, reading and a strong passion for Springboks rugby union team.

In early 2014 John visited the UK to celebrate his mother's 100th Birthday. He took time out to share his recollections of Bobby Moore over a spot of lunch.

Best drink in the world!

I have given this a lot of thought since I received your letter. I was the youngest member of the team when I first played and was very naïve. Bobby was more like a mentor to me. He really was a figure that I looked up to and was a hero of mine even before I turned professional. Then all of a sudden, I found myself playing with him in the first team and winning the FA Cup and European Cup Winners Cup. It was a dream come true.

My debut came at home to Blackburn Rovers in 1963 and Ron Greenwood picked myself, John Charles and Martin Britt. We were involved in our successful FA Youth Cup run at the time and had just beaten Aston Villa 4-2 to make it to the semi-final.

Both 'Britto' and I had scored two each against Villa and 'Charlo' was our captain so Ron gave us our chance in the first team. We were safe in the league and Ron wanted to

blood a few of the youngsters. Unfortunately, we lost that game 0-1 on a rock hard pitch with no grass and the ball bouncing all over the place.

I remember my second game, up at Hillsborough against Sheffield Wednesday, really well. I believe Peter Swan was making his comeback for The Owls after the betting controversy, so there was a lot of interest in the game. As I got off the team bus and went into the players' entrance the steward said: 'Sorry son, you are not allowed in here.' I was being pushed aside but Bobby was right behind me and he put his arm around my shoulder and said: 'He's with me.' Bobby then took me through to the dressing room. I think the steward must have thought that I was an autograph hunter!

My relationship with Bobby was a little bit distant because he was living in Chigwell, while I was living in Hornchurch near players such as Geoff Hurst, Martin Peters, and Brian Dear. They called us the 'Hornchurch Hornets.'

In those days, the younger generation tended to stick together as a group; that would be Geoff Hurst, Ronnie Boyce, Brian Dear and myself as opposed to the older players in the side such as Bobby, Budgie, Eddie Bovington, Ken Brown, John Bond and Jim Standen. Bobby had a different lifestyle to the rest of us.

When I first played in the youth side Ron Greenwood set up a game with the first team. I ran home to tell my dad that I had played against Bobby Moore. I was that excited.

Training with Alan Stephenson and Bobby Moore.

Bobby's defensive partnership with Ken Brown was special and easily the best pairing he enjoyed during his time at West Ham. Ken was a traditional defender and he knew what his strengths and weaknesses were. I rarely saw Ken on a mazy dribble or bringing the ball out past the half-way line. If ever he did try something like that, one of the players would say: 'Browny, where are you going?' He would reply: 'Sorry son, I must have lost my head for a moment!' Ken was a fearless, no-nonsense type of player. He had the perfect physique for a centre-half and, although he wasn't blessed with pace, he was a great header of the ball. Back then, there was more aerial play than you see today which was great for Ken. He trained like a Trojan and was an absolute professional. Bobby, being the great player that he was, knew exactly where Ken would be and was the master at putting himself into positions which looked after his own space and Ken's, too.

Ken was a bit of a subtle assassin, too, and would sometimes whisper something into an opponent's ear if he didn't like how they were playing. Bobby never got involved like that so they each brought different aspects to their game. You only have to look at the medals they won to see that it worked well.

Winning the FA Cup in 1964 was a big highlight for me and I have vivid memories of the game up at Hillsborough in the semi-final against Manchester United. The big heroes that day were Bobby Moore and Ron Boyce. Bobby was absolutely fantastic and I can't think of anybody else who could have kept United's forward line of Charlton, Law and Best as quiet as he did. We were big underdogs going into the game having lost 0-2 at home to United the previous Saturday when they fielded a team without Charlton, Law and Best! In fact, after

that game their keeper David Gaskell had famously told us not to bother turning up for the semi-final!

The final itself was just tremendous. Greenwood had told us the team line-up on the previous Monday ahead of John Lyall's testimonial game so we could all relax and prepare ourselves for the biggest match of our lives.

Beating a very hard working Preston North End side 3-2 was the best feeling and to score a goal was the cherry on the cake. Bobby actually set me on my way for the goal. He passed it up to me around about the half-way line and I ran with it for a while before playing a one-two with Budgie. I received his return pass on the edge of the box and I knew my left foot always had a chance of finding the bottom corner of the net if I hit it sweetly. Fortunately for me, I looked up and saw the ball nestling in the back of the net. I have a lovely photo of Bobby and me embracing after the goal. It was a very special moment for me. As a young boy, I had dreamt about winning the FA Cup and when the final whistle blew I just didn't want to leave the pitch.

At the time, I was earning £15-per-week, with an additional £10 appearance money and a £10 win bonus. The FA Cup changed all that. After the final I received an increase to £30-per-week and, by Christmas, that had risen again to £50. That was the highest I earned during my time at West Ham.

For a regular league match the players were also given five tickets and most of us would sell those on for a few extra quid. However, we were given 100 tickets for the FA Cup final and I had a lot left over after I had ensured all my family and friends were going so Bobby gave me £600 and took them off my hands. I used that money to buy a brand new Morris 1100 so it really was a very special time.

There is a sad postscript to my FA Cup story. Later in life I had all my medals stolen from my house in South Africa. The thieves took my FA Cup medal, my European Cup Winners Cup medal, my Junior World Cup medal and a watch that was given to each of the players by the Borough of West Ham, as it was then. There was also a beautiful ring that I had won with the Tampa Bay Rowdies. I was devastated but thankfully, I still have my shirts from all those finals and my England schoolboy caps.

As time went on, and I became that little bit older and got married and had children, I became a lot closer to Bobby. He was a fantastic guy to be with when you got him in an environment he loved, such as at his home or up the West End. This was a massive highlight for me because going to a restaurant with Bobby was a fantastic experience. Heads would turn and it was a weird feeling that you were with someone who was like royalty. But even though he had such an incredible aura about him he was just a normal guy. He never had a bad word to say about anybody and, in terms of knowing how to treat people, he was in a league of his own.

After training, Bobby was often very busy with his various businesses, so the best time to catch him was at a social event or if I was invited to his house. He was the most amazing host. Just walking into a restaurant with him was like a film star experience. Everyone would say: 'Who's that with Johnny Sissons?' Well, something along those lines!

I would have loved to have played with Bobby for England and it should have happened. Alf Ramsey picked me to play when I was about 19, maybe 20, but Ron Greenwood intervened and said I wasn't quite ready. So although I was in the squad, Alf didn't play me and that was the closest I came.

Bobby was a fantastic professional and a superb trainer and because we both played on the left hand side of the pitch he was always available to me. If I got myself into a corner Bobby would be there to give an option, a way out. Just knowing that he was always there behind me was a tremendous boost.

He dominated most of the games I played in, with either his playing ability or his presence and usually both. This was even more apparent in the bigger games and, in particular, the cup semi-finals and finals.

Bobby was instrumental in my move to South Africa. Budgie had called me and asked me to join him at Hellenic, the team he was managing at the time. I also had a

call from Frank Lord who was in charge at Cape Town City and he doubled the offer I had on the table from Budgie. I went to both Bobby and Geoff Hurst because they had guested as players in South Africa and they both urged me to go. 'Sisso, you'll love it!' they said and they were absolutely right. I was a very indecisive person and quite insecure so Bobby and Geoff had a great influence on my move to South Africa.

The last time I saw Bobby was when he was very ill and I had returned to England to see my mum and my sisters. I went to a game and Bobby was doing some radio work and I saw him there. He was terribly thin and he died shortly afterwards. It may have been an England game but I'm not absolutely sure. He was asking all about me and was so very interested in what I was doing with my life.

The man had such an incredible aura and the application he showed to both his football and personal life was flawless. Today's footballers just do not seem to have the word 'professionalism' written through them. For them, football seems to be all about their lifestyle, the cars they drive and the money that comes their way. These are the key motivating factors. There isn't a shred of loyalty nowadays or, at the very least, anything like the commitment that Bobby showed to West Ham United every day of the 16 years he was at the club. West Ham fans adored him because of that. He was totally bonded to the club they loved. The club he loved. There just isn't anyone like that in today's game. He was a humble man, a good listener, a terrific mentor and generous beyond all measure. Bobby Moore was a man to look up to.

John Sissons

'Sisso'.

Bobby and Tina's wedding held at St Clements Church, Ilford, Essex on June 30, 1962.

Back row L-R Bond, Brown, Kirkup, Peters, Standen, Dickie, Burkett, Bovington, Moore. Front row L-R Brabrook, Sealey, Boyce, Byrne, Hurst, Scott, Sissons.

CHAPTER SIX
1963-64

Bobby Moore's total appearances (July 1963-June 1964): 62 games (3 goals)
League Division One: 37 (2 goals), England: 10, FA Cup: 7, League Cup: 6, Friendlies: 2 (1 goal)

1964 is a golden year on the West Ham United timeline. A 23-year-old Bobby Moore captained the team to FA Cup glory over Preston North End to win the trophy for the very first time in the club's history.

It is difficult to overstate just how important the FA Cup was to the domestic game back in 1964. It was the only chance that most players ever had of playing at Wembley Stadium. The League Cup final and FA Cup semi-finals were not played there and the concept of play-off football was decades away.

For the majority of fans, lifting the FA Cup was bigger than winning the league. It was the only time an entire match was aired live on television and a growing hysteria accompanied a team as it progressed through each round until the scramble for final tickets became the single most important pre-occupation of every fan destined to walk down Wembley Way. Indeed, back in 1964, West Ham's allocation of 15,000 tickets was wholly insufficient.

It was one of the greatest seasons in the club's history and the highest-priced season ticket for the enjoyment of a lifetime was just £10. For those supporters who took the 'football special' from St Pancras station to Sheffield for the FA Cup semi-final victory over Manchester United, the memories will never die. Some are still drying out from the Hillsborough experience! Later in his career, Moore wrote for the Ilford Recorder and following are his recollections on that marvellous night: 'That is the one game I am never likely to forget. It was virtually a home game for the Old Trafford side, and we went up there as complete underdogs, especially as they had beaten us two nothing at our ground the week before. On the day we outclassed them.'

On the Thursday prior to the FA Cup final, Moore was voted the Football Writers' Association Footballer of the Year. However, he missed out on the Hammer of the Year award to his good friend, Budgie Byrne.

It was testament to the family nature of the club that, shortly after beating Manchester United in the semi-final, the matchday programme reported how they were hoping the surviving members of West Ham's 1923 FA Cup final team would join them for the final against Preston North End. Victor Watson, Jimmy Ruffell, Billy Brown and Billy Moore were referenced in the piece along with regret that legendary goalkeeper, Ted Hufton, was too poorly to attend.

Footballer of the Year.

During the 1963-64 season, Moore played in 10 internationals and, following Jimmy Armfield's final England appearance on April 11, 1964 – versus Scotland at Hampden Park – Bobby became the nation's permanent captain.

As Ron Greenwood began to develop a winning formula, the debut opportunities for other players became somewhat limited and only three 'new' Hammers lined up with Bobby Moore in the first team – Dave Bickles, Roger Hugo and Peter Bennett.

Here is their story...

44 – DAVE BICKLES
April 6, 1944 – November 1, 1999

Born: West Ham, London

Position: Centre-half

Games played with Bobby Moore: 26 (1963-67)

Games played for West ham United: 28 (1963-67)

First game with Bobby Moore (Debut): September 14, 1963 Liverpool (a) W 2-1

Scorers: Liverpool: Hunt
West Ham United: Peters, Hurst

Liverpool: Furnell, Byrne G, Moran, Milne, Yeats, Ferns, Callaghan, Hunt, St John, Melia, Thompson

West Ham United: Standen, Kirkup, Burkett, Peters, **Bickles**, Moore, Brabrook, Boyce, Byrne, Hurst, Dear

David Bickles could not have imagined that his first team debut for West Ham United – a 2-1 victory over Liverpool in 1963 – would stand as the only success the Hammers would enjoy at Anfield for over 50 years.

Press reports compared Bickles' performance that day to that of a veteran after he had replaced an injured Ken Brown in the line-up. It is a record which Bickles took to his grave in 1999 and an achievement of which the Bickles family are

Young Hammers scaling new heights. L-R Brian Dear, John Charles, Derek Woodley, John Cartwright (obscured), Mickey Beesley, Dave Bickles, Martin Peters and Ron Boyce.

tremendously proud. Dave's three sons continue to keep a close eye on events up at Anfield each year, often attending the game with friends.

'Bicks' joined the club in 1959 and signed professional forms in August 1960. He skippered the West Ham boys team and gained two England Youth caps. He was also part of West Ham's successful tour of America in 1963, just a few months before his magical league debut.

A mis-diagnosed shoulder injury meant that Dave was transferred to Crystal Palace on September 30, 1967. He later played for Colchester United and became player-manager at Romford Borough, right up to the point when 'The Boro' became defunct in 1978. He later managed Collier Row.

Standing tall in the heart of defence at Stamford Bridge, April 1966.

Previously, Bickles had been awarded a joint testimonial by the non-leaguers, and West Ham United were the visitors to Brooklands in November 1975.

Whilst teaching PE in various schools in East Ham, most notably Brampton Manor, he was invited to join the coaching staff at West Ham United by ex-reserve team player, Tony Carr.

Sadly, in 1997 Dave contracted kidney cancer and passed away two years later, aged 55.

He is survived by his wife Lynda and their three boys, Glen – who was an apprentice at West Ham and played centre-half for the reserves, Craig – who was an apprentice at Spurs during the Paul Gascoigne era, and Gary, who, was rated by his father to be the best player of the three. Gary works for the Dutch financial institution ING and kindly took the time to discuss his father's career at West Ham United and his friendship with Bobby Moore.

Bobby Moore, like everybody else at West Ham, called my dad, 'Bicks.' They were good friends and if Bobby was here today he would describe my dad as being very laid back, always holding a rolled-up newspaper in one hand, which he would bang on his thigh, while holding his keys in the other. That was the classic image of my father. They used to go to the Slater's Arms together after training for a few beers and Bobby was a great help on the pitch.

My father had a dream debut, winning up at Liverpool in 1963. He told me how Bobby sat next to him on the train journey up there in order to settle his nerves. He also sat next to Bobby in the dressing room, too. Those two simple things had a big calming influence on my dad.

Bobby was only 22 at the time and my dad was 19. Just *being close to the great man's stature helped to settle my dad and Mooro was saying to him: 'Once you get out there it will be just like a game in the park. Just block out the noise and concentrate on doing what you are good at.' That is what he did. He kept his focus, had a good game and continues to hold his place in the West Ham record books.*

Afterwards, in the dressing room, all the players came over to him and were saying: 'Well done Bicks!' They were slapping his back and ruffling his hair. When they got back to London they all went out to a casino up the West End.

We lived at number 14 Charles Road, near Green Street, very close to the ground. Once a week after training, a few of the players – including Bobby – would come round and play cards all afternoon. Harry Redknapp would be there, as would Charlo, Brian Dear and Colin Mackleworth. The winner would always leave a little tip on the mantelpiece for my mum.

Brian Dear used to joke that West Ham signed my dad from Tel Aviv schoolboys and while there is some Jewish blood in our family, it has never played a strong part in our lives. Dave's father was Jewish and got married to a Catholic girl. His dad originated from Poland and was called 'Bickless,' but after moving to England he dropped an 's' and we have been called Bickles ever since. My dad was the youngest of nine kids!

According to my mum and dad, after the 1964 FA Cup, the club raffled the actual ball from the final – and they won it! A few years later, when I was old enough to kick a ball I punted it over the garden fence and it has never been seen since!

Ron Greenwood went off my dad and sold him to Crystal Palace in 1967. It was unnecessary really because it was later shown that he had a serious shoulder injury which, ironically, he had picked up at home to Liverpool in September 1965.

He was jumping for a ball with Ian St John, who stayed rooted to the ground leaving my dad to somersault over him and he badly injured his shoulder. He would later have a steel plate and pins inserted to shore up that part of his body.

It was disappointing because Ron lost faith in my dad, who was also suffering from serious migraine at the time. It was all related to the injury and he was missing a lot of games. My dad had come up through the ranks, made a wining debut at 19-years-old and had also played for England Youth, so he had looked all set for a good career. Sadly, it just wasn't to be.

When I was about eight-years old I have a vivid memory of going to a match with my dad and sitting next to me was Bobby Moore and sitting next to my dad was Jimmy Greaves. I can't recall the ground but it was a ramshackle old place with just one stand. I believe they were watching Jimmy's son, Danny, playing.

My dad was 100% into football and was a coach at West Ham for many, many years. He was part of Tony Carr's coaching team. He became very good friends with Jimmy Frith, who has been at West Ham since the old king died! Jimmy was one of the pallbearers at my dad's funeral and is a fantastic guy. Because my dad was a games coach at several local schools he kept his eye out for any young, talented footballers.

There is a big story in our family about West Ham winning the 1975 FA Cup final. When my dad was player-manager at Romford, they arranged a joint testimonial for him and long-serving striker Robin Chandler, the following November. West Ham were the opponents and brought a full-strength team down to Brooklands to play. A few days before the game, my dad was at Chadwell Heath coaching the kids, when a club official came over and gave him a big holdall to look after. He told my dad to bring it to his testimonial the following Tuesday. When he got home and opened it up it was the FA Cup.

When me and my brothers woke up in the morning and went downstairs, sitting on top of the telly was the FA Cup! I was 10-years-old at the time and my dad told me to keep it quiet at school and that he was going to arrange police protection at the house. I ran home from class and there were about a dozen kids queuing up at my house to see the cup! No 10-year-old is capable of keeping a story like that secret and all our school mates were in my house parading up and down with the FA Cup. I actually took it to bed and slept with it one night.

A couple of days later, my brother Craig was walking around the house with the cup when he tripped over my dad's outstretched legs. The cup went flying through the air, before crashing on the floor. When we picked it up and put it on the table it was completely bent. Panic ensued and my dad went and got our neighbour Bob. The pair of them had the FA Cup underneath the settee trying to bend the thing back into shape! They did quite a good job but it wasn't perfect and nothing was said when my dad returned the cup after his testimonial match. Six months later when Southampton beat Manchester United to win the famous old trophy, it was reported in the newspapers that someone had bent the FA Cup!

In 1997, doctors diagnosed my father with kidney cancer. It soon spread everywhere and they gave him six months to live,

When football was fun! Dave with John Charles.

but he carried on for another two-and-half years. Because he was a PE coach, he was super-fit and I think that's what kept him alive that bit longer. Brian Dear visited him and there is a funny story about a visit to Oldchurch Hospital in Romford, made by both Harry Redknapp and Frank Lampard senior. Harry was managing West Ham at the time and Frank was his assistant. When they arrived at the hospital, rumour soon spread about who was on the premises and it wasn't long before my dad's bed was surrounded by a good many people. The nurses commented that some of them hadn't walked for months but shuffled down to see Harry and Frank!

I've got a lot of respect for Harry. When my dad was dying of cancer he came round one Sunday to see him. They were laughing because Harry had put a few quid on the live game – Southampton, I think – and they were four down after 20 minutes! While he was there our washing machine packed up and two days later a brand new one arrived courtesy of Harry.

One story my dad shared with me before he died was about Harry's bust up with Billy Bonds. My dad was coaching the kids at Chadwell Heath and was with Harry in the canteen when he said he had received a call from the board and they wanted him to go in to see them. 'I know what they want,' he said. 'They want to offer Billy's job to me but I don't want it,' he insisted. Meanwhile the board had told Billy of their intention to move him upstairs and install Harry. Billy sensed foul play by then but my dad was convinced that his gripe should have been with the board and the way they handled matters. He felt it was a tragedy that two great mates, with their friendship roots dating back to the 1960s, should become estranged over something that had no ill intention.

Dad was very proud of his record of being in the last West Ham United team to win at Anfield and we are all so pleased he took that to his grave. In the February before he died my two brothers and I went up to Anfield for the very first time. When the players came out of the tunnel I called him up and held up the phone and said: 'Dad, do you remember this?' He got quite upset but it was a really nice moment. We actually drew 2-2 and could have won it late on. We walked out of that game saying: 'Bicksy is still unbeaten at Anfield!'
Gary Bickles

The following recollections are provided courtesy of Dave's former friends and team-mates:

When Dave lived in Custom House I knocked on his door with Charlo and Roger Hugo. We wanted him to come out with us for the day. He always seemed to be in bed and when his mum answered, we asked if Dave was in? 'What are your names?' she asked and I told her it was Brian Dear, John Charles and Roger Hugo. She turned round and shouted up the stairs: 'Dave, there are three blokes here to see you!'

Dave always came in to training with a rolled up newspaper in his hand. He would be tapping it on his leg. He was often late and Ernie Gregory got the hump with it one day and shouted at him; 'Where have you been?'

'Sorry Ern,' he said. 'My bus got caught behind a funeral!'

Another time, when Dave was playing away in an A Team game, Ernie caught him having a cigarette in the toilet at half time. He loved a fag did Dave.

A lot of the players went to his wedding in the Princess Alice pub in Forest Gate.

After the team won the FA Cup in 1964, Dave and I joined them at the Hilton Hotel for a party. We nicked all the tailor made cigarettes, with the West Ham colours on them, from the tables and, later, made our way back to Charlo's flat on the Barking Road, where we had our own knees-up!

Ernie Gregory liked Dave and always said that playing for England youth had ruined him. He thought they played too much football, which was too strenuous and burnt out a lot of players.

Poor old Dave, I went to see him one day with my dad, at his holiday home in Wallasea, near Rochford. He was very ill then, thin as a stick.

A teacher read the eulogy at his funeral and said some lovely things about him. Bicksy was a very popular lad.
Brian Dear

We called him 'Dave the Schmo' because it sounded a bit Jewish. We used to play cards at his house. He lived right next to the ground so me and my good pal, Colin Mackleworth, plus a few others would go round there and play three-card brag for money. If Dave was doing his money he wouldn't let us leave!

I can still picture the Schmo now, walking to the ground with a rolled up newspaper in one hand which he would bang on his leg, while holding his keys in his other hand. That is the image a lot of the players will have of him.
Harry Redknapp

'Bicks' played centre-half but would have probably been better off as a sweeper because he liked to get the ball down and play it. As big as he was, I don't think he really liked the physical aspect of the game.
Trevor Dawkins

Dave was a loveable rogue
Carol Charles

We used to coach the kids at the Pretoria Road School in the afternoons. 'Bicks' always had a rolled-up newspaper in his hand and was about five years older than me. He would have a quick chat with the kids and then hand the session over to me. Off he would go, out of the gates, with his newspaper, on his way to the betting shop over the road. He'd then come back two hours later and say to all the boys: 'Well done, that was a great session.' He made it look like he had run the whole thing!
Frank Lampard

Handing out an award to West Ham United midfielder Lee Hodges in 1995.

45 – ROGER HUGO

Born: Woking, Surrey, September 6, 1942
Position: Inside or outside-left
Games played with Bobby Moore: 1 (1964)
Games played for West Ham United: 3 (1964)
First game with Bobby Moore: March 28, 1964
West Bromwich Albion (a) W 1-0
Scorer: West Ham United: **Hugo**

West Bromwich Albion: Potter, Howe, Williams (G), Fraser, Jones, Simpson, Foggo, Fenton, Kaye, Jackson, Clark
West Ham United: Dickie, Kirkup, Burkett, Peters, Brown, Moore, Brabrook, Boyce, Byrne, **Hugo**, Sealey

Roger Victor Hugo's scoring record at West Ham United was played three and scored two. Curiously, all three games were away from home in the Midlands – against Leicester City, West Bromwich Albion and Stoke City, respectively.

Bobby Moore missed two of those games but did line up alongside Hugo when the striker scored the only goal against West Bromwich Albion at The Hawthorns on March 28, 1964.

Previously, Hugo had become a member of the scoring

Roger (far right) lining up in the West Ham reserve team.

They Played With Bobby Moore – The West Ham Years

Roger (far left) at Brian Dear's 70th birthday party with Ron Boyce, Ken Brown, Jack Burkett and Mike Beesley.

debutant club at West Ham United when finding the net at Leicester City on March 18, 1964 in a 2-2 draw.

He played schoolboy football for South London, London and Surrey before signing apprentice forms with West Ham United. After scoring a hat-trick for the youth team against Millwall Colts in a Southern Junior Floodlit game, he was asked to sign professional forms in October 1960.

Roger was a very popular player amongst his peers and was noted for having a lethal left foot which found the net on many occasions for the reserve team. Sir Geoff Hurst also recalls his golfing prowess: 'Roger was the reason I didn't get into golf. He played off six so I decided to stick with football!'

Hugo left the club in the summer of 1965 and joined Watford before playing in South Africa for Port Elizabeth. Another ex-Hammer, Andy Malcolm, was also at the Eastern Cape side.

Roger continues to live in South Africa but visited these shores in autumn 2013 and attended Brian Dear's 70th Birthday celebrations in Southend-on-Sea. He continues to run a successful DVD rental business with his brother in South Africa called Video Spot.

It was great playing with Bobby Moore. He made things happen and brought the best out of those around him. The biggest trouble with West Ham players nowadays is that they simply do not have the basic skills like passing. Bobby could

find anyone on the pitch with either foot and was always two or three moves ahead of the general play.

He loved to find Budgie who, in turn would play it to Boyce or back to Bobby or sometimes he would turn and send Peter Brabrook off down the wing. Things were happening, it was exciting. We got the best out of each other and Bobby initiated most things.

When I joined West Ham they had so much talent it was frightening. Bobby Moore, Johnny Cartwright, Andy Smillie, Joe Kirkup and many others, who just oozed talent.

Bobby was an organiser, a great passer, someone who got things moving but so very quiet, a bit of a closed book.

One of the earliest times I met Bobby was at the meeting to abolish the maximum wage. Jimmy Hill, who went to my school – Henry Thornton on Clapham Common – was very involved and did a lot for the players. All the top players were there including Johnny Haynes and, of course, they relaxed the maximum wage which revolutionised the game as we knew it.

I remember seeing Stuart Leary there with the Charlton brothers – Jack and Bobby. Stuart had come over from South Africa and played for Charlton Athletic. He took his own life in his 50s. They found his body on top of Table Mountain, Cape Town.

Bobby was very fortunate in that the best player in his position was put in jail! Tony Kay of Everton was a top, top, player but got done for taking a bung to throw a game. He

BURKETT, HUGO EARN A POINT

Leicester City 2, West Ham 2

LEFT-BACK Jack Burkett scored his first goal in League football. Roger Hugo, drafted into the first team after a lengthy wait, celebrated with a debut goal. And West Ham's "trial" team minus Moore, Byrne, and Sissons, gave the Filbert-street men the fright of their lives for the second time this year.

Leicester 2, W. Ham 2

LEFT back Jack Burkett popped up with a goal-saving act for West Ham nine minutes from the end of this scrappy Filbert-street match.

Industrious inside right Ron Boyce worked the ball to left half Martin Peters, whose shot was blocked ... but Burkett promptly crashed home a sizzling 18-yarder.

The below-strength FA Cup Finalists—without Bobby Moore, Johnny Byrne and John Sissons — deserved the point if only for the way they fought.

Just Over

Twice they were behind and twice they stormed back. In fact, they might easily have grabbed both points.

With seconds to go a shot from inside left debutant Roger Hugo hit 'keeper George Hayes and the ball spun over the bar.

Leicester opened the scoring after seven minutes — through inside left David Gibson.

Hugo equalised in the 30th minute. Leicester's second goal came ten minutes later through Ken Keyworth.

Here indeed was evidence that Hammers have adequate resources to meet and beat the long wait to Wembley, writes REAPER.

Hugo gave an encouraging display at inside-left to add his name to the growing list of men who will be challenging for cup places. Once he had settled in to the extra pace of first team soccer he linked up well with danger man Peter Brabrook and almost added to his tally as Hammers piled on tremendous pressure in the second half.

This was the third all-action clash between the sides this season—and set the scene for Monday's fourth, the League Cup semi-final second leg.

Hammers start one down at Upton Park. But if this game is any guide they will wipe that out convincingly.

Leicester caught Hammers as they did in the first League Cup match—on the hop. Inspired by Gibson they attacked with speed and precision from the start and Gibson fired them ahead in seven minutes.

Twenty-one-year-old Hugo pounced on a Brabrook pass to make it 1—1 in 32 minutes but Keyworth put Leicester ahead before the break.

Then Hammers began to get a grip on the game. Bovington and Peters policed the menacing Gibson and new boy Heath out of the game and Boyce moved more freely into attack.

It took Burkett to finish off a barrage of shots in 82 minutes to equalise but Brown scraped a header inches wide. Hurst missed a good chance and Hugo had a shot saved.

West Ham: Standen; Bond. Burkett; Bovington, Brown, Peters; Sealey, Boyce, Hurst, Hugo, Brabrook.

Making the headlines.

was a different player to Bobby Moore. Bobby got the team moving but what a player Tony Kay was!

I met Bobby out in South Africa a few times after our West Ham playing days. We had some good fun together. He came over in the 1970s with Terry Venables, Geoff Hurst and Bill McGarry, the Wolves manager. They put on a lot of coaching sessions for Macabbi which was a Jewish concern.

It was funny how I first met Bobby over there because he was doing a book signing and I queued up and shoved a book under his nose and said: 'Sign that me old mate!' He looked up and smiled: 'Roger, what are you doing here?' I had to remind him that I lived there! Anyway, Bob, Geoff

and I went out and had a great time.

I'll tell you a story about Pele and how much he loved Mooro. My brother, Michael, has two boys, both mad on football and both are avid West Ham fans. Like me they live in South Africa.

They all went to Sun City for a holiday and had heard that Pele was going to be there. They called me up and told me they couldn't get close to him because there were thousands of people all trying to see him. I told them to shout out: 'Bobby Moore!' when they next saw him.

They tried it and said that Pele stopped as though he had been shot. Well, Pele invited them into his entourage and Michael told him about me and how I played with Bobby at West Ham. They had a lovely chat and have some wonderful photos with the great man.

Quite a few have now passed away from my time at West Ham. Bobby was the first to go, of course, but all those that looked after me – John Bond, Noel Cantwell and Malcolm Allison – have all since passed on, too. In South Africa we have a saying: 'They are starting to cut the trees down in our part of the forest,' Sadly that applies to the boys I knew at West Ham.

Roger Hugo

During a visit from South Africa.

46 – PETER BENNETT

Born: Hillingdon, Middlesex, June 24, 1946

Position: Midfield

Games played with Bobby Moore: 43 (1964-70)

Games played for West Ham United: 47 (1964-70)

First game with Bobby Moore (Debut): April 4, 1964
Bolton Wanderers (h) L 2-3

Scorers: West Ham United: Sealey, Byrne
Bolton Wanderers: Taylor, Lee, Bromley

West Ham United: Standen, Bond. Burkett, Bovington, Peters, Moore, Brabrook, **Bennett**, Byrne, Hurst, Sealey

Bolton Wanderers: Hopkinson, Hartle, Farrimond, Rimmer, Edwards, Lennard, Davison, Bromley, Lee, Hill, Taylor

Peter Leigh Bennett was West Ham United's first ever substitute. He replaced Jack Burkett in a 2-1 home victory against Leeds United on August 28, 1965.

John Sissons' wedding. L-R Peter Brabrook, Terry Needham, Peter Bennett and Bobby Moore.

Bennett is described by many of his peers as a stylish, ball-playing midfielder, who made his name as a member of the victorious West Ham United Youth team which beat Liverpool 6-5 on aggregate in the 1963 FA Youth Cup final. For good measure he was also in the West Ham teams which won the London Challenge Cup in both 1967 and 1968, overcoming Dagenham and Tottenham Hotspur, respectively.

Bennett played for Middlesex and England Boys before signing as an apprentice professional with West Ham in July 1961. He signed full professional forms in the summer of 1963. He had been spotted by Charlie Faulkner, one of Wally St Pier's scouts, who also signed John Sissons.

'Les', as he was commonly known, was over five years younger than Bobby Moore and played 42 league games and five cup games in the first team. His cultured style of football hasn't been forgotten by former players such as Sir Geoff Hurst, who thought that Bennett could have been another Martin Peters.

He was on the scoresheet with Jimmy Greaves when, in 1970, the pair of them lined up against Tottenham Hotspur in front of 53,000 fans at White Hart Lane. Sadly, he was transferred to Leyton Orient shortly afterwards in a deal which saw Tommy Taylor move to Upton Park.

Bennett also had a spell in the States playing for the St Louis Soccer Stars and played against Pele as part of the experience.

Today, Peter is an experienced carpenter whose son, Wayne, has played golf on the PGA Tour. He lives in Ruislip with his beautiful wife, Carina.

I used to watch Bobby a lot more than I played with him and there was one thing that really stood out for me. It was the fact that he could perform in any position. He could play up front as well as anybody and I remember a game when he did just that. He stayed up there for the last 20 minutes and was fantastic.

As an apprentice, one of our tasks was to paint the ground in the close-season. I remember a time when I was painting the old rails at the back of the goal when Bobby had just been picked to play for England for the very first time. It was like watching this god run around the pitch, all on his own, putting in a bit of extra training ahead of the Chile World Cup in 1962. We were in different worlds and yet we were inside the same stadium.

When I was an apprentice, Ernie Gregory used to tell us how Mooro almost didn't make it as a player. Apparently, it was touch and go if they were going to take him on. There were so many really capable players at West Ham at that time. The three-year period from 1963 until 1966 will never be bettered in my opinion. There was so much talent at junior, A Team, reserve team and first team level. I lacked a bit of confidence and didn't play as well as I could while I was at West Ham.

Rob Jenkins' clinic in Green Street was incredible. Bobby Moore used to go there regularly on Sundays. If a player picked up an injury he would pop in to see Rob, and the local police would be sitting in there having a good old drink. Rob is a one off. His dad, Bill, was brilliant as well.

The week before the European Cup Winners Cup final in 1965, we were playing a friendly at Shamrock Rovers in Ireland and Ron Greenwood fielded the team that he wanted to line up at Wembley. At half-time, we were losing 0-1 and he brought me on in place of Brian Dear and we ended up winning 3-1. I got one and Hursty got two. Ron Greenwood called me over after the game and told me to stand by my phone. Now, I was nowhere near getting into that team but that is what he said to me. Nothing happened, obviously – I wasn't good enough anyway and, remember, Deary was a terrific player, too.

I remember a time at West Ham which wasn't very pleasant. Bobby had a contractual dispute with the club and Greenwood basically held him to ransom before the World Cup. He forced him to sign a contract which wasn't giving him what he wanted with the ultimatum: 'Sign or miss out on the World Cup.'

I think it was only an extra tenner that Bobby was after. It created a really bad atmosphere around the club and, when we went on a pre-season tour to Switzerland, you could cut the air with a knife it was so tense. It was a horrible time.

After they had won the World Cup in '66, Moore, Hurst and Peters returned to training at Chadwell Heath a couple of weeks later than the rest of us. I've never seen so many photographers in one place and it was like a full West Ham crowd. It was a proper heroes homecoming and absolutely amazing.

In his England Youth strip.

In action (No. 8) against Manchester United.

Flying high against Nottingham Forest with Moore looking on.

I remember playing against Mooro when he was at Fulham and I was at Orient. They thrashed us 0-4, I think, and we were chatting on the pitch. I remember we finally got a corner and he said: 'Is there going to be a lap of honour?'

I suppose my claim to fame with Bobby Moore is that I used to get changed next to him. In fact he copied me. He copied the way I used to hang my clothes up nice and neat on the peg and meticulously fold up my strip afterwards as though it hadn't even been worn. Mooro learned all that from me...I wish!

Seriously, I used to bung my clothes anywhere like all the other lads. Mooro had a hanger rather than a peg. Neat and tidy and in control, that was Bobby.

I still can't believe that he lifted the World Cup but ended his life writing a few articles and commentating on the radio. The country totally failed him.

When I think of Bobby Moore there is one very clear image that springs to mind. One day I was walking back from Chadwell Heath to the station with John Dryden who played in the reserves at West Ham. We used to call him 'Legsy' because he was so skinny. Brian Dear used to say that if he didn't move around in the shower he wouldn't get wet, he was that thin! All of a sudden we heard a 'toot toot!' behind us and it was Mooro in his red convertible Triumph Vitesse. The sun was shining, the roof was down and Bobby was there, with his blond hair, driving around in this beautiful car.

'Les.'

'Want a lift lads?' he said, and gave us a lift to the station. Jeez, it was fantastic. It is an image I've always carried with me. He looked so content with life and just oozed class.

Peter Bennett

Back row L-R Brown, Bond, Standen, Burkett, Bovington, Moore. Front row L-R Brabrook, Boyce, Byrne, Hurst, Sissons.

CHAPTER SEVEN
1964-65

Bobby Moore's total appearances (July 1964-June 1965): 54 games (2 goals)

League Division One: 28 (1 goal), England: 7, ECWC: 7, American Tour: 6, Friendlies: 4 (1 goal), Charity Shield: 1, Reserves: 1

On January 24, 1965, Tina and Bobby Moore became parents following the birth of their baby daughter, Roberta. Their personal joy contrasted starkly with Great Britain's mourning, following the passing of its national hero Winston Churchill on the very same day.

Although it was not widely known at the time, Moore had been fighting against testicular cancer during these times and did not play for club or country between November 1964 and March 1965. Despite that prolonged absence, he still ran Martin Peters close for the 1965 Hammer of the Year award.

His return to first team action saw him play a crucial role in West Ham United's greatest-ever achievement – beating TSV Munich 1860 2-0 at Wembley in the final of the European Cup Winners Cup on May 19, 1965. It catapulted the club onto the international stage and Ron Greenwood famously described the Hammers victory as the best technical performance from any West Ham United team.

At the celebratory dinner following the Wembley triumph, both Alan Sealey and Brian Dear performed on the microphone as part of the evening's entertainment. 'Sammy' sung a version of Tony Bennett's 'San Francisco' while 'Stag' opted for 'Lazy River,' by Louis Armstrong. The fact that both players soon had their legs in plaster, following pre-season injuries, was not related to the quality of their vocal performances…

The season started with the first team returning from a pre-season tour of Austria and Germany to play Liverpool, at Anfield, in the FA Charity Shield. A crowd of 38,858 watched the 2-2 draw courtesy of goals from Gordon Wallace (28 mins), Johnny Byrne (41 mins), Gerry Byrne (49) and Geoff Hurst (84). The trophy was shared between the two clubs.

The youth team continued their fine achievement of winning the Augsburg Youth Tournament for the third consecutive season. Harry Redknapp was voted player of the tournament in Germany and was rewarded with a radio!

Bobby Moore with West Ham United's finest ever trophy – The European Cup Winners Cup.

Not surprisingly, first-team opportunities were scarce and only two Hammers made their debuts with Bobby Moore during the 1964-65 season – Eddie Presland and Trevor Dawkins.

Here is their story…

47 – EDDIE PRESLAND

Born: Loughton, Essex, March 27, 1943

Position: Left-back

Games played with Bobby Moore: 6 (1965-66)

Games played for West Ham United: 6 (1965-66)

First game with Bobby Moore (Debut): February 27, 1965 Liverpool (h) W 2-1

Scorers: West Ham United: **Presland**, Hurst
Liverpool: Hunt

WEST HAM UNITED

BOLEYN GROUND : LONDON E.13

No. 35

LIVERPOOL

FOOTBALL LEAGUE—Division One

SATURDAY 27th FEBRUARY 1965 at 3 pm

OFFICIAL PROGRAMME   6d

West Ham United: Standen, Kirkup, **Presland**, Bovington, Moore, Peters, Brabrook, Boyce, Byrne, Hurst, Sissons

Liverpool: Lawrence, Lawler, Byrne (G), Milne, Smith, Stevenson, Graham, Hunt, St John, Arrowsmith, Wallace

Edward Robert Presland is a member of a very select band of West Ham United players – those who scored on their first team debut with Bobby Moore in the line up. Presland's 30-yard strike on 48 minutes, against Liverpool in February 1965, emulated the achievement of Mike Beesley in 1960. This exclusive club was subsequently joined by Jimmy Greaves (1970), Bryan Robson (1971) and Ade Coker (1971). Footage of Presland's goal was captured on film and is amongst his most prized possessions.

Presland signed professional forms at West Ham United in October 1960, aged 17. He played for East Ham, London and Essex Boys whilst attending Thomas Lethaby School.

Eddie was also a fine cricketer having been a member of the England Boys team and the Essex County youngsters. He made his County debut for Essex in 1962 and is one of a handful of players who played both football and cricket with Bobby Moore. Competition for the Number 3 shirt resulted in Presland being transferred to Crystal Palace on January 13, 1967.

Sir Geoff Hurst is one of many who has fond memories of Eddie: 'He was the best man at my wedding and I enjoyed his company at both football and cricket.'

Eddie enjoyed seven years at West Ham United and cherishes the experience. He possesses an impressive knowledge of the club and relishes keeping alive the memories from that unforgettable era.

He spent 35 years working at Stepney Green School in London's East End and managed Dagenham FC to a 2-1 FA Trophy success over Mossley at Wembley Stadium in 1980, with another former Hammer – Joe Durrell – in the side.

Eddie lives in Braintree with his wife, Celia. He continues to clock up the mileage, scouting for Norwich City, and loves a round of golf in his spare time.

The interview with Eddie took place in the fitting surroundings of the Boleyn Ground.

Eddie in the dressing room before his debut.

Eddie (far left) lining up with Essex CCC at Brentwood in 1964.

I knew Bobby before we both joined West Ham United. We had played cricket together for London. He was a very good cricketer, better than he was a footballer at the time. He would have joined the staff at Essex without a doubt because he was a very competent opening batsman. It is interesting that Bobby didn't play football for London or Essex Boys but he did through playing cricket. Alan Sealey also played cricket for London Boys.

We had so many laughs together because I was an East Ham lad and Bobby was a Barking boy and we would get a little card sent through from the London Cricket Association saying: 'You have been selected to play against Eton'...and then 'Harrow' or 'Winchester' etc. Can you imagine both of us going there to play?

Bobby used to take the mickey out of those public schoolboys something rotten. They were being taught by the best in the country and had their super posh accents; 'Oh, I say!' and the like while Bobby would be saying: 'Wotcha cock!' to everyone.

We played their under-15 side and they were only allowed to wear these grey flannel trousers and dark brown cricket boots, all very stylish as you can imagine from such a school as Eton. Bobby would pull their legs by saying: 'Can't your mum and dad afford whites?' It was all such a big laugh to us.

The first time I played football with Bobby, he was 11 and I was 10. He played for Barking Boys and I was playing for East Ham Boys. Bobby's mum Doris was working at William Warnes rubber factory at the time and she always called him

On his debut against Liverpool with Bobby Moore in February 1965.

Defending against Sunderland in March 1965.

'Robert'. Both his mother and father Bob doted on him as you would expect with Bobby being an only child. The first time I saw him he was a shy, little, tubby, curly haired boy.

I used to meet him at Barking station to go to the Bat and Ball ground at Gravesend to play cricket. He was 15 and I was 14. We would get on the steam train from Barking to Tilbury and then take the ferry across the river Thames before walking the rest of the way to the ground. I can still see Bobby now with his bat tied up in his pads carrying them over his shoulder. He always gave me his money because I was just young enough to get a half-fare but he wasn't. I would always ask for two halves. We felt like the Great Train robbers and yet all we had done was get on the train for half fare! For years later, right up until the last time I saw him he would always come up to me and say: 'Are you still getting half-fare?' People around us obviously wondered what we were laughing at but it was just a shared joke we took through life together. He had a brilliant sense of humour.

When I joined West Ham I remember playing a five-a-side game in 1964 just before Bobby was diagnosed with testicular cancer. Ronnie Boyce hit this ball as hard as you like and it hit Bobby in the crotch and he was doubled over in pain. I think that must have been the start of it although nobody ever sat us down and told us about his condition. There wasn't any publicity about it whatsoever. It was all kept hush-hush and Bobby was always the last one to complain. I think the club's official line was a groin injury.

I played a few games with Bobby in the reserves when he was making his comeback after his cancer operation in the mid-60s. He played in the reserves as though he was playing for England, absolutely totally committed.

The memories of my debut are as clear as day. I pulled up in the car park and instead of playing in front of five or six thousand for the reserves, which was a good crowd back then, I was going to be playing in front of a full house against Liverpool. I knew on the Friday I was playing and I went into the dressing room to get changed. The shirts were hanging up with the numbers facing outwards and they started with the goalkeepers jersey and went round, Number 2, 3, 4 etc. I remember Bobby saying to me: 'I bet you're nervous aren't you?' as a sort of a joke to relax me.

Jack Burkett was out with an injury and Ron Greenwood brought me in to play left back even though I was right-footed. Ron used to say that the great Brazilian left back, Nilton Santos, was right footed and I used to think: 'Yeah, that is all well and good but this is Eddie Presland!'

Ron was an amazing coach. I would walk past him in the corridor and he would say: 'One minute 27 seconds.' When I looked at him confused he explained how that was the length of time it took before I gave the ball away in Saturday's game! The following week he would say: 'Two minutes 12 seconds' so I felt well chuffed!

On reflection it was good that I was on the left side because I was next to Bobby and he told me to keep my ears open and that he would never be more than 10 yards away from me. 'It's just another game of football,' he kept saying. Anyway, I managed to score on my debut and had a good game and I always used to joke with Bobby afterwards because the Stratford Express gave me 8 out of 10 and he only got 7. I said to him: 'I don't need you anymore, I'm alright now!'

Greenwood was very good at encouraging players to pass their coaching badges and urged them to get involved with

Young Eddie.

I eventually ended up as chief scout at Tottenham Hotspur and now work with Norwich City in a scouting capacity, too. I often use Bobby as an example in discussions with other scouts. Many clubs are quick to discard players because of their size or their speed or their lack of heading ability but I always say it was lucky these scouts weren't around in the 50s and 60s because Bobby would have been crossed off many a list!

Far too many scouts are looking for the end product which is never there in the beginning and the art of scouting is being able to spot potential. West Ham owe a great debt to both Noel Cantwell and Malcolm Allison for seeing potential in Bobby and pushing and developing him.

I cried my eyes out when Bobby died. I was at home and it came on the news. It wasn't a case of thinking Bobby's dead and now I'm going to be sad, it was an involuntary, natural act of just bursting into tears. I have a Bobby Moore DVD at home and I find myself putting it on even now because I love hearing what other people say about him.

Eddie Presland

Eddie with his debut programme.

the local schools. I ended up having a 35-year association with Stepney Green School.

I would take the school kids to Oakfield Sports Centre next to Fairlop station but on one occasion I couldn't get my car back in time from a garage and was waiting at Ilford Broadway to get a bus to make my way over to Fairlop. Now, I hadn't seen Bobby for ages at the time but all of a sudden this big red Jaguar XJS spun around in the road and pulled up in front of me. It was Bobby. 'Jump in,' he said, 'I'll take you wherever you're going.' He was just a naturally helpful person and we had a lovely chat and probably didn't see each other again for another year or so after that.

48 – TREVOR DAWKINS

Born: Thorpe Bay, Essex, October 7, 1945

Position: Midfielder

Games played with Bobby Moore: 3 (1965-67)

Games played for West ham United: 6 (1965-67)

First game with Bobby Moore (Debut): April 19, 1965
West Bromwich Albion (a) L 2-4

Scorers: West Bromwich Albion: Foggo, Astle, Brown (2)
West Ham United: Hurst, Boyce

West Bromwich Albion: Potter, Cram, Williams (G), Howshall, Jones, Fraser, Foggo, Astle, Crawford, Hope, Brown

West Ham United: Standen, Kirkup. Peters, **Dawkins**, Brown, Moore, Bennett, Boyce, Hurst, Dear, Sissons

Trevor Andrew Dawkins is widely appreciated as being the best player in West Ham United's successful 1963 FA Youth Cup winning team. His former team-mates describe him as possessing great skill and first class technique, although a little too laid back to make it to the very top.

Perhaps the most enduring description of Dawkins' talent comes from his former youth team-mate, Harry Redknapp: 'If you could have combined the fluent ball skills of Trevor Dawkins with the engine of Bobby Howe, then you would have produced one very special player indeed.'

1963 FA Youth Cup winners – Back row L-R Needham, Britt, Burnett, Mackleworth, Kitchener Bennett, Howe. Front row L-R Redknapp, Dawkins, Charles, Sissons and Dryden.

It is a sentiment echoed by former team-mate, Brian Dear: 'Trevor Dawkins and Martin Peters were two of the most skilful players at West Ham. They could chip the ball, curl the ball and find anyone on the pitch. It was terrific to watch.'

Dawkins played for Southend, Essex and London Boys before being selected for the English Schools FA trials.

He joined West Ham as an apprentice during the summer of 1961 and signed professional forms in October, 1962 at the same time as both Peter Brabrook and Dennis Burnett.

Former West Ham left back, Joe Kirkup, is one of many former Hammers with glowing praise for Trevor: 'I thought he was going to be a first class player. He was so comfortable on the ball and everything

FA Youth team reunion in August, 2014. L-R David James, Peter Bennett, Dennis Burnett, Harry Redknapp, Martin Britt, Carol Charles (wife of John Charles, holding the 51 year old match ball!), Alan Herbage, John Dryden, Trevor Dawkins and Colin Mackleworth.

seemed to come so easy to him. You never saw him run, a bit like Bobby Moore, but I thought he could have been a possible replacement for Martin Peters. He wasn't as good as Martin but he was very skilful.'

Ron Boyce supports this view: 'Technically, he was a very good player and it was something of a mystery that he didn't make it at West Ham. He was probably a bit too laid back to go all the way.'

After just a handful of games in the claret and blue, Dawkins joined Crystal Palace on September 30, 1967. He also spent three years in the mid-1970s playing in South Africa for Durban United, where he caught up with his good pal, Budgie Byrne.

Trevor's football legacy is largely to be found overseas in the United States, where he played indoor football for Cleveland Force between 1980 and 1984. He also won several indoor soccer league accolades as coach of Canton Invaders, Cleveland Crunch and Houston Hotshots.

Trevor still lives in Texas and makes an annual visit to Leigh-on-Sea, in his native Essex, to see his mother. He has been enjoying retirement for quite a few years and keeps fit by playing racquet ball three-times-per-week.

In August 2014, he met up with his former team-mates for a reunion of the FA Youth Cup winning side of 1963. Colin Mackleworth, Dennis Burnett, Carol Charles (wife of captain Charlo), Peter Bennett, Harry Redknapp, John Dryden and four-goal hero Martin Britt each enjoyed an evening of nostalgia at Montpeliano restaurant in Knightsbridge. Former youth team players Alan Herbage and David James put the icing on a perfect evening, which produced a super-charged moment when 'Britto' produced the actual ball

from the game – a little worse for wear after 51 years in his garden shed!

Bobby was five years older so I don't really know why he took a shine to me. I think he liked the way I played and the fact that I was easy going, so we got on quite well. He called me 'T' or 'Trev'. Like Bobby, I hated giving the ball away, was very confident in possession and preferred the simple over the elaborate.

He really looked after me at West Ham and, before I had even signed for the club, I got selected to play for the England Youth team against Ireland at the old Vetch Field in Swansea. The first person I received a telegram from was Bobby. Both Phil Woosnam and Malcolm Musgrove also sent me telegrams.

On reflection, I was probably around Bobby a bit too much. When I was 17 he used to drag me off everywhere and we went to see all the European matches at Tottenham in 1962-63. Inevitably, we would then go on to a club afterwards. Alan Sealey would join us and we just loved watching a match and then going out for drinks.

Both Dave Mackay and Danny Blanchflower played for Spurs at the time and they really were terrific times over at White Hart Lane. My idol was Johnny White, who sadly died young after being struck by lightning on a golf course. When I was 15, I used to train here, there and everywhere and got to know 'Whitey' quite well.

We used to drink with the players from Arsenal, Chelsea and Spurs in whatever club was popular at the time. We also went to Carnaby Street quite a bit. There wasn't the paparazzi like there is today so it largely went unnoticed. We used to go to the Café Royal to watch boxing. There was so much happening in London back then and everything just seemed to be there for us to enjoy. So we did!

One night Harry Redknapp and I went for a beer in The Blind Beggar, at Whitechapel but it was so busy we decided to leave it and went somewhere else. The next day the newspapers were full of headlines like: 'Gangland Slaying!' It was the night when Ronnie Kray shot dead George Cornell. We literally dodged a bullet that night!

By the time I made my debut for West Ham, against West Bromwich Albion, I had known Bobby for five years so it wasn't a daunting experience at all because we had hung out together so much during that time. We were just mates playing football.

I actually had a few words with Bobby on my debut because I felt he had made a few mistakes and I had really wanted to win. We knew each other really well at that stage so I had no reservations about voicing my opinion and telling him straight – he could have done a lot better! There were no hard feelings.

I probably should have established myself in the first team a bit more before enjoying the lifestyle so much but, when you are a young kid, a wise head isn't always there.

I drove down to Torremolinos once with Bobby and Malcolm Allison. It was about 1964 and Malcolm wasn't at West Ham anymore, of course, but we all went down there on holiday. I had a place in Marbella which I used to drive down to in my MGB but we decided to give somewhere else a try a bit further along the coast. We were all driving our own MGBs, fully stacked with beer, and the music blaring, when all of a sudden Bobby signalled over to me and was frantically pointing at something. When I looked, there was Ron Greenwood sitting in a bar! We couldn't believe our eyes. Of all the places in the world, we had chosen the same place and the same time to go on holiday!

There was such a great camaraderie at the club and the best way I can sum it up was when the old physio, Bill Jenkins, passed away. To this day I have never been to a funeral attended by so many people as there were that day – easily over 100 cars lined the streets. Everyone loved Bill and it was just like losing a relative. That was typical of the depth of feeling around West Ham United at the time.

After I left West Ham, I went to Crystal Palace before heading down to South Africa, where I spent a few years playing for both Durban United and Durban City. Mooro had urged me to go because he knew Budgie Byrne was down there and he said that I would enjoy myself. He was absolutely right! I had the time of my life seeing Budgie, Frank McLintock and Johnny Haynes pretty much every day I was there. Bizarrely, I actually won a cap playing for South Africa against Argentina in 1976. God only knows how I qualified to play! It was the first mixed-race South African team to play an international and the supporters were still segregated. We put on a show for them, though, and ran out 5-0 winners, courtesy of four goals from the great Jomo Sono, who went on to play for the New York Cosmos.

I was living in the States when I heard the news of Bobby's death. I knew he had been poorly and had problems but I didn't think it was life-threatening. It took me weeks to get over the shock of it. I was in a place called Wichita, in Kansas, when one of the players came up to me and told me the news. It completely wiped me out for some time.

I loved my time at West Ham and should have gone a bit further with the club than I did but, as everyone always tells me, I didn't take it seriously enough. I think I will have the words: 'Too laid back' chiselled on my headstone – and tilt it backwards a little bit!

Trevor Dawkins

Trevor visiting Rob Jenkins' clinic in Green Street during a visit from Texas in 2014.

Bobby Moore with the FA Cup and Charity Shield.

Back row L-R Brown, Peters, Kirkup, Standen, Dear, Moore. Front row L-R Sealey, Boyce, Hurst, Burkett Sissons.

They Played With Bobby Moore – The West Ham Years

CHAPTER EIGHT
1965-66

Bobby Moore's total appearances (July 1965-June 1966): 77 games (4 goals)

League Division One: 37, England: 16, (2 goals), League Cup: 9 (2 goals), ECWC: 6, Friendlies: 5, FA Cup: 4

Having lifted both the FA Cup and European Cup Winners Cup in the previous two seasons, Bobby Moore completed an imperious hat-trick when he climbed Wembley's 39 steps to raise the Jules Rimet Trophy on July 30, 1966. It was an achievement which will never be bettered. The whole nation was in raptures as the blond-haired boy from Barking trod a familiar path to the Royal Box to receive the World Cup form Her Majesty the Queen.

England were world champions and a 25-year-old Geoff Hurst eclipsed the 40 league and cup goals he scored for West Ham United during the 1965-66 season with three of the most celebrated goals in world football. Moore always maintained that England's fourth goal, in the 4-2 victory over West Germany, was his finest moment in football.

Hurst had only gained his first full England cap – ironically against West Germany – in February, just five months before his historic performance. Fellow Hammer Budgie Byrne missed the final cut to be part of Alf Ramsey's England squad, denying West Ham fans a fourth World Cup Hammer.

His finest achievement...receiving the Jules Rimet trophy from Queen Elizabeth II.

Martin Peters confirmed his status as one of the greatest utility players in world football and it is remarkable that all three players cost absolutely no transfer fee, whatsoever. They remain the finest testament to West Ham United's youth academy.

Controversial Russian linesman Tofiq Bahramov had previously officiated West Ham's European Cup Winners Cup match against Olympiakos at the Kariaskis Stadium earlier in December 1965. Bahramov was born in Azerbaijan and his decision to allow Geoff Hurst's second goal in extra time, which set up England's victory, is widely regarded as the most significant decision in English football.

In December 1965, West Ham United were voted BBC Television's Team of the Year, in recognition of their 2-0 victory over TSV Munich 1860 at Wembley during the previous May. Captain Moore and his team-mates, along with club personnel such as physio Bill Jenkins and trainer Albert Walker, were beamed into living rooms throughout the United Kingdom.

Interestingly, there was no place for Moore on the Hammer of the Year podium, with Geoff Hurst gaining most votes ahead of Martin Peters and Peter Brabrook. However, Moore was voted Sportsman of the Year by the British Sports Writers Association. His contract dispute with West Ham was finally resolved and his weekly wage increased to £150.

Back on the pitch, West Ham relinquished its hold on the European Cup Winners Cup after losing in the semi-final against Borussia Dortmund. Defeat in the League Cup final against West Bromwich Albion, which would have meant qualification to the Fairs Cup tournament (a forerunner to the UEFA Cup and Europa League) meant there would be no more European football during the Bobby Moore era.

Once again, Ron Greenwood selected a consistent line up throughout the season and Moore – who played in a staggering 77 matches for club and country – lined up with only three new debutants – Harry Redknapp, Jimmy Bloomfield and Dennis Burnett.

Here is their story...

49 – HARRY REDKNAPP

Born: Poplar, London, March 2, 1947

Position: Right-wing

Games played with Bobby Moore: 164 (1965–72)

Games played for West Ham United: 175 (1965-72)

First game with Bobby Moore (Debut): August 23, 1965 Sunderland (h) D 1-1

Scorers: West Ham United: Peters
Sunderland: Herd

West Ham United: Dickie, Kirkup. Burkett, Peters, Bickles, Moore, **Redknapp**, Boyce, Byrne Hurst, Sissons

Sunderland: McLaughlan, Irwin, Ashurst, Harvey, Hurley, Baxter, Hellawell, Herd, O'Hare, McNab, Mulhall

Henry James Redknapp was almost six years younger than Bobby Moore and played in 164 first-team matches with him. He was a member of West Ham United's successful FA Youth Cup final team which overcame Liverpool 6-5 in 1963 and was still at the club almost a decade later, playing in all four matches of the epic League Cup semi-final against Stoke City in 1972. His former team-mates are unanimous in their assessment of his core skill: 'Harry had a terrific ability to put in first class crosses.'

Harry with Bobby, Rob Jenkins and Frank Lampard.

Harry (centre), training with England Youth along with fellow Hammers Martin Britt (on Harry's right) and Peter Bennett (fourth from the right).

Redknapp and Moore remained great friends throughout their lives and played together whilst in Seattle in the late 1970s after Harry had finished his four year spell with AFC Bournemouth. When returning to these shores they would share their first coaching role in England, at Isthmian League club Oxford City.

In 1994, Redknapp became only the eighth manager in West Ham United's long history and continues his managerial odyssey today with Queens Park Rangers. He narrowly missed out to Roy Hodgson on becoming England manager. It would have been the ultimate journey for the Poplar-born winger.

Along with George Kay, Dave Sexton, Ken Brown, Malcolm Allison, John Lyall and Bobby Gould, Redknapp is one of the few former West Ham players to win a major trophy as a manager – when leading Portsmouth to FA Cup success in 2008.

Harry's reputation of being a wheeler dealer in the transfer market has its roots in his time at West Ham where he sold anything from mohair suits to new cars. His brother-in-law, Frank Lampard senior, holds Harry in the very highest esteem: 'There have been three great coaches in my life; Ron Greenwood, John Lyall and Harry Redknapp and if I had to work with one of them I would choose Harry.'

In stark contrast Sir Geoff Hurst highlights Harry as the personification of just how unpredictable football can be: 'If you asked me to nominate one player from the 89 who played with Bobby Moore that wouldn't make it as a coach, I would have said Harry Redknapp. He didn't show any interest in that side of the game when he was at the club and was always quick to get away after training. Now, he is one of the most successful English managers in recent times and just missed out on the England job which would have been absolutely fantastic for the country. We spent some time together out in Seattle and that is when I started to notice his man-management skills.'

Former West Ham striker, Clyde Best, is another to hold Harry in high regard: 'I call him the 'Kenny Rogers of football' because he is a gambler. He was a typical Cockney guy that liked to have a laugh, loved to play cards, was mad about the horses but all the time was just a very down to earth person. We stay in touch, which is important to me.'

Harry still resides in the 'Millionaire's playground' of Sandbanks in Bournemouth with his wife, Sandra, but walking the dog, checking the racing results and winding down with a glass of red wine suggests an altogether different lifestyle. You can take the boy out of Poplar…

When I went to West Ham I was only 15 and Bobby took a shine to me. He was 20 at the time and well established in the first team. We got on well and I always felt he liked me. Bobby, Frank Lampard and I would go out for a drink and spend a lot of time together socially. We'd come back from an away game and pop into a good East End pub like The Globe or The Blind Beggar for a few beers.

In 1971 we were on tour in America and we travelled around a bit and ended up in Los Angeles. Kent Gavin, who, at the time, was a top photographer for the Daily Mirror was following Bobby all around the States taking photos.

Kent got tickets for Mooro and Geoff Hurst to see Frank Sinatra and a photo shoot was arranged for Bobby with Sinatra a couple of days before the concert. We all loved Sinatra, he was the guvnor. We were all keen to hear all about it and when Bobby came back we all rushed to him to hear how it went: 'He didn't have a f****** clue who I was!' he said. Apparently, Sinatra just kept saying: 'Hurry up man I've got a busy schedule' and was ushering in various people to have their photo taken with him. Bobby said: 'He looked at me as if to say: 'Who the f*** are you?'

Incredibly, I was lucky enough to get a ticket for the concert because two of Kent's reporter friends were fogged in at Heathrow and couldn't get over so he put them in a hat at our hotel on Sunset Boulevard. We were already having the time of our lives and then this opportunity arose.

It was billed as Sinatra's farewell concert so everyone wanted to be there. Pop Robson won one of the tickets and Clyde Best won the other but Clyde wasn't a fan of Sinatra's music and he knew I loved him so he gave me his ticket.

When we arrived, the whole place was full of stars. Anyone who was anyone was there to see Sinatra. There was Princess Grace, Gene Kelly and Joe Namath the famous quarter-back of the New York Jets. Dean Martin and Barbara Streisand were amongst his guest singers. Clint Eastwood was sitting near us and Pop knew all the actors and was pointing them out to me. I was 24 years old and it was just terrific to be there with Mooro, Hursty and Pop. I'll never forget it.

I played in the League Cup semi-final in 1972 when Bobby went in goal against Stoke City up at Old Trafford but I have more vivid recollections of the game we played before that when we drew 0-0 in the first replay at Hillsborough.

We were waiting for a coach outside our hotel in Buxton and it was getting later and later and clearly something was wrong. Finally it arrived and Ron Greenwood started shouting at the driver, he told him to go faster, and get up the inside, switch lane and put his foot down. There were no police escorts in those days and the driver just lost it completely. He hit about seven cars on the way and was a nervous wreck. We were being chased by cars and the police eventually got involved.

I was one of the card players at West Ham. Bobby wasn't a card player, he was more of a drinker but I loved a game of three-card brag. Trevor Brooking liked to play as did Billy Bonds, Peter Bennett, Tony Scott and Jimmy Lindsay.

'The guvnors' – Photos provided with the kind permission of Kent Gavin.

Bobby joined me out in America with the Seattle Sounders. Geoff Hurst was also there along with another Hammer, Bobby Howe, who was the coach. Mooro took it all very seriously and moved his family – Tina, Roberta and Dean – over there. We enjoyed the training under Bobby Howe and we all had a great time.

Training at Chadwell Heath. Bobby Moore wearing the Number 5 shirt in the bakground.

Mooro and I always said that if either of us got a job in coaching the other would join and that's how the job at Oxford City came about. At the time I was in Phoenix, Arizona where I had signed a five-year deal but the owner of the club reneged on everything and suddenly there wasn't any football club.

I didn't really know what to do but thankfully Bobby called me up to say he was manager of Oxford and he wanted me to join him. He saw it as a stepping stone to get established but it was very difficult because, it was Oxford City – not Oxford United – and they were in the Isthmian League.

Bobby's only other job in management was with Southend United and he had no chance there. I actually got Bobby the job at Roots Hall. Anton Johnson who owned Bournemouth, where I was installed as manager, called me in one day to say he was buying Southend instead and asked me if I had any ideas who to make manager. I said: 'Bobby Moore.' That was that.

Unfortunately, Anton didn't stay long at Southend and a club needs stability if it's got any chance to succeed. So, because it didn't work out for Bobby there, people say he wasn't a good manager, which is rubbish. If Bobby had become the manager of West Ham he may have been the best manager in the club's history, who knows? I still think he could have been a great manager. He had so much knowledge of the game and knew everyone and who wouldn't want to play for Bobby Moore?

It was such a diabolical waste that West Ham had this man who could have been the greatest ambassador in English football but they didn't want to know him. All I can think of is that sometimes in football people are reluctant to employ big names and prefer to have people around them that can be kept in their place and pose no threat to their own position.

Another way of looking at it, of course, is that most people thought Bobby was such a big character that he was being looked after and didn't need to be offered anything. It's a little bit like when Bobby told me that Ron Greenwood never once said: 'Well done' to him in all the time he was at West Ham. Perhaps Ron was another that just thought Bobby didn't

need it but believe me everyone needs it. Who doesn't want to be told they are different class at whatever it is they do?

When Mooro was ill he came down to Bournemouth and I picked him up at the Royal Bath Hotel. It made me cry to see him like that. His big thighs had withered away. In all the years I've been in football I've never met anyone like Mooro, so to see him as a shadow of the impressive character he had been was absolutely heart breaking.

Bobby was a class act, everything he did was class and he was everyone's role model. If he wore a key ring on his belt one day everyone else would start to do the same. He was fantastic company and loved a night out and a drink with the boys. We all had so much fun with him. Frank, Stag, Charlo, Cushley, Eddie Bov and all the boys will all have so many special memories. He never had a bad word for anybody and wasn't an aggressive guy. He was just a lovely, lovely, person.

Harry Redknapp

Following are a few comments about Harry from his former team-mates:

Whenever I meet up with Harry, we often talk about our West Ham days and he always keeps Bobby's memory alive. Harry is such a great character and he told me a very funny story about a recent trip he made to a physiotherapist. He suffers with his knee and his son, Jamie, recommended a top-class physio. Harry went along to a state-of-the-art clinic and took a seat and lost himself in a newspaper. However, he was recognised by a chap sitting across the room who politely said: 'Alright Harry?'

Now, Harry just glanced quickly in the chap's direction and said: 'Yeah, I'm alright mate,' and went back to his paper. Then it started nagging at him that he knew the fella and when the chap went in for his appointment Harry got up and asked the receptionist if she knew who he was because he looked very familiar. 'That was Prince Harry' she replied. Harry was so embarrassed: 'But I called him 'Mate!'

Colin Mackleworth

The night we went to see Frank Sinatra was magnificent. Geoff and Bobby were dressed up in their tuxedos because they knew they were going but Harry and I just turned up in our casual clothes sitting next to the rich and famous of Hollywood. Afterwards, there were drinks and canapes by a swimming pool and Harry and I were standing there with Clint Eastwood and Sammy Davis Junior. It was crazy.
Bryan Pop Robson

Whenever I see him he always asks about my wife and our boys. He never forgets me and he's always got time for me. He's different class.
Keith Miller

He must be the longest serving manager now that Sir Alex Ferguson has retired. He is terrific to me and every year I bring some young kids over from the States and no matter where Harry is, he opens up the training ground to us and the lads love it.
Ted MacDougall

Harry really looked after me at West Ham especially after Stuart Morgan and Stephen Death left for Reading, which sort of left me on my own. The best crosser of the ball at West Ham was Harry Redknapp. His crossing was as good as Beckham's if not better and you can tell him that.
Dave Llewelyn

Flying down the wing.

I took Harry's place when I made my debut against Arsenal and I remember he came up to me before the game and wished me all the best. When I went onto the pitch Arsenal's George Armstrong ran across the pitch to wish me well and I remember thinking how I had seen him make his debut for Arsenal.
Pat Holland

We were apprentices together and Harry's old man had a caravan down at Leysdown-on-Sea. One summer, Harry, Terry Needham, Colin Mackleworth and me went down there for a week away. Next door to our place was one of those Butlins-type holiday camps and Harry found out that they had a party every week to say goodbye to all those that were about to leave. So over the wall we went and into the dance hall where we had a great time. Anyway, we eventually got collared by the bouncers and pulled in to the office to see the manager: 'Right then lads,' he said, 'I need to know the number of your chalet.' Harry answered: '225,' and sounded very convincing. 'It only goes up to 180' replied the manager and we were swiftly asked to leave!

There are so many stories with Harry. One that sticks in my mind was when he bought a knocked-off television set. When he switched it on it didn't work so he opened up the back and there was nothing there except a brick!

He used to sell cars to the players. 'Don't buy them off the forecourt,' he would say. 'I can get you a better deal.' He ended up selling about five cars to the players which meant he got a free one for himself.

Harry had a similar deal with a tailors shop outside Mile End station called Rosemans. If he sold five mohair suits he got a free one.

Sadly, Harry hasn't done much with himself and the last I heard he was living on a council estate in Sandbanks!
Peter Bennett

Harry and Billy Bonds were really good mates when I was at West Ham. They owned a greyhound and one day Harry was getting all the players to have a punt on it: 'It's been laid out for this race,' he said. At the time I was taking home £7.50-per-week so a few quid was quite a bit for me at the time but I decided to get involved. I had a rough night's sleep and woke up to check the results in the newspaper only to find the dog had finished nowhere! At the training ground the following day Harry was describing to quite a few others, who were also out-of-pocket, just how he had to pull Bonzo off the trainer because the dog hadn't tried at all. 'We decided to take the dog back. We've had to leave it on my dad's balcony in Poplar!'
Joe Durrell

I was lucky in that I had Harry as a team-mate. He was tremendous and we knew exactly what each other was likely to do on the pitch. He made it easy for the midfield players at West Ham. It was in the days when you gave the ball to the wingers and you didn't do much else. Harry wasn't the best player away from home but at Upton Park he was a really good winger. I remember when Harry was manager at Bournemouth in the early 1980s and I went down there to play in a golf tournament. He took me and all my pals out while we were there.
Jimmy Lindsay

We were coached by Jim Barrett jnr at West Ham and one day one of the players locked him in the medical room. They left him there for ages and when he finally got out he mistakenly took Harry to be the culprit and smacked him around the face. Ron Greenwood found out about it and I think Jim lost his job over it.
Roger Cross

I coached Harry for a while and he got up to all sorts of mischief. I took him along to an England Youth training session at Lilleshall and he must have been playing up because I was taken to one side and told to keep a close eye on him. Thankfully, he knew how to get down that wing and put a cross in.
Bill Lansdowne

He always had something to sell. He is a diamond of a person and what you see is what you get. If you call him up now no matter where he is or what he is doing he'll always open up his door and have a cup of tea with you.
Tommy Taylor

Harry was absolutely brilliant to me when I joined West Ham. I was having difficulty settling in and he drove me everywhere to help me find a place to buy. Albert Walker did the same and I really must say that I can't speak highly enough of the players and staff at West Ham at that time.
Peter Eustace

I think the FA missed an opportunity when overlooking Harry for the England manager's job. He would have taken away the fear of playing for the country which handicaps so many players. He can handle the press, knows every player in the land and has that rare talent of getting the best out of them.
Frank Lampard

At a reunion of the 1963 FA Youth Cup winning team in August 2014.

50 – JIMMY BLOOMFIELD
February 15, 1934 – April 3, 1983

Born: Notting Hill, London

Position: Midfield/Inside-forward

Games played with Bobby Moore: 12 (1965-66)

Games played for West ham United: 14 (1965-65)

First game with Bobby Moore (Debut): October 9, 1965 Nottingham Forest L 0-5

Scorers: Nottingham Forest: Hinton, Wignall, Storey-Moore, Addison, Wilson

Nottingham Forest: Grummitt, Hindley, Mochan, Newton, McKinlay, Whitefoot, Storey-Moore, Addison, Wignall, Barnwell, Hinton

West Ham United: Standen, Kirkup, Charles*, Peters, Bovington, Moore, Redknapp, **Bloomfield**, Hurst, Bennett, Brabrook Sub: Bickles*

James Henry Bloomfield almost became a West Ham United player in 1960, some five years before he actually signed for the club. In November 1960, Bloomfield and David Herd, both of Arsenal, were being lined up to form part of a deal that would take popular Hammer Phil Woosnam to Highbury. In the end the deal fell through and Jimmy moved instead to Birmingham City, while Phil was eventually transferred to Aston Villa. Interestingly, going into the 2014-15 season, West Ham United had not transferred a player to Arsenal in over 100 years – since both Charles Satterthwaite and James Bigden went to Woolwich Arsenal in 1904.

Bloomfield (bottom row, second from the right) before the ECWC semi-final second leg against Borussia Dortmund on April 13, 1966.

Bloomfield (centre left), watching Brian Dear flex his left peg against Blackpool on March 19, 1966. John Sissons (centre) and Martin Peters (centre right) also look on.

Bloomfield eventually signed for West Ham, from Brentford, on September 30, 1965.

He had started his career with The Bees and was, coincidentally, there at the same time as Ron Greenwood in the early 1950s. Jimmy also gained England Under-23 experience while playing for Arsenal.

Moore did not play in Bloomfield's debut game away at Fulham in October 1965, so their first game together was up at the City Ground against Nottingham Forest, one week later.

Jimmy's time at West Ham was brief – six days shy of one year – and he moved on to Plymouth Argyle in September 1966. Interestingly, former Hammer Peter Shearing was also playing for the Pilgrims.

Bloomfield entered management with Leyton Orient in 1968 and guided them back to the second tier of league football. He would subsequently manage Leicester City, when following in the footsteps of ex-Hammer Frank O'Farrell, after his ill-fated spell in charge of Manchester United in 1971. After six years at Filbert Street, Jimmy returned to Orient for a second spell which, after four years, ended in 1981.

Jimmy was diagnosed with lung cancer in the late 1970s, a cruel irony for someone who was a non-smoker. He passed away on April 3, 1983. He was just 49-years-old.

We are indebted to his widow, Susan and their son, David – a former youth team player at Upton Park – who shared the following memories of Jimmy's time with Bobby Moore at West Ham United:

When my dad joined West Ham United and started training with the team, he used to say to my mum that Bobby Moore could find Geoff Hurst anywhere on the pitch even if he was wearing a blindfold.

Ron Greenwood knew my father from his coaching days at Arsenal and liked the way he played. He was looking for an experienced player and although my dad was 31 at the time, he felt he could make a positive difference. My dad was actually earning more money at Brentford and took a pay cut to play at West Ham in the first division. It wasn't about the money, of course, and Ron had put into words precisely how my dad had felt about the game of football so there was a real synergy between the two men.

If I had to assess my father as a player, I would say he was a creative inside-forward, who notched up over 100 career goals from 500 professional matches, which wasn't a bad return for a midfielder. He was very adept at making incisive passes to release the wingers. My grandad used to say that a bit more pace, however, wouldn't have done him any harm!

One day, my dad was chatting with Bobby and revealed that their paths could have crossed a few years earlier. In 1962, my dad was part of the squad of 40 selected by England as potentials for the World Cup in Chile. Unfortunately, my dad broke his arm around that time and never made it to the 22 but he told Bobby just how passionate he had always been about playing for his country. It was one of his life's ambitions.

He believed that to play for England and be the best person in your position in the country was the very pinnacle of any player's career. The following day, Bobby gave my dad one of his international shirts. We still have it today and it is something of a family treasure. We don't know which game the shirt is from but it was definitely before the 1966 World Cup. It is pure white with the lions on the front and a red Number 6 on the back. We keep it with my father's England Under-23 shirt and the jersey he wore when playing for the Football League representative team. When my dad played for Arsenal in the 1950s the England team was selected by a committee and Arsenal didn't have anyone on that so there

Alas, Jimmy's effort effort at Blackpool was ruled out for offside. Martin Peters looks on.

was a feeling that good players were missing out. My dad fell into that category.

Another possession we have from my father's career is a player of the month trophy he was awarded by the Evening Standard while playing for West Ham. It is a cigarette lighter and yet another treasured family heir loom.

My dad wasn't at the club very long but he always spoke very highly of Ron Greenwood, the players and the way West Ham United was run. The highlight of his time there was playing in both legs of the semi-final of the European Cup Winners Cup in 1966. West Ham were the holders so it was a big deal but their opponents, Borussia Dortmund, were a very good side and won both legs.

I remember my dad brought home a leather football for me and I was struck by how futuristic it looked. It was a black and white speckled one whereas, in England, we played with a plain white ball or an orange one when it snowed!

My mum also tells the story about the time my dad said that he had played in a game in which Bobby had not made a single mistake. He described it as the 'Perfect game.' I was reminded of that in recent years when Iniesta and Xavi of Barcelona were described as having perfect games. Little did they know that Bobby had already done it 50 years earlier!
David Bloomfield

Despite his short spell at West Ham United there were many ex-Hammers keen to share their memories of Jimmy:

When Jimmy Bloomfield played for Birmingham City he was treated like Bobby Moore. He was a god to them, he was that good a player.
Harry Redknapp

We got him from Brentford. He was a bloody good player, one of the best. He was a very nice fella.
Jim Barrett jnr

Jimmy was an absolutely unbelievable player. I played with him in the reserves a few times and he was superb. That is how we got to know each other and he later signed me for Orient. He had cancer during his later days and had to wear a colostomy bag. Despite this, he was still curling in free kicks past John Jackson. He was an incredible bloke. I really liked him. He was like an old fashioned Johnny Haynes, he had everything.
Peter Bennett

Jimmy was very comfortable on the ball. He didn't have any pace but read the game well. He was an unflappable and mild mannered guy.
Trevor Dawkins

Jimmy Bloomfield was the reason I signed for Orient in 1968. I had played with him at West Ham and, before that, against him when he was with Arsenal and I was playing for Chelsea. He was a good midfield player and a lovely, lovely man, who was a pleasure to talk to. He never lost his rag. We used to play in front of crowds of 15,000 so they liked his style of football at Orient. We won the old third division.
Peter Brabrook

I played with Jim at both Arsenal and West Ham. He was a great ball player and had brilliant control. Sadly, I remember seeing him shortly before he died. He was at West Ham's training ground, when I was visiting from the States in 1982. It was hard to see someone I was very fond of, suffering like that, but Jimmy was very upbeat.
Jim Standen

They Played With Bobby Moore – The West Ham Years

51 – DENNIS BURNETT

Born: Bermondsey, London, September 27, 1944

Position: Right-back

Games played with Bobby Moore: 59 (1965-67)

Games played for West Ham United: 66 (1965-67)

Honours with Bobby Moore: 1966 League Cup finalist

First game with Bobby Moore: October 13, 1965 Mansfield Town (h) W 4-0 (League Cup 3rd round)

Scorers: West Ham United: Hurst (2), Brabrook, **Burnett**

West Ham United: Standen, **Burnett**, Charles, Bovington, Brown, Moore, Brabrook, Peters, Britt, Hurst, Sissons

Mansfield Town: Treharne, Nelson, Humble, Hall, Gill, Morris, Gregson, Macready, Middleton, Cheesebrough, Scanlon

Dennis Henry Burnett scored one of the great goals in West Ham United's history – an 80-yard strike on a frozen pitch at Boundary Park against Oldham Athletic in the FA Cup third round, 1966. Alongside Ronnie Boyce's celebrated strike against Manchester City at Maine Road in 1970, Burnett's goal is one of the most remarkable strikes Bobby Moore saw during his time at West Ham.

Burnett signed professional forms in October 1962 and was a member of the victorious 1963 FA Youth Cup team which defeated Liverpool, 6-5, in the two-legged final.

His former youth team-mate and best man, Colin Mackleworth, recalls Dennis fondly: 'He was a better player than he got credit for at West Ham.' Another member of the 1963 Youth team, Trevor Dawkins, highlights a particular feature of Burnett's play: 'I thought he read the game very well and didn't panic in tight situations.'

Burnett played over 50 league games and 16 cup games for the Hammers and also scored in the 1966 League Cup semi-final first leg at Cardiff City. He kept his place, ahead of Joe Kirkup, for the final which West Ham eventually lost, 3-5, to West Bromwich Albion. It was the last two-legged final before the competition was moved to Wembley Stadium.

The arrival of Billy Bonds in the summer of 1967 saw Burnett transferred to Millwall, where he formed a resolute defensive line with former Hammers, Lawrie Leslie and Harry Cripps.

Later in his career, he played in the North American Soccer League for St Louis Storm and came up against Moore's great friend, Pele, on three occasions.

Dennis is highly revered in Norway, following a successful spell as a coach during the 1990s.

Bobby does the honours for Dennis and another former Hammer, Harry Cripps, at a shop opening.

In action against Sheffield Wednesday, October 1965.

The World Cup wedding! L-R Bobby Howe, Colin Mackleworth, Trevor Dawkins, Dennis, Jean, Peter Brabrook, Alan Sealey and Bill Kitchener.

They Played With Bobby Moore – The West Ham Years

Today, he resides in Sussex with his 'World Cup wife', Jean, and keeps active with various building projects:

Bobby Moore always called me 'Denboy'. He was an icon to me. I was a young lad at West Ham when Bobby was there and I simply couldn't talk to him on the same level as I would speak to, say, Harry Redknapp or Colin Mackleworth.

It reminds me of a good friend of mine, George Shillian, who was in the army and found it very difficult to speak to the officers. George and I are in the Masons now and there is a similar feeling there. You just wouldn't speak to the very top people at a lodge meeting. It was a bit like that at West Ham. You are in the same team and on the same side but there is a hierarchy and being over familiar with someone like Bobby Moore just wouldn't have been appropriate. Bobby Moore was the captain of West Ham United and England and I felt it was only right that I should speak to him when spoken to.

My wife Jean and I got married on World Cup final day in 1966. Most of the team were there apart from Bobby, Geoff and Martin, of course, who had other things on their minds! Obviously, these things are booked a long way in advance and we couldn't change it. Ironically, we were able to make it a bit later in the day, but, typically, the game then went to extra time! The Canon of Rochester conducted the service and he wasn't best pleased because there were quite a few of the lads at the back listening to the final on transistor radios – there weren't any mobile phones back then, of course.

Bobby was the best out and out defender I ever saw but Pele is the best player I have seen. I actually played against him when I was in the States with St Louis Storm. Pele played over 1200 games, scored over 1000 goals and, in every game, someone was trying to stop him by good means or foul. He came through all that and still performed at the very highest level so I would make him my greatest ever player. Bobby faced the best in the league and the world and won trophies for both club and country. Most people who played with or against him salute him as the best.

Bobby was very quiet in the changing room before a game and I can still see him now, standing at the door holding his shorts in his hands because they were the last item of his strip to be worn. He would say: 'Come on lads, let's go, are you ready Denboy?' And off we'd go.

West Ham were playing up at Oldham Athletic in the FA Cup and it was a very cold day and the pitch was icy. Their striker ran through on our goal but over-played the ball so I went for it and absolutely leathered it as hard as I could. The ball went flying over the half-way line, took a bounce on the hard surface and went over the goalie's head into the net. It was literally about 80-yards. I was just happy that I had cleared it so the goal was a big bonus. Bobby and all the lads were congratulating me in the dressing room afterwards.

After I left West Ham I still returned to the club to see Jack Turner, who helped the players with their mortgages and insurance and was a bit of a confidant to some of the lads. I was still living in Goodmayes at the time and usually saw Bobby in Jack's office. We would have a chat. Jack was very

close to Bobby and Trevor Brooking.

When I was playing for Millwall, Harry Cripps and I opened a wallpaper shop together in Ilford High Road. It sold Magicote, Crown and Dulux paint. We had a grand opening and invited Bobby along to open the shop. David Webb and Frank Lampard were also there. Bobby was terrific in those situations and helped in every way he could.

The last time I saw Bobby was about six months before he died. I was coaching out in Norway and was invited over to cover a game at Wembley between the Norwegians and England. I was working for Norwegian radio and I think the Norwegians won the game 1-0. Bobby was sitting just across the way from me in the commentary box. He was wearing a big sheepskin coat and I popped over for a chat.

I watch players now and think my god they are not good enough to lace Bobby's boots. Most of them are just not very good or do a couple of things over a short period of time and earn an obscene amount of money as a consequence. Bobby did exceptional things week-in, week-out, during his 16 years at West Ham.

Dennis Burnett

Dennis at a reunion of the 1963 FA Youth cup winning team in August 2014.

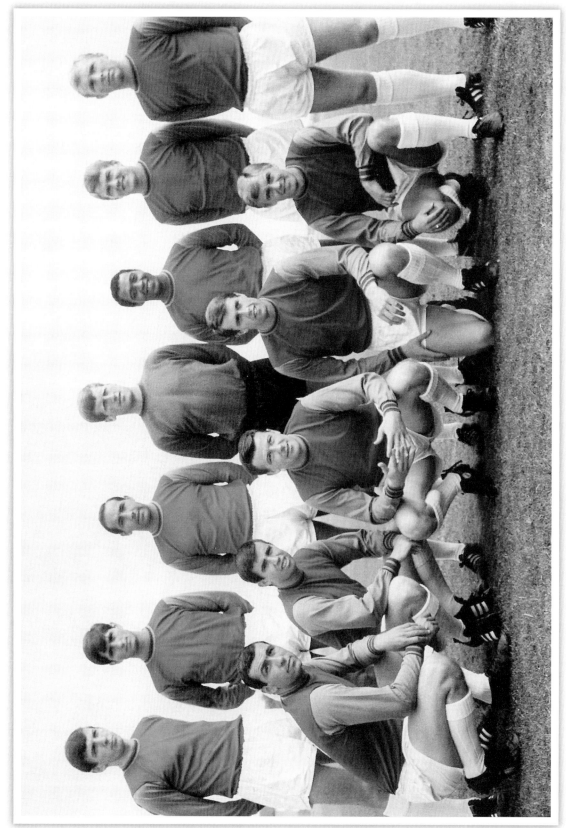

Back row L-R Peters, Burnett, Bovington, Standen, Charles, Burkett, Moore. Front Row L-R Brabrook, Boyce, Byrne, Hurst, Sissons.

They Played With Bobby Moore – The West Ham Years

CHAPTER NINE
1966-67

Bobby Moore's total appearances (July 1966-June 1967): 67 games (3 goals)

League Division One: 40 (2 goals), England: 6, Friendlies: 13 (1 goal), League Cup: 6, FA Cup: 2

Bobby Moore was made an Officer of the Order of the British Empire in the Queen's New Year's Honours list. In doing so he became the first representative of West Ham United Football Club to receive such a royal honour. He also became the first footballer to be voted BBC Sports Personality of the Year, ahead of Portuguese legend Eusebio and fellow team-mate Geoff Hurst.

Hurst bagged 41 goals for the season across the league (29), FA Cup (3) and League Cup (9) and narrowly missed out to Jack Charlton for the Football Writers Sportsman of the Year award.

Sadly, just one week before the start of the new season, popular club physio Bill Jenkins suddenly and unexpectedly passed away. His son Rob, who had been in charge of the reserves for two years, stepped up to become first team physio, a position he held for the next 25 years.

Ken Brown also played his final match for West Ham United and registered a post-war record of 456 appearances, overcoming the 406 posted by Ernie Gregory. He was the final player from Bobby Moore's debut, more than nine years earlier, to leave the club. The great Budgie Byrne and cup hero Alan Sealey also left the club, marking the end of a golden era at Upton Park.

In April, the Hammers visited the United States and participated in a small piece of football history – they played Real Madrid in the Houston Astrodome, Texas. It was the first ever match to be played on a full sized pitch completely under cover. The game ended in a 2-3 defeat with Geoff Hurst and John Sissons scoring for West Ham. Former Hammer Phil Woosnam travelled from Atlanta, Georgia to attend the game and caught up with his team-mates.

1966-67 was West Ham United's first season without a major youth team or first team

trophy since 1963. Fortunes were starting to hide, once more, and perhaps it was no coincidence, when news filtered through that James Brockman, the man who co-wrote *I'm Forever Blowing Bubbles* in the 1920s, had passed away on May 22. The low point came with an FA Cup third round replay defeat at the hands of Swindon Town – two divisions lower than the Hammers. As a result, angry fans smashed windows in Bobby Moore's sports shop on Green Street.

There was one beacon of excellence – a 7-0 trouncing of Leeds United in the League Cup on November 7.

Six Hammers made their debuts in the first team alongside Bobby Moore OBE. They were Bobby Howe, Colin Mackleworth, Bill Kitchener, Paul Heffer, Trevor Hartley and Doug Eadie.

Here is their story...

1966 BBC Sports Personality of the Year - Bobby Moore with Eusebio.

52 – BOBBY HOWE

Born: Chadwell St Mary, Essex, December 22, 1945

Position: Left-back

Games played with Bobby Moore: 78 (1966-71)

Games played for West Ham United: 82 (1966-71)

First game with Bobby Moore (Debut): September 24, 1966 Southampton (h) D 2-2

Scorers: West Ham United: Hurst, Peters
Southampton: Chivers, Davies

West Ham United: West Ham United: Standen, Burnett, Charles, Peters, Brown, Moore, Brabrook*, Boyce, Byrne, Hurst, Sissons Sub: **Howe***

Southampton: MacLaren, Webb, Hollywood, Wimshurst, Knapp, Walker, Paine, Chivers, Davies, Melia, Sydenham

Robert John Howe was the first Hammer to make his debut from the substitutes' bench. He came on for Peter Brabrook against Southampton on September 24, 1966. Interestingly, Bobby Moore came on as a substitute on only one occasion throughout his 16-years at West Ham United – against Derby County on February 6, 1971 when, ironically, he replaced Bobby Howe. Bobby on for Bobby.

Bobby (centre) watching Moore clear his lines against Manchester United on March 29, 1969.

Howe played for Thurrock, Essex and London Boys before joining West Ham's youth section in August 1962. He signed professional forms five months later, eventually pulling on the shirt in 75 league games and seven cup ties. He also played cricket as an all-rounder for his local club Aveley C.C.

Bobby played in West Ham's successful FA Youth Cup final team of 1963, who unforgettably beat Liverpool 6-5 over two legs.

Howe was almost five years younger than Bobby Moore and appeared in the teams that both played up at Blackpool in the 1971 FA Cup debacle and, before that, Jimmy Greaves' glittering West Ham debut against Manchester City at Maine Road the season before.

While at West Ham, Howe undertook his FA coaching course and gained his full badge at the Lilleshall centre. Little did he know that some 10 years later he would be coaching Bobby Moore himself when both players were starring for Seattle Sounders in the North America Soccer League.

Perhaps Howe's greatest claim to fame is that he is the only West Ham player ever to man-mark Pele in a club game. It happened during West Ham's 2-2 draw with Santos at Randall's Island, New York in September, 1970. Frank Lampard, who also played in that game, commented: 'I think he is still chasing Pele now!'

Bobby in action against Spurs.

Howe's brother-in-law is former Hammer, Trevor Hartley, who shared the following thoughts about the left-back: 'We've always got on well and I married his sister, Julie, in 1969. Bobby and I used to go to the shows together. We'd go and see Lon Satton, who stood in for Sammy Davis Jnr. One time we met Tina Moore, Cathy Peters and Judith Hurst in a night club. It was pure coincidence and we ended up dancing with them. Mooro, Martin and Geoff were away on international duty at the time but I remember them all saying they wanted a word with us and jokingly accused us of taking their wives dancing behind their backs! Bobby Howe was a hard-working player with a good engine. He wasn't a typical West Ham player. He was Mr Reliable, which is why John Bond took him to Bournemouth. He has always been a great friend and we have coached together both here and in the States.'

Howe's fitness is another area of his game that has not been forgotten. Former keeper Peter Grotier recalls a particular example of his stamina: 'I remember going to a party at Bobby Ferguson's house one Saturday night and all the lads were having a good time and then someone brought out a broom handle and challenged us to see how many sit-ups we could do with it behind our necks. Jimmy Greaves wasn't the fittest of people and he couldn't do it and I think I managed about two but then Bobby Howe had a go and racked up over 50, just like that.'

Bobby left West Ham in January 1971 and joined John Bond's AFC Bournemouth. His eventual destiny would be the United States of America and he remains a very well respected coach out there today.

Clyde Best describes Bobby as: 'A wonderful fella and my room-mate during our West Ham days. He went on to do great things for football in the United States.'

Nowadays, Bobby lives and coaches in Seattle. He visits the Hartley family in Bedfordshire each year.

When I joined the club as a 16-year-old in 1962, Bobby had just returned from Chile in the World Cup and although both

In attacking mode against Coventry City.

Martin Peters and Geoff Hurst had not yet pulled on the England shirt, there was a feeling at the club that things were starting to move.

The start of it all really was our FA Youth Cup triumph in 1963. For me, to be a part of that youth team in my first year and beat a very good Liverpool side, 6-5 over two-legs, was the best start imaginable. I think 10 from that youth side also played in the first team for West Ham. John Dryden was, unfortunately, the only one to miss out, which is a remarkable statistic.

I remember the club hadn't long since moved to Chadwell Heath which, at the time, was largely a converted cricket pavilion and the whole of my training at West Ham took place there. The first team dressing room was separate from the one we used as apprentices and youth players. It was an incredibly intimidating experience to walk from your dressing room into the first team dressing room with Bobby Moore, Geoff Hurst and Martin Peters. You just wanted to get in there, pick up their sweaty gear and get out!

My debut game was against Southampton in 1966 when I came on as a sub and played a cameo role for 10 minutes. I remember being absolutely exhausted!

My full debut came against Coventry City and I remember Ron Greenwood telling me the evening before so I played that game about four times over in my head during my sleep

that night. It's funny because once you have your first touch in a game it's just football again and you get on with it. The level is obviously higher and you are playing against well-established players and internationals. I had been training with internationals of course so I had nothing to fear really.

When someone like Bobby Moore comes up to you after a game and says: 'Well done!' it really does mean so much to a young player. I was never part of Bobby's social group at West Ham. 'The Black Lion crowd' would have been difficult for me to be involved with because I lived out in Essex, 25 miles away from the ground, and I usually drove home.

I remember watching Bobby from the stands once and I can't recall the game or the year but I don't think he actually put a foot wrong throughout the entire match. Nowadays they produce all these stats on possession rate and passing accuracy, well Bobby didn't misplace a pass and he hit balls to the front men with brilliant precision. In Baseball over here, there is something called the 'perfect game' and if we had something like that in football, Bobby's performance that day would have set a new standard.

Bobby was the quintessential captain, not only at West Ham but for his country. He was the player everyone wanted to be and the person everyone wanted to emulate. If I had to assess him as a player I would simply say: 'Magnificent.' He was a pre-planner rather than a crisis manager. He was rarely exposed in a game and because he wasn't fast he had to be deadly accurate. His ability with the ball was simply phenomenal as he demonstrated on the biggest stage of all when he played that ball to Geoff Hurst for the fourth goal – and his hat-trick – in the 1966 World Cup final at Wembley.

One of the great things about playing for West Ham at that time was that it gave me and others the opportunity to play with and against world class players. To be in a team that included Bobby Moore, Geoff Hurst and Martin Peters and then play against other true legends of the game in George Best, Bobby Charlton and Dennis Law was just phenomenal. We mustn't forget Pele in all this because a personal highlight for me was when we played Santos in the States and Ron asked me to man-mark him!

I played against George Best three times and, on two occasions, I did alright. The other time we got taught a lesson up at Old Trafford, losing 2-5. My theory is that great players decide on whether or not we mere mortals have a good game. If they bring their 'A' game, then we have no chance.

I'm a little bit surprised that Bobby didn't get into management a lot earlier and was very disappointed with the England set up, in so much as, he meant at least as much to England as Franz Beckenbauer meant to the German football federation. Beckenbauer was looked after and became the manager of the German national team. He was incredibly well respected and his experience and expertise was used to maximum benefit for German football. Even as a figurehead, Bobby would have had a tremendous impact on the psyche of the game in this country. Admittedly, he was only 51 when he passed away and might have been given a more prominent role in the England set up but there was no indication that the FA was planning such a move, was there? Bobby was certainly worth more than Oxford City and Southend United and I don't mean that in a disrespectful way to those clubs.

Some might think that Ron Greenwood could have utilised Bobby when he took over the England manager's role. I am no expert on the relationship between those two people but my hunch is that, while a mutual respect existed between them for their undoubted talents, that is as far as it went. They certainly weren't close friends.

In 1979, Bobby came over here to play for Seattle Sounders. Harry Redknapp was instrumental in getting Bobby to the United States. Jimmy Gabriel was the manager and Harry and I were the assistant coaches. Of course, you can't coach a player like Bobby Moore you just have to ensure his fitness levels are good and say: 'Go out there and do what you do well.'

He was well past his prime of course but he was absolutely first-class in the way that he carried himself. He really was tremendous. The club asked him where he wanted to live and obviously he could have chosen anywhere but he asked to be wherever the other players were. He seriously wanted to be one of the lads and really and truly assimilated himself into the players' community.

I remember being with Bobby out there and we were chatting about our days at West Ham and he told me that in all the time he was there Ron Greenwood never once said 'well done' to him. Now when you think of how many matches he played for West Ham and how many good games he played, that really was an amazing thing to hear. He was expected to be brilliant in every game and that was taken for granted but Bobby's words made it clear that no matter who you are – the very best or otherwise – you still need a pat on the back. It is a lesson for people in all walks of life, not just managers and coaches but everyone – a bit of praise when someone has done something worthy of praise is essential.

I'm delighted that statues of Bobby have been erected at Upton Park and Wembley Stadium. What would be magnificent for his memory, would be for all the players that knew him to be reunited for the first game in the Olympic Stadium. It is always a fantastic feeling for the players to go back to West Ham and hopefully bump into some old friends. What a commendable project this is to keep alive the memory of someone who contributed so much to the game of football, not only at West Ham United but for England and globally as well.

I played for West Ham and Bournemouth and have coached in both England and the United States but I think you always remember your first club and to be involved at West Ham throughout the 1960s with players like Bobby Moore, Geoff Hurst and Martin Peters was a privilege.

When I think of Bobby Moore I think of a classy footballer, a first class role model and an inspiration for all players, young and old. It is not a bad life's legacy that everyone wants to be like you.

Bobby Howe

During a visit from his home in Seattle.

53 – COLIN MACKLEWORTH

Born: Bow, London, March 24, 1947

Position: Goalkeeper

Games played with Bobby Moore: 3 (1966-67)

Games played for West Ham United: 3 (1966-67)

First game with Bobby Moore (Debut): December 27, 1966 Blackpool (h) W 4-0

Scorers: West Ham United: Byrne, Moore, Hurst, Peters

West Ham United: Mackleworth, Bovington, Burnett, Peters, Brown, Moore, Brabrook, Dear, Byrne, Hurst, Sissons

Blackpool: Waiters, Thompson, Hughes, Fisher, James, McPhee, Skirton, Robson, Charnley, Suddick, Lea

Colin Mackleworth is the only West Ham United goalkeeper to keep a clean sheet on his debut during the Bobby Moore era. It came at home to Blackpool in a 4-0 victory on December 27, 1966. For good measure, Moore scored from 30 yards.

Somewhat unfairly, Mackleworth is largely remembered for being on the receiving end of a 1-6 defeat against Champions-elect Manchester United at the Boleyn Ground, led by a rampant Dennis Law, George Best and Bobby Charlton, just four months after his debut. Mackleworth is philosophical about the experience: 'I went to the right club – I just didn't do the right things!'

Colin joined West Ham as an apprentice in April 1962 after playing for East London, Middlesex and London Boys. His finest moment at the club came when he lined up with the 1963 FA Youth Cup final team which overcame Liverpool.

Former team-mate Trevor Hartley considers Colin to be: 'The best half-volley kicker at the club. Jim Standen was excellent at it and so was Colin. Rather than hit high balls to me, which I'm not going to win, he would ping them to me like an arrow which was easier for me to control. I really liked Colin and he was very good mates with Harry Redknapp. They drove everywhere together.'

Former West Ham forward Dave Llewelyn expands on Mackleworth's friendship with Redknapp: 'Sometimes after training at Chadwell Heath, we used to have a race to see who could get back to Upton Park the quickest. Now I didn't have a car, so I would sometimes jump in with Harry and Colin and they would be tearing down the Barking Road, over-taking cars and when they got to East Ham Town Hall, rather than wait for the lights, Colin would cut through the car park and come out the other side!

Fellow Youth Cup winner Trevor Dawkins is another with fond memories of Mackleworth: 'He was a very steady goalkeeper and I actually thought he would have done a lot better. I always felt confident when he was in goal behind me. He actually dated the Queen of the Isle of Dogs!'

With the youth team holding the FA Cup – Stevenage 1964.

Colin was transferred to Leicester City in late-November 1967, where the departure of Gordon Banks seemed likely to herald a prime opportunity for regular first team football. However, the fates once again conspired to deal a cruel hand as Mackleworth became an understudy to none other than Peter Shilton, one of the greatest goalkeepers in the history of the game.

Colin is one of four Hammers from the Bobby Moore era to enter the police force after his playing days. Alan Dickie, John Dryden and Bill Kitchener are the other three. Colin's final job before retirement was as an undertaker for Dignity in 2012. He moved from Leytonstone to Suffolk in order to maximise the opportunities for relaxation. His good pal Harry Redknapp stays in touch and recently invited him along for a catch up at a Queens Park Rangers match. The pair were again reunited in August 2014 for a gathering of the 1963 FA Youth Cup winning team.

One of the big highlights during my time at West Ham came when we won the FA Youth Cup in 1963. We had also won the London Minor Cup, an Augsburg Tournament trophy and the South East Counties League award. During the photo-shoot for the 1963-64 season Ron Greenwood asked for the FA Youth cup we had won to be included in the first team photo. I have a clear memory of Mooro coming up to me afterwards and saying: 'Ron thinks more of the youth team than he does the first team.'

Bobby was great to me on my debut against Blackpool. I didn't know I was playing until an hour before kick-off but I remember

With Bobby and Martin Peters in action against Denis Law of Manchester United, May 1967.

That game against George Best.

Mooro coming over to me after the game and saying: 'Well done, Macca.' That doesn't sound like much but it meant a lot to me.

Out of all the experienced players Mooro was always helping me and, even after the 1-6 defeat against Manchester United in 1967, he never lambasted me. In fact there was a photo in the Daily Mail which showed Bobby looking after me when I was injured in that game.

An interesting caveat to the Manchester United story is that in later life, when I left the police force, I became an undertaker for the firm Dignity and one of the final jobs I handled was preparing the coffin of George Best before it was taken back to Northern Ireland.

The game against Manchester United was a low point in my career but just a few days later Jim Standen asked me to play in an Evening Standard five-a-side competition at

Wembley Arena. Jim said he didn't like playing on the hard surface and that I would be on telly because it was to be shown on Sportsview. I jumped at the chance and I played with Mooro, Martin Peters, Ron Boyce and Geoff Hurst.

We beat QPR 3-0 in the first game and I didn't even touch the ball. Some chap from the Evening Standard came into our dressing room with a wad of notes and gave us each £20. I was only on £12-a-week at the time so I was over the moon. A few of the West Ham players had come along to watch including Jim himself, who was pleased I'd won a few quid and I said I'd get him a drink afterwards.

Next up we beat Crystal Palace, 2-1, and once again the chap came in with an even bigger wad of notes and gave us all £30 each. I can remember Jim looking a bit sick at this stage because he saw that I had hardly touched the ball. In the final we beat Arsenal easily – 4-0 – and I ended up taking home £150 for doing next to nothing. We were all celebrating when all of a sudden Johnny Byrne came into our dressing room absolutely beaming. Budgie had played that night for Crystal Palace and being young and naïve I thought it a bit odd that he was so elated having lost in the earlier rounds. Mooro explained to me that Budgie had put £500 on us at 7/1 to win the tournament! He took us all to the Playboy club in Park Lane and treated us to whatever we wanted.

Bobby did the little things really well and once when we went on tour to Switzerland, Harry Redknapp and I were in a bar having a quiet drink when Mooro came over and asked us what we were up to. We had a brief chat and he disappeared only to return shortly afterwards with two bottles of champagne. 'Enjoy your evening lads' he said and off he went.

I appeared in an advert with Mooro. We were down at the ground and he asked me if I wanted to earn a few bob being in an advert for liquid hair cream called Vitalis. Bobby Howe and Trevor Hartley were also in it and we had to walk into the showers at the ground with towels around us while Bobby did the talking. I remember it was supposed to take half-a-day but ended up taking two days. Ron Greenwood wasn't amused at all but we had a great time. When it was shown on the television, Bobby took a load of stick up at places like Manchester and Liverpool.

When my football career ended I became a policeman and was actually on duty at Wembley Stadium for the 1975 FA Cup final between West Ham and Fulham. It was quite surreal really for me to be in a copper's uniform and Bobby in a Fulham shirt. There was one stage when I caught the ball and threw it back to Frank Lampard. 'Hello Macca!' he said.

Bobby got into coaching with Harry Redknapp at Oxford City and I went along once to watch them play Aveley, which is close to Romford, where I was living at the time. I had always been very close to Harry and he always says I was the reason he joined West Ham instead of Arsenal. Anyway, I hadn't seen him for a while so I went over to the game but they lost 0-2. Harry has never handled defeat particularly well so he wasn't in the mood to hang around for a drink but I had a nice chat with Bobby.

In the 1980s, my wife met Mooro at a book signing in Debenhams and it was a measure of the man that he took the time to ask all about me and whether or not I was still in the police force. He always had such a strong and genuine interest in the welfare of others.

The last time I saw him was in Bethnal Green in the 1980s. I was on my way to the police station and he was standing outside The Salmon and Ball pub. He recognised me and came over for a chat.

Colin Mackleworth

'Macca'.

54 – BILL KITCHENER

Born: Arlesey, Bedfordshire, November 3, 1946

Position: Left-back

Games played with Bobby Moore: 12 (1967)

Games played for West Ham United: 12 (1967)

First game with Bobby Moore (Debut): March 18, 1967 Nottingham Forest (a) L 0-1

Scorer: Nottingham Forest: Baker

Nottingham Forest: Grummitt, Hindley, Winfield, Hennessey, McKinlay, Newton, Lyons, Barnwell, Baker, Wignall, Storey-Moore

West Ham United: Standen, Burkett, **Kitchener**, Peters, Heffer, Moore, Brabrook, Boyce, Bennett*, Hurst, Sissons, Sub: Redknapp*

William Harry Kitchener was at West Ham United between 1962-67 and was another to play in the famous FA Youth Cup final against Liverpool in 1963. Kitchener was almost six years younger than Moore and was 19-years-old when making his debut alongside him – away at Nottingham Forest on March 18, 1967.

Previously, Kitchener had signed apprentice forms on May 16, 1962, having captained the Bedfordshire schools side and he became a full professional in November 1963, just after his 17th Birthday.

Former team-mate Trevor Hartley recalls Bill: 'He had a good left foot and Ron Greenwood liked him. Afterwards, he came down to Bournemouth and we got on very well together. He came to my wedding.'

Harry Redknapp still lives near Bill and recalled a funny incident with his former youth team-mate: 'A few years ago I went to watch my local village cricket team in Bournemouth and I parked up on the quietest country lane you are ever likely to see, when this copper pulled up on his motorbike, got off and started telling me I was in breach of some parking law and that he

was going to have to fine me. I started protesting but when he took his helmet off it was 'Kitch.' Bloody sod, had me right over!'

Kitchener also had spells at both Torquay United with former Hammer Frank O'Farrell and AFC Bournemouth with Bobby Moore's great friend, John Bond. Sadly, a back

Bill's testimonial at AFC Bournemouth with Bobby Moore, March 13, 1973.

injury cut short Bill's football career. Bond wasted no time arranging a testimonial for his tall defender. It took place at Dean Court, against a full-strength West Ham team led by Bobby Moore. The game was played in March 1973, just one year before Bobby was to leave West Ham.

After his playing days, Bill spent a total of 33 years as a police constable and civilian police worker with both the Hampshire and Dorset police forces. He is now enjoying retirement near Christchurch, Bournemouth. Two replacement hips, a replacement knee and a replacement ankle have not prevented him from using both the gym and swimming pool to keep fit. Bill has a love of dogs and other hobbies include cycling, gardening and antiques. He enjoys the occasional P&O cruise as well as a nice glass of red wine.

Bobby Moore was the tops and I was in awe of him. I was just a country boy from Bedfordshire and it felt like all the players at West Ham were city slickers. Bobby was so authoritative you just couldn't help but look up to him. I used to travel from my home town of Arlesey in Bedfordshire so didn't do much socialising at West Ham.

As a kid, I only ever went to watch one game – to see the great Stanley Matthews play for Stoke City against Luton Town – and then all of a sudden I found myself at Upton Park playing with the England captain.

Getting the better of Derek Dougan of Wolves.

Bobby was like a god to me. I only spoke to him when he spoke to me. It was so great to play with him because he did everything right and he never gave the ball away. He was just the boss, wasn't he? He was a stalwart, a gentleman and someone to model your game on. He knew a lot about coaching and how the game should be played.

I played my debut at Nottingham Forest and we ended up losing 0-1 late on. The game was so fast and furious, it was energy-sapping stuff. I played left-back so it helped having

Bobby close to me in that game because he paced himself so much better and I learned from that. I played well and we went on a bit of a winning run taking maximum points from our next three matches.

One of the big highlights for me was playing with Bobby against Denis Law, George Best and Bobby Charlton at Old Trafford. I must admit to feeling a bit anxious because I was expecting it to be even faster than the Forest game but it was so much slower. There was less frenetic movement and more skill. Law, Best and Charlton each scored and we lost 0-3.

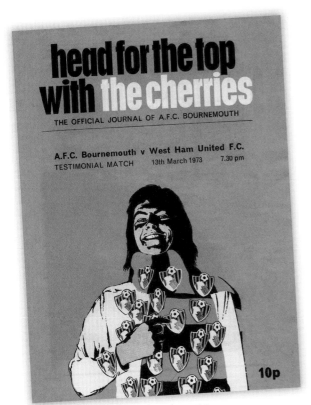

March 13, 1973. Bill Kitchener's tesitmonial programme versus West Ham United.

I never went out socially with Bobby and, to be honest, I was so in awe of him I found it difficult to talk to him. Harry Redknapp got on really well with him. They were East End boys, whereas I was a kid from the sticks and a bit quieter. Bobby was so reliable and was always thinking ahead and analysing the game. He let me know what I was expected to do and because of that I felt part of a solid unit. He was a natural born leader. West Ham was a club full of characters when I was there and they all looked up to Bobby. Everyone respected him.

Another big highlight was playing against Real Madrid in the Houston Astrodome during a visit to the United States. It was an exhibition game, which we lost 2-3, but playing against the likes of their captain Francisco Gento was unforgettable. I felt really tired on the flight home but played in West Ham's

next match – a 0-1 defeat at home to Leeds United. After the game I discovered I had German measles. I bet Bobby didn't play football with too many measles sufferers!

Bobby played in my testimonial match when I was at Bournemouth. The entire West Ham team came down to Dean Court and the atmosphere was terrific. Unfortunately, I couldn't play because I had a suspect back but I went out afterwards with Bobby and all the boys for a few beers. They made me feel so welcome and it was like I had never been away.

It was an absolute privilege to play with Bobby Moore. He was such a superb reader of the game. I couldn't help but learn from him in every game we played together. Up the Irons!

Bill Kitchener

'Kitch'.

55 – PAUL HEFFER

Born: Upton Park, London, July 21, 1947

Position: Centre-half

Games played with Bobby Moore: 16 (1967-70)

Games played for West Ham United: 17 (1967-70)

First game with Bobby Moore (Debut): March 18, 1967 Nottingham Forest (a) L 0-1

Scorer: Nottingham Forest: Baker

Nottingham Forest: Grummitt, Hindley, Winfield, Hennessey, McKinley, Newton, Lyons, Barnwell, Baker, Wignall, Storey-Moore

West Ham United: Standen, Burkett, Kitchener, Peters, **Heffer**, Moore, Brabrook, Boyce, Bennett,* Hurst, Sissons Used Sub: Redknapp*

Paul Victor Heffer has enjoyed a lifetime association with West Ham United. He played 16 games with Bobby Moore spread over five seasons and was almost seven years his junior.

Moore never forgot Heffer and gave him his first major role in coaching – at Southend United in the early 1980s.

Heffer's former youth team-mate, Tony Carr, subsequently installed him as Assistant Academy Director at West Ham

Setting off to America in 1969. L-R Ferguson, Stephenson, Boyce, Charles, Sissons, Dear, Brooking, Moore, Heffer, Redknapp, Peters and Howe.

They Played With Bobby Moore – The West Ham Years

Paul Heffer thwarting the attacking intentions of Manchester United's Denis Law.

over 20 years ago and Paul has seen a steady stream of young talent fall under his charge ever since.

Born in Upton Park, Heffer soon moved to Southend where he played schoolboy football, eventually signing professional forms for the Hammers in August 1965. He played 15 league games and two FA Cup ties for the club before a series of leg injuries forced early retirement from the game.

The club arranged a testimonial match for Paul which took place on April 4, 1973 against an Israel National XI. Although the Israeli international, Mordechai Spiegler, did not play in the game, he had been training with West Ham and was instrumental in arranging the match. Speigler did not play for West Ham United but was a forerunner to the other Israelis who have pulled on the first team shirt – Eyal Berkovic, Yossi Benayoun and Yaniv Katan.

Whilst at West Ham Paul got on particularly well with both Dave Llewelyn and Trevor Hartley. His nickname was 'Spangles.'

Today, Paul lives in Southend with his wife, Lorraine, a former hockey player for Essex. They have three children; John, Steve (a former West Ham youth player) and Jane. There is also a very healthy future generation of Hammers

with their six grandchildren; twins Isabella & Jessica plus Liberty, Sam, Ronnie and Jack.

Paul shared his memories of Bobby Moore at Chadwell Heath:

West Ham United was my team and Bobby Moore was my idol. I first went to Upton Park in the late 1950s, when old Ernie Gregory, Malcolm Musgrove and John Dick were in the side. Vic Keeble was my first hero. Everyone seemed to walk to the matches back then. I was from a large family and about 20 of us would stand on the North Bank and because I was so young and so small they would pick me up and pass me down to stand on the beer crates at the front. At the end of the game I'd be picked up again and handed back to my family and they'd walk to their various homes in Green Street, Plashet Road, Creedon Road, Raymond Road and Gwendon Avenue. My grandmother had 11 children so we were scattered all over the place.

I had a memorable initiation at West Ham. Basically, as a youngster you weren't allowed in the first team dressing room unless, of course, you were tidying it up or collecting the dirty shirts. If you were invited in, you knew you had made it.

When Ron first picked me, I noticed the first team players were being super kind but it was all just a front for their cunning plan. Alan Sealey was the main ring-leader but Martin Peters and Geoff Hurst also invited me in and sat me down. I had never been in there on a matchday before and had no idea that I was sitting in Bobby's area. When the great man came in, he gave me a right dressing down and was asking me who the hell I thought I was? I can still hear him today: 'You've been here five minutes and you think you can sit in my place!' Then of course all the players just had a big laugh at my expense so you can imagine how I felt. They set me up good and proper with that one because everyone knew Bobby was my hero. I had grown up at Upton Park, I had his picture on my bedroom wall and when he walked past me I was trembling with nerves.

Later on, Bobby got himself involved with people he shouldn't have been involved with and lost a lot of money which is why he had to make the move to Fulham, to keep his finances afloat really.

With Bobby, everyone says he lacked pace, which is true, but the first five yards were in his head.

The job with Bobby at Southend came about when a mutual friend of ours, Dave Patience, called me up to say that they were looking for a coach and that Bobby knew me and wanted me to take the role. That was the start of everything for me and I have been in coaching ever since, mainly at West Ham.

I would say I learned a lot of my coaching from Ron Greenwood and John Lyall and that Bobby gave me another chance to employ that knowledge at Southend United, working with the youth team. But for Bobby I would probably have carried on as a greengrocer which is what I was doing before I went to Roots Hall.

Bobby wasn't having a very good time at Southend United and I remember he came to me for a chat around the time of the 1986 World Cup, when he had received offers of a role in media. He said he could either be Bobby Moore the World Cup winner and go back on radio and TV as a pundit or be Bobby Moore the failed Southend United manager. So he said he was leaving and wished me the best of luck.

I always like to think that Bobby Moore had an input – even though he wasn't here – on the development of players such as Rio Ferdinand, Frank Lampard, Joe Cole, Michael Carrick and others. Bobby gave me my first major job in coaching and what I learned from him, I have tried to pass on to others.
Paul Heffer

Part of the West Ham United Academy – a link to the Bobby Moore era.

56 – TREVOR HARTLEY

Born: Doncaster, South Yorkshire, March 16, 1947

Position: Midfield/right-wing

Games played with Bobby Moore: 5 (1967-69)

Games played for West Ham United: 5 (1967-69)

First game with Bobby Moore (Debut): April 28, 1967 West Bromwich Albion (a) L 1-3

Scorers: West Bromwich Albion: Brown (2 pens), Astle
West Ham United: Bennett

West Bromwich Albion: Osborne, Fairfax, Williams, Talbot, Colquhoun, Brown, Foggo, Astle, Kaye, Hope, Clark

West Ham United: Standen, Charles, Burkett, Peters, Heffer, Moore, Redknapp, Bennett, **Hartley**, Hurst, Boyce

Trevor John Hartley was the first Yorkshire-born West Ham United player to line-up with Bobby Moore. He played five games in the first team with him and the experience has endured ever since.

Hartley signed professional for West Ham in summer 1964, having played for Islington Boys, London Grammar schools and London Youth. He played tennis at Wimbledon in the English Schools Championship and also excelled at both cricket and badminton.

He gained his full FA coaching badge at West Ham and has had a long and distinguished career in football both in England, Singapore, Malaysia and the United States of America.

Trevor (right) watching Geoff Hurst and John Holsgrove of Wolves, November 1968.

Hartley partners Geoff Hurst on his debut against West Bromwich Albion at The Hawthorns in April 1967.

He left West Ham for AFC Bournemouth in 1969 and managed the Cherries in the mid-1970s following the departure of both John Bond and Ken Brown to Norwich City.

Today, Trevor is enjoying retirement in Bedfordshire. He still puts in a round of golf and meets up with his brother-in-law, Bobby Howe, who resides in America.

We were the blonds at the club. There was Mooro, George Andrew and myself. John Sissons claimed to be blond so we'll let him in as well! I think I was actually blonder than Bobby but it's nice to have one thing in common with the great man!

I met Bobby on my first day at the club. I went to the training ground at Chadwell Heath and he had just arrived in the car park with Alan Sealey. 'Sammy' gave me the nod and Bobby wished me all the best. He had something about him which was impressive. He was never late. He could drink like a fish and still be the first one in the following day. Other players, like Johnny Byrne didn't carry it off so well. They looked like they were struggling with a hangover but Bobby would be immaculate and totally engaged.

On the ball.

I was never in Bobby Moore's dressing room, I was always in with the reserve team. I also lived in Highbury so didn't really spend a lot of time with Bobby, socially.

It is strange the small things you see that stay with you for a lifetime. During my first training session with the first team, I remember seeing Bobby going down on one knee and dispossessing Martin Peters with his other leg. I just thought that was too easy but it couldn't have been because it was Martin Peters?

The only criticism I would have of Bobby is that sometimes he took chances passing the ball back to Jim Standen. But on those few occasions when he left it short, nobody ever said a word. Everyone admired him too much to criticise him. He expensively got caught in possession for England away at Poland in a World Cup qualifier in 1973 but it never gets mentioned for exactly the same reason.

I was one of the few players at West Ham to go and watch England in the 1966 World Cup finals. Ron Greenwood said to me how disappointed he was that more people from the club didn't go along to all the games at Wembley and White City. I was with a couple of school friends and we went to all the London matches. Ron just couldn't believe that with three of our boys in the England team, more West Ham players didn't go along to the matches. They were happy watching it on the television.

I only played five first team games at West Ham but I did set up a goal for Mooro in our 4-3 win over QPR in the 68-69 season. When I say 'set up' all I did was pass him the ball and he took it on a few strides before scoring from 25 yards. Ron Springett was in goal for them. Harry Redknapp scored a great volley to win it. There is film footage of it somewhere. A funny thing from that game was that I heard Bobby liked to take a warmish shower before a game so I started doing the same thing.

One year, we went on tour to the States. We were based in Baltimore and, for some reason, I was the only player who took his driver's licence with him. Therefore, I had the responsibility of driving the team minibus to the various venues. I got so much stick from Mooro and the lads because I was a bit sharp on the brakes and jerky on the clutch. They were shouting things at me like: 'We're all going to die!'

Bobby Moore was the best player I ever played with and Glenn Hoddle was the best player I ever coached.

I have played and coached all over the world but if anyone asks me what I did in football I always say: 'I played with Bobby Moore.'

Trevor Hartley

Trevor with the programme from his favourite match – a 4-3 win over QPR.

57 – DOUG EADIE
September 22, 1946 – January 7, 2013

Born: Edinburgh

Position: Midfielder

Games played with Bobby Moore: 2 (1967)

Games played for West Ham United: 2 (1967)

First game with Bobby Moore (Debut): May 9, 1967 Tottenham Hotspur (h) L 0-2

Scorers: Tottenham Hotspur: Greaves, Gilzean

West Ham United: Standen, Burnett, Charles, Bovington, Bickles, Moore, Peters, Boyce, Hurst, Sealey, **Eadie**

Tottenham Hotspur: Jennings, Kinnear, Knowles, Mullery, England, Mackay, Robertson, Greaves, Gilzean, Venables, Saul

Douglas Eadie was a member of the West Ham United reserve team that won the London Challenge Cup on November 20, 1967. He played in the final two league games of the 1966-67 season, at home to both Tottenham Hotspur and Manchester City, both of which included Bobby Moore in the line-up. He enjoyed only a brief spell at the club but the memories stayed with him throughout his fascinating life.

Eadie, who was spotted playing youth team football in Scotland, was 19 when he signed for West Ham on September 2, 1966.

Former West Ham physio Rob Jenkins provides some insight into the circumstances surrounding Eadie's arrival at West Ham: 'I used to pick up Kenny Dalglish when he came down from Celtic. He was about 16-years-old and he was with another lad called Jimmy Mullen. They were

Doug holding the London Challenge Cup in 1967.

staying in the Hartley Hotel at the top of Green Street by the junction with Romford Road. I used to drive them both to Chadwell Heath to train. Greenwood loved Dalglish and wanted to sign him but he was homesick so he went back to Scotland and joined Celtic. Everyone could see what a wonderful football player he was. Later on, Doug Eadie came down with Jimmy Lindsay. I would say Jimmy had a bit more skill than Doug although they were both good players. They weren't the most disciplined of boys and I know Doug had a disagreement with Ron because he called me up and said he didn't want to leave and could I do anything to change Ron's mind? I told him I was only the physio.'

Cutting in from the wing against Manchester City, May 1967.

Jimmy Lindsay also has very clear memories of Doug: 'He was a fellow jock and we played at least 30-40 reserve games together. We shared digs and I remember he and Frank Lampard didn't like each other and they had a fight on the training ground. Most Saturday nights, Dougie and I would be driving around, late on, and we always knew Rob Jenkins would be in a pub that would have a lock-in somewhere, so we would knock on the door and sure enough he would get us in.'

Eadie was one of the very first West Ham players to go out on loan. Under new rules which were introduced ahead of the 1967-68 season, Ron Greenwood sent him to Leyton Orient for the maximum period of three months. He was 20-years-old.

Eadie's life story after his playing career is a fascinating tale of alcoholism, poverty and then film and television success.

Doug Eadie passed away on January 7, 2013 and we extend our warmest gratitude to his son, David, for the following recollections:

My father would tell all that knew him about his days playing for the Hammers. He only had four photographs in his house, three of his grandchildren and one of him cutting in from the wing at the Boleyn Ground. They were his proudest achievements.

Bobby Moore wasn't just captain of the first team, he knew everyone in the reserves and the youth team. He was the captain of the whole club. My dad's impression of Bobby Moore was that he was a gentleman, a really, really nice guy and someone about whom he always spoke very highly. He said West Ham was a great family club where you

got to know the players' wives and went out socially with your team-mates. I played centre-half when I was a lad, so I used to love the stories my dad told me me about Bobby Moore. People often go on about Franz Beckenbauer and how brilliant he was but I have a theory that if you look at the way he played and the way he stroked the ball he had obviously been watching Bobby Moore.

Dougie played for Celtic reserves at the time of the great 'Lisbon Lions' team of 1967 and it was Jock Stein who sent him down to West Ham United for a trial. Ron Greenwood was looking for a winger that would eventually take over from an ageing John Sissons, and my father fitted the bill.

Dad thrived in London. He was put in comfortable digs with other apprentices and was looked after by a matronly, club-approved, landlady. He had new friends such as Harry Redknapp, who showed him the sights of London as well as how to have a good night out! Harry always stayed in touch with my father.

He was surrounded by great players like Martin Peters and Geoff Hurst, a superb club captain in Bobby Moore and a good, yet fickle manager, in Ron Greenwood.

Dougie was a regular in the reserves and youth team, often scoring and, more often than not, being a provider for the prolific Trevor Brooking. The team was successful, winning the London Challenge Cup in 1967 when overcoming giant-killers Dagenham in the final.

Ron Greenwood was pushing the youths through to the first team, too. Most of the heralded 1963 FA Youth Cup winners got their chance. It sent out the right message – with the right application everyone could play in the top division. Eventually, the call to Ron Greenwood's office came and Dougie was told that he was in the first team for the penultimate game of the 1966-67 season against Spurs. At the time, they had Jimmy Greaves, Alan Gilzean and Dave Mackay, but Dougie still felt confident. After all, we had Bobby Moore, Geoff Hurst and Martin Peters.

That Saturday, Dougie ran for every ball and tackled like a lion, high on nervous energy. Even his mistakes were paying off. After mis-kicking a corner kick, the ball soared nearer the centre spot than the penalty spot, but luckily it landed on the foot of Martin Peters, who volleyed a 30-yard shot just over the bar. Ron Greenwood mentioned, during his half-time rant at the team, that Dougie's corner kick to Martin Peters was the only moment of skill West Ham had demonstrated in the first half. My dad just supped his tea and said nothing! He managed to hit the post during the second half but West Ham failed to score, eventually losing 0-2, in front of a 35,000 crowd.

Dougie had done enough to keep his place in the first team for the following week against Manchester City. This was West Ham's final game of the season, but little did Dougie know that this was to be his last for the Hammers, too.

Overall it was a dull game which ended in a 1-1 draw, although Dougie had played well. After the game, he was called in to the manager's office. He'd played well, so he wasn't expecting any disappointments. Unfortunately, Douglas had forgotten the fickle nature of Ron Greenwood:

'Tottenham have made a bid for you,' said the manager.

'Oh, really?' came Dougie's reply.

'But you're not going. League rules mean I have to tell you about approaches but we own your contract so we say what happens, and you're staying here for now.'

My dad accepted it but as he left Greenwood's office he asked a question that effectively ended his time at the club: 'How much are they offering to pay me?'

Ron told Dougie in no uncertain terms that by asking such a question he was being disloyal to the club. The following season Dougie found himself on loan to Leyton Orient. He regretted asking that question to his final days.

An injury caused Dougie to retire from football and he found work with the Daily Record in Scotland, part of Robert Maxwell's dynasty. When Maxwell died in 1991 my dad lost his job and fell on very hard times. He developed a serious drinking habit.

Whilst battling his addiction and poverty, he realised that he must find himself some focus. A friend told him about the potential to earn money as an extra on television so he joined Equity, the actor's union, and secured the services of an agent. He then set off looking to start a new career.

Initially, he got parts in Trainspotting, Taggart, Monarch of the Glen and became the regular postman in Take the High Road. He then moved on to credited roles in The Plan Man starring Robbie Coltrane, Strictly Sinatra with Ian Hart and even played a murdered referee in the Taggart episode 'Football Crazy.' In total, he appeared in 86 films and TV productions. He was still a handsome man and managed to get modelling work well into his fifties. He became the face on many Prudential posters and billboards at this time.

Sadly, Dougie never did overcome his hardest battle – against alcohol – which ravaged the last two decades of his life. Some days he won and some days he lost. He was forever a loving father and grandfather, who would do any job to help support his family. We later found out that before he died he took a train down to London and watched the Hammers for one last time.

He sadly passed away on January 7, 2013. He was discovered in bed next to an unfinished script of what would have been his best ever work – that of his life story.

David Eadie

Doug Eadie the actor.

Ken Brown, the last survivor from Bobby Moore's debut in 1958, finally hangs up his West Ham boots in 1967.

Back row L-R Heffer, Bonds, Peters, Cushley, Ferguson, Bovington, Hurst, Kitchener, Moore. Front row L-R Redknapp, Brabrook, Boyce, Dear, Bennett, Charles, Sissons.

CHAPTER TEN
1967-68

Bobby Moore's total appearances (July 1967-June 1968): 64 games (6 goals)

League Division One: 40 (4 goals), England: 10, Friendlies: 8 (2 goals), FA Cup: 3, League Cup: 3

The summer tours included trips to Dublin, Finland, Switzerland and Germany. New signing Billy Bonds followed up his first appearance in Ken Brown's testimonial by playing in all eight games across the four countries. The other members of the party included Standen, Ferguson, J Charles, Peters, Heffer, Moore, Redknapp, Boyce, Dear, Hurst, Sissons, Kitchener, Brabrook, Bovington, Bennett, Cushley, Howe and Hartley.

Construction started on a new East Stand which, when completed, provided standing room for 4,000 fans and seating for another 3,500 supporters. The £150,000 estimated to build the stand was set to increase the ground capacity to 42,000. It was clearly time for change given the Chicken Run stand was the oldest remaining part of the Boleyn Ground.

The season was defined by a 12th place finish in the league and early exits in both the FA Cup, at home to Sheffield United, and League Cup, away at Huddersfield Town. One of the few highlights came when Geoff Hurst scored his 100th goal for the club.

On March 28, 1968 Bobby and Tina Moore's son Dean was born. The Moore family was complete.

At the Ilford Palais on April 23, Bobby received his third

End of an era.

Leading the Hammers out at Stamford Bridge in October, 1967.

Hammer of the Year award, ahead of both Trevor Brooking and Geoff Hurst.

Mention should be made of George Andrew, another of West Ham United's bright blond players. After four seasons at the club, George was transferred to Crystal Palace where he was reunited with both Johnny Byrne and Eddie Presland. He played two first team games for West Ham United but Moore was absent on both occasions.

Ron Greenwood made his biggest splash in the transfer market since his arrival at the club. Bobby Ferguson (£65,000), Billy Bonds (£50,000) and John Cushley (£10,000) wore the claret and blue for the very first time. Moore also played in the first-team debuts of Trevor Brooking and Frank Lampard, both of whom continued the club's impressive development of local talent.

Here is their story...

58 – BOBBY FERGUSON

Born: Ardrossan, Ayrshire, Scotland, March 1, 1945

Position: Goalkeeper

Games played with Bobby Moore: 229 (1967-73)

Games played for West Ham United: 276 (1967-79)

First game with Bobby Moore (Debut): August 19, 1967 Sheffield Wednesday (h) L 2-3

Scorers: West Ham United: Hurst, Peters
Sheffield Wednesday: Fantham, Ritchie, McCalliog

West Ham United: Ferguson, Bonds, Charles, Bovington, Cushley, Moore, Redknapp, Peters, Hurst, Boyce, Sissons

Sheffield Wednesday: Springett, Smith, Megson, Mobley, Ellis, Young, Fantham, McCalliog, Ritchie, Usher, Quinn*, Used Sub Eustace*

Robert Ferguson played more games with Bobby Moore than any other goalkeeper at West Ham United. He was one of the club's most controversial signings when Ron Greenwood decided to pay a record transfer fee of £65,000 for him instead of £50,000 for World Cup winner Gordon Banks. The transaction has been debated long and hard by West Ham fans the world over.

'Fester', as he was commonly known, was four years younger than Moore and joined the club on May 25, 1967. He had a good reputation having replaced Campbell Forsyth in goal at Kilmarnock and Tottenham's Bill Brown of Spurs in the Scotland team. In 1964-65 he had won the Scottish League with Kilmarnock and gained seven full caps with Scotland – one against a Bobby Moore-led England team.

Former West Ham United keeper Alan Dickie recalls the moment when Ferguson joined the Hammers: 'I was in goal for West Ham in a friendly against Kilmarnock and Bobby Ferguson played for them. Greenwood liked what he saw and signed him soon afterwards. Jimmy Hill came to watch me in that match and I subsequently joined Coventry City.'

Ferguson ended up spending 15-years at the club and enjoyed a testimonial – against Southampton – in 1981. He was famously replaced in goal by Moore, after suffering from concussion, during the epic League Cup semi-final second replay against Stoke City at Old Trafford in 1972.

He emigrated to Adelaide in the 1980s, and joined Adelaide City. He had various business interests including a marine complex and a carpet & tiling concern.

Today, Bobby still resides in Adelaide. He is semi-retired and combines a little bit of work with a little bit of golf. He plays off 12. There are four grandchildren and he still pursues another hobby close to his heart: 'I'm still trying to find the perfect red wine!'

Moore takes the gloves from Ferguson in the epic League Cup semi-final second replay versus Stoke City in 1972

I actually played against Bobby Moore when Scotland played England up at Hampden Park in 1966. There were only 120,000 people there! Someone sent me a photo of the teams walking out and I am behind John Greig and just a couple of feet away from Bobby. Little did I know then that we would become great mates.

Another early memory I have of Bobby also came before I joined West Ham United. I was on international duty with Scotland and Greig, the great Rangers' captain, was talking to me about Moore. At the time I was being linked with a move to West Ham and he said: 'That guy can really hurt you in a tackle. He's a very, very hard tackler.' I was surprised to hear that because Bobby didn't have a reputation of being a hard man but his timing was so good he could stop you dead in your tracks. He was a very strong man.

When I came down from

The two Bobbys guard West Ham's goal.

Scotland to join West Ham we went on a pre-season tour and Ron Greenwood paired me with Bobby so we roomed together. It was the best welcome I could have wished for and the first time I ever saw anyone fold their underpants!

Bobby was a dream to play with and was one of the few players to really listen to my instructions. Whatever you told him to do, move left or right or close down a player, he automatically did it.

Most West Ham fans remember the epic tussle we had against Stoke City in the League Cup semi-final second replay when I was concussed and Bobby took the gloves to face a penalty. I'm always grateful to Bobby for calling my wife Greer afterwards to let her know I was okay, just in case she heard something to alarm her on the television or radio. I don't recall much about the incident but remember the ball coming through and me diving at somebody's feet. The next thing I knew I was flat on my back. I was still groggy a couple of days afterwards. The other thing I remember from that night was back in the Midland Hotel and being under a table drowning my sorrows with Bobby over a bottle of brandy.

Afterwards, there was an end of season trip to Toronto, Canada and Ron Greenwood decided to take only two goalkeepers, Peter Grotier and myself. Peter fell sick on the tour which left me as the only option and Mooro said something funny that I always remember. We were at a party one night in a tower and were easily about 30-floors up on an outside balcony. I was looking over the edge and Bobby said: 'Don't fall over Bob – I'm not playing in goal for you again!'

Bobby was always doing kind things for people and I recall he bought a suit for a young reporter called Michael Hart, to help him get more interviews with the players. Michael ended up working for the London Evening Standard and has a great knowledge of West Ham.

Bobby had an instinct that made it natural for him to help other people and share great experiences. I remember I was wandering around a hotel in Berlin once and he called me over to introduce me to Franz Beckenbauer and his wife.

The last time I spoke to him was over here, in Australia. I think someone had brought him over on a promotional venture in the late 1980s and I got a few reporters here to track him down but he was a few hours flight away so instead I spoke to him on the phone. I think he was on a golf course at the time. As usual he asked me if I had everything I needed and I asked him the same. He seemed very happy.

Bobby loved a drink and loved a laugh. There wasn't any badness in the guy. He had a superb sense of humour and you could see a twinkle in his eye when he was being sarcastic or mischievous. You just knew he was laughing inside behind that cool façade.

His favourite joke was about a guy who came out of the pub and jumped into his car and started hitting cars all over the place. He mounted the pavement and knocked down people before smashing through a shop window. The cops arrived, grabbed him and asked him if he was drunk to which he answered: 'Of course I'm pissed, what do you think I am a f****** stunt driver?'

Bobby was a funny man. He always had a gin & tonic in a tall glass with lots of ice and: 'Some limes please, sir. Thank you.'
Bobby Furguson

There are no shortage of memories from Ferguson's former team-mates:

Bobby Ferguson saved my life! We were over in Spain on tour and all on the beach. They had just pulled out some guy who had drowned and put him under a couple of deck chairs and left him there. We went into the sea but I can't swim very well and got caught in a rip tide, up to my neck. I was forcing myself back to shore one step at a time but I was being forced back out and found myself getting sucked under the water. I shouted out to Bobby Ferguson for help and he pulled me back in to where I could reach shore, otherwise I would have died.
Bertie Lutton

We went on a six week tour of the States and ended up in Bermuda. We had a competition to see who could grow the most facial hair while we were out there and Bobby Ferguson won it easily. I had this little wispy blond moustache but he looked like Black Beard!
Trevor Hartley

Aerial battle against Manchester City in November, 1968 under the watchful gaze of Bobby Moore and John Cushley.

I think even he was surprised when Greenwood spent £65,000 on him when we could have bought Gordon Banks for £50,000.
Jimmy Lindsay

Fester was my great mate at West Ham. We still keep in touch now. I'm half Scottish so we got on well and shared a room together, when we went on tour. He was a great reaction keeper.
Bobby Gould

'Fergy' saved more with his feet than he did with his hands and was one of the best strikers of the ball I have seen for a goalkeeper.
Tommy Taylor

I was thirteenth man for the second replay with Stoke City so travelled with the team. After Bobby Ferguson sustained an injury, Rob Jenkins, the physio, took him to the tunnel and asked both me and Johnny Ayris to throw some balls at him to see the seriousness of the concussion. We were throwing these balls at him and they were bouncing off his head and shoulders. His eyes were rolling in his head and he was completely out of it.
Joe Durrell

At home in Adelaide with his wife Greer and their family.

59 – BILLY BONDS

Born: Woolwich, London, September 17, 1946

Position: Defender/Midfielder

Games played with Bobby Moore: 287 (1967-74)

Games played for West Ham United: 794 (1967-88)

Honours with Bobby Moore: Hammer of the Year 1971, 1974

First game with Bobby Moore (Debut): August 19, 1967 Sheffield Wednesday (h) L 2-3

Scorers: West Ham United: Hurst, Peters
Sheffield Wednesday: Fantham, Ritchie, McCalliog

West Ham United: Ferguson, **Bonds**, Charles, Bovington, Cushley, Moore, Redknapp, Peters, Hurst, Boyce, Sissons

Sheffield Wednesday: Springett, Smith, Megson, Mobley, Ellis, Young, Fantham, McCalliog, Ritchie, Usher, Quinn*, Used Sub Eustace*

William Arthur Bonds took over the captaincy from Bobby Moore – legend replacing legend.

Bonds started his football journey with Woolwich Boys and Kent Boys. He worked for a propeller-making factory after school but soon signed for Charlton Athletic and turned professional in 1962. The £50,000 paid to the Valiants for his services on May 13, 1967 stands as one of the best signings in the club's history.

Billy played 794 games for West Ham United, captained the side to two FA Cup successes, a European Cup Winners Cup final, three promotions as a player and manager and left the fans with a multitude of indelible memories. He was only denied a full England cap due to injury – twice.

Bonds was five years younger than Moore and played with him in almost 300 games, most notably in the epic, four-game, League Cup semi-final, tussle with Stoke City in 1972.

Bonds set a new standard at West Ham United. He overtook Moore's all-time appearance record during the 1982-83 season and became the club's oldest-ever player when running out for his final game on April 30, 1988, at Southampton, aged 41 years and 226 days. On May 8, 2013 the club presented him with a Lifetime Achievement award.

Bill has finally hung up his running boots and, instead, dabbles with an American Football fantasy team and reads the occasional cowboy book. He is enjoying retirement with his wife, Lynne and their family, both in Chiselhurst, Kent and at their holiday home in Dorset.

The West Ham faithful still queue in their droves to see him at various reunions in both London and Essex. In keeping with Bill's high regard for the history of West Ham, he enthusiastically gave his time to meet and talk about Bobby Moore.

The first time I met Mooro, I was just a kid of about 14-years-old. I was at Moatbridge School with my brother, Michael,

and our football team had won a cup. A relatively unknown Bobby Moore came along to present the medals. I didn't really know who he was but when he came in he looked like a film star. I was living on a council estate at the time and was struck by the presence of this blond-haired, smartly dressed man with a beautiful blonde woman on his arm. Some of the boys were a bit disappointed that nobody famous had turned up!

I was a Charlton Athletic supporter as a kid and the first time I came across West Ham was in 1964. I was on the ground staff at The Valley and we were drawn against them in the third round of the FA Cup. West Ham had a lot of star players in that team and were captained by Mooro. They beat us 3-0 on their way to winning the cup.

When I first started playing for West Ham I wore the Number 2 shirt and it was so reassuring to look across at Bobby in that Number 6 jersey, always unflustered regardless of the game. He wasn't a bawler or a shouter. He didn't need to be. I think most players thought: 'Christ, I'm playing with Bobby Moore.' That was enough. He was that special.

We were very different types of player. Bobby wasn't a power-tackler, he was more of a Cool Hand Luke type whereas people have described me more as a warrior-type, a viking or a gladiator. He used to call me 'Daffy' after Daffodil, the Cockney rhyming slang for Bill.

I never saw Bobby in a bad mood or angry. I even saw Trevor Brooking swipe John McDowell once!

We had a really good side back then but probably suffered from a lack of discipline and depth in the squad. I remember relations between Ron Greenwood and Mooro being at a low ebb around then, when on a pre-season tour of Germany, Bobby injured his leg coming home after the curfew and climbing over a fence. He'd caught it on some barbed wire. Although they had a professional respect for each other, I think that is as far as it went.

Moatbridge School Team – Billy (far left) next to his brother Michael (bottom left) with Bobby Moore at the back.

Another big memory I have of Mooro came in the four matches we had against Stoke City in the semi-final of the League Cup. We put so much into those games and, personally, I felt I had reached a peak in my own performance over those four games. I was running everywhere and gave it my all and Rob Jenkins, our physio, is right when he says it was the only time I cried after a football match. The defeat at Old Trafford was a bitter pill to take. We would have played Chelsea in the final at Wembley. What a day for the fans that would have been? But it wasn't meant to be and Stoke, who had a good side, went on to beat Chelsea in the final.

Obviously, a big moment came up at Old Trafford when Mooro went in goal after Bobby Ferguson was concussed and Clyde Best didn't fancy taking the gloves. It was a brave decision and not one I would have taken. You can ask me to play anywhere on the pitch and I'll give it a go but not in goal. I just couldn't do it. All credit to Mooro for stepping up. He saved Mike Bernard's penalty but sadly could not get the rebound.

Another big occasion with Mooro came in the 1975 FA Cup final after he had moved to Fulham. I've got to be honest about it, on that day we wanted to stuff 'em, with or without Mooro. I was only 70% fit but John Lyall wanted me out there and I don't think we played particularly well and only won it because of a couple of goalkeeping errors. After the game, Mooro was the first one we consoled.

The last time I spoke with Mooro was when I was manager of West Ham and we were playing up at Grimsby in November 1992. He was commentating, with Jonathan Pearce, for Capital Gold and we drew 1-1. After the game I came out of the dressing room and sat on the wall outside. The stadium was empty and it was freezing cold and I heard this shout: 'Bonzo!' It was Mooro. He was wearing a flat cap and I'd never seen him with one like that before. He looked very ill and had lost a lot of weight. We sat there together for 10 minutes or so discussing the game and football in general and then he said he had better be off back down the motorway. Now, he would have got home about 2am or 3am in the morning and I often think to myself: 'Why on earth was Bobby Moore doing something like that?'

After Mooro passed away, West Ham's next match was up at Roker Park against Sunderland. I was the manager at the time. Now, Sunderland fans can make a lot of noise, up there, but it was the most impeccably observed minute's silence I have ever witnessed. Not one person made a sound. I've always felt a lot of respect for Sunderland fans and, because of that I will always remember that game. It was even more poignant to me than the tribute at Upton Park in our next game when Geoff Hurst and Martin Peters carried the floral Number 6 shirt to the centre circle before the game with Wolverhampton Wanderers.

One of the biggest regrets I have from my management days is that I never brought Mooro back to West Ham in some kind of ambassadorial role. To have a man like him around the club for the kids to see and look up to would have been

On the goal line with Bobby Moore against Leeds United, December 1968. Bobby Ferguson and John Cushley try to contain Billy Bremner and Jack Charlton.

fantastic. He represented how far you can go in the game. I had a lot of influence at the club back then and it would have been so easy for me to bring him back but it simply never occurred to me. Can you imagine me asking Bobby Moore, who knew all the film stars and everybody, if he wanted a job? He would probably have just laughed at me? But as it turned out, that wouldn't have been the case at all and I realised this when I met his first wife, Tina, a few years back and she kindly signed her book for my wife, Lynne. Tina tells how their daughter Roberta was out with Bobby when he was very ill during the final few months and some fella came up to Mooro and told him how much he loved him and what he had meant to him. Roberta said it really affected her dad and he was so pleased that someone had said that to him. When I heard that I was shocked that he may have left this world uncertain as to his status in the game and the incredible contribution he made. It was then that I started to think how I might have been able to have done that bit more for him.

I've never been one for that whole celebrity scene and I prefer to take people on their own merits. I wouldn't say I was close to Mooro but that was due to me not allowing myself to get too close to anyone really. I got on great with most of the lads and would go to the dogs or have a drink when we were away, but I preferred to go home after training and games at Upton Park. Having said that, out of all the footballers and film stars I've played with or met, Bobby was the one person I was in awe of. Maybe it was because of the impression he made on me when I was that young Moatbridge School kid?
Billy Bonds

Following are some player recollections of Billy Bonds:

I love Bonzo, which is why it is so disappointing to me that we probably won't talk again. I'd like to think we'll meet up again but I can't see it happening. I used to room with him. We were great mates but you know what happens. He left the club when he was manager and people started saying things and it bred ill feeling and you can't get back to where your friendship once was. When he left, I wanted to go back to Bournemouth, I didn't want to manage West Ham.
Harry Redknapp

The physical side of football has largely been removed from the current interpretation of the game but it was a major component during the 1960s and 70s in particular. There were some real hard men in the game but they co-existed with many players who had flare and skill in abundance. It was like beauty and the beast being played out on a football

Celebrations at the end of the 1975 FA Cup final, as Moore (far right) calls time on Wembley.

pitch sometimes. Consequently, many teams had protectors in their sides who made sure no real harm came to the ball-players. Billy was my protector on the pitch and without him around I am convinced my number of appearances would have been significantly reduced due to injury. Obviously, I thank Bill for that but wince at the amount of hard knocks he must have suffered for those around him.
Sir Trevor Brooking

I talk about him all the time and if I had to draw up a team sheet Billy would be the first name on it. I consider him very highly indeed.
Clyde Best

Billy was great, a fantastic guy, he was like a race horse, a very quick race horse. I remember him and Steve Kindon, the old Wolves player, who could run like lightning as well. Billy was even quicker than him, the man could catch pigeons. I always remember that after training he would be in his car and gone before I had even got in the shower!

He chucked me out of the card school. I was earning about £18 a week but could easily lose £30 on the coach to and from a game. Billy called an end to it because I was definitely gambling more than I should. I think I owed Billy some money

and he had already fallen out with Harry over money. Billy used to put his bets on with Harry and one day stood to win a lot of money – and I mean a lot of money – and Harry said he had forgotten to put them on. They didn't speak after that.
Jimmy Lindsay

I remember we were playing in a tournament in Spain and were up against a German or Spanish team, I can't recall precisely, and I was running for a ball with this big guy who was well over six feet tall. Anyway, he lost his balance and went over like a sack of s***. Then he started towering over me and threatening me. Billy Bonds came tearing over in a flash and grabbed the guy to keep him away from me but the bloke turned round and slapped him across the face. All hell let loose then and players piled in from everywhere.
Bertie Lutton

Before Ron Greenwood bought Billy Bonds, he wanted to sign John Gilchrist from Millwall but their manager, Benny Fenton, wanted too much money so we ended up getting Billy. John Gilchrist was absolutely gutted because he was desperate to play for West Ham and then he ended up having his career cut short due to injury.
Rob Jenkins

Bill was the great protector at West Ham. Each player was like his own son so he wouldn't let any harm come to them.
Pat Holland

The fittest person I have ever met in my life. He used to strip off and was like a god. He won all the races, all the sprints, everything. You name it and he won it.
Dave Llewelyn

You rarely got the better of Billy in a one-on-one but I think I frustrated him a bit in our practice matches. I didn't have the pace to take him on so would try to go past him with a one-two. Billy preferred the confrontation of someone trying to take him on.
Trevor Hartley

I owe my only hat-trick at West Ham to Billy Bonds. We were playing Tranmere in the League Cup and both Billy and I had scored two each. In the last minute we got a penalty and I heard Greenwood and Lyall in the dugout shouting: 'Don't give it to that twat!' But Bill handed me the ball and I hit it home. I've still got the ball indoors. Thanks Bill!

Bonzo loved a game of cards and I started playing with him, Trevor Brooking and Frank Lampard. If I had been winning I would stick a twenty pound note to my forehead and say: 'See you later, lads!' They wouldn't have a chance to win it back, because I was the first off the train on my way home to Bristol. Bonzo was such a great captain and right up there with the best trainers you are ever likely to see. Simply phenomenal. I love him.
Bobby Gould

An unbelievable person, a family man through and through. Always the first to arrive and the first to leave. An absolute monster of a player.
Tommy Taylor

I was regularly the 13th man so I went with the team to many games and I remember going to the old Baseball Ground in the year Derby County won the league. It was a mid-week game and Billy Bonds came up to me and gave me 20 or 30 tickets and said: 'Joe, go outside and find as many West Ham fans as

you can and give them these tickets.' I went out in the old backstreets around the Baseball Ground and looked around for Hammers scarves and gave them all away.

I know West Ham fans revere Billy but I sometimes wonder if they truly know just how much he did for them and the club.
Joe Durrell

Finally, a fan's eye view…
Everyone knows that Billy Bonds was famous for being the first one out of the club after a game. He would grab a four-pack of lager and shoot home through the Blackwall Tunnel. But there was one occasion, when the club invited all the great players from Mooro's era to mark the opening of the Bobby Moore Stand in 1994. Billy stood in the bar afterwards chatting with the great Budgie Byrne until the early hours of the morning.
Terry Connelly

The great Billy Bonds.

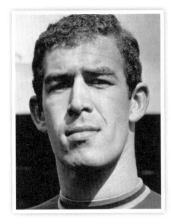

60 – JOHN CUSHLEY
January 21, 1943 – March 24, 2008

Born: Blantyre, Lanarkshire

Position: Centre-half

Games played with Bobby Moore: 43 (1967- 70)

Games played for West Ham United: 46 (1967-70)

First game with Bobby Moore (Debut): August 19, 1967 Sheffield Wednesday (h) L 2-3

Scorers: West Ham United: Hurst, Peters
Sheffield Wednesday: Fantham, Ritchie, McCalliog

West Ham United: Ferguson, Bonds, Charles, Bovington, **Cushley**, Moore, Redknapp, Peters, Hurst, Boyce, Sissons

Sheffield Wednesday: Springett, Smith, Megson, Mobley, Ellis, Young, Fantham, McCalliog, Ritchie, Usher, Quinn*, Used Sub: Eustace*

John Cushley spent three years at West Ham United and developed a close friendship with Bobby Moore. The Scotsman brought a combative style of play and a steel to the club, which was not typical of the famed 'West Ham way.'

Unfortunately for John, Ron Greenwood brought in another central-defender – Alan Stephenson – which restricted the number of games Cushley played. His final tally for the Hammers was 46 league and cup games but his experience with Bobby Moore remained with him for a lifetime.

Cushley studied for a Master of Arts in English and History at the University of Glasgow, two subjects that he would teach, both as a player and after his football career was over.

John had been at Celtic since 1960 and won a Championship medal in 1965-66. He was also a finalist in the Scottish Cup the previous season. The reality for John was that he was an understudy to one of Celtic's greatest ever centre-halves

Clearing his lines under the watchful gaze of Bobby Moore at Anfield in December 1968.

– Billy McNeil – so the move to West Ham United and the chance of regular first team football held big appeal.

Cushley signed for West Ham on July 17, 1967 having started his footballing journey with Lanarkshire Boys and Scottish Schools. He played twice for the Scotland Youth team and Ron Greenwood paid £25,000 for his services.

When playing at West Ham, Cushley taught part-time at St Bonaventures Grammar School in Forest Gate. He possessed a flair for languages, played golf and was a keen swimmer.

John was eventually transferred to Dunfermline Athletic in September 1970 and played out the rest of his career with The Pars and Dumbarton, eventually hanging up his boots in 1976. He returned to Upton Park, between 1993-95, as a scout during the Harry Redknapp era, before continuing his involvement with Celtic's youth set up.

In 2008 John Cushley passed away having been diagnosed with Motor Neurone Disease the previous year.

The following recollections of John's time with Bobby Moore were kindly provided by his wife, Mary, from the family home in Bothwell, near Glasgow:

John and Bobby were very good friends and I must add that I have very fond memories of Mooro, too. John had enormous respect and fondness for Bobby Moore but he never called him 'Bobby.' It was always 'Mooro.'

John and I got married on October 20, 1969 while he was at West Ham. We had met in Scotland at the Trocadero in Hamilton. He had spotted me out on the floor, asked me to dance and then said he would like to see me again. That is how we met.

When John was transferred to West Ham we were living on Clayhall Avenue in Barkingside. Unfortunately, Bobby couldn't make it to our wedding but he did send a very beautiful crystal decanter as a gift, which I still have to this day.

Very soon after our wedding there was a knock at the door and it was Bobby asking John to go out for a drink. John thought it wise to decline given that we were just a couple of days into our marriage!

We spent a lot of time in both Bobby and Tina's company. She was so glamourous and we really enjoyed our time together. West Ham was a very sociable club at that time and the players' and their wives spent a lot of time together at various functions and social gatherings. It was great fun!

John bought a beautiful pale blue jaguar which, apparently, had previously belonged to Sean Connery. Bobby was instrumental in ensuring that John got it.

John had a great time at West Ham and was very good friends with John Charles and Brian Dear. In fact, 'Charlo' and his wife, Carol, were very hospitable people and they used to let me stay with them before John and I found our own place after we were married. They all came to our wedding at the Silvertrees Hotel up in Bothwell, near Glasgow. It was a place that John and I used to frequent both for Jazz nights and its lovely restaurant.

Bobby Moore's style was another aspect that impressed John. One day he came home looking very handsome in

'Cush' the teacher.

a leather coat which he had bought from one of Bobby's businesses. He also had his shirts handmade, just like Bobby.

John was very much a part of the drinking culture at West Ham and would often go out with Bobby, John Charles, Brian Dear, Jimmy Lindsay and a few others. They made John very welcome at West Ham and his landlady, when he first arrived, was a lovely lady called Glad Gladstone. I think Bobby liked John's wicked sense of humour and his love of music.

John admired Ron Greenwood very much and viewed him as a gentleman. He always laughed that Ron was initially looking for a hard man to play in defence at West Ham but when he saw John in action he asked him not to play quite so hard! Poor John didn't know whether he was coming or going. But all said and done, John had tremendous respect for Ron.

John always maintained that one of the best performances he ever saw by a player was Mooro's against Brazil in the 1970 World Cup, especially after all the nonsense with the bracelet in Bogota beforehand.

After his playing days, John returned to Celtic where he was employed as their Health and Education officer, which he loved. It was very, very, out of the blue when he was diagnosed with Motor Neurone Disease. It is an illness which gradually prevents you from doing anything but John was so courageous in carrying on with his work with the youth at Celtic and his appearances on Celtic TV.

In the end, he had to stop driving and eventually became house-bound. He never complained at all which I found so inspiring and amazing. I've heard that Mooro was the same with his illness and there is something about such men, which makes them so very special.

John had a huge funeral in St Bride's Church in Bothwell. The surviving members of Celtic's Lisbon Lions attended and the great Tommy Burns read the eulogy.

The things I miss most about John are his love of fun and his keen sense of humour. We had been together for over 40 years and had two boys and two girls together. I just miss his presence. I called him my Braveheart.
Mary Cushley

The Player's View of John Cushley:

I remember we were playing Spurs and Cushley must have kicked Jimmy Greaves about four or five times. In those days, it was a different game in terms of physical contact. There was none of this tap a player and you get a yellow card, push a player and you're off. At half time, Ron went mad. 'What are you doing?' He said. 'You can't keep kicking them!' I remember thinking, what is 'Cush' supposed to do? That was his game. He couldn't play, he couldn't pass it, he couldn't trap his fingers in a door so all he could do was kick people. He was great at it! Cush and I always used to laugh about that.
Jimmy Lindsay

I really liked John. He came into the club and was a different type of player to the typical West Ham mould. Ron Greenwood always liked players who could pass the ball and take it out of defence but John wasn't that type of player at all. He was more likely to bring a bit of Scottish steel to the defence and play well in the air. So it was a bit unfair to ask John to change his style of play so dramatically.
Bobby Howe

John always wore really smart shirts with cufflinks that had 'JC' on them. When he played for West Ham he used to kick everyone which was great for Mooro!
Dave Llewelyn

I couldn't believe it when Ron signed John Cushley because he was such a football purist and John was a crash, bang, wallop type of defender, a bit of a hard man.
Joe Kirkup

After West Ham signed Cush we went on tour to Germany and played Borussia Dortmund. John was kicking holes in their great players – Sigi Held and Emmerich – but at half-time Ron told him to take it easy and to not be so rough!
Brian Dear

He came to the club from Scotland and I had to play against him during a practise match. Now it so happened I was on my game and I gave him a roasting. It was his first game

in a West Ham shirt and although I didn't give him the best introduction to English football I got on well with him.
Trevor Hartley

Because John played alongside Billy McNeil in the Celtic side Ron Greenwood thought he was a better player than he actually was. He became a very devout religious guy later on in life but had been one of the heavy drinkers when he was at West Ham.
Rob Jenkins

Like Don Revie, John also died from Motor Neurone Disease. I'd be interested to know just how many ex-footballers have suffered from that condition. Dementia is another illness that a lot of footballers succumb to later on in life and I'm not surprised given the amount of times a lot of those guys were heading the old style footballs, which were like bricks.
Peter Eustace

I'll never forget my first reserve team game against the first team because Cushley was marking me. I tried to go past him and he knocked me up in the air and stood over me saying: 'Welcome to the big leagues!'
Clyde Best

John the family man.

61 – SIR TREVOR BROOKING

Born: Barking, Essex, October 2, 1948

Position: Midfielder

Games played with Bobby Moore: 218 (1967-74)

Games played for West Ham United: 637 (1967-84)

Honours with Bobby Moore: 1972 Hammer of the Year

First game with Bobby Moore (Debut): August 29, 1967 Burnley (a) D 3-3

Scorers: West Ham United: Moore, Peters, Hurst
Burnley: Lochhead, Bellamy, Harris (pen)

West Ham United: Ferguson, Bonds, Charles, Peters, Cushley, Moore, Redknapp, **Brooking**, Hurst, Boyce, Sissons
Burnley: Thomson, Latcham, Buxton, O'Neil, Angus, Bellamy, Morgan, Lochhead, Irvine, Harris, Casper

Trevor David Brooking spent 17 years as a player at West Ham United and the first six of those were played in front of Bobby Moore.

Trevor played as a schoolboy for Ilford, London and Essex Boys before winning his first England Schoolboys cap in the 1963-64 season. He signed as an apprentice professional on July 24, 1965, full professional forms on May 2, 1966 and also gained six England Youth caps.

Brooking's first season playing for the Hammers came in 1967-68 when he scored nine league goals from 25 games, including a hat-trick against Newcastle United in April 1968. He is, therefore, one of only 10 West Ham players to bag a treble during the Bobby Moore era.

Trevor Brooking would of course become one of West Ham United's greatest ever legends, winning the FA Cup twice and being awarded the Hammer of the Year on no fewer than five occasions, a record at the club. Indeed, at the end of his inaugural season in the first team, 1967-68, he was runner-up to Bobby Moore for that particular award. He is also the last Hammer to register double-figure England caps. In addition to his colossal contribution to West Ham United as a player he also served as the club's caretaker manager on two occasions during 2003.

Clyde Best is one of many to recall Brooking's skill set: 'Trevor was Mr Smooth. He had oodles of talent, was very flamboyant and he made the game look so easy. It was no surprise when he went on to play numerous times for England because we all knew at an early age that Trevor was a bit special.'

Brooking is one of the most decorated players in the club's history and won the FA Cup twice (1975 and 1980), promotion once (1981) and appeared in both a European Cup Winners Cup final (1976) and a League Cup final (1981). His international record of 47 caps (five goals) is third, in terms of appearances, only to Bobby Moore (108) and Geoff Hurst (49) in West Ham United's history.

Trevor was honoured with an MBE (1981) a CBE (1999) and a Knighthood (2004). In 2009, the club changed the name of the Centenary Stand (formerly the North Bank) to the Sir Trevor Brooking Stand in honour of his contribution to the club and he still attends most home matches.

In 2014, Sir Trevor announced his retirement from his role as Director of Football Development with the Football Association, a position he had held since 2003. He still resides in Shenfield with his wife of 45 years, Hilkka, with whom he has two children, Warren and Colette. Colette's four year old son, Harry, will doubtless have the best possible chance of being comfortable on the ball with both feet!

The following memories were shared from Trevor's office at the new Wembly Stadium:

All my family supported West Ham and I was taken over there as a lad in the late 1950s. I watched Andy Malcolm who was known as 'The Shadow', Phil Woosnam ('The Professor'), Ernie Gregory ('Uncle Ern'), Malcolm Musgrove ('Mad Muzzie') and Vic Keeble and John Dick up front with the great defensive duo of John Bond and Noel Cantwell.

I first met Bobby Moore when I was still at school. I needed some treatment and went along one Sunday to see Bill Jenkins, West Ham's physio, in his clinic on Green Street. It was about 1965.

When I saw Bobby I was too shy to speak to him but, after a few more visits, I felt more comfortable to ask him why he was there because he was usually the only one training on a Sunday. Little did I know that that Bobby was a social animal as well as a great player and would come in every Sunday after being out the night before and run laps around the pitch in his sweat suit. It was a good lesson to experience because I was a youngster and Bobby's commitment to fitness really was something very impressive to witness.

My debut is an amazing memory because we drew 3-3 up at Burnley and our goal scorers were Bobby Moore, Geoff Hurst and Martin Peters, which is pretty unique. Burnley were a top side back then and regularly finished in the top half of the table.

It was very tough to break into the reserves at West Ham let alone the first team. I was in the A Team under Jim Barrett junior for a long while before I got into Ernie Gregory's reserve team. I owe a lot to Jim Barrett because he switched me into a more attacking midfielder, which was my best position. Of course, a similar thing happened to Geoff Hurst, who was an up and down wing-half, but Ron saw something in Geoff and gave him an outstanding career as a striker. Both Ron and Jim underlined the importance and benefit of good coaching at West Ham and the club had it in abundance. I soon started setting up and scoring goals and, after six months playing in the reserves, I was in the first team.

Bobby Moore wasn't a ranter or raver and he led by example, although I do remember one occasion when he knocked the ball into me in midfield and came out to take the return but instead I decided to turn. As I did, I got caught in possession and Bob gave me an almighty mouthful which wasn't a regular occurrence but was a good lesson. There were a few expletives but the message was clear: 'There is no point in me coming out of defence to set up an attacking situation if I don't get the ball back.'

In my early days in the first team it was touch-and-go whether or not I was going to become an established player in the senior side. Geoff obviously had the Number 10 shirt at the time and, naturally, I used to watch Martin Peters more than any other player because he was a midfielder and that was my position. Because of the World Cup triumvirate of Moore, Hurst and Peters there was a tendency to give them the ball rather than express oneself. It was probably the case for many of the younger players coming through at the time that they afforded the bigger stars too much respect at the cost of their own development.

Soon after I broke into the team, I was told that I may form part of the deal that would take Bobby to Derby County

Elegance defined.

under their manager, Brian Clough. I never met with the representatives of Derby but Bob did meet up with Clough. At the time there was tremendous competition for the midfield places at West Ham with Ron Boyce and Martin Peters being the regulars with myself. Jimmy Lindsay and Peter Bennett trying to hold down a place. The transfer may well have had some involvement from Jack Turner, who knew both Bobby

Controlling Alan Mullery of Spurs with John Sissons on hand.

and I really well but, in the end, Ron Greenwood went to the board and said he would resign if they sold Bobby.

On reflection it was undoubtedly the best thing for me that I stayed at West Ham. I would guess that every player who passed through the club during the Ron Greenwood era had their game improved. A player is certainly born with various skills but a good coach can bring out so much more and develop raw talent into something exceptional. Ron certainly did it with Geoff and to a lesser extent with Bobby and Martin. All three would applaud Ron's coaching expertise and I would add my voice to those accolades.

Ron said a couple of things to me which I used to some effect throughout my career. The first was to receive the ball sideways on. You have probably seen footage from my playing days where I let the ball run across me before picking a pass or shot. That was all Ron and something he tried to instil in every West Ham player. It helped that I was already comfortable with either foot by the time I joined West Ham. I was naturally right footed but my father, Harry, who was a hard hitting centre-half, taught me from an early age at our home in Salisbury Avenue to play with both feet. I went to Ripple Road School which was about a 30-minute walk from my home. My dad gave me a tennis ball to kick there and back and I had to negotiate a bridge and played it off the wall with both feet so I became very comfortable with a football.

Part of the sideways-on philosophy was the importance of the weight and angle of pass. Nobody can receive the ball sideways on if it is being whacked in at tremendous speed so Ron's theory was to perfect the weight of the pass a player was making. A player should never put a team-mate under pressure with a pass. The object is to make the play easier. If you watch Barcelona and Spain, most of the time they are caressing the ball to their team-mates and making quick, deft touches in tight spaces to create space, and, in turn, chances.

Everything about the West Ham way, or the Ron Greenwood way, was weight and angle of pass and Bobby Moore was a master of this and could put the ball anywhere on the pitch at any pace.

The second thing that Ron developed with all the players was awareness. He would simply click his fingers and shout: 'Stop!' We were then expected to close our eyes tight shut and tell him where we thought our team-mates were positioned on the pitch. Stevie Gerrard and Frank Lampard are very good at that as was Dennis Bergkamp before them. Their brains are not only calculating the best position to be in on the pitch but also where their team-mates are likely to be. It is not a natural ability and is learned through hours and hours of practice. Any West Ham player who spent two years at the club instinctively knew where to pass the ball and how to create space.

At the unveiling of the Bobby Moore statue in 2007 with L-R Tony Blair, Stephanie Moore, Bobby Charlton (hidden), Jeff Powell and sculptor Philip Jackson.

I got to know Bob a lot more after our playing days, particularly in the late 1980s when we both got into radio punditry. I was with the BBC and he was with Jonathan Pearce at Capital Radio. I used to see him on trips abroad and one of my favourite memories of Bob came when we were both covering a club European match in Germany. Bob wasn't a regular golfer but he was starting to enjoy the game later on in life. He was the type of golfer that took a three or four iron off the tee rather than a wood. One day he called me up in my hotel and asked me if I wanted to play a round of golf with himself and one other. He wouldn't tell me the name of the other person but when I got to the course there was Franz Beckenbauer.

Now, if I was asked to name my top five legendary football figures in my lifetime both Bobby and Franz would be there so to play a round of golf with both of them was something I'll never forget.

If you look at West Ham during the Bobby Moore years, he epitomised Ron Greenwood's coaching philosophy. When people talk about the West Ham way of playing football, what they are actually saying is the Ron Greenwood way of playing football and Bobby Moore was the greatest manifestation of Ron's vision on how the game should be played. Bobby's distribution from the back was absolutely pivotal to everything West Ham achieved.

Bob's speed of thought on the pitch was something I tried to develop in my own style of play and I like to believe that I was a quick thinker on the pitch, which is something I learned from Bobby. Another trait he had was that he never panicked on the ball. A little shimmy into space was how he dealt with pressurised situations and calmness on the ball is another characteristic I learned from Bobby.

You never saw Bobby remonstrate or lose his head on the field. He may have bounced the ball off the surface to reveal a little frustration but he knew that a hot head did more harm than good. We tried to teach Bonzo the benefits of this because he could really blow hot in certain situations! Bill never lost that particular character trait and he became the great protector of so many players at the club, including myself, thankfully.

By winning the European Cup Winners Cup in 1965, Ron gave West Ham a massive international reputation which still lingers to this day. Bobby added to that status with his achievements in the England shirt. Between them, they helped transform a parochial family club in London's East End into a star-studded outfit playing a European style of football with international repute. Anyone will tell you that if a team is going to be successful when adopting that style of play it all starts at the back and Bobby's distribution was such a big cog in the whole process.

Showing his style and class at Southampton.

West Ham fans will see similarities between Bobby and I in terms of pace and heading ability! I like to think that I overcame any deficiencies in those areas with quickness of thought and application. I learned to read the game more ably from Bobby. You couldn't help but learn from his style of play. His philosophy which became my philosophy was not to retaliate when the opposition is trying to kick lumps out of you but to gain the sweetest revenge of all by creating or scoring a goal.

The last time I saw Bobby was at Wembley Stadium in 1993 when we were both reporting on the England versus San Marino match. After the game we all went back to a media centre inside a hotel and I noticed then just how poorly he was. But he wanted to go to that game and must have viewed it as a final farewell to the venue that he graced with such distinction throughout his playing career.

If Bobby was alive today I believe he would be enjoying all the accolade and status his profile deserved. He was beginning to become very comfortable in a media environment and had left behind the years he had spent with various pub and club involvements.

I believe he would have received all the recognition he so richly deserved. With each passing World Cup, the success of the 1966 team becomes more ingrained in the English consciousness and Bobby would have been at the centre of all that. He was only 51 when he died

so everything was extinguished prematurely and there has been a lot of criticism towards both the FA and West Ham for not acting sooner.

If you were fortunate enough to have played with Bobby Moore you will never forget the experience because he had such a huge impact on football at both club and international level.
Sir Trevor Brooking

Following are a few recollections of Trevor from those who coached and played with him during the Bobby Moore era:

I saw many kids come through West Ham's A team but if you ask me who was the best, you wouldn't have to look any further than Trevor Brooking.
Jim Barrett jnr (1960s youth team coach)

We always knew he was going to be a player. He joined the club in 1965, a year after me. I played with him in the reserves and he put me through and I scored with the lowest chip over a goalkeeper, ever. I always felt we had a bit of telepathy between us in the reserves and I can understand Kevin Keegan when he says Trevor was the best player with whom he played. He had the physique and could do things other players couldn't do.
Trevor Hartley

Even after I left the club, my parents, Charlie and Florence, still went over to watch Trevor from the vantage point of the old West Stand. My uncle 'Smiler,' – who also loved to watch Trevor play – said he would always do something in a game that you thought about on your way home. If ever I spoke to Smiler I would only ask how Trevor played because I knew that he was the only reason he went over there.
Bobby Howe

He was usually in the card school with Billy Bonds and Pop Robson. When we were on tour I was always the one to go and get their drinks because they couldn't spare time away from the table. They used to play for silly money and lose a week's wages, no problem. I got on well with Trevor and it was probably because I brought his drink back first! He did things with the ball that you didn't see anyone else do in the league at that time. The one story I remember about Trevor Brooking is that when we played up at Old Trafford in the 1972-73 season he was injured and, on the Friday morning, Ron came up to me and told me I was playing in Trevor's position on the left side of midfield. Now, when you think I was a speedy winger, nine stone seven ounces wringing wet, this was quite a daunting prospect.
Dudley Tyler

I must have put Bacardi in Brooking's Coke over 100 times at West Ham but he always knew it had been laced. Coke, what a thing to drink! It's worse than drinking beer when you think about it. I look at Trevor in a similar way to Mooro. He wasn't very quick and couldn't head the ball but he was a class act. I marked him in a youth tournament between Scotland and England. I kicked him all round the pitch and he kept saying in his posh voice: 'Jimmy, don't keep doing that'. It was played at Southampton and we lost 0-1.
Jimmy Lindsay

I used to kick about with Trevor Brooking, Harry Redknapp and Billy Bonds. We played a lot of cards together. We went on tour to America and were at a baseball game in Baltimore when out came this big fat guy called Boog Powell. Now, Trevor used to have a bit of trouble with his weight so when Boog ran out Harry said 'Look, there's Trevor!' and it stuck ever since. Now we have to call him 'Sir Boog!'
Peter Bennett

'Boogaloo' was different class! I travelled up from Bristol every day so would have to get up at 5am. Trevor picked me up from various

stations and took me to the training ground. It was funny because if I was late I had to take the train to Chadwell Heath, which actually passed the training ground. All the players would be out there waving and shouting: 'You're getting fined Gouldy!' Trevor was very kind to me and I used to room with him. He sympathised with my daily journey in from Bristol. 'Come and stay with us for a night,' he said. I went back to his house and had a meal and a Coke because he is tee-total. At about 10 o'clock I said I was going to bed, so went up to my room and pulled the curtains and the whole lot just fell on top of me! 'Just my luck!' I thought. I had to sheepishly go back downstairs and explain what had happened. 'Don't worry about it,' said Boog. 'Hilkka, Go and get the tool box, please.' And off she went. When she returned she walked past us and kept on going up the stairs and started fixing the curtain rail. She was the DIY expert in the family!
Bobby Gould

A true legend.

62 – FRANK LAMPARD

Born: East Ham, London, September 20, 1948

Position: Left-back

Games played with Bobby Moore: 213 (1967-74)

Games played for West Ham United: 664 (1967-85)

First game with Bobby Moore (Debut): November 18, 1967 Manchester City (h) L 2-3

Scorers: West Ham United: Peters, Hurst
Manchester City: Lee (2), Summerbee

West Ham United: Ferguson, **Lampard**, Burkett, Peters, Cushley, Moore, Redknapp, Boyce, Brabrook, Hurst, Sissons

Manchester City: Mulhearn, Book, Pardoe, Doyle, Heslop, Oakes, Lee, Bell, Summerbee, Young, Coleman

---

Frank Richard George Lampard played more games with Bobby Moore than any other left-back. Furthermore, he is part of a very select band of four Hammers – along with Johnny Byrne, Geoff Hurst and Martin Peters – who lined up with Moore for both club and country.

The first of Lampard's two full England caps came against Yugoslavia on October 11, 1972. Bobby captained the team and was gaining his 97th international cap in the process. Interestingly, Lampard's second and final cap came seven years later, against Australia, in 1980. It remains a record for the longest gap between England caps.

Lampard attended Pretoria Road school in Canning Town and won medals for swimming, badminton and athletics. He excelled at football and played for West Ham schools, Essex Boys and also represented Essex and the South at schoolboy cricket.

Frank signed apprentice forms for West Ham United in 1964, graduating to professional status in September 1966. The 19-year-old's impressive early progress was temporarily halted when suffering a broken leg in a game against Sheffield United at Bramall Lane. The tackle from Willie Carlin occurred with just a few minutes remaining in the game. Sheer hard work and dedication resulted in Lampard establishing himself as the club's left-back for the next 15 years, picking up two FA Cup winners medals (1975 and 1980) and a promotion along the way. A European Cup Winners Cup final in 1976 and a League Cup final in 1981 add to his impressive legacy.

Despite being over seven years younger than Moore, Lampard was amongst his greatest friends and joined him as coach of Southend United in the early 1980s. Lampard also became Harry Redknapp's number two at West Ham United during the 1990s. They remain very close brothers-in-law having married sisters Pat and Sandra Harris. Sadly, Frank's wife, Pat, passed away on April 24, 2008.

Remarkably, Frank's son, Frank junior became the most decorated player in Chelsea's history and the Blues' all-time leading scorer. His 106 England caps, just two short of Bobby Moore, marks the most perfect, fittingly respectful, end to young Frank's legendary status.

Frank senior contributed many stories about his great friend Bobby Moore, over a glass of beer in Wanstead.

I was quite a few years younger than Bobby but I think we had a similar mentality. I remember the time when we first connected as friends. I had just got into the first team and we were playing away. It was always a dash to get on the train for London after a game and we normally tried to board the 6pm special.

I was just a kid from Canning Town and was in awe of Bobby, who would be sitting with all the other senior players. I was four or five seats away from him but he caught sight of me and motioned for me to sit at his table where he handed me a bottle of lager. That was the start of our friendship. I can remember going straight out the next day and buying my first car! It was a red Vauxhall Victor with column change and a bench seat.

To me, Bobby was the ultimate player. He worked hard to make himself the best he could be. As a young lad he was a decent player but he turned himself into a legend. I wanted to be like him and always told young Frank that if he wanted to be a top player he had to conduct himself in much the same way as Bobby.

I think about Bobby a lot and he has got a special place in my heart and that will never change. Anyone coming into football should know about Bobby Moore and what he achieved. He was the absolute pinnacle of what a footballer should strive to be. He was a gentleman, he had no inhibitions and just got on with things and treated everyone around him with the utmost respect throughout his entire career.

He wasn't a ranter and raver and if I ever gave the ball away

Dealing with Liverpool's John Toshack, along with Billy Bonds, Bobby Ferguson, Bobby Moore and Tommy Taylor.

needlessly he would just look at me in a way that said: 'You know you shouldn't be doing that.' Just a glance from his eyes was enough. Maybe I'm not the best person to talk to about Bobby because I can't say enough good things about him. He had everything. He was everything a young lad coming out of the East End of London would want to be, a world figure who lifted the World Cup and left a flawless trail of gentlemanly behaviour all along the way.

Derby County wanted to sign Mooro in the late 1960s and I was sharing a room with him around that time. He received a phone call from reception saying that someone from Derby was there to see him, I don't know who. Anyway, Bobby just said: 'I don't want to see him,' and put the phone down. Then, there was a knock at the door with someone saying that a man from Derby was still downstairs waiting for Bobby but he just brushed it off and never went to see him. It could have been Brian Clough for all I know.

Why Bobby went in goal against Stoke City up at Old Trafford in the League Cup I do not know. He couldn't dive

because he didn't like getting dirty! Anyone could dive better than him.

I remember when I got my first cap for England against Yugoslavia. Bobby was captain, of course, and Sir Alf Ramsey was the manager at the time and we trained on the Friday morning before the game the next day. Afterwards we got on the coach and Alf sat next to me and said: 'You're going to play tomorrow.' I was quite surprised and then Alf said I would be the first player with a beard to play for England. I still don't know if this was true but that's what he said.

When I got off the coach, Bobby was there and he knew what had happened and said: 'Well done.' The next day I was walking out behind him at Wembley Stadium. After the game we ended up in The City Arms on the Isle of Dogs having a few beers. Fantastic really, and an experience which is right up there with winning the FA Cups and scoring the goal in 1980, against Everton in the semi-final replay at Elland Road.

I might have played for England with Bobby a lot earlier if I hadn't broken my leg in 1968 against Sheffield United.

Ron told me that before the break I had been selected to play for England Under-23s and that would have put me on the map a lot earlier. I was quite sad when he told me that and I may have had an outside squeak of going to the 1970 World Cup finals but Terry Cooper ruled the roost instead. He was the best left-back in the country by a mile so they made the right decision anyway.

Bobby and I spent quite a bit of time together at West Ham and had a lot of fun, especially during the trips abroad. At home I have a large canvass of Mooro and me, on a camel in Israel, with Ted MacDougall and Bobby Ferguson. It is one of many memories with Bobby I like to look back on.

I could never even dream that I was going to play against Bobby in the 1975 FA Cup final, just a year after he left West Ham. How did that happen? It just can't happen can it? But then I was walking out alongside him at Wembley and he's wearing a Fulham shirt, totally mad really.

I was with Bobby as player-coach at Southend. Harry Cripps, who Bobby thought a lot of, was there too. I'm not sure what Harry did but he would turn up in a small van on Fridays and sell picture frames to the players. He had a stall down the Romford Road. I used to say: 'Crippsy, it's Friday, we've got to do some training.' Mooro was so laid back and never confronted people about such behaviour.

In classic pose.

We had a fine start at Southend and went on a good run for the first 15 or so games but then things took a turn for the worse. One day, Bobby asked me to take training because the chairman wanted to have a chat with him so I did and Bobby didn't show up at all. After training I saw him having a shower and I asked him how he was and he said: 'Not good.' The chairman had told him that he didn't want two players in the team the following day. I had just told the lads the line up and said to Bobby we would look like mugs if we changed things for no reason. Obviously we couldn't tell them the chairman was picking the team. 'Yeah I know' he said, 'But it's not easy.'

Bobby could be a bit soft in these situations so I told him it was an easy decision and that he was the manager and he picked the team. 'Let's sleep on it,' he said. That was no good for me so I told him that I'd be calling it a day if he dropped the two players. 'Alright,' he said. Which wasn't the best response I was hoping for! He didn't say: 'Frank, don't be too hasty' or

'I want you to stay.' I ended up leaving on the Monday after he had gone with the chairman's line-up on the Saturday. 10 days later they sacked Bobby, too.

As a manager he never quite came up to what he could have been. I think West Ham as a club could have helped him more, they could have taken him in and looked after him. It would have benefited everyone.

I feel a lot of people, particularly at smaller clubs, might have been a little bit in awe of him. I think that some people might have also been a bit threatened by him because of what he was, who he was and how he was.

He was a mate of mine rather than just a football mate. We got on very well and I learned a lot from him, especially how to conduct yourself in certain situations both on and off the pitch. Bobby could come across as a bit shy at times and I can be like that sometimes, although, as I've got older maybe I've changed a bit. I always looked up to him and he

With Bobby Moore and Harry Redknapp at the opening of Harry Cripps (far left) and Dennis Burnett's shop in Ilford, Essex.

never had a bad word for anyone. It was a pleasure to be with Bobby and he just brought out the best in everyone around him. He was a massive world figure, right up there with Pele and Beckenbauer, so it was a privilege to spend so much time with him. He was so cool and calm and hardly ever put a foot wrong. He enjoyed his socialising and I'm really proud to have known him. I always talked about him when I went on to become a coach. I also tried to use a lot of Ron Greenwood's teachings because to me he was the Bobby Moore of the coaching world.

One of the great things about Bobby was how he would always get on with things. He would never make too much noise about his problems. Going back to when he was ill, you could see he wasn't well but he would never moan about anything and would just carry on as if nothing was happening. He played like that as well, as though nothing was happening which is probably why you never saw him panic and always had that coolness about him. A fantastic person and we are yet to see another like him.
Frank Lampard

Following are some player reminiscences of Frank Lampard:

He was like Bobby in that he liked to learn from the senior pros and worked really hard to improve his game. Frank wasn't the fastest but his work ethic meant he played at West Ham for almost 20 years and won two FA Cups and two England caps.
Brian Dear

He used to be so professional at such a young age. He would always do that bit extra in training. He knew what he wanted to be and he worked really hard to get there. I remember West Ham came down to Bournemouth for a pre-season game and John Bond sat in our dressing room after the game and said: 'What a good player Frank Lampard has become.' I always look at those players like Frank, Trevor Brooking and Billy Bonds, who carved out successful careers for themselves and hold my hand up and say: 'Well done!'
Trevor Hartley

Frank was unbelievable, he was the hardest working pro I have ever seen in my life. He was naturally a right-back but he knew Billy Bonds was in that position so he worked hard to become a left-back because he rightly assumed John Charles wouldn't last long in that position. Sure enough, every afternoon, Frank would be putting in crosses from the left for Roger Cross. Frank was a very ordinary player who carved out a very good career through sheer hard graft. Some of that work ethic has rubbed off on young Frank, who I think has been the best player in England for the past 15 years. He doesn't get nearly enough praise for what he has achieved.
Jimmy Lindsay

There was one game when I went through on Frank and put my studs down his legs. He wasn't wearing any shin pads so I completely zipped him. Mooro came over to me and

said: 'Now, Mike, that wasn't very nice was it?' It made me feel awful that I had upset Bobby.
Mike Summerbee (Manchester City and England)

When I played for Sheffield Wednesday I would sometimes go and watch Sheffield United play midweek games, especially if a good team like West Ham were the visitors. I was at the game when Willie Carlin broke Frank Lampard's leg. It was an awful challenge.
Peter Eustace

Frank has always got on well with Rob Jenkins, our physio at West Ham. When we travelled abroad, Jenko absolutely hated flying and Frank had to put him in a headlock to keep him from freaking out!
Bobby Gould

He was a very good professional. Nobody trained harder and nobody did more extra training than Frank. When I joined, he had broken his leg and needed to work extra hard to get back into shape. He did that superbly. Frank was a model professional.
Clyde Best

The way they've treated the Lampard family at West Ham is unreal, an absolute disgrace. Young Frank is a fantastic boy, a superb player and he's been treated appallingly. He's had bastards singing: 'Where's your mother gone?' It's scary that people like that are out there.
Harry Redknapp

Frank at his home in Gidea Park, Essex with a special memory of Bobby Moore, Frank, Ted MacDougall and Bobby Ferguson in Israel.

63 – ALAN STEPHENSON

Born: Buckinghamshire, September 26, 1944

Position: Centre-half

Games played with Bobby Moore: 116 (1968-72)

Games played for West Ham United: 118 (1968-72)

First game with Bobby Moore (Debut): March 16, 1968 Southampton (a) D 0-0

Southampton: Martin, Kirkup, Jones, Walker, McGrath, Gabriel, Channon, Saul, Davies, Paine, Sydenham

West Ham United: Ferguson, Bonds, Lampard, Peters, **Stephenson**, Moore, Dear, Boyce, Brooking, Hurst, Sissons

Alan Charles Stephenson was bought from Crystal Palace for a club record fee of £80,000. He signed on March 12, 1968 and, at the time, the Hammers were languishing fifth from bottom in the league, just a single point out of the relegation zone. The following week, Stephenson helped to keep a clean sheet on his debut at Southampton alongside Bobby Moore. The club would eventually finish comfortably in mid-table. 'I think Ron Greenwood brought me in specifically to keep West Ham from going down and, thankfully, the club stayed up.'

Stephenson began his football career as captain of Walthamstow Boys and was working in the circulation department of *The Times* before signing professional forms for Crystal Palace. Whilst with the Eagles, he gained three England Under-23 caps and after 170 games, signed for the Hammers. During his spell at Upton Park he played in a further four England Under-23 games.

In 1970 Stephenson played with Bobby Moore in a memorable encounter against Pele's Santos, on Randall's Island, New York. The game finished 2-2 courtesy of goals from Clyde Best (2) and Pele (2).

Clearing the threat from Bobby Tambling and Tommy Baldwin of Chelsea.

In defence with Bobby Moore against Chelsea in September 1968.

When Tommy Taylor was signed from Leyton Orient it marked the end of Stephenson's time at West Ham United. Taylor remembers the moment well: 'When I signed I went straight to the hospital to see 'Stevo' because he was having his cartilage out and I was brought in to replace him. He was really decent about it and when I eventually ended up going back to Orient, Stevo was reserve team coach there.'

Fellow defender Frank Lampard provided some insight into the difficulty Stephenson faced whilst playing at West Ham: 'When Stevo arrived at the club Ron Greenwood set up a game at Chadwell Heath to help settle him in. The ball came to Alan and he volleyed it full length of the pitch. Ron shouted: 'Stop the game!' He walked over to Stevo and said: 'Alan, you are not at Crystal Palace now. You are a West Ham player. Never do that again. You control the ball and pass it. Never hoof it up the pitch! From that moment on poor Alan, who had been a decent player at Crystal Palace, didn't know whether to, stick, bust or have his hair cut. He lost all his confidence.'

Stephenson is one of the few players to captain West Ham during the Bobby Moore era. He was handed the responsibility before a home game against Stoke City on October 6, 1969.

In 1972 he was transferred to Portsmouth for £32,000 and three years later played for Durban United in South Africa where he caught up with former Hammers, Budgie Byrne

and Trevor Dawkins On his return to the UK he coached the reserve team at Leyton Orient for four years before retiring from the game to become a publican. He also worked as a welfare and education officer for Essex County Council.

Alan is enjoying retirement in Colchester and plays the odd round of golf. He has been a keen collector of books down the years and has a strong interest in genealogy. He likes to return to watch the Hammers whenever he can and has an extensive collection of programmes and memorabilia from his playing days. After our interview he kindly drove me to the house of Vic Keeble in Earls Colne – another one of the 89 Hammers who played with Bobby Moore. Following are Alan's recollections:

Bobby called me 'Stevo' and I got on well playing alongside him. I didn't really appreciate my time with him until after I'd retired from the game.

I joined West Ham from Crystal Palace where I had a reputation for being a reasonable player, an aggressive ball-winning centre-half and a good marker, who was hard to beat. Ron Greenwood paid a record fee for me and I believe he brought me in to do a specific job – to help keep West Ham up during the 1967-68 season – and we ended up finishing 12th in the league, so it was a good start. I was a very confident character and believed I would make a positive difference.

Mooro inspired the players around him by the way he played. Technically, he was such a gifted player and although people comment on his lack of pace, he was a very clever footballer and the master at putting himself in situations where he didn't get exposed at all. He could make tackles and score goals as well.

He was utterly reliable in his play, great with both feet and his passes up to Geoff Hurst were immaculate. This was no better demonstrated than in the '66 World Cup final, the biggest stage of all. He performed week in, week out for West Ham regardless of his England commitments.

Bobby rarely lost his temper. He was a very placid type of guy on and off the field and I think the only time I saw him lose his cool was when I was badly tackled in a game against Everton in December 1969. Bobby played a pass to me and, as I played it up-field, Joe Royle came in late and put six studs across my shin. It opened up my calf and the muscle was just lying there.

That really upset Bobby and I remember him giving Joe a mouthful – it was the only time I saw him angry. I was rushed to hospital to have my leg stitched up and it kept me out for about a month. Players used to try and rile him and wind him up but he was far too professional to retaliate.

After the game against Brazil's Santos I was sitting in the dressing room, when the door opened and Bobby walked in with James Bond, who was played by Sean Connery at the time. I was a bit star-struck to say the least. I had already had the thrill of playing with Bobby, Geoff and Martin during the season and now I had played against Pele, Carlos Alberto and Garrincha in New York. So when James Bond walked into the dressing room it really was the icing on the cake – absolutely amazing! Bobby introduced me to him and we shook hands.

Ron made me skipper, once, and it was the only time I captained West Ham – at home to Stoke City in 1969-70. Bobby, Martin and Geoff all missed that game because of their international duties so Ron gave me the responsibility. We drew 3-3 but had been winning 3-0 at half-time so it was quite a baptism really.

One of the things I'll never forget about Bobby was his greeting. He would always say: 'All is well, Stevo?'

Alan Stephenson

'Stevo'.

Back row L-R Stephenson, Peters, Ferguson, Charles, Moore, Bonds. Front row L-R Redknapp, Boyce, Brooking, Hurst, Sissons.

CHAPTER ELEVEN
1968-69

Bobby Moore's total appearances (July 1968-June 1969): 67 games (3 goals)

League Division One: 41 (2 goals), England: 9, America Tour: 6 (1 goal), Friendlies: 5, FA Cup: 3, League Cup: 3

A new season and a new match day programme. The classic pocket sized shape remained but the photographic action shot with claret header and footer was gone, indefinitely.

The men in charge of the four teams at West Ham United were as follows: Ron Greenwood, Albert Walker and physio Rob Jenkins continued their charge of the first team while Ernie Gregory and physio Dave Gladstone looked after the reserves. John Lyall and Archie Wood attended to the A Team in the Metropolitan League and Bill Lansdowne was in charge of the youth section, assisted by Dick Arnold.

A promising finish of eighth in the league was offset by early exits in both cups – Coventry City knocked out the Hammers in the League Cup while lowly Mansfield Town added to the misery in the FA Cup.

Bobby Moore played in front of his largest ever away attendance in club football, when 63,274 turned up at Old Trafford for the visit of the Hammers on September 7. The *Manchester Evening News* headline read: '63,000 locked in…Goal getters locked-out,' as the teams played out a 0-0 stalemate.

Highlight of the season occurred in October when Geoff Hurst scored six goals during an 8-0 thrashing of Sunderland. Remarkably, it was his World Cup captain who scored the best goal of the game – a beautiful strike from distance, past Jim Montgomery, and into the top corner.

On January 14, 1969, former manager Charlie 'Mr West Ham' Paynter officially opened the new East Stand.

At the end of the season the team toured the USA and participated in an International Cup competition set up by NASL Commissioner and former Hammer, Phil Woosnam. West Ham represented the Baltimore Bays but attendances were poor – only 714 fans witnessed the encounter between West Ham and Dundee United at Cobb Stadium, Texas.

It was also a very busy summer for Harry Redknapp, Peter Bennett, Bobby Ferguson and Alan Stephenson, all of whom took their wedding vows.

Bobby Moore would encounter some fresh faces in the first team, including Roger Cross, Jimmy Lindsay, Keith Miller, Peter Grotier, Pat Holland and Stephen Death.

Here is their story…

Frank Clark of Newcastle United and Bobby Moore shake hands at the start of a new season.

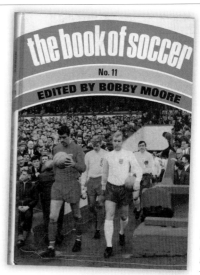

Established captain of club and country.

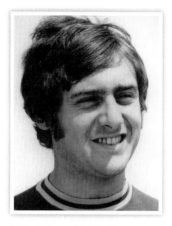

64 – ROGER CROSS

Born: East Ham, October 20, 1948

Position: Centre-forward

Games played with Bobby Moore: 7 (1968-69)

Games played for West Ham United: 8 (1968-69)

First game with Bobby Moore (Debut): August 26, 1968 Burnley (h) W 5-0

Scorers: West Ham United: Peters, Hurst (2), Brooking (2)

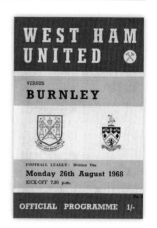

West Ham United: Ferguson, Bonds, Charles, Peters, Stephenson, Moore, Redknapp, Boyce, Brooking, Hurst, Sissons* sub: **Cross***

Burnley: Thomson, Smith, Latcham, O'Neil, Waldron, Bellamy, Coates, Lochhead, Casper, Kindon, Thomas

Roger George Cross loves West Ham United. He played just a handful of first team games for the club, having established himself as a prolific reserve team striker, and was the leading scorer in two consecutive seasons at that level.

His first team debut – a 5-0 victory over Burnley – on August 26, 1968, was the most emphatic victory experienced by any debutant during the Bobby Moore era.

His father, George, regaled him with tales of pre-War Hammers from the Ted Hufton, Jimmy Ruffell and Victor Watson era and Roger's high regard for West Ham United's history has deepened ever since. He signed apprentice forms for the Hammers in July 1964.

Cross attended Sandringham school and played for East Ham and Essex Boys and also represented Essex at schoolboy cricket.

He was over seven years younger than Bobby Moore, who was in the team when Cross scored his one and only goal for West Ham United – against Arsenal at home on August 25, 1969. Former team-mates recall how Cross really looked the part and would often straighten his shirt and shorts after a tackle.

His experience of playing with Moore under Ron Greenwood during the 1960s held him in good stead for the various coaching and scouting roles he fulfilled at the club under Harry Redknapp, Glenn Roeder, Trevor Brooking, Alan Pardew, Alan Curbishley, Gianfranco Zola and Avram Grant. It is fitting that a man with such a high regard for West Ham's history should play his own part in it.

Roger made a big name for himself at Brentford following a £12,000 move in 1969 and went on to play for Seattle Sounders in the North America Soccer League.

Nowadays, Roger is a part-time senior scout for Charlton Athletic. His hobbies include watching football, collecting records to add to his vinyl collection, antique fairs and lots of socialising with friends and family. In September 2013 he attended Brian Dear's 70th Birthday celebrations, which is

Bobby at Roger and Joy's engagement party.

They Played With Bobby Moore – The West Ham Years

typical of a man that has nothing but time for the claret and blue. Roger and his wife, Joy, are closing in on 50-years of marriage.

One of my strongest memories of Bobby came after I scored a goal at home against Sheffield Wednesday in September 1969. We won the game 3-0 and I got a header but because it skimmed the head of Ian Branfoot, who was on the line, it has always been credited as an own-goal in the record books. After the game, I remember Bobby in the dressing room saying: 'That's young Cross's goal, Ron, he scored that.' Ron replied: 'Yeah, I know, I know.' But the papers marked it down as an own-goal and it has stayed that way ever since. I was really disappointed because the ball was on its way in and Branfoot jumped on the line but it barely touched his head and carried on its way into the net. It was great that Bobby fought my corner.

I used to go to the ground on Sundays to play a bit of head tennis with Frank Lampard and Harry Redknapp. Bobby was always there and Budgie was often there, too. They would put on their T-shirts and then black plastic bags followed by a full tracksuit. Off they would go running laps of the pitch. Rob Jenkins, the physio, would often run with them and they worked up a good sweat. When you saw it you felt compelled to do that extra bit of training. I can always remember Budgie in the bath afterwards, laying the Sunday newspaper on the water, soaking wet, and reading it as it floated around the bath.

Bobby's dedication to training rubbed off on all the young players. I was at the club for six years and the professionalism he demonstrated and standards he set, were simply fantastic. It was a wonderful, wonderful era at West Ham.

On Mondays, Ron Greenwood set up training sessions to include both the seniors and the youngsters. We were each given a ball and would work our way around the pitch, performing different activities. Ron would bring players in to demonstrate different tasks and I can remember Bobby volleying balls in from the corner flag to Geoff Hurst, who

Getting the better of Everton's Sandy Brown.

Scoring for fun in the reserves – this time against QPR in 1970.

was standing on the half way line. Geoff would chest it down for someone running on to it. They would then play a one-two before having a shot at goal, which was next to the other corner flag. Bobby was so good at it he was like a machine. He had so much ability with either foot I can't find the words to tell you just how skilful he was. Geoff would also make it look so easy. He bounced the ball off his big chest, up into the air, before laying it off. It was so funny because when everyone rotated and it was someone else's turn to take Bobby's role, the balls would be flying here, there and everywhere! Ron would say: 'You saw Bobby, you saw what he did, now you do the same.' But it was a classic case of something being easier said than done!

I remember going to watch Bobby when he was in the team that got to the 1959 FA Youth Cup final against Blackburn. At the time, I was a keen collector of autographs and often stayed late after the games getting the signatures of all the players. In those days the kids cut out pictures from various magazines like Charles Buchan and Soccer Star and got them signed. I had loads and loads of Bobby and the others in that youth team including Frank Caskey, Geoff Hurst, Mickey Beesley and John Cartwright, as well as the first team players such as John Dick and Vic Keeble, who had won promotion the year before.

In 1964, the club gave me and my family tickets for the FA Cup final. I was a bundle of nerves watching that game, literally shaking. When I signed for the club the following year, it was a dream come true. Then, Bobby Moore himself came along to my engagement party, ahead of my marriage to Joy. It was simply a fantastic time in my life.

When I played my first full game in 1969 – at home against Arsenal – Bobby gave me a really good piece of advice. He said: 'Their players aren't as good as you think they are, believe me they aren't as big as you think' He was dead right. When I played and scored against Arsenal I could have easily been overwhelmed by Bob Wilson, Frank McLintock, George Graham and Terry Neill but Bobby was spot on with his advice because when I got out there and started playing the ball and making passes, I started to think things weren't too bad and that I could play my game. I have always passed on Bobby's advice to players making their debuts in the various coaching roles I have held over the years.

Another strong memory comes from a match we played up at Everton. Bobby never left me in any doubt as to the challenge ahead: 'It's tough up there,' he said to me when we were on the coach: 'Up at places like, Everton, Manchester, Liverpool, you are always going to get a tough game.' It really helped settle me because I felt a man such as Bobby Moore shared the same worries as a young lad trying to establish himself in the first team. Although the record books show we lost 0-2 to the eventual champions, we played well that day and I could have easily scored a hat-trick.

After I left West Ham I went to Brentford first and then onto Fulham just before Bobby signed for them. Unfortunately, I had returned to Brentford before he arrived but he did call me up to ask what it was like at Fulham. I told him it was a fantastic football club but that he would notice a big difference in the coaching. Alex Stock was nothing like Ron Greenwood and John Lyall but he did know how to pick a team. Alex's team talks were very regimented and he would say things like: 'Tuck your shirt in, pull your shoulders back and let's get out there.' One of the first things I remember Alex doing when I arrived was getting a barber to come down

to the ground to cut everyone's hair. Now the 1970s was the decade of long hair so it all felt a bit strange.

I was one of the first players to wear a pair of white boots when I was at Brentford but when Alex found them at Fulham he put them in the incinerator! Although I didn't get on too well with him, I still thought it was a great club.

I can remember that if Bobby ever made a mistake at West Ham there was a gasp from the crowd. If anyone else left a back pass short or made the wrong pass there would be a resounding groan from the crowd and, sometimes, all-out criticism, but when Bobby made a mistake there was just a gasp and a silence. He was that good.

The final thing I want to say about Bobby is that I am so proud to have seen him play so many times when I was a young West Ham fan at school and then to line up with him in the first team. It makes me quite emotional to think about it. When I was in the youth team we would often race back to the ground and stand in the player's pen and watch him up close. Joining West Ham was the greatest thing ever!

Roger Cross

A true Hammer.

65 – JIMMY LINDSAY

Born: Hamilton, South Lanarkshire, July 12, 1949

Position: Midfielder

Games played with Bobby Moore: 40 (1968 – 71)

Games played for West Ham United: 45 (1968-71)

First game with Bobby Moore (Debut): October 8, 1968 Burnley (a) L 1-3

Scorers: Burnley: Murray, Kindon, Dobson
West Ham United: Brooking

Burnley: Thomson, Smith, Latcham, Todd, Waldron, Blant, Thomas, Murray, Casper, Dobson, Kindon

West Ham United: Ferguson, Bonds, Charles, Peters, Stephenson, Moore, Redknapp, Boyce, Brooking*, Hurst, Sissons Sub: **Lindsay***

J ames Young Lindsay was 19-years-old and almost eight years younger than Bobby Moore when he made his first team debut for West Ham United, as a substitute for Trevor Brooking, at Burnley in October 1968.

Lindsay almost formed part of one of the biggest transfers in the club's history: 'Ron almost sold Trevor Brooking and Jimmy Lindsay to Newcastle for £75,000. They both went up and spoke with Joe Harvey but thankfully it blew over.'

Lindsay played for Glasgow Boys before signing professional forms with West Ham in July 1966. The following season he gained a Scotland Youth cap.

The Scottish midfielder arrived at the club at the same time as Tony Carr, Steven Knowles, Stephen Lay and Michael Glumart. He would be the only player from that group to pull on the first team shirt.

Former striker Clyde Best offered his view on the youngsters joining West Ham United at that time: 'The club had so much good talent back then and Jimmy Lindsay was part of that. Unfortunately, Martin Peters and Ron Boyce made it difficult for him to get into the team. There were quite a few with fantastic talent who didn't make it. Stephen Lay was exceptional in the reserves and Keith Miller was unfortunate in that he played in the same position as Bobby Moore so had to move to Bournemouth to get his chance.'

Bobby Howe is another with a view on Lindsay's time at West Ham: 'For a while it looked as if Jimmy was going to establish himself in the first team and become West Ham's regular Number 8 but injury and competition for places edged him out.'

Trevor Hartley also played with Jimmy at West Ham and viewed him as: 'a fierce competitor as you would expect from a Scotsman. He got on well with George Andrew and Doug Eadie. I thought his attitude was good and Greenwood liked him, too. Jimmy was outspoken and I think he told Ron he didn't want to play for him anymore so he was another one that didn't go as far as he should have.'

Club physio Rob Jenkins remembers a time when

Bobby Moore watches as Jimmy tussles with Willie Morgan of Manchester United, August, 1970.

Former centre-half, Tommy Taylor recalls Jimmy's humour: 'He used to joke that the only people who could play football properly were the Scottish.'

Sadly, Jimmy twice suffered a broken leg at West Ham which impeded his progress. The experience is still fresh in the memory: 'Before I broke my leg against Mansfield Town in the FA Cup I recall Boycie coming up to me in the dressing room ahead of the game and warning me about their player, Johnny Quigley. I was naïve in those days and sure enough, Quigley broke my leg. It was a tie we should have won and victory would have put us in the quarter-finals against Leicester City at home. A broken leg and a 0-3 defeat was not one of my better days at West Ham!'

In action against Paul Edwards of Manchester United.

Lindsay played 40 matches with Bobby Moore, including the notorious FA Cup tie up at Blackpool in 1971. He also lined up in Bobby Moore's testimonial against Celtic at the Boleyn Ground on November 16, 1970. He was transferred to Watford for £20,000 in May 1971.

Today, Jimmy lives in Shrewsbury having pursued a post-playing career as a publican in the area. He still puts in a round of golf and plays off an 11 handicap.

The first time I met Bobby was during one of the many running sessions we did over at Epping Forest. I ran with Clive Charles and we could run all day but Mooro and people like Eddie Presland and Brian Dear were so slow and they didn't like us going off too quickly: 'Get back!' they would shout.

At training, we would do these shuttle runs and Mooro was so very slow, my mother could run quicker than him. I remember thinking that I'd be able to go by him anytime I felt like it because he was so static. But of course I never could get by him. I can't recall one time when I managed to beat him and yet he had no pace whatsoever, he was just too clever.

When I joined the club I didn't have a clue about how much Greenwood and Mooro didn't get on. They had respect for each other but that was it. There was one occasion when Bobby's enmity towards Ron was plain to see. We went on tour to America in 1969 to promote football over there and we were representing Baltimore. Wolves and Aston Villa were over there, too. Mooro, Geoff Hurst and Martin Peters were on international duty in Mexico as part of the preparation for the 1970 World Cup. When they joined up with us a couple of weeks later, there was only one room available which Martin and Geoff shared. The only other option for Mooro was to share with Greenwood! Well, Bobby flatly refused to entertain

that idea and, in the end, Paul Heffer, who was rooming with me, moved into Greenwood's room and Mooro came in with me. Every room had an ice machine outside and Mooro told me to fill our bath up with ice while he drove off for a while, returning with 20-dozen Budweisers. Our bathroom became a makeshift bar for the rest of the trip. To top it off, we parked two cars under the window and switched on the radios for a bit of music!

It was during that tour when Bobby got asked for his ID to get into a bar. He was only about 28 at the time! They were very strict about ID out there and I used Bobby Howe's passport to get a drink. He was a lot better looking than me but they never checked it that closely.

Back then there was a big drinking culture in football. You don't get it nowadays. We finished training at 1pm and two days every week I would usually coach the kids, along with Stuart Morgan, at the nearby St Bonaventure's School.

I was easily led in those days and if Mooro asked me if I fancied a pint in the Black Lion, I would go. My digs were close to the pub so it was easy for me to get involved. Stuart Morgan was my best man and I'd like to stay in touch with him a bit better.

I was brought into the Blackpool affair and yet it was nothing to do with me. Mooro, Clyde Best, Brian Dear, Rob Jenkins and Jimmy Greaves were supposedly drinking in a club the night before the cup game but Greenwood called me up on the Sunday after the game and accused me of being out drinking on Friday night. Ironically, had Bobby asked me to go out for a quick pint, I probably would have gone. As it happened I was playing cards with Billy Bonds, Trevor Brooking, Harry Redknapp and 'Les' Bennett. Greenwood was still very upset with me: 'Jimmy, you've bloody let me down by going to that club in Blackpool.' He clearly didn't have a clue who the culprits were. I just told him I didn't know what he was going on about which was all I could say because I really didn't know anything at that time. Sadly, Brian Dear paid the ultimate price and never played for West Ham again. It was also the beginning of the end for Mooro and Greavesie.

I played in Bobby's testimonial against Celtic. We all went back to the Sportsman's Club afterwards. I thought the West Ham boys could drink but those Celtic lads were worse than us! Bobby Murdoch seemed to be drinking with both hands! Celtic never got paid to play that night so the players were determined to get the most from their free piss-up. The game ended 3-3 against a very good Celtic side, which included legends such as Jimmy Johnstone, Tommy Gemmell and Billy McNeil.

I was too big a part of the drinking culture at every club I played for and I saw some real greedy pigs around alcohol but I never saw anyone drink like Mooro. The biggest difference with Mooro was that he never got drunk. Then, every Sunday, he would put the black bags on and do 40 laps of the pitch to sweat it all out. At five past 12 he would then head back down the Black Lion and start sipping away at half a lager again.

One thing about Mooro was that he hated being beaten by Scotland. They gave him so much stick and ridiculed him with their chants: 'Bobby Moore, superstar, walks like a woman and he wears a bra!' Now, if Mooro lost a league game he would come off the pitch and you wouldn't notice too much change in him but the one game he wanted to win every year was the Home International against Scotland. He loved beating them and when he did he would let me know all about it when he came back!

I was a bit of a yard dog on the pitch and would try and nullify the attacking intentions of midfielders such as Alan Ball. One day Greenwood told me to man mark QPR's Rodney Marsh. 'He is playing much deeper these days so keep him out of the game.' The game kicked off and I started shadowing Marshy. After a while Mooro came over to me and said 'What are you doing in defence?' I told him what Ron had asked me to do. 'But he's playing up front you daft f***! I was actually marking him in our own defence! We had a good laugh about that one. I was still voted man-of-the-match in the Sunday People!

The last time I saw Bobby was when I played against him. He was at Fulham and I was at Hereford United. I couldn't get in the bar afterwards because I didn't have a ticket but we bumped into each other on the stairs and he got me in. We had a chat and that was it. He was a gentleman and a true great.

Jimmy Lindsay

At home in Shrewsbury.

66 – KEITH MILLER

Born: Lewisham, January 26, 1948

Position: Centre-half

Games played with Bobby Moore: 3 (1968-69)

Games played for West Ham United: 3 (1968-69)

First game with Bobby Moore (Debut): November 23, 1968 Ipswich Town (a) D 2-2

Scorers: Ipswich Town: Morris, Viljoen
West Ham United: Hurst (2, 1pen)

Ipswich Town: Hancock, Mills, Houghton, Morris, Baxter, Jefferson, Hegan, Viljoen, Crawford, O'Rourke, Brogan

West Ham United: Ferguson, Bonds, Charles, Cushley, Stephenson, Moore, Peters, Boyce, Dear, Hurst, Sissons*, Sub: **Miller***

Keith Raymond Miller played three times for West Ham United, all of them alongside Bobby Moore.

He was seven years younger than Moore and would go on to make his name at AFC Bournemouth, where he remains in the top ten on the all-time appearances list.

Miller played for Blackheath Boys and Walthamstow Avenue before signing professional forms for West Ham on August 31, 1965.

He spent five years with the Hammers and is largely remembered for breaking the leg of Paul Reaney, the Leeds United right-back. Ironically, Miller was wearing the Number 6 shirt in that game.

Former friend and team-mate at both West Ham and Bournemouth, Bobby Howe, describes Keith as 'a solid, dependable player and citizen.'

Harry Redknapp is another to remember Keith with fondness: 'I played a lot of games with Keith at Bournemouth. We all call him 'Dusty' and he still lives down in Bournemouth like me. He's a terrific guy and it is always good to catch up with him.'

Jimmy Lindsay was one of Dusty's best pals and has somewhat dubious proof of it: 'We played together in the A team and reserves together. I've still got the scar from one of his tackles when I was playing for Watford and he was at Bournemouth.'

In July 1970 Miller joined Bournemouth where a rich presence of former Hammers – John Bond, Ken Brown, Harry Redknapp, Tony Scott, Pat Holland and Trevor Hartley – helped shape his progress.

Nowadays Keith has fully retired from his job with *Compass* Magazine. His hobbies include walking, cycling and spending time with his grandchildren. He maintains contact with both Harry Redknapp and Ted MacDougall. In 2012, he attended John Bond's funeral and caught up with his former team-mates from both West Ham and Bournemouth.

Following are his memories of Moore:

I was actually working at Smithfield meat market in London, with my father Reg, when I got an offer to trial at West Ham.

Ready for action.

I was only 17 and went along during my two-week holiday from work. My first experience of Bobby Moore came when I was training with him over that period. At the end of it, Ron Greenwood came up to me and said he'd like to sign me. I went straight back to the market and handed in my notice. I told them I was going to be a footballer and signed amateur forms for West Ham in June 1965. It was the start of five great years at the club.

It was always going to be difficult for me because West Ham had just won the FA Cup in 1964 and the European Cup Winners Cup the following year and I played in Bobby's position! I ended up making two substitute appearances – at Ipswich and Nottingham Forest – and one start against Leeds United but it is still a big highlight in my life.

I actually wore the Number 6 shirt against Leeds and Bobby wore the Number 5 so that was a great honour in itself. It was a highly dramatic game for me because I broke Paul Reaney's leg. It was an unfortunate collision and thankfully, Paul was very magnanimous about it and saw it for the accident that it was.

Bobby could see how terribly I felt about the whole episode and was very sympathetic. Ron Greenwood suggested I went to see Paul in hospital which I did and he was as good as gold about the whole episode. We shook hands and he told me not to worry about it which was difficult for me because, before the injury, Paul was in the England squad to go to Mexico for the 1970 World Cup. We'll never know what would have happened had he went.

Even now, my mum – Eileen – remembers the occasion when Bobby Moore shook her hand. She had come to a match to see me play and Bobby took the time to meet her. She mentions it every time she hears his name or sees a picture of him. The simple act of shaking his hand has stayed with her forever.

When I was at the club, one of my friends Eric Batty who worked on various football magazines asked me to see if Bobby would give him an interview over the phone. I wanted to help but was very anxious because I had to go into the first team dressing room and ask him. I was really nervous but he just said: 'Hello, Keith, what do you need?' He was so obliging and natural that I laugh now because I was wondering if I should call him Mr Moore!

I remember when Bobby, Geoff and Martin won the World Cup and returned for pre-season training in 1966. I have never seen so many journalists at Chadwell Heath. As a teenager it was incredible to be around all that.

I didn't leave too big an imprint at West Ham United, but even though I only played the one full game, I had the master alongside me and it really doesn't get any better than that does it?

Keith Miller

Incurring the hard knocks of first team football on his debut at Ipswich Town, November, 1968.

With his good friend Ted MacDougall (right).

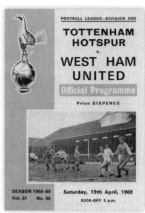

67 – PETER GROTIER

Born: Stratford, London, October 18, 1950

Position: Goalkeeper

Games played with Bobby Moore: 52 (1969-73)

Games played for West Ham United: 54 (1969-74)

First game with Bobby Moore (Debut): April 19, 1969 Tottenham Hotspur (a) L 0-1

Scorer: Tottenham Hotspur: Greaves

Tottenham Hotspur: Jennings, Beal, Knowles, Mullery, England, Pratt, Johnson, Greaves, Gilzean, Pearce, Morgan

West Ham United: Grotier, Bonds, Charles*, Howe, Stephenson, Moore, Redknapp, Boyce, Hurst, Peters, Sissons Sub: Brooking*

Peter David Grotier was over nine years younger than Bobby Moore and played in over 50 games with him over a four-year period.

Grotier signed apprentice forms on October 18, 1966 and turned professional on March 8, 1968. He attended South West Ham Technical School and had also played for Clapton juniors.

Peter shared the Number 1 shirt with Bobby Ferguson throughout his time at West Ham United. He was the 10th keeper to line up with Bobby Moore. Only Stephen Death and Mervyn Day were to follow.

'Grote' as he was commonly known, was very popular amongst his team-mates and many remember him with a wry smile. Ade Coker led the way: 'He was such a fantastic character and somehow we managed to play together again at Lincoln City. I would love to meet up with the Grote again.' 'Ernie Gregory loved the Grote,' recalls Dave Llewelyn. 'He was Ernie's favourite.'

Clyde Best has not forgotten the mischievous side of Peter: 'Grote was a clown, always playing jokes on people. He was a very nice guy, we were all mates and hung out together. I thought he was a fantastic talent.'

Peter remains very good friends with Tony Carr, former Director of Youth Development at West Ham, who played for West Ham reserves in the late 1960s. Memories from that era are never too far away.

Today, Peter works as an Operations Director for a freight forwarding company in Coggeshall, Essex. He lives with his wife, Jackie, in Colchester and they have three grandchildren – Rosie, Joseph and Mason. Peter's hobbies include travel, golf and fishing.

Saving a penalty from Birmingham City's Alan Campbell in September 1972. Bobby Moore looks on.

Saving from Denis Law at Old Trafford, August, 1970.

He shared the following memories of Moore:

On October 18, 1966 my dream came true. It was my 16th Birthday and I was sitting in Mr Ron Greenwood's office signing apprentice forms for West Ham United.

Within a month of being part of this fantastic club and training with three World Cup winning players, something happened which has stayed in my memory to this day.

We had just finished our morning training session at Chadwell Heath and, along with the other apprentices, I was clearing away all the muddy boots and wet training kit of the professional players. Albert Walker, who was the kit man at the time, called me over and said: 'Peter, you have been chosen by Mr Moore to go to Upton Park and assist him in getting his playing kit and boots ready for a TV advert he is involved in.'

Can you imagine how I felt, being asked by the England World Cup winning captain to assist him in preparation for a TV advert? I was showered and dressed in no time at all and asked Albert if he would give me a lift back to Upton Park: 'No, Mr Moore will take you in his car,' came his reply.

Looking out into the car park I could see this gleaming red Jaguar with a cream leather interior and I was going to be sitting in it with Bobby Moore at the wheel.

Are you ready, Peter?' he called and I could only respond

with: 'Er, yes, Mr Moore.' 'Let's go then' he replied.

Within only a few hundred yards of leaving Chadwell Heath there I was chatting with Bobby Moore as if we were best buddies. 'Are you enjoying the training?' he asked. 'Are all the professionals looking after you?' came the next question. 'Are you playing well?' I hardly had time to answer them.

'I have to go home before we go to Upton Park,' he said. We drove into Chigwell, passing some amazing houses and pulled onto his drive in Manor Road. There was this beautiful house with green tiles on the roof, it was like a mansion to me because I was living in a council house in Stratford at the time. I was invited inside.

'Tea or coffee, Peter?' he offered. 'Er, tea please.' 'Milk or lemon?' came the next question and Bobby obviously knew by the look on my face that I was puzzled. 'Would you like milk or lemon in your tea?' he explained. 'Milk,' I said nervously.

Then this beautiful lady appeared in the kitchen, it was Tina Moore. I remembered her from the TV coverage when the World Cup lads were celebrating. Bobby introduced me, she was stunning and so very nice.

We set off for Upton Park and the nearer we got the more people started to recognise the car and began waving and shouting: 'Good luck Saturday, Bobby!'

The closest Peter got to a cap! Repelling the attacking advances of Derby County at the Baseball Ground with John Cushley (left) and Alan Stephenson, March 1970.

Bobby's kit had been laid out in the home dressing room by yours truly and I stayed there watching him changing into it with my mouth wide open. It really was like a dream and he looked immaculate.

After the filming was over, Bobby thanked me for my help and handed me £10 which at the time was more than a week's wages to me. That day will be a lasting memory of a fantastic man, the best player I have played with or against and, remember, I played against Pele and George Best, too.

Little did I know that 18 months later I would be running out at White Hart Lane behind the great man making my debut and it will always be with me to say I was part of his career.

We had a few trips abroad during my time at West Ham and I particularly remember a visit to Israel. Ron Greenwood had arranged it as part of a plan to sign Mordechai Spiegler, the Israeli international who had trained with us for a while. We were going to play the Israeli national team. We were in a beautiful hotel but you could hear all the gunfire going off in the background because there was a conflict at the time. On one of the days the club arranged a trip to the Wailing Wall and this is something I will never ever forget. We all got on the coach from the hotel and drove down to one of the holiest places on the planet. Opposite the ticket office and entrance was a bar and it ended up that only about three people went in to see the Wailing Wall while the rest of us followed Bobby into the bar and got pissed!

Most of my memories are from the socialising we did, with Bobby always saying: 'A bottle of lager, Grote, would be lovely.'
Peter Grotier

'Grote'.

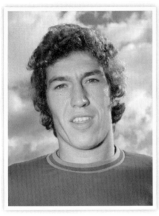

68 – PAT HOLLAND

Born: Poplar, London, September 13, 1950

Position: Left-wing

Games played with Bobby Moore: 60 (1969-74)

Games played for West Ham United: 298 (1969-81)

First game with Bobby Moore (Debut): April 21, 1969 Arsenal (h) L 1-2

Scorers: West Ham United: Sissons
Arsenal: Graham, Sammels

WEST HAM UNITED ☓

VERSUS

ARSENAL

FOOTBALL LEAGUE : Division One
Monday 21st April 1969
KICK - OFF 7.30 p.m.

No. 57

OFFICIAL PROGRAMME 1/-

West Ham United: Grotier, Bonds, Howe, Cushley, Stephenson, Moore, **Holland**, Brooking, Hurst, Peters, Sissons

Arsenal: Wilson, Storey, McNab, McLintock, Simpson*, Graham, Robertson, Sammels, Court, Radford, Armstrong
Sub: Gould*

Patrick George Holland was West Ham United's first-ever scoring substitute. It came late on in the game during Bobby Moore's final first team appearance for the club – against Hereford United in the FA Cup third round on January 5, 1974. 'Patsy' had actually replaced Moore himself on 30 minutes to unwittingly bring to a close the greatest contribution ever made by any player to West Ham United.

Former team-mate, Bobby Gould – who ironically missed out himself in 1975 – has a recurring memory of Patsy: 'He's got my Cup final shirt! Every time I see him I tell him that I want my Number 11 shirt back because he wore it in the Fulham final. He always gets back at me by saying he is going to wear it in his grave to rub salt in my wounds! I never got off the subs bench in the 1975 final despite coughing up a lung to get Ron Greenwood and John Lyall to notice me and put me on!'

Holland played in the East Ham Schools side which won the English Schools Trophy in 1966. He signed apprentice professional forms in September 1967 and became professional on September 5, 1968. Coincidentally, the former long-standing director of West Ham's Youth Academy, Tony Carr, signed on the same day.

Clyde Best declares: 'It was a treat to play with Patsy.' Indeed, the popular winger would remain at West Ham for 17 years, playing 302 games, winning a 1975 FA Cup winners medal and a runners-up medal in the 1976 European Cup Winners Cup final. Holland also formed part of the record breaking 1981 promotion team, having sadly seen a recurring knee injury prevent him from winning further honours in the 1980 FA Cup final victory over Arsenal.

Member of another fine West Ham United Youth team – winners in Zambia, May 1969.

Holland is yet another player from the Bobby Moore era to enter management, having had a spell at Leyton Orient during the mid-1990s. He also ran a wine bar – Hollands – in Shenfield, Essex.

Today, Patsy is part of the scouting team at Arsenal and still lives in Upminster with his wife Janette.

Entertaining the Chicken Run.

I remember seeing Bobby Moore play when I was just 10-years-old. I was an Arsenal supporter as a lad and I went to Upton Park on November 5, 1960 to see them play West Ham. My family were all dockers and we stood in the Chicken Run.

I got there really early and was decked out in all my red and white regalia; rosette, bobble hat, scarf, the lot. West Ham destroyed Arsenal 6-0 that day and by the end of it I was sitting down on the planks unable to watch any more. Dave Dunmore tore Arsenal to pieces and scored a hat-trick. I can also remember both John Dick and Phil Woosnam playing out of their skins. I have since learned that John Lyall wore the Number 3 shirt for the Hammers.

During pre-season, Ron Greenwood always ensured that everyone trained with the first team so it wasn't very long after I joined the club that I was training with Bobby Moore. I was a really nervous young man and always had my head down. My hands would shake when I was eating in the canteen. If I saw Bobby I couldn't even make eye contact. They were formidable men to me and talking to them was the furthest thing from my mind. I do remember going home after my first training session and my dad asking me who was the best player and I answered: 'Trevor Brooking.'

Bobby was about 10 years older than me and was in a different league altogether. It was quite daunting to be around the senior pros because they had such tremendous stature at that time in their careers. One thing Bobby did which I always remember was run over to me after I had scored a goal and shake my hand. Now I didn't score that many goals and Bobby wasn't one to shake the hand of others after they had scored, but for some reason he took the time to shake my hand which I thought was fantastic.

During the summer break, I would sometimes go to the ground and do some extra running and stairway work. One day after my shower, Bobby walked into the changing room with this tall man with big afro hair: 'Hello, Patsy boy,' he said. 'Hello, Bob,' I replied. 'This is Carlos Alberto,' he said. I shook hands with Carlos Alberto, who was over here on a photo

Getting in a shot against Manchester City in March 1970.

shoot. There I was, standing there with the captain of the greatest ever Brazilian team and the captain of the greatest ever England team. Simply fantastic!

Bobby used to write a column in the Newham Recorder and I remember he wrote some lovely things following a game for West Ham at home to Manchester United. (January 17 1970). I had a good game in that one and we drew 0-0. Bobby wrote: 'I looked over at young Patsy and he was doing his boots up. He seemed composed so there was no need to wish him well and I left him alone. Manchester United was always a big game and they were the team I had made my debut against 12 years earlier. He went out and did really well, a typical performance, he didn't let any of their players settle and chased every ball.' It was a lovely article and I have always kept it.

At West Ham, we always went out for a Christmas bash. There was a pub on the Mile End road called The Globe. Harry Garrish was the manager and Jimmy and Patsy Quill owned it. We all met there and, by that, I mean the top-to-bottom of West Ham United, from the young apprentices right through to the senior pros. Players from other clubs would also turn up and, in fact, Glenn Roeder came once and we got him drunk and put him on a train the wrong way home! At some stage in the evening, I was in the toilet and in walked Bobby. 'Tina's been calling the pub,' he said. 'We're supposed to be going out tonight and she's been telling everyone to get my arse home!' Now, I could tell he didn't want to go because Bobby was a man's man but I didn't really say anything to help. I was too busy thinking: 'That's the England captain and he's drunk like me!'

Bobby had a very good sense of humour which he took onto the field with him. I remember we went on tour to America and I was one of the youngsters along with John McDowell, Peter Grotier and Kevin Lock. We were based in Los Angeles but flew all over the States to play. One of those games was in Dallas and we were there for a few days. Like an idiot I got badly sun burned which was so bad, I could barely move. Anyway, I managed to gingerly put on my kit and played in the game. Bob and Tommy Taylor kept chipping the ball to me about chest high. I didn't realise at first but after half dozen times I could see them laughing to each other. It was agony every time I had to bring it down on my red raw chest!

I had the honour of playing in Bobby's testimonial match against Celtic at Upton Park. It was a filthy wet night and I came on with 30 minutes to go and straight away got nutmegged by Jimmy Johnstone! I then picked up the ball and went on a run, taking on three players, rounding the keeper but was just unable to finish from a tight angle. As I was running back, the Wee Man tapped me on the head and said: 'Different class, son, different class!'

Bobby had hired The Sportsman's Club for the post match-drink and we all met up there. I remember seeing Sean Connery and Bobby was in his element being surrounded by all his show biz and football pals. It was an honour to be there and I had just started courting my future wife, Janette. She was only 17 so it was just a fantastic experience for us both.

I remember going to Shoreditch once because I was into fashion and we all liked buying new gear. Green Street in Upton Park was okay but they all tended to sell the same styles. Bobby had a business relationship with a man named Maurice Keston who was a big Tottenham fan. He owned a manufacturers in Shoreditch and they sold top of the range clothes. I bought a trench coat there like the one Michael Caine used to wear. Anyway, as I went into the shop Bobby was walking out: 'What are you buying?' he said to me. 'I need a few shirts' I replied. 'Don't buy this one,' he said. He opened his bag to show me this beautiful purple shirt. I wanted one immediately so bought one in pink!

I used to sell Bobby the old-style music cassettes known as 8-tracks. They pre-dated the smaller cassette and CD. At that time they were the must-have thing for anyone into music. Now, I could get my hands on all the latest releases and Bob was interested in crooners, like Frank Sinatra. I was selling them for about £2 each but when Bobby asked me I was too scared to ask for the full price so I told him a quid. I lost on the deal but it just felt better!

Inadvertently, Bobby saved my career at West Ham. Ron Greenwood wanted to let me go to Norwich City in exchange for Graham Paddon. I didn't want to go and Ron wasn't happy and said I would never play for West Ham United again. Fortunately for me there was a bizarre run of injuries at the time, which meant Ron had to put me on the bench for an FA Cup game against Hereford United. After 30 minutes Bobby was stretchered off with a gash on his leg. So from nowhere, I was back playing in the first team and with no time left I went on a mazy run and scored the equaliser to force a replay. On the Monday, the whole atmosphere had changed and Ron thanked me for my efforts in front of everyone so I felt that he wanted to keep me which obviously he did.

I was lucky in that I played under two great captains in Bobby Moore and Billy Bonds. Bobby always called me: 'Young Patsy' or 'Patsy Boy,' but Billy called me 'Dutch.' They both led by example but had very different styles. If you did something wrong or made a mistake on the pitch, Bobby would just look at you in a certain way and that was enough. Billy was all action and would be very vocal on the pitch: 'Come on Dutch!' he would shout at me. We became very good team-mates.

After the 1975 FA Cup final, West Ham stayed at the Grosvenor Hotel on Park Lane while the Fulham boys were down the road at the Hilton. We all made our way to the Hilton because Bobby's showbiz pals were there and we knew we would have a much better time.

I was very nervous before the final. Some people can take it in their stride but I wasn't that type of player. It just so happened that I was standing next to Bobby in the tunnel as we were about to make our way onto the pitch: 'Alright, Patsy Boy?' he asked. I told

him how absolutely petrified I was – or words to that effect! 'You'll be alright,' he said, assuringly.

Bobby was highly revered even without the show business PR machine that can artificially promote a player, such as David Beckham. Bobby was famous because he was such a fantastic player and what folk nowadays might not know is just how many people outside of West Ham United absolutely loved the fella. Former Arsenal players like Bob McNab and Frank McLintock absolutely adored the man. Even now Frank talks about Mooro as if he was a god.

The last time I spoke with Bob was in the car park at West Ham. I was on scouting duty and Bob was fulfilling his radio commitments. We were locked in after the game and I was a bit frustrated. We had a chat and he said not to worry, it'll clear soon and that was it. The last time I saw him was on the telly and I phoned Terry Creasey, who was big mates with Bob, and he told me that it was serious and just a week later he had died.

Bobby Moore was the ultimate football hero. If he said 'Hello' it just lifted your day.

Pat Holland

'Patsy'.

69 – STEPHEN DEATH
September 19, 1949 – October 26, 2003

Born: Elmswell, Suffolk

Position: Goalkeeper

Games played with Bobby Moore: 1 (1969)

Games played for West Ham United: 1 (1969)

Only game with Bobby Moore: April 30, 1969
Manchester City (a) D 1-1

Scorers: West Ham United: Peters
Manchester City: Pardoe

Manchester City: Dowd, Book, Pardoe, Doyle, Booth, Oakes, Summerbee, Bell, Lee, Young, Coleman

West Ham United: Death, Bonds, Howe, Cushley, Stephenson, Moore, Holland, Brooking, Hurst, Peters, Sissons

---

Stephen Victor Death played just a solitary first team game for West Ham United – against Manchester City at Maine Road on April 30, 1969. In doing so, he lined up with seven cup winners, including three victorious 1966 World Cup legends.

Death's football path saw him keep goal for Suffolk Boys, who he helped to win the inter-county championship. He soon appeared on the radar of chief scout Wally St Pier and signed apprentice forms for West Ham on June 3, 1965 before completing professional forms two years later.

The keeper also gained three England Schoolboy caps against Wales (twice) and West Germany.

After leaving the Hammers, Stephen went on to make his name at Reading, where he set a new record of over 18 hours without conceding a goal. That English shut-out record was only broken by Manchester United's Edwin Van de Saar in 2002.

In stark contrast to his time at West Ham, Stephen played in 537 matches for Reading, straddling a 13 year period.

In 2003, at the relatively young age of 53, he passed away from cancer. There was no shortage of memories from his former team-mates at West Ham United.

I was in digs with 'Deathy' who was an absolute nutter. Fellow youth team player, Stuart Morgan, was also with us but he didn't make it to the first team and Stephen only played one first team game. I remember one time we were out in Geneva and we went to a bar and had a great night. There was Stephen, Stuart, Jimmy Lindsay and myself. We couldn't get home but some chap in a sports car said he'd drive us back to the hotel but there wasn't enough room for all of us so Deathy said; "Don't worry, I'll sit on the boot". Anyway, the car sped off and Stephen went flying off the top!

Once, Ron Greenwood told him he'd been picked for an England Youth trial but Deathy just said he didn't want to go so he never went.

If he had been six inches taller he would have played for England. He was the best goalkeeper out there. It was funny because when he moved to Reading I was at Peterborough and my first league goal was against him. He had George Best looks and all the women absolutely loved him. He was a good mate and we would go to the Black Lion in Plaistow for a few beers. He is an absolute legend at Reading and it was a shame how he ended up. Basically, he was living like a recluse before he died.
Dave Llewelyn

One day Ron Greenwood called Stephen into his office. He went up there, sat down and lit up a fag: 'Now, that is exactly why I have called you up here, Stephen,' said Ron!
Brian Dear

Stephen was a heavy smoker and didn't say much. He was like a recluse as a young kid. I felt sorry for him really because he was a bit strange but fearless as a goalkeeper, albeit a little too short to be a top, top, keeper.
Frank Lampard

Stephen had a wonderful career at Reading and was an excellent, agile, goalkeeper. He obviously grew in confidence after he left West Ham, where there was a lot of competition for the Number 1 jersey.
Bobby Howe

One of the best shot stoppers I have ever seen.
Colin Mackleworth

He always said: 'My name is Death'
Rob Jenkins

Claiming the ball against Manchester City under the watchful eye of Bobby Moore.

We were in digs together and he pulled all the women because he was so good looking. He didn't even speak to them and he still pulled! In fact he didn't speak much at all. When you went out with him you were lucky to get six words out of him all night. He was too small to be a great goalkeeper but he had the best hands of any keeper at the club and was very brave.

Jimmy Lindsay

His name absolutely suited him because he was very dark. But what a character – a total rebel! Ron Greenwood arranged a friendly at Chadwell Heath against QPR and we had Deathy and Paul Heffer running the lines. The game kicked off and, after ten minutes, Ron noticed that Deathy wasn't calling any offsides or throw-ins. In fact, he was just standing there with a fag on the go! Ron asked Tony Carr to go over to Stephen and ask him to put out his cigarette and start running the line properly. Tony went over to Stephen and passed on the instruction and returned to Ron, who asked what his response was? 'If Ron wants me to put my

fag out tell him to come and effing ask me himself!' came his reply.

Every year John Lyall took the youth team to Switzerland and Italy to play in a tournament. Deathy and I were the two keepers and this was the third year we had stayed in the same hotel which was a real doss hole. We slept three or four in a room and spent most evenings playing cards and drinking beer. One night, we were all pissed and someone dared Deathy to climb out the window and bang on the reception door to wake everyone up. Well, you only had to ask Deathy once and he'd do it. He started climbing out the window but we were three storeys up and it must have been 50-feet to the ground. As he was scaling down the drain pipe it came away from the wall and he fell flat on his back. We all thought he was dead but he just jumped up and we let him back in. When he returned to the room we were all cheering. At breakfast the following morning, John Lyall had the drain pipe running down the centre of the breakfast table! We all kept schtum but had to chip in to pay for the damages.

Peter Grotier

A VIEW FROM THE PHYSIO
MEMORIES OF BOBBY MOORE BY ROB JENKINS

Rob Jenkins became West Ham United's first team physiotherapist in August 1966 following the sudden death of his father Bill. It was a position he held for the next 25 years covering over 1400 professional games. Like his father before him Rob enjoyed a close friendship with Bobby Moore:

I socialised with Bobby a lot of the time. The East End in the 1960s was a different place to what it is now. There was virtually a pub on every corner and after a game on Saturday the Black Lion in Plaistow would be so crowded the landlady would tape off an area for the West Ham players. She would then make sausage sandwiches for us all. It wouldn't happen nowadays because the association between players and fans in the 1960s and 70s was much closer. It is practically non-existent today.

West Ham famously drew 2-2 with Pele's Santos in New York. My big memory of that occasion came after the match when Bobby saved my life. We had a drink with Pele back at the hotel before Bobby and I jumped into a big yellow taxi and went to a party. I was a smoker at the time and took a rolled-up cigarette off somebody . It soon became clear that it wasn't ordinary tobacco. I started to feel suicidal. Bobby noticed the change in me and got me back to our hotel and made sure I went to bed to sleep it off. If I hadn't been with Bobby I don't know what I would have done. I was hallucinating and not in control of my actions. Some people have said that the cigarette paper may have been impregnated with LSD and that I had been on a bad trip! Whatever it was I haven't had another cigarette since and I just thank god that Bobby was there to look after me.

I was with Bobby on the night of the so called Blackpool affair. I made a mistake really because I usually gave him a sleeping tablet the night before a game. He was a terrible insomniac but on this occasion I had forgotten to pack some so Bobby suggested we went for a walk instead. Clyde Best, Jimmy Greaves and Brian Dear joined us and we ended up in Brian London's 007 club having a quiet drink. All hell let loose after we lost the game and Greenwood found out we had been drinking. A good player called Tony Green of Blackpool made mincemeat out of us and we lost 0-4 on an unplayable pitch.

My aunt Iris – my father's sister – used to attend all the home games and would sometimes visit the lounge afterwards. She said Bobby had the bearing of a prince and that when he entered the room it sent a shiver down her spine.

Bobby was a stalwart. Not only a great footballer but a great person. Very well mannered, very tidy and very unique.

Rob on tour in 1973 with Bobby Moore. Fellow hammers Bobby Ferguson and Billy Bonds are also enjoying the sun.

Rob with his good friend Frank Lampard inside the Green Street clinic.

Back row L-R Bonds, Heffer, Stephenson, Bennett, Best, Moore, Cushley. Middle row L-R Peters, Charles, Grotier, Death, Ferguson, Lampard, Brooking. Front row L-R Redknapp, Boyce, Hurst, Lindsay, Howe, Sissons.

CHAPTER TWELVE
1969-70

Bobby Moore's total appearances (July 1969-June 1970): 60 games (0 goals)

League Division One: 40, England: 12, Friendlies: 5, League Cup: 2, FA Cup: 1

The biggest event of the season came in March, with the news that Martin Peters had left the club to join north London rivals, Tottenham Hotspur. The transfer, which brought the ageing Jimmy Greaves to Upton Park as part of a £200,000 deal, was the most high profile sale of home-grown talent in the club's history. The legendary Moore, Hurst and Peters was no more.

Peters would pick up two League Cup winners medals and a UEFA Cup winners medal during his time at White Hart Lane. It was a template for what happened at West Ham United some 30 years later when home-grown talent such as Rio Ferdinand, Michael Carrick, Frank Lampard jnr and Joe Cole helped to fill trophy cabinets at both Manchester United and Chelsea respectively.

Once again, West Ham United exited both cups in the very early stages, at Nottingham Forest in the League Cup and at Middlesbrough in the FA Cup.

Moore was voted Hammer of the Year, for the fourth and final occasion. Fittingly, Billy Bonds was runner-up for the second year running but 'Bonzo' would have his day, many times, in the future.

The season culminated with the World Cup finals in Mexico. England's pre-tournament preparations had been interrupted by the Bogota jewellery affair, which saw a shop assistant at the Hotel Tequendama, Clara Padilla, accuse Moore of stealing a £625 gold bracelet studded with emeralds.

Moore was cleared of any wrong doing and played in all four England games, eventually exiting the tournament at the hands of West Germany, 2-3.

The game between England and Brazil in the group stage is heralded by many as Moore's finest ever performance. Pele described him as: 'The best defender I have played against and a gentleman of honour.'

Moore was voted runner-up to Germany's Gerd Muller for the European Footballer of the Year award.

Ron Greenwood signed Peter Eustace from Sheffield

Guadalajara 1970 – two giants of the game.

Wednesday for £90,000 as a replacement for Peters, and, alongside Moore's great friend, Greaves, he was one of four new Hammers to make their debuts for the club - the others being Clyde Best and Dave Llewelyn.

Here is their story...

70 – CLYDE BEST

Born: Somerset, Bermuda, February 24, 1951

Position: Forward

Games played with Bobby Moore: 165 (1969-74)

Games played for West Ham United: 218 (1969-76)

First game with Bobby Moore (Debut): August 25, 1969 Arsenal (h) D 1-1

Scorers: West Ham United: Cross
Arsenal: Lampard (og)

West Ham United: Ferguson, Bonds, Lampard*, Peters, Stephenson, Moore, **Best**, Boyce, Brooking, Hurst, Cross Sub: Howe*

Arsenal: Wilson, Storey, McNab, McLintock, Neill, Simpson, Robertson, George, Court, Graham, Radford

Clyde Cyril Best is one of the most popular names in West Ham United's history. The Bermudan-born striker played over 150 games with Bobby Moore.

Best was a gentle giant who occasionally wore the goalkeeper's gloves in an emergency. He was another innocent in the 'Blackpool affair' of 1971 and his most famous legacy can probably be found in the score-line; Santos 2 (Pele 2) West Ham United 2 (Best 2).

Clyde's popularity in Bermuda can be summed up when asking for his address – 'Just send it to: 'Clyde Best, Bermuda' – and it will find me.'

Best became something of a journey man after his time playing for West Ham. Interestingly, he scored the winning goal for Tampa Bay Rowdies in the 1975 Soccer Bowl to secure their first ever North American Soccer League title. He also had spells with Feyenoord in the Dutch league before playing out his career in America's Indoor Soccer League. He also coached the Bermudan national team during the late 1990s.

In 2006, Clyde was honoured with an MBE in the New Year's Honours list. He recalls the occasion with superb humour. 'It was a great honour to be meeting the Queen and my wife insisted that I buy a tailored suit from Savile Row. I had no idea these

Between the sticks versus Leeds United with Pop Robson and Bobby Moore, April 1973.

things cost so much and I blew all our savings to buy it. There was a very anxious moment when the tailor started showing us catalogues of top hats. The prices were out of this world but my wife said we had to do it properly. That hat crippled us financially and when we got to Buckingham Palace the first thing they said was: 'Take it off!'

Clyde still lives in his native Bermuda and continues his sterling work at the Westgate Correctional Facility in Hamilton.

Bobby Moore led the way for all of us. The most important thing to me about Bobby was that for a person who had achieved so much in football, he was a great human being. He was just the ultimate and we all looked up to him. To be in the same team and company as him was a privilege and an honour. I was so young and Bobby, Geoff Hurst and Martin Peters were World Cup winners so it was an unbelievable time.

One thing about West Ham in those days was that everybody got along together. The club arranged trips abroad and Bobby was so good at getting the players to go out for a drink so we all knew each other really well. He also got tickets for the guys to see shows and boxing nights.

I remember my first game against Arsenal. I was training at Chadwell Heath and Ron Greenwood pulled me aside and told me to go home and get some rest because I was going to play. I was over the moon with that

In the famous hoops at Highbury.

and I'll never forget going into the dressing room and Bobby talking to me and making me aware of what needed to be done, but also ensuring that we went out, enjoyed it and had some fun. It was the start of my playing career at West Ham and Bobby gave me a lot of advice and a lot of help.

For me, he goes down as the greatest ever defender. People often talk about Bobby Moore and Franz Beckenbauer together. But I would always pick Bobby ahead of Beckenbauer. He read the game superbly, had two brilliant feet, was a fantastic passer of the ball and saw things so much quicker than everybody else. He would ping the perfect ball to me when I made my run and he was just a joy to play with. He trained as hard as he played, he was a wonderful trainer and would do extra running on Sundays.

I remember we went on a trip to America and played Santos at Randalls Island in New York. Pele and myself scored the goals in a 2-2 draw and, as usual, Bobby was superb.

I'll never forget the night in Blackpool. We had been told on the Friday evening that the game was going to be called off so Bobby, Brian Dear, Jimmy Greaves, Rob Jenkins and myself went to Brian London's 007 club. Sadly, some people were a bit mischievous in what they said and an innocent drink attracted all the wrong publicity. I was only drinking ginger beer and lime but that's life, I suppose. We all admitted that we had made a mistake and the fact the game went ahead, with us losing 0-4, only served to compound the situation. It was a shame that Brian Dear never played again for West Ham because one thing about Stag was that he was a tough cookie.

Another big moment in my time at West Ham came during the League Cup semi-final second replay against Stoke City. Whenever Bobby Ferguson got injured I normally took the gloves but, this time, it was simply too big a responsibility for me and I think Mooro saw that and stepped up to the plate himself. Boy, I was mightily relieved!

I try and get to a game at West Ham every year and always like to catch up with Frank Lampard, Trevor Brooking and Rob Jenkins in his clinic. I like to see as many of the guys as possible because it is nice to rekindle those relationships. The camaraderie is what I miss most. I have a very good friend called Alan Olsen, who I always see and no trip would be complete without visiting Charlo's wife, Carol and his sister Rita. They are family to me.

I will always be indebted to West Ham for giving me the opportunity to play with great people like Bobby, Geoff, Martin, Billy Bonds, Trevor Brooking, Frank Lampard and Harry Redknapp. It was a school of science.

Bobby was one of the greatest players of all time and a person that I will never, ever, forget as long as I am on the face of the earth. A true legend.

They've got some team up top right now with Bobby Moore, Georgie Best, Peter Osgood, Alan Ball and Budgie Byrne!
Clyde Best

Following are a few comments from Clyde's friends and former team-mates:

When Clyde came over to play for West Ham he lived with Charlo's mum, Jesse, at 23 Ronald Avenue. Jesse was such a big character and would call Clyde a few names, all harmless. He would say: 'Okay Big J, calm down!' Clyde towered over her, but Jesse treated him as one of her own boys. Inside her house were all the medals and trophies that Clyde, John and Clive had won during their time at West Ham. They were Jesse's pride and joy.

Scaling the heights.

When the time came to leave the home, my son Keith was asked to help clear away a lot of stuff which wasn't going to the new house so he and a couple of his mates disposed of it all. Some years later it came to light that all the medals and trophies had been packed inside one of the black bags which were thrown away. Keith was devastated and it still hurts the family now.
Carol Charles

Bestie was one of the loveliest people I have ever had the privilege to know. It was strange because he was the

first person I ever saw with a toiletry bag. He used to moisturise his hands. To see his pearly white teeth just made you feel good.
Bobby Gould

Both myself and Tony Carr travelled out to see Clyde in Bermuda and he has sent over a few kids to train and play in the youth side at West Ham. Djair Parfitt-Williams was one of those.
Paul Heffer

PC Best and Worzel Grotier at a fancy dress party.

We used to live close to each other, I was in San Diego and he was in Los Angeles and we would meet up and go out together. He has been so laid back his whole lifetime. It is easy to lose touch with him but tell him I'd love to see him.
Ade Coker

He was a good lad. He wasn't a heavy drinker and would only have Champagne when he did go out. He used to say it was the purest drink you could put in your body.
Dave Llewelyn

I remember being out with Clyde and buying a few rounds of drinks. After a while of doing this it became noticeable that Clyde wasn't actually getting a round in for anyone at all. I thought to myself: 'That's the last time I get him a drink,' but the next evening he bought the drinks for everyone all night long and we didn't get a single round in. Apparently, in Bermuda there is a custom where a person buys the drinks by the evening rather than by the round!
Jimmy Lindsay

Clyde was so huge that we called him the bear. He couldn't drive so the last person out after a game had to take the bear home!
Tommy Taylor

In the early 1970s there was a fancy dress party at Tommy Taylor's house and all the players got involved and made a real effort to get into the spirit of things. Peter Grotier came as one of the Worzels, Patsy Holland dressed up as a woman, Mervyn Day came as a vicar and Clyde Best was a very convincing police officer. During the evening there was a disturbance down the street so we sent Clyde out to deal with it. He calmed everything down!
Rob Jenkins

With his debut programme during a visit from Bermuda.

71 – PETER EUSTACE

Born: Stocksbridge, Yorkshire, July 31, 1944

Position: Midfielder

Games played with Bobby Moore: 45 (1970-72)

Games played for West Ham United: 48 (1970-72)

First game with Bobby Moore (Debut): January 10, 1970 Sheffield Wednesday (a) W 3-2

Scorers: West Ham United: Peters (2), Hurst (pen)
Sheffield Wednesday: Craig, Prophett

Sheffield Wednesday: Springett, Wilcockson, Megson, Pugh, Prophett, Craig, Sinclair, Whitham*, Downes, Smith, Coleman Sub: Warboys*

West Ham United: Ferguson, Bonds, Howe, Peters, Stephenson, Moore, Holland, Lindsay, Hurst, **Eustace**, Best

---

Peter Eustace was some three years younger than Bobby Moore and played in over 40 games with him at West Ham United. He was signed from Sheffield Wednesday for a club-record fee of £90.000 and, with Martin Peters soon to be departing, was thought to be an ideal replacement. He certainly got off to the best possible start when beating his former club 3-2 at Hillsborough.

Born in Stocksbridge near Sheffield, Eustace came to West Ham with a lofty reputation Former West Ham physio Rob Jenkins recalls Eustace joining the club: 'Peter was a gentleman. He lodged with Dave Gladstone's mum. Dave was the physio for the reserves. Peter had a good reputation when he joined West Ham because he'd helped Sheffield Wednesday get to the FA Cup final in 1966. He used to say that he and his team-mate, Jim McCalliog, played all the football in the first half and they took a 2-0 lead. Trouble was, in the second half the whole team thought they could play football, too, and they ended up losing 2-3!'

Peter played in Bobby Moore's testimonial match – against Celtic at the Boleyn Ground on November 16, 1970. One of his final games for the club was when he came on as a substitute for Harry Redknapp in the 1972 classic League Cup semi-final second replay versus Stoke City. Some 28 years later Harry would be employing Eustace as a scout when manager of West Ham United.

Peter's stay at West Ham was not a happy one and his relationship with Ron Greenwood soon deteriorated. He returned to Sheffield Wednesday after just two seasons.

Happier times – Ron Greenwood welcomes Peter to West Ham.

In action during Bobby Moore's testimonial versus Celtic, November 1970.

Peter is another former Hammer to try his hand as both a publican – at the Cheshire Cheese Inn, Derbyshire – and a manager – with both Sheffield Wednesday and Leyton Orient.

Today Peter is enjoying retirement in Castleton, North Yorkshire.

My former team-mate, Peter Swan, at Sheffield Wednesday was the first to alert me to the special talent that was Bobby Moore. He had been to Chile with Bobby for the 1962 World Cup and was talking to me about him in the dressing room before a game at Hillsborough. He was saying what a very good player he was and that West Ham had a very special talent. Ironically, the only other time talk of a special player went around the dressing room came during a tour of West Germany when Wednesday played against the national side just prior to the World Cup in 1966.

A certain player by the name of Franz Beckenbauer was all the talk in our dressing room afterwards. The game came about because Wednesday's manager, Alan Brown was very good friends with Helmut Schön, the famous coach of West Germany as it was known back then.

When I joined West Ham, Bobby came up to me and said: 'Welcome to the club.' He wished me well and hoped that we would have a successful time. He said all the right things to me.

Then he went on to say that with all new players, the boys

usually took them out for a drink after training and he asked me if I liked to drink. I said I'd love to join them for a little drink to get to know everyone but when I got there only seven players had turned up and they clearly liked a drink. I got the first round and I wasn't a lager drinker but I ordered seven lagers. By the time it came round to my turn again I said my farewells and started to leave. 'Where are you going?' Bobby said, so I got another round in. When it came round to my turn the second time I was in a terrible state but they seemed to handle it a lot better than me. In the end I was having to pour pints in flower pots just to keep up!

My first game with Bobby should have come in the FA Cup up at Middlesbrough in January, 1970 but I signed too late so didn't travel down until afterwards. Instead, I went and saw Sheffield Wednesday get taken apart by a little lad with dark hair called Kevin Keegan, who was playing for Scunthorpe United at the time.

I saw so many things at West Ham that I hadn't seen anywhere else. We played up at Newcastle United on a freezing winter night. It was the coldest conditions we ever played in. Before the game, I was looking around the dressing room in amazement because three or four of the players were wearing nylon stockings and gloves. I thought to myself surely they are not going out on a football field like this? At Sheffield Wednesday we always played in short sleeves because the manager, Alan Brown, insisted we didn't need something to keep us warm and that we should keep ourselves warm through hard work.

My first home game was a 0-0 draw against Manchester United and I was interviewed on the radio afterwards. I said that one of the reasons I had come to West Ham was to play in front of packed houses because people will always come to see Bobby Charlton, Dennis Law and George Best. Afterwards, Ron came up to me and gave me my first telling off: 'Never say that again' he said. 'People come here to see Bobby Moore, Geoff Hurst and Martin Peters and possibly you.' It was my first reprimand and things then got a lot worse.

I had been used to playing with really tough captains up at Sheffield Wednesday like Tony Kay, Peter Swan and Don Megson. They were all really aggressive people who were always shouting and telling you in no uncertain terms what they thought about you. They would think nothing of poking you in the chest and giving you a real dressing down. Now Bobby was the complete opposite and I kept waiting for him to show his mettle, his tough side, but it never happened. I had played against him a few times before I joined West Ham and I knew he was a very strong guy so this was a surprise to me.

At Manchester City once, Francis

Patrolling the midfield.

Lee was causing us all sorts of problems and I said to Bobby: 'Why don't you say something to these lads, why don't you have a go at us and try and get us going?' He looked at me for a moment before replying: 'What do you want me to say?' to which I responded: 'Just say anything to them. Whatever you say to these players they'll do it.' Then something happened which I will never forget. All of a sudden he started singing: 'We wish you a Merry Christmas,' inside the penalty box at Maine Road! I took his point, which was that no matter what you said to some of the players in that West Ham team it wouldn't have had any effect on them, whatsoever.

Bobby had complete control over that ball. He could run it out on both sides, which is a skill you just don't see in today's game. He could dart left and stroke it upfield or dart right and start a move that way.

He was the first person I found who really looked after himself. He wasn't a big eater and we know he liked a drink

but he would take vitamin pills and minerals well before anybody else was taking them. He kept them in a special box. He had no fat on him at all and trained in bin liners every day. In fact, my first experience of Bobby came at the training ground. He was asking someone for a pair of scissors to cut holes in a black bin liner. I thought why is he doing that and then he put it on and started wearing it.

One of the things Bobby used to say was: 'Be there or be square.' One time, he took me to see Top of the Pops at the BBC studios. They used to record it on Wednesday nights and air it on the Thursday. If you wanted to have a good time, Bobby was your man.

I was invited out by Bobby to join him, Jimmy Greaves, Rob Jenkins, Clyde Best and Brian Dear on that infamous night up at Blackpool but I had enjoyed my trip to Wembley with Sheffield Wednesday a few years earlier and wanted to go back there with West Ham.

The conditions were awful and it should never have been

played but I think the BBC had taken their cameras so they forced the game to be played. A typical West Ham player back then was tallish, elegant and very skilful and to play on a pitch like that nullified all those things. The players had a big argument after the game, it was a total shambles and Ron Greenwood used the previous night's drinking session as an excuse for the defeat. He clearly had a motive because he had never used it on other occasions when he knew we had been out prior to a game. We all went out before we beat Manchester City 5-1 when Ronnie Boyce scored his wonder goal from the halfway line but nothing was said.

One of the terrible things they did to Bobby when I was at West Ham was to leave him out of the team for half-a-dozen games for no reason. He had to suffer the indignity of being on the substitute's bench for a match against Derby County, even though he was fit to play and was the best player at the club. The fans didn't like it at all and it created a bad atmosphere.

The last time I saw Bobby was at Hillsborough just before he died. I couldn't believe that with all his services to football they had stuck him in the Cantilever stand at Hillsborough with the rest of the public. I saw this guy in front of me and noticed the familiar blond hair and I thought: 'That can't be Bobby Moore, it just can't be? They wouldn't put him in a seat where some idiot could say something stupid to him.' But when he turned around it was indeed him. We had a chat and he said he was still managing to get around. I said how lovely it was to see him. If that had been Beckenbauer in Germany he wouldn't have been sat in any old stand at a club, he would have been in the Directors' Box with the other dignitaries and yet here was Bobby, a national treasure, so very poorly, sitting in a seat that anyone could buy for a fiver. The whole experience was a shock to me because he would have had to climb up those big concrete steps, it just left a terrible feeling in me.

As a player, I did get quite close to Bobby because I ended up rooming with him on quite a few away trips. You wouldn't call him complex but Bobby had a lot of sides to him. He could be a real East End boy but he could also be a very gracious type of fellow.

When England won the World Cup it wasn't a footballer shaking hands with the Queen, it was someone a bit bigger than that.

Bobby Moore was like a chameleon in that his life took him to so many different places and put him in countless different environments and yet he coped with them all extremely well. From the dodgy characters who wanted to know him at the Black Lion in Plaistow, right up to Royalty itself and everything in between, Bobby was a master at coping with every situation.

Peter Eustace

With Bobby Moore's testimonial programme.

72 – JIMMY GREAVES

Born: Manor Park, London, February 20, 1940

Position: Centre-forward

Games played with Bobby Moore: 40 (1970-71)

Games played for West Ham United: 40 (1970-71)

First game with Bobby Moore (Debut): March 21, 1970 Manchester City (a) W 5-1

Scorers: Manchester City: Lee
West Ham United: Greaves (2), Hurst (2), Boyce

Manchester City: Corrigan, Book, Mann, Doyle, Booth, Oakes, Towers, Lee, Bowyer, Young, Pardoe

West Ham United: Grotier, Bonds, Lampard, Boyce, Stephenson, Moore, Holland, Eustace*, Hurst, **Greaves**, Howe Sub: Llewelyn*

James Peter Greaves scored twice on his West Ham United debut – against Manchester City at Maine Road in March, 1970. It was a feat which Bobby Moore had never witnessed and something which had not been achieved at West Ham since Ken Tucker went on to net a hat-trick against Chesterfield in 1947. Going into the 2014-15 campaign, no Hammer had scored two or more goals on his debut since Greaves. It was a professional triumph for the striker, who also scored on his debuts for Chelsea, AC Milan, Tottenham Hotspur and England.

Greaves and Moore were best mates and roomed together for England. They helped each other with their respective battles against alcoholism and cancer.

Greaves, the maverick goal-poacher, best in his field and with a penchant for socialising, was exactly the type of character to whom Moore was attracted and they often frequented the same pubs and clubs at home and abroad.

It was while Jimmy was at West Ham that he scored his final goals in top flight football. Indeed, his career league tally of 357 goals has never been bettered in the history of English top tier football. In fact, Greaves is 47 strikes ahead of the next best – Dixie Dean – and 74 ahead of Alan Shearer, the best striker the Premier League has produced to date.

Jimmy, 74, continues to enjoy retirement with his wife, Irene, but still entertains large audiences when touring with his live stand-up show. He often invites former players to be part of the show, an honour enjoyed by former West Ham United and England team-mate, Geoff Hurst. 'He actually said I was the best guest he had ever had but that was probably due to the fact that I left early!'

Jimmy kindly gave a few recollections of Bobby Moore over the phone, usually when he was walking his dog 'Lester,' who, Jimmy explains: 'Was named after the greatest jockey ever to grace a racecourse – Lester Piggott.'

I roomed with Bobby the whole time we played for England together and the icebreaker was the 1962 World Cup in Chile. It was not a very well developed country to say the least and we slept in a converted dressing room next to a sports field. We were kept awake all night by the sound of torrential rain pounding the corrugated roof. Time was hanging heavy, while we were waiting for the tournament to start and it really helped both of us to talk about our lives, ambitions and all sorts. It was the start of a lasting friendship.

Bob and I loved to unwind with a few drinks and we usually met up once a week. He wasn't 'Mr Perfect' as most people painted him and he liked to live on the edge a little.

When Alf Ramsey took over as England manager in 1964 he tried to outlaw drinking, which was a bit tricky for us because we were used to nipping out for the odd half of lager when on tour with England. The infamous occasion when Alf left our passports on our beds one night, after we had broken his curfew, certainly made us think about our behaviour but we still slipped back into our old habits. I actually believe the socialising helped Bob and I to bring the best out of each other.

Not playing in the 1966 World Cup final was a bitter blow for me but Bob was kind enough to say that the only blemish on that perfect day came from the fact that I hadn't played. 1966 had always been the optimum year for me to have a shot at winning the World Cup so to miss out felt like an end. I was 26-years-old, and at the peak of my powers, so it was hard to find any consolation in what I was going through. I wasn't selected for the 1970 World Cup, even though I was playing really well, so my fears about missing my chance were realised.

There was a remarkable twist of fate during the 1970 Mexico World Cup. I had somehow found myself participating in the London to Mexico World Cup motor rally with Tony Fall, who was an experienced British rally driver. At the time, Bob was embroiled in the nonsense with the stolen bracelet in Bogota,

Colombia and, coincidentally, was being held at the British Ambassador's home in Mexico when I was finishing the rally. I decided to see if I could visit him. I ended up scaling a wall and climbing across a roof before entering the house and finding Bobby. It really was the most bizarre encounter and the look on Bob's face when he saw me was a picture! He was a mess and hadn't shaved or taken a shower for days. It was a shock to see him like that and probably the dirtiest and most dishevelled he had ever been in his entire life.

When he played in what I consider to be his finest game – against Brazil in Guadalajara – just a week or so later, he was super human. No other defender has ever been capable of putting in a performance like that and it is always a terrific game to watch. After what Bob had been through it was an astonishing performance, really.

I don't remember too much from my time at West Ham. I went there because of Bobby but I didn't play my best football and probably made more headlines in the Slater's Arms! I did of course score on my debut, which was nice, but had spent the night before drinking and felt as rough as hell on the morning of the game. Ron Greenwood let it slide

What happened next? An all too frequent sight for West Ham fans.

because we had won the game but we weren't as fortunate when we went out the night before an FA Cup match up at Blackpool the following year. It is all water under the bridge now but I was disgusted at how the club treated Mooro after we had lost the game 0-4.

The last time I saw Bob was up at St Andrews, Birmingham. He was working on the radio and wasn't looking at all well. I had known for a while that he wasn't going to recover but it was still a shock. I asked him to meet me in one of the lounges after the game but he didn't show and must have nipped off home instead.

Everything I have ever said about Bobby is already well documented so I don't think I can add anything more. He was the greatest defender that ever played the game, had a career that was more distinguished than any other Englishman, was a great personal friend – probably my best friend in football for quite some time – and he was a lovely chap. We had a lot of fun together, that's all I can say.

Jimmy Greaves

The Player's view of Jimmy Greaves:

Jimmy was a genius. The most naturally gifted player I have ever seen. His record speaks volumes and when you hear a player in today's game being described as a genius, after scoring a single goal, they would do well to look at Jimmy's record. He scored 124 goals from 157 top flight matches for Chelsea and he hadn't quite turned 21. That is the only standard for any budding genius and you can add to that the 360 goals from 420 games he played for Spurs – an absolute football phenomenon. Before the 1966 World Cup it looked like Jimmy and I were going to be the two strikers. He was given his Number 8 shirt and I had the Number 10. Roger Hunt was given Number 22 so Jimmy and I appeared to be the preferred pairing. It didn't work out for Jimmy but his England record – 44 goals from 57 caps – is typical of the very highest standard he set. I am a huge fan of Jimmy's and whereas I wasn't a world class-player, but could play on the world stage, he was world-class.

Sir Geoff Hurst

Moore and Greaves were two of the greatest players the world has ever seen. They hailed from the same area and loved to paint the town red together. They were kindred spirits, the best players on the pitch and certainly the best company off it. If you had a night out with those two you didn't forget it for a long, long, time.
Harry Redknapp.

I played with Jimmy at Chelsea, when he was just a young pup. We played one of the great Wolves sides of the 1950s. Eddie Clamp, Peter Broadbent, Dennis Wilshaw and Ron Flowers were in their team and we still beat them 6-1 with Greaves scoring five. I set up four!
Peter Brabrook

He was my hero and it was a personal hightlight of my career when I played with him at West Ham. Old Jim was so funny. Everyone would go and warm up before a game but Jim would simply go and take a shower. He was still putting on his strip with a couple of minutes to go before kick off!
John Sissons

I used to meet up with Jimmy at West Ham. He lived in Upminster and I lived in Hornchurch. We used to go out for a beer and he would always have half a bitter so I was absolutely amazed when the press revealed his drinking problem. I had absolutely no idea. I couldn't believe it.
Ron Boyce

English football's greatest ever top tier league scorer – 357 goals.

When I left school, one of the teachers asked me to go over to Glebe Road, which was used for football on Saturdays by schools in the Dagenham area. He said there was a little player he wanted me to look at and it was Jimmy Greaves aged 14! He was only a tiny tot but I'm telling you it was like watching a player from a different universe, altogether. He was out of this world. He would control the ball, turn, beat one player and then another, shoot from distance, hit the bar and follow up. Complete control.
Harry Obeney

A big hero of mine was Jimmy Greaves. He used to say to me: 'Don't follow my example, I'm a lazy trainer. I don't train well but I can score goals.'
Ade Coker

When he left Chelsea and was signed by AC Milan he came and trained with West Ham because Milan didn't have their pre-season training until a bit later. He knew Mooro and Hurst so came and trained with us for a couple of weeks at Grange

Turning on the style.

Farm. Now, I was just a young kid in 1961 and was completely awestruck to see someone like Jimmy Greaves. I just couldn't believe I was just a matter of a few feet away from him. Grange Farm wasn't the best of surfaces to play on but it was as though the ball was tied to his foot. Greavsie was fantastic!
Peter Bennett

Before Jimmy went to Milan he came to Grange Farm to train with West Ham. My speciality had always been the overhead kick and Jimmy was good at it, too. Anyway, they wanted to take some photos of Jimmy doing it on his left foot and they wanted someone to do it on his right foot. All the lads said 'Beezo can do it' so I did stand in but I've never seen the photos.

When I joined Southend United in 1962, I had a roaring start to the season and scored 10 goals in six games which remains a club record. I was top scorer in the country at the time, with Jimmy Greaves.
Mike Beesley

It was amazing when Jimmy Greaves arrived because when I was growing up there was nobody better than Greaves and Denis Law. To be around him was simply brilliant.
Joe Durrell

Jim was fantastic when he arrived. He was this absolute superstar and yet he would stand in the bar drinking pints

of bitter, smoking a pipe! We used to drink halves of lager because it didn't look too bad. We finished training at 1pm and drink until 6pm which was long enough, when you had to drive home to have a bite to eat. I had no idea that Greavsie was then going home and opening up the spirits. When I played for Hereford United, we had a game against Gambia and our manager, John Sillett, came in and said he had one of my old pals guesting for Hereford. It was Greavsie. I popped in to see him before the game and he was drinking!
Jimmy Lindsay

When Jimmy left Chelsea for AC Milan in 1961, he joined in a few of our training sessions at Grange Farm. We were playing five-a-side and he belted the ball and broke my little finger!
Alan Dickie

Like Mooro, Jim made it look so easy and was so laid back. We went on tour to America and Greavsie trained all day with black sunglasses on. I was expecting Ron Greenwood to tell him to take them off but he didn't say a word. It was funny because Ron got sozzled on the flight over there. He was drinking gin & tonic and he must have been well gone because he was really, really nice to me, probably the only time that he was. I wish he'd drunk a bit more often!
Peter Eustace

When John was very ill, Jimmy's wife, Irene, called me up. She said: 'I'm not going to ask about John because I've heard all about his illness. I've phoned up to ask about you and how you are coping.' I really appreciated that call.
Carol Charles

I liked Jimmy but he was just seeing out his career at West Ham. People say we lost Martin Peters but he didn't want to play for West Ham anymore. Jimmy did well for us in the short time he was here, though.

On his debut up at Main Road I had to tell him at the breakfast table to keep away from Ron Greenwood and when he asked why I said: 'Because you stink of booze!'
Rob Jenkins

Just to be on the same field and playing with Jimmy Greaves was an honour. I had always heard about Jimmy as a kid and then to be in the same team was a great pleasure. You couldn't put a price on Jimmy Greaves in today's market.
Clyde Best

Leaving the Boleyn Ground after a disciplinary hearing following the Blackpool affair in 1970. Brian Dear is wearing Bobby Moore's coat.

73 – DAVE LLEWELYN

Born: Cardiff, August 9, 1949

Position: Forward

Games played with Bobby Moore: 5 (1970-72)

Games played for West Ham United: 6 (1970-72)

First game with Bobby Moore (Debut): March 21, 1970 Manchester City (a) W 5-1

Scorers: Manchester City: Lee
West Ham United: Greaves (2), Hurst (2), Boyce

Manchester City: Corrigan, Book, Mann, Doyle, Booth, Oakes, Towers, Lee, Bowyer, Young, Pardoe

West Ham United: Grotier, Bonds, Lampard, Boyce, Stephenson, Moore, Holland, Eustace*, Hurst, Greaves, Howe Sub: **Llewelyn***

David John Llewelyn was the final Welshman to play with Bobby Moore at West Ham United. He may have enjoyed greater success had his 'goal' on his debut up at Maine Road been allowed to stand in West Ham's 5-1 demolition of Manchester City in 1970. Patsy Holland was in an offside position and he has never let him forget it since.

Llewelyn signed professional forms for West Ham on August 27, 1966, aged 17. His height and strength marked him out as a potential regular up front. He was a prolific goalscorer in the reserves and once scored a hat-trick within three minutes. It came in a Combination Cup semi-final against Cardiff City – Dave's home town club.

At the age of 20, Dave won a Wales Under-23 cap whilst playing for West Ham – it came against Scotland at Aberdeen on January 26, 1972.

When Dave moved to Noel Cantwell's Peterborough United in the summer of 1972, part of the deal was for a pre-season friendly to be played between the two clubs.

Dave still resides in Peterborough and has, for the past 10 years coached the GB Medical football team, an experience which has taken him all around the world. In 2009, he coached them to a world championship victory in Korea. He is a fitness fanatic and has been involved in the gym industry for the past 30 years.

Everyone at West Ham United called me 'Llew'. Nobody called me Dave. I remember watching West Ham play Cardiff City in the early 1960s and I said to my mate, Dave Lloyd: 'They are a really good side.' They had Bobby Moore, Geoff Hurst,

Leading the line in the reserves.

Martin Peters, Peter Brabrook, and Ronnie Boyce in that side. Shortly afterwards, Dave wrote a letter to West Ham and, lo and behold, they replied and asked me to come down for a trial. It was as simple as that.

At the age of 17, Wally St Pier asked me to sign pro forms. It was the best thing ever. I loved the place, the way we played and everything. If I hadn't been to see West Ham play Cardiff that day it is very unlikely that I would have played for them.

During pre-season, the club would always have its annual club photo taken. Mooro wasn't there on this particular day and Ron Greenwood asked me to put on a shirt and stand in for Bobby. I thought: 'Brilliant, I'm going to be in the team photo.' But my happiness was cut short when Ron explained how they were going to superimpose Bobby's head onto

Playing for Peterbrough United in a pre-season friendly against a Bobby Moore-led West Ham United.

my body! And that is what they did but Bobby wasn't very happy with it so they took another photo at another time. The photo with my body in it was never used. I'd love to have that photo if anyone has it.

On one occasion the team took the train down to play Southampton. We ate our pre-match meal and the waiter came round with the coffee just as the train went into a bend and he spilt it all over Mooro. Bobby was always immaculate, so his suit was completely ruined and the kit man, Albert Walker, had to go and find a track-suit for him to wear. We all got off the train in our suits and there was Bobby in his track suit. It was probably the only time he looked casual when everyone else had their best gear on.

A big moment for me at West Ham came when I was presented with my Wales Under-23 cap. It was sent through the post and the club's physio, Rob Jenkins, called all the lads together and presented it to me personally. Rob's father, Bill, was born in Wales so it was lovely that his son did it.

Rob was great to all the players and he will probably remember better than me the time he had to stitch up Bobby Moore's shin during a game. Dr Bell was called in to look at the injury – Bobby hadn't worn shin pads – but he didn't fancy fixing it up and so he told Rob to do it, instead.

I always say to people that if the rules that exist in football today had stood in the 1960s, then West Ham would have won the league. By removing the physical side of the game it would have left the Hammers with so many skilful ball-players with the likes of Bobby, Martin, Boycie etc. I am in no doubt that we would have made a serious challenge for the title.

Tense times at Highbury, January 1971.

West Ham United 1970-71. Bobby Moore's head superimposed on Dave Llewelyn's body! (Back row far right)

There was a bit of an age gap between me and Bobby so I wasn't really in his social circle but he always behaved impeccably towards me. When my parents came to watch me play, Bobby was so welcoming and it made their day to chat with the England World Cup-winning captain. He was brilliant, a true gentleman.

I was more of a reserve team player and, if you look in the record books, you'll find that I played in every position for the reserves. Bobby knew how I played and always found me with perfect passes in training. He was the best player I have ever seen.

The last time I ever saw Bobby was when I was working in the commercial department at Peterborough United. He was playing for Fulham. It was a League Cup game and George Best and Rodney Marsh were also playing for Fulham. After the game Bobby bought me a drink in the players' bar and introduced me to George Best, who had scored that night. I remember the goal as though it was yesterday. He was on the edge of the box, flicked the ball up and volleyed it into the opposite corner of the goal. They all stayed until about midnight and we had a great time. They signed autographs for everyone all evening long. They were as good as gold.

I absolutely loved my time at West Ham United and one of the clauses in my transfer to Peterborough United

was that they would play a pre-season friendly up at London Road. It was very strange to be playing against my old side but they all made me feel very welcome.

To say that you have played with the three World Cup stars and Jimmy Greaves for good measure is something I am very proud of. It is hard to believe it really happened to me. Absolutely fantastic! If anyone asks me who I support I always say West Ham United. I am so passionate about the club and the history I have with it.

Dave Llewelyn

'Llew' (centre) with his family.

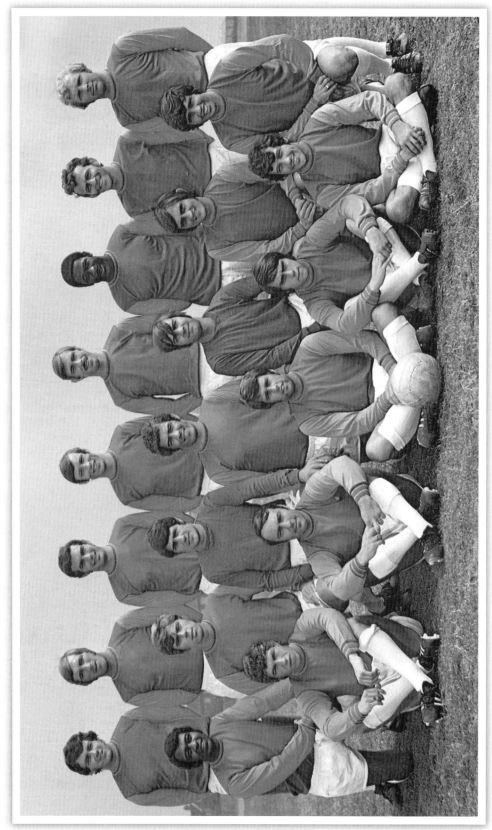

Back row L-R Bennett, Bonds, Brooking, Stephenson, Heffer, Best, Spiegler, Moore. Middle row L-R Charles, Redknapp, Ferguson, Cushley, Grotier, Lampard, Boyce. Front row L-R Holland, Greaves, Hurst, Lindsay, Howe.

CHAPTER THIRTEEN
1970-71

Bobby Moore's total appearances (July 1970-June 1971): 53 games (2 goals)

League Division One: 39 (2 goals), Friendlies: 6, England: 5, League Cup: 2, FA Cup: 1

On September 22, 1970 West Ham United added another landmark to their illustrious history – they played against Pele's Santos at Randalls Island, New York. A crowd of 22,143 spectators filled Downing Stadium and enjoyed a 2-2 draw courtesy of goals from Pele (2) and Clyde Best (2). They were Pele's 1,096th and 1,097th goals of his unique career. Bobby Howe was given the unenviable task of marking him.

In October, a post-war record attendance at the Boleyn Ground - 42,322 – witnessed a 2-2 draw between West Ham United and Tottenham Hotspur. Geoff Hurst scored his 165th league goal, which took him ahead of club legend Jimmy Ruffell and into second place on West Ham's all-time league goal scorers list. Hurst would eventually finish his Hammers career on 248 strikes in all competitions behind the peerless Victor Watson, whose career tally of 326 goals still looks safe for some considerable time to come.

On November 16, 1970 – 12 years and two months after his debut for West Ham United - Bobby Moore was awarded a testimonial match. Glasgow Celtic were the visitors and 24,448 clicked the turnstiles to watch a high-spirited encounter which ended in a 3-3 draw.

In January 1971 Moore was the surprised subject of *This is your Life*, a hugely popular, prime-time, television programme which showcased a person's life achievements. The mood of the programme was somewhat subdued following the 'Blackpool affair' a few days earlier. Moore, Jimmy Greaves, Brian Dear, Clyde Best and physio Rob Jenkins were deemed to have broken Ron Greenwood's curfew on a late night drinking session prior to an FA Cup third round tie which, disastrously, ended in a heavy 0-4 defeat at Bloomfield Road.

The already strained relationship between Moore and Greenwood was further compounded and the manager did not select Moore to play again until February 6, 1971, when his perfectly fit skipper was named as a substitute for the visit of Derby County. It was the only time that Moore came on as a substitute in a competitive game for West Ham United – replacing Bobby Howe in the second half. 'Moore sub – the final sick joke' read one particular banner in the crowd.

Moore finished runner-up to Billy Bonds as the Hammer of the Year. He also finished third in the BBC Sports Personality of the Year behind both boxer Henry Cooper and golfer Tony Jacklin. The result would have doubtless been somewhat different had England not surrendered a 2-0 lead against West Germany in the 1970 World Cup quarter-final.

Moore and Pele before West Ham United's friendly against Santos.

and the substitute is...

Greenwood gave debuts to two home-grown talents during the campaign - John Ayris and John McDowell - as well as two new signings in Tommy Taylor, from Leyton Orient and Bryan 'Pop' Robson – from Newcastle United.

Here is their story...

74 – JOHN AYRIS

Born: Wapping, London January 8, 1953

Position: Right-wing

Games played with Bobby Moore: 41 (1970-73)

Games played for West Ham United: 65 (1970-76)

First game with Bobby Moore (Debut): October 3, 1970 Burnley (h) W 3-1

Scorers: West Ham United: Hurst (3)
Burnley: Coates

West Ham United: Grotier, Bonds, Lampard, Boyce*, Eustace, Moore, **Ayris**, Brooking, Hurst, Best, Howe
Sub: Heffer*

Burnley: Waiters, Angus, Merrington, Docherty, Waldron, Probert*, Thomas, Coates, Casper, Wilson, West
Sub: Nulty*

John Patrick Ayris actually made his debut at West Ham United as an apprentice. He set up one of the goals for Geoff Hurst's hat-trick in a 3-1 victory over Burnley and duly signed professional forms the following Monday.

Ayris scored one of the three goals in Bobby Moore's testimonial game against Celtic in 1970. He was also in the line-up for the infamous FA Cup game up at Blackpool the following year.

Ayris was almost 12 years younger than Bobby and played with the great man in over 40 matches.

Previously, Johnny signed apprentice forms for West Ham on August 26, 1969 and full professional on October 6, 1970.

He pulled on an England Youth shirt on seven occasions and was widely touted as having tremendous potential until a brutal challenge from Chelsea's Ron Harris in September 1971 scuppered his progress. Former physio Rob Jenkins recalls the moment clearly: 'Chopper Harris went right through him and when I was tending to him he wanted to carry on so I did what I could and he went back out there. A few minutes later I could see he was turning grey so we took him off and sent him to hospital. He was diagnosed as having a punctured lung. John was such a great talent with a terrific sense of humour but he wasn't quite the same player after that.'

John Ayris and Graham Paddon off to work.

Ayris was one of several wingers vying for a first team place at West Ham. Joe Durrell was in the frame and remains a good friend of John's. They actually signed professional forms on the same day: 'I played for Senrab and John played for Wapping Boys', recalls Joe, 'I was more direct as a player than John but he was trickier than me. Ask him to tell the story about the time when Bobby Moore chauffeured us to the Old Globe pub in Stepney.'

Fellow winger Dudley Tyler is another who got on well with the Wapping wide boy: 'I liked John and we were both lucky in that Ron favoured his wingers and would, on occasion, play both of us.'

Ayris had a brief spell playing for Cape Town City in South Africa before winding down his career with Wimbledon.

Today, John helps to run the sports centre at South Woodham Ferrers, Chelmsford.

I used to look at Bobby in training and think to myself: 'I can take him, I'm sure of it.' But his brain was so quick I had no chance. We used to play two-against-two in the grids at Chadwell Heath and I was up against Bobby and Billy Bonds. I just couldn't get near to them. Bobby used to hold it and shield it so well. His legs were as thick as my waist at the time and I remember thinking: 'He's a strong old boy.'

I didn't have time to dwell on my debut. I was expecting to play against Chelsea reserves but Ron Greenwood called me in and told me I wasn't going with them because, instead, I was playing in the first team against Burnley. Ron was very clever to tell me on the day because I was only 17 and still an apprentice and would have worried about it and had a sleepless night. The downside was that my

The Wapping winger.

family couldn't get to the game. I didn't drive at the time so I took the train to the ground and went home afterwards to Wapping by train. I think I did okay on the day and we won 3-1 with Geoff Hurst getting a hat-trick.

I played in Bobby Moore's testimonial match against Celtic. Bobby was hated by the Scots. I think they respected him but it was the England versus Scotland rivalry and of course Bobby epitomised the very best of England so how could the Scots do anything else but despise him?

It was a great honour to play that night because Jimmy Johnstone played who, along with George Best, was one of my heroes. They were archetypal wingers, tricky, quick and loved taking on players. As usual, Celtic brought an army of fans to watch their team and half the ground was full of their supporters. I remember they were all waving these blow up mini footballers in the Celtic shirt above their heads.

I was lucky to score in that game which ended up 3-3. The ball came out and I was on the edge of the box, I never won many headers so I didn't go into the box for corners! Anyway, I chested it down and volleyed it over the top and it landed in the back of the net. I didn't score many goals so it was a fantastic feeling and I remember we all went to the Sportsman's Club afterwards and people like Sean Connery and Eric Sykes were there. Eric Sykes was wearing glasses with no lenses in them. Believe it or not, they were a hearing aid and he kept rubbing his eye through the hole where the lens should have been!

Bobby and I both scored in the same game once. It happened up at Maine Road against Manchester City. They had Lee, Bell, Summerbee and Rodney Marsh at the time and they absolutely mullered us in the first half, scoring four goals. Anyway, I got us back into the game with a 30-yarder with my left foot. Now my left foot was for show only so it really was a special moment. It seemed to give us a bit of impetus and we were unlucky to fall just short at 4-3. I think Bobby scored with his head that day which must be a collector's item!

Another time, we were playing up at Wolves and were coming home on the train. Bobby always made a point of going round all the tables and chatting with the players and asking them what they were doing that night. I used to get on well with Joe Durrell and Patsy Holland and I could have only been about 17 or 18 at the time. Joe and I had arranged to go for a beer at the Old Globe in Stepney Green and it just happened that Bobby was going there himself and he offered us a lift. So when the train pulled in to Euston, Bobby went and picked up his red Jaguar and there was Joe and I sitting on beautiful leather seats being driven by Bobby Moore. It was just the type of man he was. Obviously, West Ham fans loved him but a lot of people outside the club thought he was aloof and arrogant. He was never like that. I don't think I've met a more humble man.

Bobby never really talked to me about tactics or specific opponents but he did encourage me on a different level. Frank Lampard used to get me to stay behind after training because he wanted someone to run at him. Frank worked really hard on his game and Bobby liked it that I was doing that. He would tell me to keep doing it and even if Frank took the ball from me dozens of times I would still be learning. He would encourage me to go past people, to use my pace and to stay wide so that he could find me: 'You're not very big,' he used to say. 'So we need to look out for you.'

It was so reassuring to have Bobby on the pitch in a game and the only other player I can compare that feeling to is Billy Bonds. When you saw them out there you knew you had someone looking out for you, who cared for you, cared for the club and would run through brick walls for the West Ham shirt.

I think the best match Bobby Moore ever played has to be the one against Brazil in the 1970 World Cup. The things that happened in that game were simply unbelievable. The tackles, the passing, the pace, the goal, Jeff Astle's miss and, of course, that wonder save by Gordon Banks. Now, I may be wrong but I'd never seen Bobby congratulate a goalkeeper on a save but you can see him doing just that with Banks. It was a special moment.

I don't know what the background was to him leaving West Ham but, personally, I thought it couldn't and shouldn't have happened given his long association with the club. I just couldn't see him playing for anyone else and that he would be at West Ham forever. It wasn't a surprise to see Martin Peters and Geoff Hurst leaving but you just couldn't imagine the club selling Bobby Moore, he was just too important.

I loved West Ham United, I loved the people and, politics aside, it was a lovely club. People like Greenwood and Lyall taught me things that I teach now. I wasn't a golfer or a drinker so I used to go to a local school in East Ham called Kensington primary and coached the kids. Football is a simple game.

The thing that will always stay with me about Bobby Moore is his humility.

John Ayris

With wife Lyndsey, son Christopher and daughter Vicky.

75 – TOMMY TAYLOR

Born: Hornchurch, Essex, September 26, 1951

Position: Centre-half

Games played with Bobby Moore: 145 (1970-74)

Games played for West Ham United: 397 (1970-79)

First game with Bobby Moore (Debut): October 17, 1970 Tottenham Hotspur (h) D 2-2

Scorers: West Ham United: Eustace, Hurst
Tottenham Hotspur: Mullery, England

West Ham United: Grotier, Bonds, Lampard, Eustace, **Taylor**, Moore, Ayris, Lindsay, Hurst, Greaves, Dear

Tottenham Hotspur: Jennings, Kinnear, Knowles, Mullery, England, Beal, Gilzean, Perryman, Chivers, Peters, Pearce

Thomas Frederick Taylor was signed from Leyton Orient on October 17, 1970. The deal saw West Ham United's Peter Bennett move to Brisbane Road. Taylor would go on to play 397 games in the claret and blue, 145 of them alongside Moore. They would, of course, then face each other in the 1975 FA Cup final at Wembley.

I went to Wembley Stadium in 1964 to watch Bobby Moore lift the FA Cup so it was a great honour to be playing with him six years later.

My transfer to West Ham happened very suddenly. On the previous Saturday, I had been playing for Orient and had been responsible for the only goal of the game. It was pouring down with rain and the pitch at Brisbane Road was flooded

Taylor won 12 England Under-23 caps but a full England cap eluded him. He also played in Moore's last-ever game for West Ham United – a 1-1 draw at home to Hereford United in the FA Cup third round, on January 3, 1974.

Tommy returned to Leyton Orient in 1979, having played almost 400 games for the Hammers. He remains in the top 20 list for all-time appearances at West Ham United. Contemporary reports describe him as: 'A defender with the touch of a midfielder.'

Tommy is arguably the most-travelled coach West Ham has ever produced, having applied his knowledge throughout the UK, Caribbean, Europe, Africa and Australia. His wife, Pat, has been supporting his efforts along the way. He is currently coaching the Finnish side PS Kemi Kings.

Tommy returned to his native Hornchurch during Christmas 2013 and was very generous with his time and recollections of Bobby Moore:

Clearing his lines against Celtic during Bobby Moore's testimonial in 1970.

most of the time, anyway, and I under-hit a back pass which stopped in the slop. Their forward latched onto it and put it away. On Monday, the O's manager Jimmy Bloomfield called me into his office and I entered with my hands in the air saying: 'I know it was my fault and I'm sorry.' Jimmy, who was a diamond fella, just smiled and replied: 'I've sold you.' I looked at him and said: 'It was only a sloppy backpass! What if I don't want to go?' He just said that everything would be fine and that I was to meet him at West Ham later that day.

When I got to Upton Park and went up to Ron Greenwood's office, Jimmy was sitting there, too. 'Welcome to West Ham United Tommy, we're delighted you are joining us,' said Ron. 'I haven't signed yet,' I replied and asked him in which position he was going to play me. 'Centre-half,' was his response. But I explained that I wasn't a centre-half and preferred to wear the Number 6 shirt because I liked to bring the ball down and play it out of defence. 'Well, Bobby wears the Number 6 here,' said Ron. 'But when he moves on, in a few years, you can wear it.' So I ended up wearing the Number 5 jersey, which basically meant I had to kick people and head the ball. I ended up playing in that shirt for almost 10 years but at least my wages went up from £16-per-week at Orient to £100 at West Ham.

The first time I met Bob, I thought he was a very quiet person, very quiet. He was never the loudest on the field, either, but you always knew he was there. He was the same in the dressing room. One thing about Bobby, he wasn't a snob.

In full flow.

On my debut, we played in front of the biggest post-war home crowd at West Ham – 42,322. We drew, 2-2 with Spurs and, with the move to the Olympic Stadium, it is a record that will last forever. I saw some funny sights before that game. I was in the dressing room putting my strip on and I can still see Harry Redknapp and Ron Boyce in the corner, smoking a cheeky cigarette which they'd cut in half and shared.

After the game, there was a 24-pack of beer left on the table and, by the time everyone had showered and put their gear back on, they had to order another pack! It was a different age completely with most of the lads coming from the local area and everyone getting on really well together.

Bobby was his own man and I was never part of his drinking crowd. I would have one in the players' lounge after a game but then I would just head home to Brentwood.

My second game for West Ham was at Crystal Palace. They had an old concrete bath with about three inches of water in it. I got in and Bobby got in next to me and I asked him how many centre-halves he had played with at West Ham. He totted it all up quickly in his head and said: 'Seven.' I replied: 'Well, there's not going to be an eighth, Bob,' He looked and me and smiled: 'Good luck to you, son.' I was only joking but it turned out that I was one of the last.

Bob was a very quiet man, who did his work on the pitch and then went off to do his own thing afterwards. I got on well with him but he had his own people that he mixed with.

There wasn't any shirt sponsorship back then but can you imagine the sums of money West Ham could have gained if a large corporation had put their name on the chest of Moore, Hurst and Peters?

On the pitch, I always knew where he was and, if he had the ball, he very rarely gave it away. You can do a lot in football with a player like that. If you can't control the ball or pass the ball you shouldn't be in football.

Mooro did something in a game that I have never seen since. We were playing Derby County – it was a very good Derby side - and the winger was galloping towards Bobby and you could see that he wanted to take Bobby but Mooro positioned himself in such a way that the winger suddenly stopped and turned around away from goal. Then Bobby jockeyed and shepherded him all the way back to the half-way line. I wanted to stop and clap it was so good.

I was also on the pitch when Mooro blew the ref's whistle and stopped the game. We were playing Wolves and the ref's name was Garrard Lewis. I think Mooro clobbered him with the ball and he went down so Bobby went over, took the whistle and halted the game. We all had a good laugh about that one.

We knew Bobby was going to leave West Ham about a year before he went. It was an incredible coincidence that we were then lining up against him at Wembley in the FA Cup final. Personally, I enjoyed the European games more than the FA cup games but it was great to be playing against Bob and Alan Mullery at Wembley.

There will never be another player like Bobby Moore and I hope, deep down, that everyone appreciates what they had at that time.
Tommy Taylor

The following comments are provided by Tommy's former team-mates.

When I was playing for Orient they had a young kid call Tommy Taylor. He was only 17 and I mentioned him to Ron Greenwood. I said I thought he was a good player.
Peter Brabrook

Tommy was probably the chattiest one in West Ham's defence back then. He was a practical joker as well. I remember I shared a room with him and John McDowell out in Germany and I came back one night to find my bed frame on the balcony and the mattress in the bath!
Dudley Tyler

Tommy Taylor was the joker in the pack and he and John McDowell were as thick as thieves. I thought Tom could have been a bit nastier as a player. I would have loved to have played against him because he wouldn't have liked me kicking him one little bit!
Bobby Gould

When we flew home from Brussels after losing to Anderlecht in the 1976 European

Cup Winners Cup final, we took a coach back to Upton Park from the airport. Tommy managed to put on a tape cassette of Derek and Clive, who were a comedy duo played by Dudley Moore and Peter Cook. The coach was packed with all the Directors and their wives and the tape was full of highly offensive swearing and rude comments. Ernie Gregory was livid and got it taken off. I think there was a board meeting about it but nothing happened because Tommy stayed at the club for a few more years, after that.
Rob Jenkins

When I joined West Ham in 1973 I was travelling from Brighton every day and was thoroughly sick of it. Anyway, I mentioned it to Tommy and he said: 'Come and live with me during the week and go home at weekends.' I thought that sounds alright but he had just got married and, after one night, I thought I can't be doing this and went back to Brighton. It was a fine gesture, nevertheless.
Bertie Lutton

From Finland to Hornchurch in December 2013.

76 – JOHN MCDOWELL

Born: East Ham, London September 7, 1951

Position: Right-back

Games played with Bobby Moore: 138 (1970-74)

Games played for West ham United: 297 (1970-79)

First game with Bobby Moore (Debut): October 31, 1970 Blackpool (h) W 2-1

Scorers: West Ham United: Greaves, Eustace Blackpool: Green

West Ham United: Grotier, **McDowell**, Lampard, Eustace*, Taylor, Moore, Ayris, Lindsay, Hurst, Greaves, Dear
Sub: Heffer*

Blackpool: Thomson, Armfield, Mowbray, Craven, James, Alcock, Suddick, Green, Burns, Bentley, Hutchison

John Alfred McDowell spent 10 years at West Ham United after joining as an apprentice in 1969. He first lined up with Bobby Moore on his debut – against Blackpool – on October 31, 1970. It was the first of 138 matches they shared in the Hammers defence. Despite gaining one England Youth cap and 13 England Under-23 caps, McDowell was denied the chance to line up with Moore for England.

John attended Shaftesbury primary school and Sandringham Road secondary school, before playing for both Newham and Essex where he was spotted by West Ham's chief scout, Wally St Pier. He signed apprentice forms in 1967 and full professional two years later.

John's finest years at West Ham came after the Bobby Moore era, when putting in a fine performance during the club's 2-0 victory over Fulham in the 1975 FA Cup final. A year later he just missed out on a winners' medal in the European Cup Winners Cup final, after Anderlecht took home the trophy following their 4-2 defeat of the Hammers in Brussels.

McDowell was later transferred to Norwich City in August

Youth team abroad. Back row L-R Peter Grotier, Dave Llewelyn, Stephen Gill, Pat Holland, Terry Scales, Stephen Death, Clive Charles, Bobby Sutton. Front row L-R John McDowell, Kenny Wallace, Keith Pointer, Steve Aylott, John Ayris, Joe Durrell.

1979 for £90,000 where he played under both John Bond and Ken Brown. He was later re-united with former team-mate Bobby Gould in a coaching capacity at Bristol Rovers.

After his playing days, McDowell became an advertising sales director for a magazine before opening up a couple of shops with his wife, Carol. They moved to Tenerife in 2002 to run an English supermarket in Playa de las Americas but are once again back on these shores in Essex.

John has had two hip operations, which have restricted the pursuit of hobbies such as golf and squash. He is a keen reader and enjoys novels by Jeffrey Archer and James Patterson as well as a well-written biography. His five children and five grandchildren ensure that he remains active in semi-retirement. 'I'm busy playing grandad.'

The interview with John was the 89th and final step on a journey which had begun some 18 months earlier. He had remained an elusive part of the Bobby Moore story and we have his daughter Krystina to thank for ensuring her father's memories of Moore are shared:

My first day at Chadwell Heath was something I will always remember. I was a spotty little 16-year-old, who had only ever dreamed of playing for West Ham United, having been born around the corner from the ground in Plashet Grove. There can't be too many West Ham players who were born that close to the ground? I could actually see the floodlights from my bedroom window and would often collect autographs from Mooro and John Sissons, Brian Dear, Geoff Hurst, Martin Peters and Ron Boyce. As a young kid I used to cut out the pictures of Bobby Moore from the Newham Recorder and keep scrapbooks on West Ham.

In 1965, I went to Wembley with my father, Arthur, to see West Ham win the European Cup Winners Cup so I was a little nervous, to say the least, standing there, at Chadwell Heath, alongside Bobby Moore, who was an absolute god to me. While it was a dream come true I was still full of shock and awe. He always seemed to have plenty of time on the ball and could find anyone on the pitch. I tried to copy him by thinking what I was going to do with the ball before it came to me. I also tried to emulate the way he passed in such a way that it gave his team-mates a chance to control the ball, a delivery with which they could work. I like to think that I was a good passer at West Ham.

My dad was my biggest critic and he loved to tell a story about a game I played in against Manchester United at Old Trafford during 1971-72. Mooro was in that match, too, and I believe he saved a certain goal from Denis Law late on by heading off the line. We lost 2-4, with a limping George Best scoring a hat-trick and tearing me to shreds. My dad used to say that he was called down to the dressing room at half-time to untangle my legs!

Frizzy haired McDowell

Bob was a very approachable person and treated the apprentices with a lot of respect. There were no airs or graces and his first impulse was to assist in any way he could. He was a very tough player. People say he couldn't run and couldn't head the ball but he was over six feet tall so of course he could head it and he was quick enough over the first five yards to stay with most players. His superior intelligence did the rest but, as for his tackling, well, he was very tough indeed. I remember playing in a five-a-side against him and going for a 50-50 ball. I was young and trying to impress so I went diving in. In no time at all, I was left on my arse looking up at Bobby, who had the ball, gliding imperiously up the pitch ready for his next move. I think he had a philosophy whereby he preferred to intercept instead of tackle but, believe me, he could get stuck in as well as anybody.

I have a very clear memory of my debut against Blackpool

Life after Bobby Moore – firing in a shot against Sheffield United one year after Moore left the Hammers.

in 1970. The circumstances were that Billy Bonds had been suspended for five games. I was brought in to replace him at right-back ahead of Paul Heffer, who was also in the frame. In my mind, I had five games to prove myself. I marked Tommy Hutchison, who was a real handful. The stand-out memory from my debut – apart from winning 2-1, of course – was that for the first 15 minutes Bobby switched from left-half to right-half to help ease me into the game. Nothing was said beforehand, it was just his own initiative, but it helped settle me that bit quicker. I suppose the best compliment Ron Greenwood paid me was to give me Bonzo's right-back position after he returned from suspension and to move him into midfield. I ended up playing in most outfield positions during my time at West Ham. I played up front against Newcastle United once but I didn't enjoy it. I liked kicking people, not being kicked!

My best times at West Ham were the FA Cup success in 1975 and the European campaign the following season. Bob had obviously left the club by then and my biggest games with him were undoubtedly the four League Cup semi-final ties we played against Stoke City in 1972. I have two abiding memories from those games.

The first came in the second leg at Upton Park when we thought we were going to Wembley, having won the first leg 2-1 at the Victoria Ground. We conceded a goal but were then awarded a penalty. I would have put everything I owned on Geoff Hurst to score that penalty but it was such a tense moment I couldn't even look. The penalty was taken at the

old North Bank end and both Tommy Taylor and I were looking away, towards the South Bank end. The crowd just swayed and groaned so we knew it hadn't gone in.

The other memory came up at Old Trafford in the second replay. The pitch was an absolute quagmire. I could feel myself sinking a few inches into the mud with every step I took. It was a big disappointment for me because I gave the penalty away after under-hitting a back-pass to Mooro, who had replaced Bobby Ferguson in goal. I have tried to forget the memory because it was a needless penalty. I had time to clear it but for whatever reason tried to knock it back to Bob. Then I tried to make amends and went in clumsily on John Ritchie, which was unnecessary because Tommy Taylor was covering.

To play against Bobby in the 1975 FA Cup final was easily the strangest experience I had in football, but what a game he played! He was exceptional that day and it was almost as if he was trying to prove a point to Ron Greenwood and John Lyall. He certainly hadn't lost any of his brilliance.

He was such a superstar. I remember going to his testimonial dinner at the Grosvenor Hotel in Park Lane and Sean Connery and Jimmy Tarbuck were there. Another time, West Ham went on tour to Los Angeles and Bob was given tickets to see Frank Sinatra. He took it all in his stride and when I saw him at Chadwell Heath wearing his bin liner he was just 'Mooro.' They talk about Ronaldo and Messi today as being superstars but if Bobby was playing now he would be a megastar. I can't imagine today's elite footballers popping down the Black Lion for a pint, either!

The last contact I had with Bobby came when I left Norwich City in 1982. He called me up and asked me if I would be interested in playing for an Australian side called Newcastle, just north of Sydney. I toyed with the idea but had a young family and when Bobby Gould called me and asked if I was interested in being his number two at Bristol Rovers, I decided to join him, instead.

Mooro was the best defender I have ever played with and was always totally focussed on the match in which he was playing. We were up at Old Trafford once, and the fans there always gave him plenty of stick. 50,000 hot-headed Mancunians were swearing and shouting at Bob throughout the entire match but he just played better and better and better. It was the best way of coping with the situation. We were like a one-man team in the end.

I enjoyed playing with Bob in defence and learned so much from him. I never got tired of seeing him passing the ball out of defence and putting it anywhere he wanted.

He scored some good goals as well. He once netted a volley from 25-yards against Wolverhampton Wanderers. It happened in the same game as the one when he picked up the referee's whistle after having knocked him out with a close range header. It was quite a comical scene because the ref was a little bald fella but it could have been very serious had he swallowed his tongue or been concussed. Thankfully, he was only dazed temporarily. Nobody would have had the presence of mind to do what Bobby did and I've never seen anything like it since. It was absolutely the right thing to do but it didn't occur to anyone else.

I may have had a chance of winning an England cap had Sir Alf Ramsey stayed in charge a little longer. His successor, Don Revie, didn't fancy me, which put an end to any hopes I had. I was only 25 and Bobby had already played his final international game by then, anyway.

When I heard the news that he had passed away I was very upset and quite angry because he was never given the recognition he deserved. He was my boyhood hero. I was fortunate enough to meet him and class him as a friend and a team-mate. The best thing they could do for him would be to knight him posthumously. A few footballers have been knighted over the years but the one person who deserved it above all others was completely overlooked. He just seemed to be erased from England's Word Cup history.

I had the utmost respect for Mooro and to say that I played alongside him means everything to me. He called me 'Johnny Mac' and once gave me a great piece of advice which I have taken through life with me. It applies to both life in general as well as football. Bobby said: 'Listen to everyone on the way up because you might meet them on the way down.'
John McDowell

Following are a few views from John's former team-mates:

We were great mates and he was one hell of a full-back. It was a shame there were so many capable defenders at the time otherwise he would have won a full England cap.
Tommy Taylor

'Sweaty' we used to call him. He played in the same youth team as me, Clive Charles and Tony Carr. I really liked John because of his toughness. He wasn't afraid to get stuck in and could pick me out from distance with a good pass. He was best of buddies with Tommy Taylor.
Clyde Best

I took John to Bristol Rovers as my number two. I wanted them to see a West Ham player because apart from my time at Wimbledon my coaching philosophy at every club I served was based on everything I had been taught by 'Daffy' – we called Ron Greenwood that because he walked like Daffy Duck – and 'Tate & Lyall' at West Ham.
Bobby Gould

'No, mine was definitely curlier!' – At a West Ham reunion with Pat Holland (right) in 2005.

77 – BRYAN ROBSON

Born: Sunderland, County Durham, November 11, 1945

Position: Forward

Games played with Bobby Moore: 128 (1971-73)

Games played for West Ham United: 254 (1971-74/1976-79)

Honours with Bobby Moore: 1973 Golden Boot winner, 1973 Hammer of the Year

First game with Bobby Moore (Debut): February 24, 1971 Nottingham Forest (h) W 2-0

Scorers: West Ham United: Hurst, **Robson**

West Ham United: Ferguson, McDowell, Lampard, Bonds, Taylor, Moore, Redknapp, **Robson**, Hurst, Eustace,* Greaves Sub: Lindsay*

Nottingham Forest: Barron, Hindley, Winfield, Chapman, O'Kane, Jackson, Lyons, Fraser, Martin, Cormack, Moore

Bryan Stanley Robson joined West Ham United from Newcastle United on February 22, 1971. Three days later, he opened his account for the club, scoring on his debut against Nottingham Forest in a 2-0 victory at Upton Park. It was the first home victory for the Hammers in over three months and helped move the club permanently out of the relegation zone. 'Pop' as he is affectionately known had two spells at West Ham United – one with Bobby Moore (1971-74) and one without (1976-79).

His most successful season at the club was the 1972-73 campaign, when he won the Golden Boot for topping the scoring charts in the top flight. Bryan is the only Hammer in the history of the club to achieve the feat. Quite how a striker can score 28 goals in a single season and not win an England cap is one of the great mysteries of football.

Sunderland paid a club record fee for his services in the summer of 1974, just a few months after Bobby Moore had left West Ham.

Today, Pop resides in Hexham with his wife Maureen and is a highly respected coach and scout. He has applied his knowledge and experience of the game to the benefit of clubs such as Manchester United, Chelsea, Leeds United and Sunderland.

Pop, 69, is not officially retired but finished as Chief Scout of Sunderland in 2013 following the arrival of Paolo Di Canio. 'I am a bit disillusioned about how the game has gone,' he concedes. 'For the longest time it has been moving away from the community game for families and is driven solely by money. It will be interesting to see how it ends up.'

It is a testament to the selfless nature of Pop that when he was asked by his good friend, Peter Gurr, to contribute to this book, he and his delightful wife, Maureen, drove down from Hexham to discuss Bobby Moore in The George pub at Wanstead. In the back of his car was his Golden Boot.

My first playing experience of Bobby Moore came when I was at Newcastle United. He had a big reputation by then, of course, and made it difficult for me on the pitch. He was immaculate and read things so well but both Wyn Davies and I did manage to score a few times against West Ham.

I actually scored a goal at West Ham for Newcastle United which won the goal of the season. It came during 1970-71 when I scored both in a 2-0 victory. I took a corner on the far side at the North Bank end and Wyn Davies had a shot which was cleared to me as I was running in from the corner. David Craig was telling me to bring it down but I just volleyed it on the outside of my left foot over Peter Grotier. Five months later, I was playing for West Ham. I think Ron discussed my signing with Geoff Hurst.

I also played against Bobby on the eve of the 1969 FA Cup final when the full England side played England Under-23s at Stamford Bridge. It was a big occasion for me but Bobby was such a difficult opponent. He was anticipating things so well that I couldn't get a kick of the ball. He was intelligent on the ball and passed it really well. He was especially good for England, a top international footballer and I can remember missing a penalty in that game. I hit it well but it came back off the post.

When Newcastle United won the Inter-Cities Fairs Cup in 1969, I scored over 30 goals but had a slow start the following season and Geordie fans can give it to you big style when you are not on form. I remember playing West Ham that year and Bobby could hear all the booing and jeering and couldn't believe it: 'Is that aimed at you?' he asked. We actually won that game quite comfortably and I scored but I remember the England captain's disbelief at how I was being treated.

In 1971, I was in dispute with Joe Harvey, the Newcastle manager, and eventually ended up signing for West Ham. Ron Greenwood paid £120,000 for me and I should have received 5% of that figure but Newcastle tried to block it. Bobby Moore showed a lot of concern and support for my situation

They Played With Bobby Moore – The West Ham Years

Pop's first transfer to West Ham United in February 1971.

and I had to appear in front of the Professional Footballers' Association. I am fairly certain Bobby brought some pressure to bear and talked to Ron because it was settled in my favour.

I had a great debut against Nottingham Forest. It was a fairly crucial game because West Ham were struggling at the time. Jimmy Greaves played in midfield so that Geoff Hurst and I could play up front. That was an incredible moment for me because Jimmy Greaves was a big hero of mine. He said to me before the game that he was really, really pleased for me and I've always held that to be a very special moment in my career.

We ended up winning 2-0 and I actually thought I had scored in the first half and was dead excited but it was

disallowed for offside. I eventually got my goal after the break from a Harry Redknapp cross.

Before my debut, I had my first training session earlier in the week. We played on the concrete next to the car park near the main gates in Green Street. I remember being so impressed by the way the players were knocking the ball about with one and two-touch passing. It was so different from what I had been used to at Newcastle, where we had been knocking the ball long a lot of the time.

Bobby was at the centre of West Ham's passing game. He was telling me to come short to lose my defender and he'd put the ball there for me. It was a different level of skill altogether. It took me back to when I had played for England

Under-23s with West Ham's Johnny Sissons. He had a great left foot and would shout at me to come short but I didn't have a clue what he meant. But now I was part of the same culture and could see Geoff Hurst doing it every day.

Bobby would then be dribbling the ball out of defence and putting it on a sixpence with the outside of his foot. I was mesmerised, it was football from a completely different planet as far as I was concerned. There was so much quality and Ron would set up sessions that were so visionary. He would have defenders like Frank Lampard bombing forward and put Billy Bonds, Trevor Brooking and myself in a grid to play one-touch football. We learned so much about each other's game which we then took onto the pitch. The understanding I had with Billy and Trevor was like no other I had throughout my career. We were big pals both on and off the field and it is friendship which continues to this day.

Collecting the Hammer of the Year trophy in 1972.

My first full season at the club - 1971-72 - was fantastic and we finished in sixth place which I think was a record at the time. We should have got to Wembley as well but lost to Stoke City in the semi-final of the League Cup.

Then, in 1972-73, I asked Ron Greenwood if I could play as an out-and-out striker but he was against it. I understood his reasoning but preferred to play up front. I enjoyed that side of the game much more than a midfield role. In the end I used to go up to Billy Bonds as we ran out onto the pitch and say: 'If I go up front try and fill in for me.' I wasn't an out and out striker like a Number 9 but was more likely to make my runs from deep. Eventually, I played up front and I managed to score 28 goals which was enough to win the Golden Boot so it was a very exciting time. We were a good team and could have played in any country and competed. I particularly enjoyed playing against Manchester United and always seemed to score against them (Pop scored seven goals against the Red Devils).

I had such a fantastic supply from Bobby, Trevor and even the full-backs, Frank Lampard and John McDowell, would put in plenty of crosses. I scored 28 but I must have missed five times as many. I was getting six or seven great chances in each game. We really were a great attacking side back then.

When I joined the club I remember the players all went out for a drink to welcome me. We went to the Slater's Arms for what I thought would be a couple of halves. I was being treated for a hamstring injury and had to drive to Rob Jenkins' surgery for some treatment. Anyway, Bobby was there with Jimmy Greaves, Brian Dear and quite a few others and

I started to notice them putting away pint after pint. Peter Eustace was pouring his into the flower pots because it was turning into quite a session. I had to leave them to it even though it was my welcome party!

One funny experience I remember with Bobby came when we played Millwall at The Den in Harry Cripps' testimonial. We met at Upton Park and I was wearing a pair of puce trousers and a jacket I had bought out of the boot of Harry Redknapp's car. It was suede and cost me about a week's wages but I thought it looked really edgy. Now, when I got on the coach to go to the game it started to get really hot and I had put on an old shirt and I noticed I was starting to smell. I didn't want to take off the jacket because it would have made it worse so I just sat there getting hotter and hotter and was really starting to smell quite bad of body odour.

Anyway, we made it to the ground and into the dressing room but when I started to get changed I heard Mooro shout: 'Who's that?' I was so embarrassed I couldn't say anything but Frank Lampard chipped in with: 'Is that you, Pop?' I didn't know where to put my face and hastily took all the talcum powder and after shave I could get my hands on from Rob Jenkins, the club physio.

I was relatively new to the club and fresh down from Newcastle so this was the last thing I needed in front of the most immaculate player that has ever walked the planet! After the game when we got dropped off in Green Street I just legged it as fast as I could back to my hotel in Woodford Green, I just couldn't bear to face anybody.

My father-in-law was a lovely man called Len Heppell. He was something of an expert on posture and movement

Scoring against Manchester City in March 1973.

and was also from Hexham and had been a miner as well as the owner of a few night clubs in his time, including the Fandango in Hexham. He was always talking to me about balance and positioning on the pitch as well as helping me to improve my footwork and speed off the mark. He told me to stop playing golf and to play table tennis instead to sharpen my instincts and speed of movement. He told me to watch other players who had perfect balance like George Best and although I couldn't reach those heights I did show tremendous improvement and scored over 50 goals in two seasons at Newcastle United, winning the Fairs Cup along the way. I was fitter and sharper than I'd ever been.

Bobby and Len got to know each other, too. Bobby became very interested in his techniques and training. Although Len wasn't on the payroll at West Ham and didn't hold any official position at the club, he and Bobby had lunch together a few times.

Len studied Bobby's posture and running style very closely and said he ran as though he still had a coat hanger in his shirt! He helped him loosen his shoulders and improve his fitness. Len was a ballroom dancer and if you watch Strictly Come Dancing today you can see how fit you need to be and just how much improvement can be made from having the

right posture and balance. These were the areas where he tried to help Bobby and Mooro took it all on board and some say it improved his running and extended his career. It was funny because Mooro used to take the piss out of me when I ran onto the pitch and started loosening my shoulders but then he started doing it as well. It was typical of the man that he wanted to keep improving and stay at the top for as long as he could.

Bobby was utterly impressive and so effortlessly calm. There was a time when we played Newcastle at St James' Park and they had a player called Jimmy Smith who loved to nutmeg defenders. Anyway, in this particular game, Jimmy nutmegged Mooro in the first half but rather than rant and rave like so many defenders would have done, Bobby just took it in his stride and calmly waited for a moment in the second half when he nutmegged Jimmy Smith, not once, but twice. Now you very rarely saw any defender nutmeg anyone throughout their entire career let alone twice on the same player in the same game. West Ham won the match 2-1 and I remember Jimmy Smith leaving the field totally deflated. Bobby was the picture of composure.

As the World Cup winning captain, Bobby didn't impose himself upon you. He had confidence but no arrogance. I remember sometimes he would be having a nap on the train out of Euston or Kings Cross and people would wake him up for an autograph and he would always sign it. He was a very witty guy as well and could put you down with his one liners.

The last contact I had with Mooro was when he was working for the Sunday Sport newspaper. He called me up to see if I would write a few reports for him from games up in the north-east.
Bryan 'Pop' Robson

Pop's former team-mates contributed the following comments:

Pop was a terrific player, a great goalscorer and a really nice lad. I was quite friendly with him and we went on holiday together. He always seemed to wear shoes that squeaked!
Sir Geoff Hurst

When I joined West Ham, Ron Greenwood had a certain system and he had a top, top, finisher in Pop Robson to execute his plans. Pop is about as good as I have seen. Ron played me out on the left-wing, Clyde Best on the right-wing and Pop arrived late in the box. Back then, central defenders were like animals and were basically an ugly bunch intent on causing harm to strikers. Ron wanted to keep all his goal scorers away from them as much as possible which didn't work well for me as I liked to be in the thick of things scoring goals. It worked great for Pop, though, and he won the Golden Boot in 1972-73 but left-wing was no good for me.
Ted MacDougall

His father-in-law, Len Heppell, used to run mobility sessions at the club. He would look at how a player walked and then help them with their balance to improve the way they ran. He told me I ran like a scrap metal dealer!
Kevin Lock

Pop was another Jimmy Greaves. He scored lots of goals for West Ham and is another great human being. I have a friend that lives out here in Bermuda who has a house in Hexham, which is Pop's neighbourhood, so he keeps me in touch with what Pop is doing. He was a great player and I rate him highly.
Clyde Best

He was easily the best striker I played with and to see Pop in training hitting the ball was something else. He had a great understanding with Trevor Brooking and West Ham fans saw a lot of goals because of it. He was quick and an excellent striker of the ball. You can't teach people the skills Pop had, they were so instinctive.
Dudley Tyler

Pop was a great pro and a fantastic goal scorer. He's another one like Billy Bonds in that he should have got an England cap.
Jimmy Lindsay

I loved him. Pop was enthusiastic, happy and combined a lightning-quick instinct with a mature football brain. He was a good mate and you could treat him as a real friend. He was a proper north-east boy and you know how lovely those people can be. Pop epitomised all that was good about people from up there. At Arsenal, I played with George 'Geordie' Armstrong. If George was down to his last penny he would give it to you and Pop is the same.
Bobby Gould

West Ham United's one and only Golden Boot winner.

The Bobby Moore Testimonial

Bobby Moore's testimonial programme against Celtic on Monday November 16, 1970.

Back row L-R McDowell, Heffer, Grotier, Ferguson, Brooking, Lampard. Middle row L-R Bonds, Llewelyn, Taylor, Stephenson, Moore, Eustace. Front row L-R Ayris, Redknapp, Boyce, Hurst, Howe, Robson.

CHAPTER FOURTEEN
1971-72

Bobby Moore's total appearances (July 1971-June 1972): 66 games (1 goal)

League Division One: 40 (1 goal), League Cup: 10, England: 7, Friendlies: 5, FA Cup: 4

Bobby Moore became West Ham's last survivor of the 1966 World Cup triumvirate following the £80,000 transfer of the great Geoff Hurst to Stoke City. Having just turned 31-years-old there was still some mileage left in the tank as Hurst went on to play more than 100 games for the Potters, finding the net on 30 occasions. Hurst's departure meant that only Moore and Ron Boyce remained from the club's FA Cup and European successes of 1964-65.

Other notable characters that left the club were both Harry Redknapp – to AFC Bournemouth – and Alan Stephenson – to Portsmouth.

Moore's weekly wage was increased to £200, the maximum that he earned at West Ham United.

Power cuts brought the country to a standstill and, even worse, threatened the production of *Hammer*, West Ham's matchday programme. Thankfully, programme editor Jack Helliar continued to meet all the necessary deadlines.

The highlight and lowlight of the season was an epic League Cup semi-final saga against eventual trophy winners, Stoke City, played out over four matches during December and January. The marathon encounter was watched by a total of 171,334 paying customers. They were treated to layers and layers of drama which culminated in the second replay when Bobby Moore faced a penalty in the absence of concussed regular keeper Bobby Ferguson. The Hammers

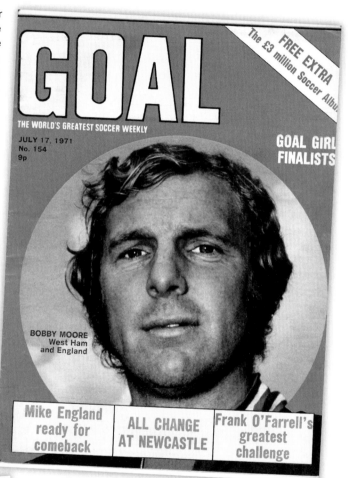

Goal Magazine 1971.

League Cup Semi-Final Replay

BRAVE MOORE TURNS GOALKEEPER BUT STOKE GO THROUGH

By DONALD SAUNDERS

Stoke City 3   West Ham 2

STOKE CITY staggered tiredly, happily and a little luckily into the League Cup final last night after removing stubborn, courageous West Ham from their path in a semi-final marathon that came to a memorable climax at Old Trafford.

eventually lost the four-game thriller and missed out on a glamourous all-London cup final against Chelsea at Wembley.

Ron Greenwood gave debuts solely to home-grown talent during the 1971-72 season. Former youth team and reserve team stars, Joe Durrell, Ade Coker, Kevin Lock and Clive Charles were the next Hammers to line up with Moore in the first team. Indeed, Moore scored his only goal of the season in Joe Durrell's debut – the winner in a 2-1 victory over Stoke City on September 25.

Here is their story...

78 – JOE DURRELL

Born: Stepney, London, March 15, 1953

Position: Left-wing

Games played with Bobby Moore: 4 (1971-72)

Games played for West Ham United: 6 (1971-72)

First game with Bobby Moore (Debut): September 25, 1971 Stoke City (h) W 2-1

Scorers: West Ham United: Best, Moore
Stoke City: Ritchie

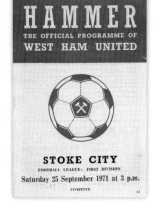

West Ham United: Ferguson, McDowell, Lampard, Bonds, Taylor, Moore, **Durrell**, Best, Hurst, Brooking, Robson
Stoke City: Banks, Marsh, Pejic, Bernard, Smith, Bloor, Conroy*, Greenhoff, Ritchie, Dobing, Jump
Sub: Stevenson*

Joseph Timothy Durrell, played six first team games for West Ham United, four of which included Bobby Moore. Indeed, the Stepney boy's pure elation at being told he is one of only 89 Hammers to have played first team football with Bobby Moore is the inspiration behind this book.

It is a bizarre statistic that such a period in history should produce four wingers for West Ham United from the borough of Tower Hamlets – Joe Durrell, Pat Holland, John Ayris and Harry Redknapp. Joe still lives in Stepney and remains the player from Bobby Moore's era to live closest to the ground. Bill Lansdowne in Barkingside runs him close.

Joe played for East London, Middlesex and London Boys before having a final England trial. He was discovered by Wally St Pier and Wilf Chitty, both of whom Joe holds in very high regard: 'Absolute gentlemen. My parents loved them from day one and it was never in doubt that I would play for the Hammers.'

Durrell is fondly remembered by his former team-mates. Ade Coker sent a message from his home on the west coast of America: 'I played in the youth team with Joe as well as Johnny Ayris and Kevin Lock. I cannot believe Joe still lives in Stepney! I read in the *EX Hammers* magazine that he came over to Seattle recently. That's where I live! Tell him that he must come and see me next time.'

Clyde Best was just as keen to talk about the boy from Stepney from the somewhat sunnier climes of Bermuda: 'Joe had a tough journey to the first team which was no mean feat in those days. You had to progress through four teams – the south east counties, A team, youth team and reserves – before making it into the first team.'

Joe was only 28-years-old when he retired from the game. He followed his time at West Ham with spells at Bristol City, Cardiff City, Gillingham and Dagenham. The Essex club was managed by former Hammer, Eddie Presland, and Joe played his part in their successful FA Trophy run of 1980. Joe

remembers the time well: 'To play at Wembley Stadium with Dagenham in front of 26,000 fans was a great way to sign off from football. West Ham won the FA Cup in the same year so it was special all round. Dagenham beat Moseley 2-1 in the final and I set up a goal for George Duck.'

Unlike so many other West Ham players from the Bobby Moore era Joe did not pursue a post-playing career in football: 'The reason I didn't get into coaching was because football and boxing are not the working class way out. Education is the way out. You will only get one David Beckham in 40 million people and only one like me in hundreds of thousands. One of the most important things that happened to me in my life was my old mum sending me back to school to get five O-levels in 1968. Without those qualifications I wouldn't have got into Goldsmiths College to gain my teaching qualifications. That to me was everything and I tried to pass it on to the next generation.' This is no more clearly evident than with his own children – daughter Jessica, who is a primary school teacher and son Jack – who completed a PHD in the United States.

Today, Joe resides in the same street in Stepney where his grandfather (a docker) and father (a postman) both lived. He also drinks in the same pub – The Grapes in Narrow Street – where they both frequented, too.

He has been married to his wife, Denise, for over 40 years and, up until his retirement in 2013, had served the teaching profession for more than 30 years.

Running in tandem with Joe's passion for education is a life long love of West Ham United. The fact that he pulled on the first team shirt on six occasions is the icing on the cake and his four years at the club during the Bobby Moore era continues to fire the senses. Naturally, our interview took place in The Grapes:

All my family are West Ham supporters and we all went along to see Bobby Moore lift the FA Cup at Wembley in 1964 and the Cup Winners Cup the following year. To think that six

Joe (Back row, second left) lining up with Bobby Moore prior to Geoff Hurst's testimonial match – November 23, 1971.

years later I would be lining up with Bobby in the first team is just incredible. The great man also scored on my winning debut so it doesn't get much better than that.

As a kid you just can't compute the full magnitude of what is going on. He was one of my idols so to actually get onto the same pitch with him leaves me lost for words really.

Ron Greenwood told me the day before that I would be making my debut against Stoke City. On the day, I took the train from Mile End and arrived at the ground about an hour and half before kick-off. I was sitting next to all the fans that I would soon be playing in front of.

In the dressing room Bobby came up to me, shook my hand and wished me luck. He told me to just carry on doing what I had been doing in the reserves because I had been setting up and scoring goals at that level. When I ran out, the first thing that hit me was the sound from all four sides of the ground. They only ever opened up one stand for reserve team matches, so 30,000 people making a lot of noise was terrific.

Early on in the game, we got a free kick over on the left and very casually Bobby said: 'Joe, keep it away from the big fella in green.' Now, that is the best thing he could have told me because if he had said anything with the words 'Gordon' and 'Banks' in it, I would have felt far less confident!

The game couldn't have gone any better, with us winning 2-1 and Bobby scoring one of the goals. They showed it on Match of the Day and my wife, Denise, called up the BBC so we have got a copy of it at home. It only shows the goals but

is priceless to me. It is a pity that West Ham's greatest era was largely missed by the cameras. It was nothing like the saturation coverage we have today.

I didn't mix with Bobby Moore socially because I was too young. Instead I would go out to places like Kate Hodders and the Jug House with Patsy Holland and John Ayris.

My best game for the Hammers came against Wolverhampton Wanderers in October 1971. I have a scrapbook at home and the headlines read: 'Durrell put on a super show' and 'Hammered by a kid named Joe.' I did play well in that game and I think I got rated 9/10 in one of the newspapers. Wolves had a very strong team with players such as Derek Dougan, Peter Knowles and John Richards. I went up against Bernard Shaw, their full-back. I put in quite a few good crosses and set up Clyde Best for the only goal of the game. Afterwards my parents were having a party so the whole day was full of special memories. Sadly, I only played a couple of games after that before Ron moved me on.

I wasn't happy to be leaving West Ham but I am not the type of person to say: 'Could've, should've, would've,' about my life and absolutely loved every minute I spent at the club. I wouldn't change a thing. Six games for West Ham and four of them with Bobby Moore in the side, I'll take that every day of the week. I love looking back on those days and feel very privileged to have done what I did.

The coaching at West Ham was top, top, level. John Lyall looked after the reserves and nurtured the players with perfect preparation for Ron Greenwood and the first team. They taught you not to just pass the ball, but instead to pass the ball in the right way so that the player receiving it either had an easy pass to make, or could run onto it at pace. Making it easy for first time passing was a big part of it and Bobby was the maestro. Seeing him put the ball anywhere he wanted was a privilege to watch. You were always taught to be mindful of the defender and pass it on his wrong side. Put it where he isn't sort of thing. I was taught to nick half-a-yard on the defender and curl in the cross around the defence to the near post. Hearing John Lyall and Ron Greenwood explain all this was fantastic to my young mind. Seeing Bobby putting it all into action was just perfect. It wasn't like that anywhere else. On the contrary, at my other clubs – Bristol City, Cardiff and Gillingham – it was more like getting the ball to the front men as quickly as possible and not worrying too much about how you did it.

Fitness was also a big priority and I used to get terrible blisters during pre-season training, running around Epping Forest. I would always be at the back with Bobby Moore and Jimmy Greaves. All the greats together really! Billy Bonds was easily the best runner at the club. He would just keep going. Harry Redknapp was also quite good.

Bobby was an absolute hero, a true gentleman. When Johnny Ayris or Patsy Holland and I used to return to Euston from away games he would give us a lift back in his red Jag. 'Are you going back to Stepney?' he would ask: 'Jump in the car, then, I'll take you home.' Can you imagine that as a 17-year-old? Being dropped off by the England World Cup winning captain?

He would drop us off at The Globe pub in Stepney where we would meet up with the boys who had been playing in the reserves that day. Bobby would catch up with the senior pros but would always send over some drinks to us kids. He was just a true gent.

I am so delighted to be on the list of players to have lined up with Bobby Moore. I was almost on the list of players who scored for West Ham United. It came against Crystal Palace in a game which finished 1-1. I hit the post but was convinced it was going in. It was in all the way as far as I was concerned! But for some reason it bounced out. After the game I went back out onto the pitch to take a look. It was a muddy pitch and there was a big splodge of mud on the post at the North Bank and I can still see it now and the position of the splodge and the shape of the post meant it should have gone in but it just wasn't to be. I still think it's going in now! That would have been fantastic because I had stood on the North Bank as a youngster.

West Ham was such a big family club at the time. The people there wanted to do the right thing and put you on the right path. Even people you didn't know wanted to help. I remember my mum calling John Lyall when I had an outbreak of boils and hearing back from his wife, Yvonne, with advice to drink some glucose.

Everyone at West Ham wanted to help purely out of a natural desire to help. Yvonne didn't know me from Adam but it was so typical of the caring attitude, which was at the heart of West Ham United at the time.

It was a privilege to play with those players – Bobby Moore, Geoff Hurst, Trevor Brooking, Pop Robson and Ron Boyce. They all treated me really well. Straight after a match in the dressing room, Bobby, Boycey and others would be discussing the game and what had happened. As a young kid, I was in that dressing room listening to all those guys dissecting the game, analysing what had worked, what hadn't and then proposing improvements. Terrific days!

Joe Durrell

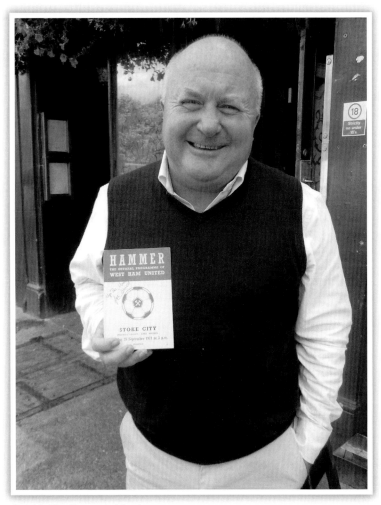

Outside The Grapes in Limehouse.

79 – ADE COKER

Born: Lagos, Nigeria, May 19, 1954

Position: Forward

Games played with Bobby Moore: 10 (1971-74)

Games played for West ham United: 11 (1971-74)

First game with Bobby Moore (Debut): October 30, 1971 Crystal Palace (a) W 3-0

Scorers: West Ham United: **Coker**, Bonds, Best

Crystal Palace: Jackson, Payne, Wall, Goodwin, McCormick, Blyth, Tambling, Craven, Hughes* Kellard, Taylor Sub: Wallace*

West Ham United: Grotier, McDowell, Lampard, Bonds, T. Taylor, Moore, Redknapp, Best, **Coker**, Brooking, Robson

Adewunmi Olarewaju Coker was the first African-born player to line up with Bobby Moore at West Ham United. The Nigerian was hugely popular during his three seasons with the club and is part of a very select band of Hammers to score on their first team debut. The goal came after just seven minutes against Crystal Palace at Selhurst Park on October 30, 1971.

'Ade' was the final West Ham player to score on his debut with Bobby Moore in the team. It ended a line which started with Mike Beesley in 1960 and continued with Eddie Presland in 1965, Jimmy Greaves in 1970 and Bryan Robson in 1971.[1]

Ade went on to sign professional forms in early December that year having played for Henry Compton School, West London district and London Schoolboys.

Former team-mate and good friend Clyde Best is in no doubt about his ability: 'At the time Ade had a wealth of talent but the game back then was very physical and he had quite a small stature which didn't help him. I think if Ade was playing today he would be a very big name in the game because he had everything.' It is a sentiment echoed by former winger, Dudley Tyler: 'If you had to compare Ade with a modern day player he reminds me of Jermain Defoe, very quick over the first couple of yards.'

Coker is also one of only a handful of Hammers to get on the scoresheet with Moore, in a 5-2 win at home to Leicester City in August 1972. He also played in Moore's final game for West Ham, against Hereford United in the FA Cup in January 1974. He played a total

On his scoring debut, clashing with John McCormick of Crystal Palace on October 30, 1971. The Hammers won 3-0.

1. It should be noted that Roger Hugo did score on his West Ham United debut – at Leicester City in March, 1964 – but Bobby Moore did not play.

Heading West Ham's second goal in a 5-2 victory over Leicester City on August 19, 1972.

of 11 games for West Ham before having spells with Lincoln City and a plethora of clubs in the North American Soccer League and the Major Indoor Soccer League. He won five caps playing for the United States national side.

Today, Ade is as bright and bubbly as ever and lives on the west coast of the United States in Kirkland, Washington. Residing almost 5,000 miles away from Upton Park has not diminished his unbridled enthusiasm for all things West Ham United.

I can't mention Bobby Moore without putting 'Sir' in front of his name because it is so well deserved. 'Sir' Bobby Moore was amazing to me as far as my career was concerned. I was completely star-struck when I joined West Ham and to be around Bobby, Geoff Hurst, Billy Bonds and Trevor Brooking was mind blowing. They were so kind to the younger players and I just wanted to be like them.

I was so impressed by their attitude towards the game, their dedication to training and their behaviour away from the club, that I just wanted to emulate them and that is the way I have tried to live my life ever since.

There were so many characters at the club. Ronnie Boyce would easily smoke a few packs of cigarettes each day and he'd still be the best player on the pitch. Bertie Lutton was the

heaviest smoker I ever saw at West Ham. Boy, oh boy, that man could smoke and yet he could run everyone – except Billy Bonds – into the ground.

I always use Bobby as my greatest example to everyone I know in the States and around the world. Everyone thinks that a player with speed will always do well and can beat a defender that doesn't have pace. Well, as we all know, Bobby didn't have any speed and, in fact, when I was a young kid, I could run backwards faster than him!

But he had master intelligence and his brain was quicker than any pair of legs on any player in the land. That's how he won the ball, picked up the pieces and kept West Ham and England on the front foot. He instinctively knew how to put a striker exactly where he didn't want to be and that is a unique skill.

When I made my debut at Crystal Palace I was in a total state of shock. Geoff Hurst had an injury and couldn't play, so I was only told an hour before the game in the dressing room. I actually turned as white as a ghost! I was so excited I needed help to calm down. Geoff was the first to come over and say: 'Just go out there and do it. We know you can and now is your chance.' Then Bobby approached and said: 'Go out and do it for yourself and for all of us. We're all behind you.'

Now, when you hear words like that from your hero, you run out onto the pitch feeling jet-propelled. I may as well have been Concorde! I actually felt invincible and had the game of my life. We beat Crystal Palace 3-0 and I scored in the seventh minute. Now, in my mind, after I scored I ran back towards Bobby. I may have taken a few diversions along the way but I needed to go to him. 'See,' he said. 'We knew you could do it, now let's have some more.' I've never forgotten those words.

I always carry 'Sir' Bobby Moore in my heart because one of the things I always remember him saying was: 'This game is bigger than all of us.' Now I didn't understand what he meant by this until he explained it to me: 'Football has been here long before us and it will be here long after we have gone and the biggest thing we can do is be a representative or an ambassador to the game. No matter what it is we do, we can do it in a good way or a bad way.'

For me, you cannot get a better explanation of the duty a player has to this great game of ours and I have shared Bobby's words with thousands of young players during my coaching career in the United States.

I was in San Diego when I heard that Bobby was ill. I called my brother, who was living in England, and told him to keep me in touch with any news. Even though I hadn't seen Bobby since I played for West Ham I needed to know what was going on.

It's always a pleasure to talk about 'Sir' Bobby Moore. As I always say, once a Hammer always a Hammer! When you run out at the Boleyn Ground and you hear the 'Bubbles' song, oh my God, you cannot help but be a proud Hammer. It still gives me goose bumps and I've taught my children to sing it.

I have nothing but time for West Ham United, always and forever. I've tried to be a good ambassador for my club over

Playing in Moore's last ever senior game for West Ham United – against Hereford United in the FA Cup third round, January 1974.

here in the States because of the influence Bobby had on my career. He was the biggest hero to the game, the greatest ambassador in the game, a true gentleman, a mentor and a person who I admired and aspired to be.

He was my hero and you never forget your heroes.

Ade Coker

80 – KEVIN LOCK

Born: Plaistow, London December 27, 1953

Position: Left-back/Centre-back

Games played with Bobby Moore: 32 (1972-73)

Games played for West Ham United: 162 (1973-77)

First game with Bobby Moore (Debut): February 29, 1972 Sheffield United (a) L 0-3

Scorers: Sheffield United: Dearden (3)

Sheffield United: Hope, Badger, Hemsley, MacKenzie, Colquhoun, Salmons, Woodward, Scullion, Dearden, Currie, Ford

West Ham United: Ferguson, McDowell, Lampard, Bonds, Taylor, Moore, Eustace, Best, Llewelyn* Brooking, Robson, Sub: **Lock***

Kevin Joseph Lock was tagged 'The next Bobby Moore,' by the British media. It was a tremendous amount of pressure to place on the shoulders of a 19-year-old but inevitable given that he played in the same position, was born locally and sported a shock of blond hair. Lock would eventually take over the Number 6 shirt and wear it with great success in the 1975 FA Cup final against Moore's Fulham. Sadly, it was a shirt which was to meet an unfortunate end.

Embracing Bobby after the 1975 FA Cup final.

Kevin signed professional forms in December 1971 and made his debut with Moore when coming on as a substitute – against Sheffield United – two months later. He would go on to gain four England Under-23 caps, also.

Former team-mate Bobby Gould is in no doubt about Kevin's ability: 'Locky was a proper West Ham player, a lovely left foot and someone who could play. Sadly the weight of wearing the Number 6 shirt after Mooro had left the club fell on his shoulders so it was a tough responsibility for him. It would have been for any West Ham player wearing the Number 6 jersey after Bobby.'

Lock's career would shadow that of Moore's in that he followed him to both Fulham and Southend United, where he played 10 matches under Bobby's management. He eventually went on to coach the youth team under Moore's successor, Dave Webb. After retiring from the game he ran The Prince of Wales pub in Mountnessing, which was opened by Trevor Brooking.

Nowadays, Kevin is a highly respected usher at Chelmsford Magistrates Court. He is an avid reader of crime thrillers with a particular interest in John Grisham. He lives in Maldon, Essex.

I was and still am a massive West Ham United fan and lived in Plaistow, close to the ground, as a young boy. The players were more accessible in those days and I remember going over to Upton Park or Chadwell Heath to collect autographs. Bobby was always one that would sign for everybody regardless of how long it took. He would get all us youngsters to form an orderly line before signing everything. Some of us would get a bit cute and line up for a second time but he would be too clever for that and single us out as already having his autograph. He would never refuse once but would never sign twice, either. I used to practice Bobby's

Playing it out of defence.

autograph at home. I could do Bobby's, Geoff's and Martin's. I used to love trying to copy them and it's a shame today's kids are denied such childhood pleasures given the squiggles that pass for autographs nowadays. Bobby Moore's signature, like the man himself, was in a different league altogether. The big bold 'B' and 'M' with the other letters clearly set down. – It just felt good looking at it. I always wanted to be a footballer and watched Bobby because I wanted to be like him.

As a kid I was too young to go and watch him play in the night games but we lived in Jenkins Road, just off Prince Regent Lane, and I could hear the crowd from my bedroom window. My bedroom was a shrine to Bobby Moore and

West Ham, with posters, books, sticker albums, autograph albums, the lot, and I would sit there with the windows open following the game based on the noise of the crowd. I wouldn't close my window until the floodlights went off.

I was absolutely fanatical about West Ham. I idolised that entire team from the mid-1960s, especially Budgie Byrne, who was a real character and a massively underrated player. I just loved him and loved watching him play.

I would queue up on Saturday at the crack of dawn outside the West Stand to get on the wall right by the players' tunnel. I always took a stool with me to get a good view. Once, when I was in the South Bank, Johnny Sissons overran the

Life without Moore: In the thick of it against Stoke City on March 28, 1975.

ball and clattered into the hoardings. His muddy hand covered my own as he tried to steady himself. Weeks later you could still see traces of the mud as I tried to preserve it and told everyone at school what had happened!

Then all of a sudden I joined West Ham and I am watching Bobby train and cleaning his boots every day. As things progressed I started training with him and then, best of all, being out on the pitch with him for the first team. For me it was a dream come true. I remember my first full start for West Ham, at Arsenal, and Bobby coming over to me in the dressing room and wishing me luck.

I learned a lot from the senior pros just by watching them both on and off the pitch. Bobby used to pick up abandoned kit in the dressing room, fold it up and lay everything neatly on the bench – and these were the good habits that I picked up on. Obviously, Bobby was my idol and he was the one I always looked at and learned from. He kept in touch with me on the pitch which was so valuable to me in those early games.

It was a little unfair to describe me as the next Bobby

Moore because no one could replace Bobby or be as good as him. I think it was because of the fact we were both local lads with blond hair and defenders, who had come up through the ranks. That's where the comparisons end really because he was 108 England caps ahead of me!

I actually got into the full England squad for a Euro Championship qualifier against Portugal in Lisbon. My hopes of playing were high when Kevin Beattie went down with an injury and I was told to warm up. Then the bugger got up and carried on, leaving me on the bench! I never got another chance.

Some of Ron Greenwood's training techniques were a little unorthodox. Once he tried to introduce ear pieces to the players so that he could communicate with them during the practice sessions. Bobby wore his for about five minutes before discarding them – and that was that.

After Bobby left West Ham it felt strange not having him around the club. To me, he was West Ham United and anything the club had ever achieved and that England had ever achieved, was all down to Bobby.

I think everyone thought he would end his playing days at West Ham and I don't know the reasons behind him leaving but he obviously felt he had a few years left in him which he did. Ironically, I would play against my idol in the biggest game of my career, versus Fulham at Wembley in the 1975 FA Cup final. I was only 21 at the time so it was a terrific experience. I was up against Viv Busby and Jimmy Conway. It was so very strange facing Bobby, though.

My fondest memories are after the game when Bobby congratulated me. He was very magnanimous. I have a lovely photo of us together after the final whistle. If you watch the match on DVD you will notice what a terrific game he had.

Sadly, I no longer have my shirt from that final. I later moved house and stored a few things in my garden shed – including my shirt and medal. A few years later, when I was having a clear out, I found the shirt, which was completely full of holes. All manner of moths and rodents had dined out on it! Thankfully, the medal was fine!

Later on in my career when I was playing for Fulham I received a call from Jim Smith, who was managing QPR. I was due to go there to see him on the following Monday but Bobby called me on Sunday and offered me a player-coach position with him at Southend United. At the time I was interested in getting into coaching so I accepted Bobby's offer.

People often question why Bobby didn't really make it as a manager? I firmly believe it was because he was asking people to do things that he could do with ease but which they simply weren't capable of doing.

I watched him run countless training sessions at Southend where he was asking the players to perform certain things – quite basic tasks really, such as how to control and pass, etc. Bobby would demonstrate each skill but the players would be kicking it out of play or controlling it badly and I could see he was genuinely frustrated. I think that if he had gone to a top club with decent players then he would have been a fantastic influence because those players would have been capable of carrying out his vision of how the game should be played. Bobby was still the best player at Southend and he was over 40-years-old.

I played with Bobby at West Ham and then I also moved on to Fulham although by that time he had left.

Then we worked together at Southend so my life shadowed his quite a bit which is amazing, really.

I was at home when I received a phone call from one of the reporters at the Southend Evening Echo. He shared the news that Bobby had died. It hit me really hard. He'd been a big part of my football life from when I was a young boy right through to when I got into coaching, so it was really, really, difficult to cope with that news.

I could remember queuing for his autograph as a young boy and how I was almost being groomed to take over from Bobby. That season we played a dozen or so games together but I think he knew that his time at West Ham was coming to an end. I still get affected now, just thinking about him. What a great man!

I could talk about Bobby forever. He was, and still is, the greatest player I have ever seen.

Kevin Lock

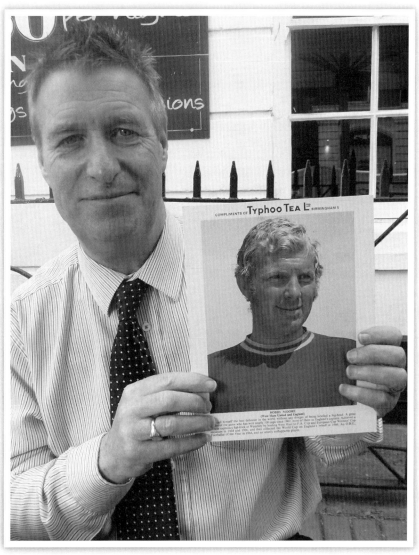

With his hero.

81 – CLIVE CHARLES
October 3, 1951 – August 26, 2003

Born: Bow, London

Position: Left-back

Games played with Bobby Moore: 13 (1972-73)

Games played for West Ham United: 15 (1972-73)

First game with Bobby Moore (Debut): March 21, 1972 Coventry City (a) D 1-1

Scorers: Coventry City: Smith
West Ham United: Best

Coventry City: Glazier, Smith, Cattlin, Machin, Blockley, Barry, McGuire, Carr, Chilton, Graham, Hunt

West Ham United: Ferguson, McDowell, **Charles**, Bonds, Taylor, Moore, Holland, Best, Hurst, Brooking, Robson

Clive Michael Charles was the younger brother of West Ham United favourite, John Charles. Despite only playing 14 league games and one cup tie for the Hammers, Clive went on to establish himself as a top-class coach in the United States of America. He was posthumously inducted into the Portland Hall of Fame in 2005 while a purpose-built stadium – The Clive Charles Soccer Center – can also be found in his adopted city of Portland, Oregon.

Clive had six years at West Ham and previously played for Newham Boys before signing as an apprentice in Easter, 1968. He gained three England Youth caps.

The form of Frank Lampard at left-back resulted in Clive being sent out on loan to Cardiff City. Bluebirds' manager and ex-Hammer, Jimmy Andrews, was suitably impressed and the move became permanent in 1973.

A transfer to Portland Timbers of the North America Soccer League in 1978 started a 25-year love affair with soccer in the United States. It culminated in Clive forming part of the United States coaching team for the 1998 World Cup in France. His burgeoning reputation never faltered and he is highly regarded for making a colossal contribution to both men and women's soccer in America. He was also a soccer pundit for ESPN at the 1994 World Cup.

His coaching credentials far outweighed his playing talents and Clive stands as the only Hammer to have been invited to the White House by a President. George W. Bush extended the courtesy to Clive in 2002.

Warming up at Highbury, April 1972.

Clive Charles passed away from prostate cancer in Portland on August 26, 2003. He was 52.

Following are the recollections of those that knew him:

After John came out of hospital in 2000, Clive bought us tickets to visit him in Portland. When we got over there it was amazing just how big a reputation Clive had. He was like the Bobby Moore of America, he'd done so well for himself. We went to one of the games he was coaching and he told us to bring along an overnight bag and our passport. Well, John and I didn't think anything of it. We were a bit like Dilly and Dolly! Before we knew it we were at the airport on our way to Las Vegas. 'I'm taking you out for lunch!' he said.

Carol Charles

Clive lived in Portland so I saw more of him than I did Charlo after our West Ham days. Thanks to his involvement with the Olympic national soccer team in 2000 he made a really terrific name for himself both on the men's side and the women's side. He was assistant coach of Team USA for the 1998 World Cup in France.

I had an enormous amount of interaction with Clive because when he first went to the University of Portland I was the director of coaching for the Washington State Soccer Association. Part of our responsibility was to produce a State team so I used to put a lot of good players Clive's way. In fact he used to call me Wally St Pier!

I wanted to steer these kids towards Clive because I knew he would look after them properly. He treated them all as professionals and he made sure they carried themselves professionally. These were his firm principles which he would have seen in abundance through people like Bobby Moore at West Ham.

He developed a terrific reputation at the University. A couple of years before he passed away they won a national college championship on the girls side. He brought that East

Wembley 5-A-Side L-R David Danson, Clive Charles, Gary Oakes, Ron Boyce, David Llewelyn, Joe Durrell and Bill Lansdowne.

Former team-mate Joe Durrell outside the Clive Charles Soccer Academy in Portland, Oregon.

End sense of humour to the west coast of the States and they loved him. Nothing was too much trouble for Clive.

He was an enormous help to me getting the role as head coach of the Portland Timbers for five years. Clive could have taken that job for himself if he had wanted it, no problem, but he had such a fantastic set-up at the University that he actually put my name forward instead. It was largely based on his recommendation that I got the job.

His funeral was absolutely packed and there were people there from all over the States including the National Soccer Federation. Former Millwall and Leicester great, Keith Weller also attended the service. Sadly he has since passed on, too.
Bobby Howe

I used to help run West Ham's five-a-side teams and Clive played in a couple of the London Evening Standard tournaments which were run in the 1960s and 70s. He played well in those competitions.
Bill Lansdowne

I spoke to Clive just before he died. I liked both Clive and Charlo and lived near to them in Barkingside. We had some great times together.
Ted MacDougall

I thought Clive was fantastic. He invited me over to help coach the US women's team and I stayed at his house. We played Scrabble which he loved. In fact Clive got me into Scrabble.
Trevor Hartley

Clive played cards with me, Trevor Brooking, Billy Bonds and Tommy Taylor. He lived near the ground and took me round to his house once. I met his mum Jesse and the rest of his large family. Clive was a likeable guy and very funny. We went on tour to Israel and, as usual, were playing cards. Clive got up and went to the toilet and when he came back he had his privates hanging out and two pounds worth of silver coins in his foreskin! 'Anyone need any change?' he asked. We all fell about laughing.
Bertie Lutton

Clive took his driving test at West Ham but failed so, naturally, I asked him why? He said he had put one hand out of the window to indicate a right turn and the other hand on the stick to change the gear. The instructor obviously saw that he had no hands on the steering wheel!

Clive was in charge of the meal tickets at West Ham. We used them to eat at Cassettari's Café. We were supposed to get one each with that day's date stamped on it and they were usually worth about 25p. Clive used to stamp three or four for everyone so we could have whatever we wanted.
Joe Durrell

Clive was a lovely little player who understood the game and went on to become a great coach at the University of Portland and with the US women's team. He was a true Hammer and shared his knowledge with many others.
Clyde Best

With his brother John (right) on thier final visit to the Boleyn Ground at Christmas 1997.

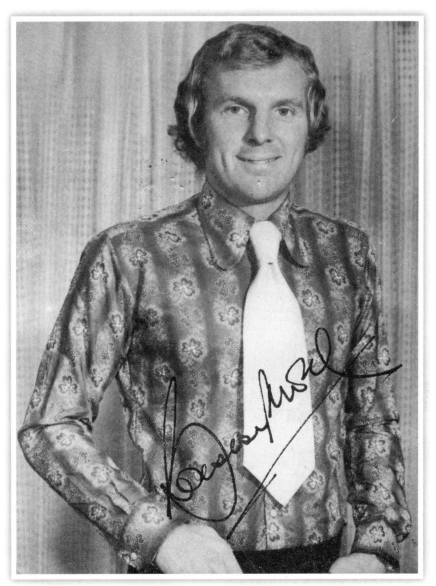

Bobby Moore the businessman.

Back row L-R Llewelyn, Heffer, Best, Grotier, Ferguson, Taylor, Moore, Bonds. Middle row L-R Tyler, McDowell, Eustace, Robson, Lock, Brooking, Lampard. Front row L-R Durrell, Boyce, Ayris, C.Charles, Holland, Coker.

CHAPTER FIFTEEN
1972-73

Bobby Moore's total appearances (July 1972-June 1973): 70 games (3 goals)

League Division One: 42 (3 goals), Friendlies: 13, England: 11, FA Cup: 2, League Cup: 2

Bobby Moore's penultimate season at Upton Park saw him enjoy the one and only ever-present league campaign of his playing career at West Ham United. He scored his final goal for the club against Manchester City on October 21, 1972 – a rare header. Sadly, it would be his final full season with both West Ham United and England.

Bryan 'Pop' Robson won the November Goal-of-the-Month competition for his acrobatic effort against Derby County. He finished the season with the Golden Boot after a highly impressive 28-goal haul. Incredibly he was still overlooked by England manager Sir Alf Ramsey and remains a member of the 'Billy Bonds club' for great players never to win an England cap.

On February 10, 1973 Moore played in his 509th league game for the Hammers – against Norwich City at Carrow Road. In doing so he established an all-time club record. Before West Ham's next match – at home to West Bromwich Albion – Moore was joined on the pitch by the very man whose record he bettered, the unforgettable free-scoring winger from the pre-war era, Jimmy Ruffell. Going into the 2014-15 season, he remains the club's most prolific winger with a staggering 166 goals.

Four days later, Moore reached another landmark when pulling on the England shirt for his 100th cap. A 5-0 thumping of Scotland at Hampden Park provided an extra layer of satisfaction.

The Hammers continued their awful run in the FA Cup, losing 0-1 away at Hull City in the fourth round. They fared no better in the League Cup, having lost 1-2 to Stockport County in the third round.

In a lasting tribute to both Moore and Trevor Brooking,

Newham Borough had streets named after them both in the Oakhurst Road area of Forest Gate.

In contrast to the previous season, Ron Greenwood gave debuts to only those players who were brought in via transfer activity - Dudley Tyler (Hereford United) Bertie Lutton (Brighton & Hove Albion), and Ted MacDougall (Manchester United), who was Greenwood's most expensive signing at £170,000.

Here is their story...

February 1973 - Bobby Moore exceeds Jimmy Ruffell's record for most league appearances in a West Ham United shirt (509).

82 – DUDLEY TYLER

Born: Salisbury, Wiltshire September 21, 1944

Position: Right-wing

Games played with Bobby Moore: 33 (1972-73)

Games played for West Ham United: 34 (1972-73)

First game with Bobby Moore (Debut): August 12, 1972 West Bromwich Albion (a) D 0-0

West Bromwich Albion: Smith, Nisbet, Wilson, Cantello, Wile, Robertson, Brown T, Brown A, Gould, Suggett, Hartford

West Ham United: Ferguson, McDowell, Lampard, Bonds, Taylor, Moore, **Tyler**, Best, Coker, Brooking, Robson

Dudley Hugh John Tyler was on the same score sheet as Bobby Moore when West Ham United beat Leicester City 5-2 at the beginning of the 1972-73 season. It was his only goal for the club. He also played in Bobby's final League Cup game for West Ham – a 0-1 defeat at Liverpool, in October 1973.

Remarkably, Dudley underwent an eight-hour operation on his heart when playing at junior level but soon made a name for himself at non-league Hereford United alongside other club legends, Ricky George and Ronnie Radford.

Former West Ham physio, Rob Jenkins, picks up the story of how Tyler joined the Hammers: 'Dudley was a very intelligent man and had been part of that famous giant-killing Hereford United team which knocked Newcastle United out of the FA Cup. He had a problem with his heart but Ron Greenwood took a £25,000 gamble on him.'

Ex-midfielder, Bertie Lutton, recalled a funny moment with Dudley during their time at West Ham: 'I had a couple of strange experiences at Upton Park. I remember being on the Underground on my way to the ground when some guy came up to me and asked me if I was Gunter Netzer the German striker! I could have laughed it off but it happened overseas as well when I was in a café with Dudley Tyler. A few of the lads started calling me Gunter! Dudley was a good man. I seem to recall he liked to play chess.'

Flexing his left peg.

Dudley's holiday snap of Bobby in Sweden.

Putting in a corner for Clyde Best and Pop Robson.

Tyler's spell with the Hammers was short lived and he returned to Hereford United in 1973 where he stayed until injury brought a close to his playing career four years later.

Dudley continues to live in Hereford with his wife Margaret and has recently retired from his part-time job as a driver for an Audi and Volkswagen dealership. He is suffering from painful hips or 'footballer's disease' as he prefers to call it. Consequently, he has put his hobbies – playing squash and tennis – on hold for a while but took the time to visit London to discuss Bobby Moore:

I was absolutely star-struck when I joined West Ham United. I had only played amateur football and part-time as a pro but had always dreamed of being a full-time professional footballer ever since I was a kid.

At the time I was beginning to think it might not happen for me because I wasn't very big and had undergone a heart operation, which would have made most clubs think twice but West Ham did come in for me. I was gobsmacked and immediately said: 'Yes.'

West Ham was the first team to play at Munich's Olympic Stadium after the 1972 Games. We went over there and played a mid-week match against TSV Munich 1860.

We also went to Sweden to play and, while we were over there, I remember playing tennis with Frank Lampard while Mooro was the umpire. I have a photo from that experience which I love because Bobby looks so relaxed.

The one story that really sticks in my mind happened when I first came from Hereford United to join West Ham. I had been working in an office playing part-time football and was as raw as you like and still very wet behind the ears. I went on those tours with the team to Sweden and Germany and, when we got back, Ron said to me I was in the first team to face West Bromwich Albion at The Hawthorns. I asked him what the match day dress code was and he said a collar and tie with a jacket. I didn't have anything like that in my wardrobe. I was staying in a hotel and only had casual kit for training. So I went up to the West End and bought what I thought was a very

Tyler–just tremendous

By DENNIS SIGNY

West Ham 5 Leicester 2

DUDLEY TYLER, the 27-year-old hole-in-the-heart forward West Ham manager, Ron Greenwood plucked from Southern League obscurity, arrived on the First Division scene with a vengeance.

Tyler is "the most refreshing thing that has happened to me in

GREENWOOD VERDICT

years," says Greenwood.

No wonder! He certainly sent 25,000 Upton Park fans wild as he scored his first League goal and teed-up two more.

What is more, Tyler gave a £200,000 rated David Nish a chasing and beat man after man in runs at the City defence.

Jittery

West Ham survived a jittery start, in which they twice fell behind, to turn in a vintage performance that had the fans chanting their "Bubbles" theme and forecasting they were going to win the League.

Can the unbeaten Ham-

mers mount a serious challenge?

Manager Greenwood told me: "Bobby Moore has got the bit between his teeth. He has played well in all three games and might have had a hat-trick against Leicester.

"He senses something is on. I told them they were a good team before the season and that they could win something."

I have never seen Moore do so much attacking in over a decade of football.

Once he went through showing ball control that could not have been bettered by a Brazilian or continental master.

Whatever else happens, both West Ham and Leicester will certainly win praise from fans and

referees for entertainment and sportsmanship.

Both Bobby Ferguson and City skipper Keith Weller kicked the ball into touch when opponents were injured.

Goals ... flowing football ... no cautions or hooliganism. What lovely way to spend a Saturday afternoon.

My notebook is full of incident and near-misses. From the moment, 155 seconds from the start, when rangy Mike Stringfellow who has been injured on and off for three years, and did not play a League match last season, scored a comeback goal, there was something happening.

Stringfellow, deputising for injured Alan Birchenall, scored with a shot that spun off Ferguson's foot.

Deflected

Moore equalised with a shot deflected off a defender.

Len Glover put Leicester ahead again and five minutes later young Ade Coker headed West Ham level.

In the second half Pop Robson put West Ham in front for the first time. Tyler brought the house down with that headed goal and two minutes later — 10 minutes from time — Robson made it five.

WEST HAM. — Ferguson, McDowell, Lampard, Bonds, Taylor, Moore, Tyler, Best, Coker, Brooking, Robson. Sub: Gould.

LEICESTER CITY. — Shilton, Whitworth, Nish, Woollett, Sjoberg, Cross, Farrington, Sammels, Weller, Stringfellow, Glover. Sub: Partridge.

DUDLEY WILL DO

ALBION 0
WEST HAM UTD. 0

THERE WAS MORE than enough to encourage Hammers' fans about this well-worn point of the season's curtain-raiser at The Hawthorns last Saturday — even if the final outcome produced more headaches than plaudits from the critics.

Certainly, neither side suggested that the Leeds and Liverpools would need to lose sleep over them just at present. But West Ham with their untried, new-look attack, showed sufficient form to dispel doubts about their chances of avoiding troubled times this year.

For a start, Dudley Tyler took to Division One like a duck to water. In fact he was, for my money anyway, the man of the match for Hammers. Fast, skilful and full of running, he has clearly settled smoothly into the scheme of things. His workrate here was impressive, especially in a readiness to help out in defence, while he also displayed a keen eye for the

By Trevor Smith

open space. On top of that he never very close to marking his scalper debut with a goal, a blistering drive from outside the box flashing inches wide. The other new boy" in attack, Ade Coker, was perhaps less noticeable. Yet his best moments brought gasps of admiration from the home crowd and underlined once again what rich potential is here. He, too, all but grabbed both points for Hammers with a whiplash shot two minutes from the end which beat Smith's full-length dive and flicked the outside of an upright. This effort, which climaxed West

Ham's best mounted attack, was later, as I read, described as a "mask" Hawk criticism, indeed. Coker's speed off the mark won him the split second shooting chance on the edge of the box at the expense of two defenders!

These factors apart, however, there was also a healthy resolution and confidence about West Ham's play. They withstood Albion's opening surge with calm efficiency, grouping effectively in defence around Taylor's lofty head, and going forward with real purpose at every opportunity.

Referee Hockey's swift penalising of crash tackling played its part in all this and the hectic command soon gave up the unrewarding ploy of fouling Best and Coker.

Hammers' goals-from-everywhere policy led to the energetic Bonds turning up in the Albion box to dribble by two men and fire inches outside as a third tackled early in the game. Best later brought the save of the day out of Smith with a 35-yard rocket, while Tyler ghosted away from a defence appealing vainly for offside to round Smith, only to have his finish blocked out.

Albion's most agonising moments came early in the second half when they put West Ham's defence under some pressure. During this period Gould squandered a clear-cut opening from six yards, a miss which seemed to dishearten the home side. Almost the only other anxious moment for Ferguson came just before the break when Hartford shot fiercely just wide after studding Moore's tackle superbly.

The longer the game went on the more unsettled Albion's fans became and their favourites responded in kind to the point, even when you could actually brush aside the uneasy suspicion that, as so often in the past, a late goal was going to set much sound West Ham play in naught. Yes, encouraging enough.

Best, Hammers

W.B.A. 0 West Ham 0

Impressive Bonds and Clyde and menace ng a midthrough at and Clyde and menace

ect approach, build-ups, national Asa Albion show

a chance for that wide, ed round the Smith to dive line, as Hammers

With the Albion defence looking stretched Dudley Tyler, the new boy from Hereford, slipped round Smith only to find his cross hastily cleared. Then Pop Robson given a golden opportunity, planted the ball into Smith's hands from only 10 yards. But that miss could not compare with two glaring chances Albion squandered at the beginning of the second half.

Sliced

Hartford found Tony Brown well inside the box but he miscued from right in front of goal. Within seconds a Len Cantello cross was headed from to Bobby Gould, who sliced wide from heade six yards

Dudley is well received by the media.

Visiting London to discuss Bobby Moore.

I didn't have the impression that Bobby was a big drinker at the club although he did like a slug of brandy about 15 minutes before a game!

I do remember going to the opening of Bobby Moore's country club – Woolston Manor – in Chigwell. I believe he went into partnership with Sean Connery. My wife, Margaret, always remembers it because she was heavily pregnant with our son and Tina Moore took her under her wing and made sure she was alright. They got on very well together and used to sit next to each other at West Ham's home matches.

I also played against Bobby when he was at Fulham and I had returned to Hereford. We had won promotion and were up against a Fulham side which also boasted both George Best and Rodney Marsh. They stuffed us 1-4.

The coaching at West Ham was something else and you appreciated just how good it was when you played for a different club. At Hereford, the manager, John Sillett, called me over, put me in the corner of the pitch and asked me to kick the ball as hard as I could down the line. Once I had done it he said: 'Good, you're marking George Best on Saturday.' So I ended up playing right-back and Besty was outside-left.

Bobby saw things so early on the pitch and I can't recall him ever being taken to the cleaners by anyone. He never, ever, seemed to have an off day.

Dudley Tyler

expensive but very smart looking sports jacket. I paid £30 for it but was only earning £50-a-week. I've still got it hanging up in the loft at home. On the Saturday I walked towards the coach wearing the collar, tie and the jacket when Bobby came over to me, felt the lapel and said 'Why pay more?'

To be honest it was a bit of a struggle financially at West Ham. I needed to be playing in the first-team regularly to make decent money and I had a wife and a baby on the way so playing in London was quite difficult. I was living in Stanford-Le-Hope so didn't tend to go out a lot with the lads. However, Bobby always made the point that I should go along to The Black Lion in Plaistow for a quick pint after training. Mooro would be sitting on a stall in the corner holding court with a half-pint in his hand.

83 – BERTIE LUTTON

Born: Banbridge, Northern Ireland August 13, 1950

Position: Midfielder

Games played with Bobby Moore: 9 (1973)

Games played for West Ham United: 13 (1973)

First game with Bobby Moore (Debut): February 10, 1973 Norwich City (a) W 1-0

Scorer: West Ham United: Robson

Norwich City: Keelan, Payne, Butler, Stringer, Anderson, Briggs, Livermore, Bone, Cross, Paddon, Howard Sub: O'Donnell*

West Ham United: Ferguson, McDowell, Lampard, Bonds, Taylor, Moore, Ayris, Best, **Lutton**, Brooking, Robson

Robert John Lutton will always hold a special place in West Ham United's history. He was the first Hammer to win a cap for Northern Ireland – coming on as a second half substitute for Bryan Hamilton in a 3-0 victory over Cyprus on May 8, 1973. He was also the only Ulsterman to play with Bobby Moore at West Ham United.

Previously with Wolverhampton Wanderers and Brighton & Hove Albion, Lutton felt he was 'Back in the big time,' when Ron Greenwood paid £25,000 for his services.

A crippling back problem limited Lutton's opportunities and he eventually requested a free transfer after just one year with the club.

'Bertie' certainly left his mark on his former team-mates and there was no shortage of comments about the midfielder. Clyde Best declared: 'Everyone who played with Bertie Lutton will remember him. He gave it his all but it didn't work out for him.'

Another striker, Bobby Gould also played with Bertie at Wolves: 'Bertie was as mad as a March hare. He was the only one at West Ham who was madder than me! At Wolves we used to do our pre-season training at Wolverhampton racecourse. The manager Bill McGarry told us to run two laps of the track. Bertie sped off and left us all for dead. He must have won it by a furlong, easily. He absolutely romped home and had pace to burn but we didn't see him again. He'd ran so quickly that he'd pulled his hamstrings and groin and was basically lame for months!'

Former West Ham physio, Rob Jenkins smiles when he remembers Bertie: 'He smoked more than John Lyall and Ron Boyce put together!'

Bertie recently visited the UK from his home in Melbourne, Australia and, despite having only played 13 games in the West Ham United shirt, he had many a tale to tell.

Nowadays, Bertie works in a warehouse for a transport company. 'My two daughters, Lisa and Kylie, live over there with me but my son, Lee, married an English girl and he lives in Wolverhampton. I pop over to see him when I can and it is always good to visit my sisters Irene and Frances in Northern Ireland. I don't watch any football and prefer to follow rugby league in Australia. I support Melbourne Storm.

When I signed for West Ham United I got picked to play for Northern Ireland against England. At training one day I asked Bobby Moore if we could swap shirts after the game and he said: 'No problem, I'll keep it for you.' I was on the bench for the game and didn't play but, at full time, I headed down the tunnel and there were people everywhere. I could see Bobby up ahead going into the England dressing room so I shouted after him: 'Bobby, shall we swap our shirts?' He then apologised and explained how he had given it to Bryan Hamilton at the whistle. I didn't swear but I wasn't happy about it and saw it as a bit of bad luck. However, when we returned for pre-season training, Bobby walked in and threw one of his England shirts at me: 'There's the shirt I promised you,' he said and I was stunned: 'Would you like one of my Northern Ireland shirts?' I suggested. He politely declined. The shirt he gave to me was from the 1970 World Cup but I don't know from which game exactly.

I ended up selling it in 2006 because it was only sitting in a cupboard in Australia and was almost thrown out once with all my caps and other shirts, when my daughter had a clear out!

I took two shirts to auction – the one Bobby gave me and one that Billy Bremner wore for Scotland. I think they valued Bobby's at £10,000 and Bremner's at £3,500. I wasn't happy with the way it was sold and felt I was had over. The bidding went £5,000, £5,500, £6,000, £6,500, £7,000, £7,500, £8,000, £8,500, £9,000 SOLD! They didn't give anyone a chance to bid higher than nine thousand! A few years later it appeared on eBay for £40,000 but I don't know if it sold. The Bremner shirt was similarly hurried and very quickly announced as a no sale at £900. A couple of days later I got a letter from the auctioneer saying that £2,250 had been offered, then £2,500 and finally £2,750. I felt I was being swindled and didn't sell so I've still got Bremner's shirt.

I only went out a couple of times with Bobby. At the end of the 1972-73 season we were beaten at home by Arsenal, 1-2. I had a couple of mates, Dennis Gray and Sid, who were visiting me from Brighton. Bobby asked me if I wanted to join him and a few of the lads for a beer and I explained about my mates and he said: 'Just bring them along.' He gave us a lift and I was sitting in the front of his Jaguar with my two pals in the back. When we got to the pub he asked us each for one pound and we drank all night long for a quid! Dennis and Sid haven't stopped talking about it since.

The other time I went out with Bobby was when we had lunch together with Trevor Brooking and Frank Lampard at a little restaurant beside the ground. The four of us went in there and Trevor paid thank Christ because I had no money! I was paying a week's wages for a month's train ticket from Brighton so I was always skint. We were earning nothing at the time, perhaps £60-a-week? Even Bobby was only on about £200-a-week. The money was poor compared to what you could get elsewhere. I was paid more playing part-time in Australia.

Bertie on the ball.

I actually signed on the dole after West Ham because I thought my playing days were over. I struggled with sciatica and could barely move at times. Then one day I received a phone call from Dave MacLaren, the former Wolves goalkeeper. He invited me to play for Sydney City in Australia so I went. I was sent to see the best doctors and they gave me a course of drugs which were banned in England but fine over there and, remarkably, I was given an extension to my career. I've been living in Melbourne ever since.

I only scored one league goal for West Ham and it came up at Derby County in 72-73. It was quite funny really because Derby had pushed up to the half way line and Ted MacDougall put the ball through and I beat the offside trap and ran onto it. The keeper came out and I just stroked it passed him and felt sure it was going in and wheeled away to the corner flag to celebrate. Anyway, I must have scuffed it because it started going slower and slower and I began to think that maybe it wasn't going in. Their big centre-back Roy McFarland started tearing after it and he nearly got there but it just rolled over the line. It didn't even touch the back of the net! We should have won 1-0 but Bobby gave away a penalty and we ended up drawing, 1-1. It was a needless penalty. I was right there and shouted: 'Don't tackle him Bobby, I have him covered,' but it was too late.

My worst game for West Ham was at home to Burnley when we lost 0-1. I was taken off and as I was walking down the tunnel a West Ham fan reached over and punched me.

Bobby was my team-mate and you look at your team-mates differently. He was a great guy to me and treated me really well. I didn't really look up to him because I had been lucky enough to have played with other great players like George Best for Northern Ireland and both Derek Dougan and Peter Knowles at Wolves. Peter was a fantastic player but he chucked it all in to become a Jehovah's Witness.

I joined West Ham with nothing and I left with nothing. In fact, Bobby inadvertently gave me my best pay-day by giving me his shirt. Thanks Bob!

Bertie Lutton

Bertie Lutton in the centre of his family.

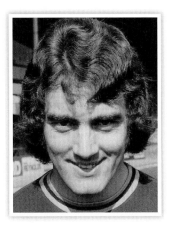

84 – TED MACDOUGALL

Born: Inverness, January 8, 1947

Position: Forward

Games played with Bobby Moore: 21 (1973)

Games played for West Ham United: 25 (1973)

First game with Bobby Moore (Debut): March 10, 1973 Sheffield United (a) D 0-0

Sheffield United: McAlister, Badger, Hemsley, Flynn, Colquhoun, Eddy, Woodward, Salmons, Dearden, Currie, Bone

West Ham United: Ferguson, McDowell, Lampard, Bonds, Taylor, Moore, Best, Lock, **MacDougall**, Brooking, Robson

Edward John MacDougall spent 10 turbulent months with West Ham United but forged a life-long friendship with Bobby Moore.

MacDougall plied his trade at the other end of the pitch to Moore but they did have one thing in common. They were both sent off while at West Ham – Ted was dissmissed on October 6, 1973 against Burnley, while Bobby received his marching orders 12 years earlier, on November 4, 1961, away at Manchester City. Billy Bonds and Harry Redknapp were the only other Hammers to be sent off in the Bobby Moore era.

Ted signed for West Ham United after failing to settle at Manchester United. He had already had the West Ham experience when playing in Geoff Hurst's testimonial on November 23, 1971.

He joined the club with a fine reputation for scoring goals in the lower divisions – including a record-breaking nine against Margate in the FA Cup in 1971 – but was still largely unproven in top flight football.

Former AFC Bournemouth team-mate, Keith Miller offers his own assessment of MacDougall: 'He was a lovely player. He was a greedy bugger but he had an eye for goal. He wouldn't do any work and would hang around the penalty area converting our crosses. He didn't do any chasing back but he was a great guy to have in the team because he never missed.'

One of the players putting in those crosses was former Hammer, Tony Scott: 'I had two wonderful season at Bourne-

On his scoring home debut with Mike Doyle of Manchester City, March 1973.

mouth. John Bond played me to my strengths, told me to concentrate on putting in crosses and not to worry about tackling or defending. Ted converted most of my crosses. He was a nasty piece of work and upset a lot of people but he got the job done.'

Perhaps MacDougall's biggest legacy at West Ham was his altercation with Billy Bonds up at Elland Road following a 1-4 defeat at the hands of Don Revie's Leeds United. Ted remembers the confrontation as though it was yesterday. 'More and more people ask me about the fight I had with Bonzo up at Leeds. I remember getting the one and only blow in. At the time there were a lot of cliques at the club. I mis-played a pass from Billy and the ball ended up going to Lorimer who set up Mick Jones to score. Billy was effing and blinding and I just told him to 'piss off' and we went in at half-time but nothing was said. Anyway, at the end of the game we had been well and truly stuffed by a Leeds side that were in their pomp. I had scored our goal so I had done my job but we were in the big bath and Billy started up again so I said to him: 'Why don't you stop talking and do something about it?' Anyway, he took one step forward and I smacked him across the chest and he fell in the bath. The players kept hold of him thank god otherwise he would have probably eaten me alive. Then, in walked Lyall and Greenwood and they held me down and I shouted at them: 'That's what's wrong with your effing club – too many cliques!' I didn't last much longer after that episode. I think I was gone within a month. To be fair to Bill, he had always treated me well and when I was at Norwich City I went back a couple of times, while my house was being sold and he was one of the very few who came over and asked me how things were going.'

MacDougall played in Moore's final league game on New Year's Day 1974 but for West Ham's opponents Norwich City, to whom he had been transferred for £140,000, a few days earlier. A deal which had seen classy Norwich midfielder Graham Paddon move the other way. Coincidentally, Bobby's former FA Cup and European Cup Winners cup team-mate, John Sissons, also played for the Canaries on that fateful day. Despite Ted scoring twice the Hammers won 4-2.

Ted followed the path of many other footballers from the 1960s and 70s, when opening up various retail outlets – 'Ted MacDougall Sports' – before spending time as a publican at the Mill Arms at Dunbridge, Hampshire. He later had a period working in property development out in Vancouver. In 2013 Bournemouth named their South Stand after the legendary striker.

Today, Ted lives south of Jacksonville, Florida and visits these shores every year with a group of young players who, courtesy of Harry Redknapp, get the opportunity to train at a Premier League club.

The many sides of Ted MacDougal.

It was in his spiritual homeland of Bournemouth that Ted shared the following recollections of Bobby Moore:

I never had a great relationship with West Ham but I loved Bobby Moore.
I was so upset when he passed away. I loved Bob dearly. He had an aura about him. His manner, his style, the way he made you feel special, everything about him. He was one of the greatest people I have ever met.

The decision to sign for West Ham happened in a car park near Stoke. Paddy Crerand, Manchester United's famous midfielder, gave me a lift down from Manchester. There were no agents or anything like that and the whole process was a lot simpler. I sat in Ron Greenwood's car and we shook hands on a deal to take me to West Ham United.

It was funny because when I got home that evening I was thinking about what lay ahead and what it was going to be like playing in a team with Bobby Moore, when I received a telephone call from Bill Nicholson, the manager at Spurs. He asked if I'd shaken Ron Greenwood's hand and I said I had and he said: 'Ok, well just don't score too many goals against us.' Those days have gone and men with integrity like Bill Nicholson are just not around anymore.

I actually played in Geoff Hurst's testimonial at Upton Park before I signed for West Ham. I had scored nine goals for Bournemouth against Margate the weekend before and Geoff phoned up John Bond, who was Bournemouth manager at the time, and asked if I could play in an All Star XI. So, one minute I was playing in the old third division and the next thing I was on the same pitch as Bobby Moore, Eusebio, Jimmy Johnstone, Uwe Seeler, Jimmy Greaves and Rodney Marsh. I actually scored in the first half before I was subbed at half-time by Tommy Docherty, who was our manager for the game and another one who didn't like me!

There were two groups of people at West Ham; 'The golfers' and 'The half-lagers!' I was with Bob, Charlo, Lampard, big Clyde and one or two others. The golfers were Trevor, Pop, Ferguson, McDowell and Mervyn Day.

I had a roaring start at West Ham, scoring four goals in five games and we went on a long unbeaten run. In the beginning, my touch was poor but Greenwood and Lyall put on training sessions in grids at Chadwell Heath and it was all one-touch passing which really improved my game. Being around players like Bob couldn't help but improve my touch and I got a lot better.

I stayed with both Bob and Frank Lampard at their houses. They both really looked after me. Socially, Bob was very discreet and composed and because he only ever drunk half-a-lager you never felt he was out of control. When he spoke to you he made you feel very special. He would talk to you and you felt as though you were the only person that mattered to him. That is a hard skill to develop but he had it naturally. I was also very good friends with Alan Ball and he used to talk so highly about Bobby at England because he roomed with him. 'He irons his money,' he used to say.

To be fair, my problem wasn't with West Ham, rather it was with the manager, Ron Greenwood. When it came to football, he was obviously ahead of his time but when it came to man-management, I think he found me a complex character. To be honest, I was a bit of an asshole back then and have had to apologise to a lot of people but I think I am actually a nice person now. It was best for all concerned when John Bond signed me for Norwich City, bringing my time at West Ham to an end.

Prior to the 1975 FA Cup final between West Ham United and Fulham, Brian Moore, who was a great commentator, was covering a game with Norwich City and he got a few ex-Hammers together to discuss the final. There was me and John Bond, Ken Brown, Martin Peters and I think John Sissons might have been there, too. It was supposed to be a West Ham love-in and Bondy was saying how pleased he was for Ron Greenwood and John Lyall and how great it was for the club and the fans. He eventually came to me and I just said I wasn't bothered and that I only cared about Bobby Moore and Frank Lampard and that I hoped Bobby and Fulham won it. That went down like a lead balloon!

Now that wasn't the end of it. Incredibly, Dave Stringer of Norwich was lined up to play his testimonial against West Ham after the Cup final and he came up to me after the Brian Moore interview and said that Ron Greenwood had called and was threatening not to bring West Ham if I was down to play. It was because of what I had said. I couldn't believe it and in the end I didn't play so that the game could go ahead!

In the 1980s, Bob was coaching out in Hong Kong for a team called Easter AA. I went and stayed with him on my way to Australia. It was quite a funny story because I was watching Bobby in Escape to Victory on the plane and then he was picking me up at the airport! I stayed at his apartment, which was overlooking the South China Sea and we sat out reminiscing whilst drinking a 1966 vintage Taylor Port! It was one of the most magnificent nights of my life.

Ted MacDougall

Visiting from Florida.

THE FOOTBALL ASSOCIATION
INTERNATIONAL MATCH

ENGLAND
VERSUS
ITALY

Wednesday, 14th November, 1973   Kick-off 7.45 p.m.

EMPIRE **WEMBLEY** STADIUM

Official Programme . . . Ten pence

The final international appearance. 108 caps, 90 as captain.

Back row L-R Charles, Lutton, Grotier, Ferguson, Best, Brooking. Middle row L-R Bonds, Taylor, Lock, Day, McDowell, Lampard, Moore. Front row L-R Ayris, Holland, MacDougall, Tyler, Coker, Robson, Boyce.

CHAPTER SIXTEEN
1973-74

Bobby Moore's total appearances (July 1973-June 1974): 30 games (0 goals)

League Division One: 22, Friendlies: 2, Reserves: 2, England: 1, Watney Cup: 1, FA Cup: 1, League Cup: 1

My considered opinion of my 16-years at Upton Park, now that I am no longer a Hammer, is that I do not regret a minute of it. You can never be poor if you have the right experiences. They can never take those away from you.
Bobby Moore

After 16 years and 642 league and cup games Bobby Moore's West Ham United career came to an end. On January 5, 1974, in an FA Cup third round clash at home to Hereford United, West Ham's greatest-ever player left the pitch with an injury on 30 minutes. He was replaced by Pat Holland who, incidentally, would score a late equaliser to become West Ham's first-ever scoring substitute.

The Bobby Moore era at West Ham United has a million hearts pinned to it. It is often the case that simple phrases encapsulate the right mood and there are a couple from the great Bobby Charlton of Manchester United and England which spring to mind – 'Bobby Moore was a friend to everyone he played with' – will doubtless resonate with an emphatic majority of the 89 Hammers in this book.

The final farewell. Bobby Moore says goodbye to the fans on March 16, 1974, prior to a home game against Coventry City. Ron Greenwood accompanies his captain.

Charlton also shared the following insight: 'If Bobby Moore played well, then everyone played well.' It is a sentiment which will chime loudly with the vast majority of fans who clicked through the Upton Park turnstiles during the late 1950s, 1960s and early 1970s.

On November 14, six weeks prior to the game against Hereford, Moore had made his farewell international bow for England, against Italy at Wembley Stadium. It would not be his final competitive visit to the twin towers. Ironically, that would come, in beautiful harmony, against the claret and blue of West Ham United, whilst wearing the white and black of Fulham some 16 months later.

Even though Moore's final season with West Ham United was prematurely cut short, there was still sufficient time for him to be involved in first team action with five fresh Hammers – Mervyn Day, Keith Coleman, Bobby Gould, Mick McGiven and the 89th and final Hammer, Graham Paddon.

Here is their story…

85 – MERVYN DAY

Born: Chelmsford, June 26, 1955

Position: Goalkeeper

Games played with Bobby Moore: 16 (1973-74)

Games played for West Ham United: 232 (1973-79)

First game with Bobby Moore (Debut): August 27, 1973 Ipswich Town (h) D 3-3

Scorers: West Ham United: Bonds, Brooking, Best
Ipswich Town: Whymark, Johnson (2)

West Ham United: Day, Lampard, Lock, Bonds, Taylor, Moore, Best, Holland, MacDougall, Brooking, Robson

Ipswich Town: Best, Mills, Harper, Morris, Keeley, Beattie, Hamilton, Viljoen, Johnson, Whymark, Lambert

Mervyn Richard Day was Bobby Moore's 12th and final goalkeeper at West Ham United. He ended a line that began with Ernie Gregory in 1958. Day was the only one of those 12 goalkeepers to face Bobby in an FA Cup final, keeping a clean sheet against Fulham in the 1975 showpiece, a feat which proved to be his finest 90 minutes in the green jersey.

Mervyn played for Chelmsford and Essex Boys before signing as an apprentice on July 20, 1971. He was an all-round sportsman as a boy representing Essex at cricket, hockey and athletics. Despite playing over 200 career matches for the Hammers, only 16 of them were during the Bobby Moore era.

After being transferred to Leyton Orient in 1979, Day became something of a journeyman keeper, also playing for

Safe hands against Burnley on October 6, 1973.

Aston Villa, Leeds United, Luton Town, Sheffield United and, finally, Carlisle United. He returned to Upton Park as a coach during the Alan Curbishley era (2006-08).

Today, Mervyn, is the head of recruitment at West Bromwich Albion and was previously a Scouting and Talent Identification Manager at Brighton & Hove Albion. Indeed, it was at the American Express Community Stadium in Falmer, East Sussex that Mervyn shared his memories of Bobby Moore:

I have a few vivid memories of Bobby Moore. I was 16 when I joined West Ham as an apprentice and, in that era, apprentices were expected to do everything. That meant cleaning the toilets, sweeping up and then painting the dressing rooms in the summer. There was no dedicated maintenance team.

It was quite amazing that the training kit was only cleaned once-a-week which was bad news for me being a goalkeeper as I obviously got dirtier than most of the other players. West Ham had giant ovens at the ground which dried all the kit but they didn't actually clean it, so you knew you would be wearing dirty gear the next day. I tried to clean mine in the shower, without Ernie Gregory seeing me, because Ernie was in charge of all the apprentices and didn't like the kit being soaking wet.

Now, when I went into the first team dressing room, I was expected to arrange all the kit. The first team knew it was our job to keep everything tidy and they would throw their kit all over the place. It was easy to see which kit was Bobby's because he would take off his socks, shorts, slip, shirt, sweater and track-suit and place them in orderly lines on the massage table. He would say to the others: 'At least try and do this for the kids.' He was all about standards and everything he did was consistent with that. He really was someone you could look up to.

When West Ham were trying to sign me, Ernie took me into a little gym they had in the main stand. I was only 15-years-old and hadn't signed apprentice forms. He introduced me to Geoff Hurst, who went to my old school – Kings Road primary in Chelmsford. Then, I was introduced to Bobby Moore and was a bit tongue-tied to say the least! Finally, Ernie called out to a figure at the other end of the gym, who was kicking a ball and heading it with perfect control: 'Martin, can you fire a few shots at this lad?' It must have been one of Martin's final days at the club because he moved to Spurs shortly afterwards and wasn't there when I signed apprentice forms. The memory of

meeting all three World Cup stars and keeping goal against Martin Peters is something I have never forgotten.

My debut against Ipswich Town in 1973 was completely out of the blue. It was a Monday evening and I was walking down Barking Road eating a hamburger. When I got to the ground, about 50-minutes before kick-off, Ernie hurried me in and told me I was playing. Bobby Ferguson's wife, Greer, was poorly and substitute goalkeeper, Peter Grotier had a very high temperature. I didn't have time to think about anything but I remember Ernie saying: 'You'll be fine, just listen to what Mooro says in front of you and go out and enjoy it.' In those days you didn't warm up on the pitch. The first time you took the field was to play, but there was a little gym where we could go to do some stretches and warm up. Some of the players would nip out the back for a couple of cheeky drags on a cigarette but I'm not naming any names. I wouldn't want to drop Boycey and Harry in it!

The first two weeks of pre-season training were spent in Epping Forest. We never saw a ball and instead would do plenty of running through the woods with a professional runner. I used to stay at the back with Mooro, Bobby Ferguson and Ronnie Boyce. They had been doing it for years, knew every short-cut throughout the forest and found a route to save about half a mile of running which was a blessing, believe me!

I never saw much of Bobby after he left West Ham but will never forget the brief time we spent together.

Mervyn Day

Bobby Moore's final West Ham goalkeeper.

86 – KEITH COLEMAN

Born: Washington, County Durham, May 24, 1951

Position: Right-back

Games played with Bobby Moore: 15 (1973-74)

Games played for West ham United: 118 (1973-77)

First game with Bobby Moore (Debut): October 6, 1973 Burnley (h) L 0-1

Scorer: Burnley: Waldron

HAMMER
OFFICIAL PROGRAMME

WEST HAM UNITED
VERSUS
BURNLEY
FOOTBALL LEAGUE : FIRST DIVISION
Saturday 6 October 1973 at 3 p.m.
FIVEPENCE

West Ham United: Day, **Coleman**, Lampard, Bonds, McDowell, Moore, Lutton*, Holland, MacDougall, Brooking, Robson Sub: Lock*

Burnley: Stevenson, Noble, Newton, Dobson, Waldron, Thomson, Nulty, Hankin, Fletcher, Collins, James

Keith Coleman joined West Ham United from Sunderland for £20,000 in September, 1973. He played 118 first team matches for the Hammers, 16 of them with Bobby Moore who was soon destined to play out his final days in English football with Fulham.

Coleman played in Moore's final League Cup match for West Ham – against Liverpool at Anfield on October 29, 1973. Two months later he would also play in Moore's final league game for the club – against Norwich City at the Boleyn Ground on New Year's Day 1974.

Coleman was Moore's final right-back at West Ham, a journey which had started some 16-years earlier with John Bond. Coleman would eventually go on to play in the Hammers' European Cup Winners Cup final versus RSC Anderlecht at the Heysel Stadium, Brussels in 1976. Despite the 2-4 defeat, it proved to be the pinnacle of his playing career having missed out on the FA Cup final the previous year.

After leaving West Ham, Keith played for Belgian side Mechelen before returning to England to play out the rest of his career with Darlington and, finally, Hendon. He later managed leisure centres and golf courses for Brentwood Council before taking voluntary redundancy.

For the past 10 years Keith has been living near Pathos, Cyprus. He is enjoying his retirement in the sun and had the following recollections of Bobby Moore:

I didn't know Bobby that well. I arrived in September 1973 and played a few reserve team games before making my first team debut at home to Burnley. We lost 0-1. It was part of the worst start to a season West Ham has ever had. I think they went 11 games without winning.

I wasn't part of Bobby's social set because a lot of the players lived far apart. Bobby was in Woodford and I lived in Brentwood, Essex.

He was always very quiet in the dressing room and would never shout at anybody. Bonzo was more the type to cajole people and get them fired up for the game. Bobby did it in his own, quiet, reserved way. He was always very encouraging and supportive of people. We all know that he read the game

On the ball in front of the Chicken Run.

Bobby Moore's final right back at West Ham United.

It was an eye-opener for me when I first joined West Ham because at Sunderland it had basically been physical work and five-a-side, whereas at Upton Park everything revolved around the ball. That's how Greenwood wanted it done and that came through in their play, which was designed to entertain. It was not always successful but that was the style Ron believed in and Bobby took that onto the pitch as captain and encouraged everyone else to play that way.

I used to socialise with Patsy Holland, Mervyn Day and John Ayris, the younger lads really, as opposed to the more established players such as Bobby and Frank Lampard. Bobby had no airs or graces and he never behaved as though he was better than anyone else. He always spoke to you with civility and treated you in the same manner as anybody else. I did play in a match against Bobby when he was at Fulham. We drew them in the League Cup and they beat us 1-2 (October 1974). It would have been nice to have played against him in the 1975 FA Cup final but John Lyall preferred to play with John McDowell and Frank Lampard so I missed out. My crowning moment in the West Ham shirt, of course, was reaching the final of the European Cup Winners Cup against Anderlecht in 1976. I still have my shirt and medal.

Bobby and I were never in a team photo together because Bobby had left for Fulham before the start of the 1974-75 season. However, there is a photo of me out there somewhere playing with Bobby. I can't remember the opposition but Bobby is defending a corner and I am on one of the posts.

Keith Coleman

very well and his great positional sense and awareness meant he could stop others playing.

I hail from the north-east and joined Sunderland in 1964, aged 13, at the same time as Mick McGiven. We spent nine years together at Roker Park before we both joined West Ham. We enjoyed a further five years together there.

Mick took over the Number 6 shirt along with Kevin Lock when Bobby left for Fulham. Mick was a very different player to Bobby, he was quite physical and tough in the tackle. He was a good player but had a few bad injuries so we never saw the best of him.

I remember when I was playing for Sunderland reserves in the late 1960s, Bobby Moore's West Ham visited Roker Park. I went along to watch and West Ham were fantastic that day. They won easily, 5-1, and Bobby scored.

A stand-out memory of Bobby, of course, came in the game against Brazil during the 1970 World Cup. To be able to limit the influence of Pele in that game showed what a great player he was. He had worked in line with the West Ham philosophy, first as a youth player and then in the reserves and, finally, under the tutelage of Ron Greenwood in the first team.

In Cyprus with the programme from Bobby Moore's final legue game for West Ham United.

87 – BOBBY GOULD

Born: Coventry, West Midlands, June 12, 1946

Position: Centre-forward

Games played with Bobby Moore: 8 (1973-74)

Games played for West Ham United: 59 (1973-75)

First game with Bobby Moore (Debut): November 24, 1973 Arsenal (h) L 1-3

Scorers: West Ham United: Bonds
Arsenal: George, Ball (2)

HAMMER
OFFICIAL PROGRAMME

WEST HAM UNITED
versus
ARSENAL
FOOTBALL LEAGUE : FIRST DIVISION
Saturday 24 November 1973 at 3 p.m.
FIVEPENCE

West Ham United: Day, Coleman, Lampard, Bonds, Taylor, Moore, **Gould**, McDowell, MacDougall, Brooking, Robson

Arsenal: Wilson, Rice, McNab, Storey, Simpson, Kelly, Ball, George, Hornsby, Kennedy, Armstrong

Robert Hewitt Gould is football's quintessential journey man. His career portfolio as a player and manager falls just shy of the 20-club mark and, part of that journey was a spell with West Ham United from 1973-1975, after Ron Greenwood paid Bristol City £80,000 for his services.

Gould played eight first-team games with Bobby Moore, including both his final league game – at home to Norwich City on New Year's Day, 1974 – and the great man's last ever, first team outing for West Ham United – at home to Hereford United in the FA Cup third round a few days later.

He is the first to admit that he wasn't a typical West Ham player, a view shared by his former team-mate, Clyde Best: 'When you looked at West Ham players they were usually quite polished and could play but Bobby wasn't the most skilful. It was his enthusiasm and the fact that he always gave 100% that got him through. Bill Shankly famously said that Gouldy couldn't trap a bag of cement!'

Former Hammer, Joe Durrell, recalls the time when Gould joined West Ham: 'I was playing at Bristol City with Gouldy and one day he came up to me and asked what it was like to play for West Ham. I told him I absolutely loved the place and that I was a West Ham man through and through. The next thing I knew he had signed for them so they had obviously been talking to him. I wanted him to take me with him!'

Perhaps the best compliment paid to Gould comes from one of the club's great workhorses, Ron Boyce: 'He always gave you 100%. He was whole-hearted and learned a lot from his time at West Ham. His attitude changed and he developed a good technique from his experience and hard work.'

Bobby also forms part of the rich vein of West Ham United players who have gone on to enjoy success as a manager – winning the FA Cup with Wimbledon in 1988. He is a regular Friday night guest on Talksport radio and lives in Portishead, Bristol with his wife, Marjorie.

Before I joined West Ham United I spent all my life trying to kick Bobby Moore. Whether I was playing for Coventry City, Wolverhampton Wanderers, Arsenal or West Bromwich Albion, I was always trying to kick Mooro because I had never seen him get riled. I was a really nasty player but I could never get near him. His football brain was just too clever. I did score a few goals against him but I would have loved to have given him a good kick as well!

It was sacrilege that I was ever allowed to play for West

All the tricks in the book.

Ham in the first place. The club had a reputation for producing players that were so much more technically advanced than me. I used to just kick and maul people and Bill Shankly's quip about me being unable to trap a bag of cement was spot on! I was never a West Ham type of player.

Ron Greenwood once told me that he wanted to sign me, when I was playing for Coventry City in the late 60s, but manager Jimmy Hill, turned him down. I have no doubt that if I had been under Ron's charge at an early age and playing with players such as Mooro, Geoff Hurst and Martin Peters, then I would have played for England because I was so eager to learn.

When I signed in November 1973, I remember going to Chadwell Heath for my first training session and I saw Bobby Moore cutting holes in a black bin liner and wearing it under his kit. I'd never seen anything like it and it was the last thing I expected the captain of England to be doing.

Mooro played in my debut game at home to Arsenal that month. My transfer from Bristol City had been lightning-quick and, just like that, I was pulling on the West Ham shirt in the dressing room with Bobby Moore. I sat down and started to look around to get a feel for the vibe, when all of a sudden, I noticed this really strong smell – it was unmistakably alcohol. My curiosity led me to a room where I found the club physio Rob Jenkins. I said to him: 'Rob, there's a really strong smell of

Keeping his heels white on the touchline.

alcohol in the dressing room.' 'Yeah, do you want one?' he replied pointing to a fridge! I opened it and it was like a bar. There was scotch, brandy and beer. Mooro, Bonzo and the others were all having a slug before the game. I'd never seen anything like it in my life.

The training at West Ham United was a revelation to me. Mooro was great on the training pitch and he always seemed to have so much time to do things. The training sessions were

designed to be all about passing but with certain conditions – one-touch passing or two-touch passing or two-touch passing below head height, weakest foot only, keep-ball and it went on like that. Pass, pass, pass – I had never done anything like that at Wolverhampton Wanderers or Arsenal, so one day I tried to have a laugh with Ron Greenwood.

Mooro and the boys were all giggling when, sarcastically, I asked Ron if he knew what five-a-side was? 'What do you mean?' he replied. 'Well,' I said sarcastically, 'I pick a team and you pick a team and we play a game of football and my team tries to put the ball in your net and your team tries to put the ball in my net.' So we're all having a good laugh and Ron came back with: 'We are well past that here Bobby, and you should be thinking more about why you have got to 28 years of age without being able to use your left foot. Now go and practice the training we do day-in, day-out, week-in, week-out and month-in, month-out and pass, pass, pass with your left foot and see how you get on.' Well, it transformed me. My touch, vision and passing with either foot all improved and I became a different player. Ron was a giant in the coaching world.

A couple of years later we won 5-3 up at Burnley but I hadn't scored. Afterwards, I was seething with myself when all of a sudden an arm came around my shoulder and it was Daffy – We used to call Ron, 'Daffy' because he walked like Daffy Duck. 'I know you didn't score, Bobby,' he said. 'But the biggest compliment I can pay you is that you looked like a West Ham United player out there today.'

It's because of Greenwood and John Lyall that I firmly believe you can go anywhere in the world and understand quite quickly if a player is going to be good, excellent or otherwise just by playing one-touch.

John Lyall converted me from a forward into a wide right player. One day he said to me: 'Do you fancy getting your heels white?' He then stood me out on the touchline and I immediately noticed I only had to worry about what was in front of me which gave me a new lease of life. It is easy to see how West Ham got the best out of Bobby Moore. Ron and John were light years ahead of any other club. The biggest mistake that I ever made in football was when I declined John Lyall's offer of becoming his number two as a coach at West Ham. At the time I wanted to carry on playing football but, later, I regretted my decision.

I never thought Mooro would make it as a manager. He was too nice and good managers have to know how and when to give a player some stick. Sometimes you've got to make hard decisions and say things people don't want to hear and Mooro just wasn't like that. He was never vocal. He was Mr West Ham United and you did it his way, the West Ham United way, the right way. As soon as you saw him you knew you were at the right club.

Bobby Gould

'Gouldy'.

88 – MICK MCGIVEN

Born: Newcastle-upon-Tyne, February 7, 1951

Position: Defender

Games played with Bobby Moore: 5 (1973)

Games played for West Ham United: 55 (1973-74)

First game with Bobby Moore (Debut): December 1, 1973 Liverpool (a) L 0-1

Scorer: Liverpool: Cormack

Liverpool: Clemence, Smith, Lindsay, Thompson, Lloyd, Hughes, Keegan, Cormack, Heighway, Waddle, Callaghan

West Ham United: Day, Coleman, Lampard, Bonds, **McGiven**, Moore, Gould, McDowell, MacDougall, Brooking, Holland

---

Michael McGiven spent 17 years at West Ham United as a player and coach. He describes himself as an honest, hard-working player and smiles when recalling wearing the Number 6 shirt after Bobby Moore had left for Fulham in 1974.

On his debut away at Liverpool in December 1973.

Signed from Sunderland for £20,000 by Ron Greenwood, McGiven arguably had the most physical of debuts during the Bobby Moore era – suffering a broken jaw after a collision with Phil Thompson up at Anfield on December 1, 1973.

Despite playing only five games with Bobby Moore they included the great man's final league game – against Norwich City on January 1, 1974 – and his last ever match for the Hammers – against Hereford United on January 5, 1974.

Clyde Best recalls 'Mick' with affection: 'We used to call him 'Coco' after the clown because of his curly hair. He stayed at the club for a long time and is one of those with West Ham in his heart.'

McGiven would go on to play 55 games for West Ham United and he continued his association with the club in a coaching capacity, working alongside future manager, John Lyall, and his staff of Ron Boyce and Ernie Gregory. Mick would accompany Lyall to Ipswich Town, eventually replacing him as Town's manager.

Nowadays, Mick works as an assistant coach at Chelsea, submitting scouting reports and analysing the opposition. His love of the West Ham he knew has never diminished and he opened the door to his home in Woodford to discuss his memories of Bobby Moore. His wife, Maureen, poignantly mentioned: 'You have certainly got a captive audience with West Ham United fans because they never forget.'

My earliest memory of Bobby Moore at West Ham came during my first few training sessions at Chadwell Heath. They were unbelievable. At the start of the training session, Ron Greenwood called a team talk. Now I had never seen anything like this. There was the England captain, various other internationals and the future England manager, all congregated near an old cricket pavilion by the railway track. We were all sitting on an old mattress and the club physio, Rob Jenkins, was treating one or two of the players, while

Ron delivered his talk. I couldn't hear a word of it because the London to Ipswich train was chugging behind and all I could see was Ron's mouth moving and the deafening sound of the train! The whole place actually shook when the train went by and because I was new to the club, I was keen to hear every word but just couldn't hear a thing.

The training was all one and two-touch football and it was great to see Bobby Moore, Frank Lampard, Pop Robson, Trevor Brooking and Billy Bonds mastering the ball. They were so relaxed in possession and effortless in control.

Bobby was very close to Frank Lampard and Rob Jenkins. They enjoyed a drink together. Pop Robson was a great mate of mine from the north-east and he also became good pals with both Trevor Brooking and Billy Bonds.

After one training session, Ron told me that Tommy Taylor had taken a knock and that I was going to make my debut against Liverpool, up at Anfield, in the Number 5 shirt.

My debut is a memory that will stay with me forever. I

Mick (right) challenges Willie Morgan of Manchester United during a 2-1 victory at the Boleyn Ground in January 1974. Alan Wooler (centre) wore the Number 6 shirt that day.

was a youngster from the north-east and I was sitting in the dressing room next to the West Ham and England captain. He was not only the West Ham and England captain but a guy, who has been described as the best defender in the world by none other than the greatest player on earth – Pele.

I remember thinking how phenomenal that was for a lad from a council estate in Newcastle and what a privilege it was to come down and play in the same team as Bobby. It was just fantastic for me.

Bobby was very quiet and so very meticulous. I've never seen anyone like him before or since. He would take his socks off, pull them out one by one and then pair them up and place them on his folded shirt and shorts. He would even fold up his tie ups and place them in his boots. Human nature being what it is I started to do the same. You just couldn't help being positively affected by him.

First and foremost, I would put his intelligence on the pitch as his number one attribute. His passing was like a laser, it just found its target all the time and his positional play was phenomenal.

During my debut we conceded early – Peter Cormack from a Tommy Smith cross after two minutes – but then Ted MacDougall missed three great chances and two of the three were a direct result of Bobby's passing.

There are far better men than me, who have described Bobby as the most intelligent player there has ever been and I would go along with that 100%. His intelligence shone out like a beacon. Jock Stein used to say they should lock him up because he saw things 20 minutes before anyone else.

We should have beaten Liverpool that day but the thing I remember most was Phil Thompson and I going for a 50-50 ball in the first half and his knee hitting me in the jaw. I was led to the dressing room and my face was numb. When I looked in the mirror, all my teeth had been pushed back, one had fallen out. My jaw was broken but Rob Jenkins patched me up and I went out for the second half!

I have never seen a West Ham team dominate a Liverpool side at Anfield like we did in the second half, that afternoon. It was a travesty that we left there with nothing.

There has only ever been one Number 6 at West Ham

United and that's Bobby Moore. Even though I spent 17 years at the club, as player and coach, I was only there for a couple of months before Bobby moved to Fulham. I was privileged not only to be there with him and the other players but also to be there with the best management team the club has ever had.

Ron Greenwood and John Lyall were really, really good people and I mean good people. Not only intelligent people but they were in football for all the right reasons – to help other people, to make the club bigger, better and stronger in all ways. There are so many instances that I look back on which substantiate their philosophy. I remember we beat Leicester in a cup game and their coach wouldn't start so John Lyall invited all their players and staff into the boardroom and looked after them.

Ron showed us how to run a football club and John Lyall kept alive his legacy. They knew what a community football club was all about and they produced players that achieved things, which are unlikely to be repeated in our lifetime.

Another product of the great coaching club that was West Ham United.

The club was so cohesive, just like a big family. Ron and John were always praising Mr Pratt, the club chairman. Every home game, religiously at 2pm, Mr Pratt would come into the dressing room, puffing on his pipe, doff his hat and say: 'Good luck boys!' He owned a timber company, which wasn't too far from the ground and he would occasionally pop along to see the players training. He would say: 'Hello Mick, how are you? It's a lovely day isn't it?' There was never any mention of football, he employed others to deal with that side of the club. He was simply interested in our general welfare. A true gentleman. I heard he set up an Old Players Association in the 1950s. Now that is class and the action of a man who was way ahead of his time. It is the right thing to do and something that is largely lacking in today's game. There's no respect for, or investment in, what has gone before.

Bobby didn't stay at the club very long after I arrived but it was clear to see the fantastic set up he had benefitted from during his time at West Ham United. I'll always remember Bobby Moore – how can you forget someone like that?

Mick McGiven

The Geordie Hammer.

89 – GRAHAM PADDON
August 24, 1950 – November 19, 2007

Born: Manchester

Position: Midfield

Games played with Bobby Moore: 6 (1973-74)

Games played for West ham United: 147 (1973-76)

First game with Bobby Moore (Debut): December 8, 1973 Manchester City (h) W 2-1

Scorers: West Ham United: Brooking, Doyle (og) Manchester City: Lee

West Ham United: Day, McDowell, Lampard, Bonds, Taylor, Moore, Ayris, **Paddon**, Gould, Brooking,* Best Sub: Coleman*

Manchester City: MacRae, Pardoe, Donachie, Doyle, Booth, Towers, Summerbee, Bell, Lee, Leman, Marsh

Graham Charles Paddon was the final Hammer to line up with Bobby Moore – the 89th man. He joined in December 1973, just one month before Moore made his last appearance for the club. During that brief spell they still managed to play in six matches together including Moore's final league and cup games.

Manchester-born Paddon had played for Coventry City and Norwich City before exhibiting his silky midfield class and cultured left foot, in front of the East End faithful. Ron Greenwood paid the Canaries £170,000 including out-of-favour striker, Ted MacDougall, for his services.

Paddon's three-year spell with the Hammers resulted in FA Cup glory in 1975 and a European campaign the following season, which concluded with a thrilling final against Anderlecht at Heysel Stadium, Brussels.

Graham's goal away at Eintracht Frankfurt in the semi-final stands as one of the all-time greatest goals scored by a West Ham United player.

He rejoined Norwich City in Autumn 1976 and took the well-trodden route of playing in the United States – with Tampa Bay Rowdies – before coaching various clubs, most notably Portsmouth, Stoke City and Derby County.

At the end of his playing career, he had also been reunited with Moore, who was managing Hong Kong side, Eastern AA.

In 2005, Graham attended a reunion of West Ham United's great cup winning teams of 1975 and 1980, in London Docklands.

Graham died suddenly from a heart attack in his bed at home on November 19, 2007. He was 57. Frank Lampard, Trevor Brooking, Keith Robson and Alan Taylor were amongst

Graham on his debut against Manchester City on December 8, 1973. Glyn Pardoe challenges while Bobby Moore looks on.

his former West Ham United team-mates to attend his funeral in Norwich.

The interview with Graham's son, Guy, easily outstrips all others in terms of surrealism. Guy works as a deep-sea saturation diver and shared his reminiscences of his father and Bobby Moore from a helium tank on the bed of the North Sea!

Hearty thanks are also extended to Graham's first wife, Pam, for her memories and photographs from their time in Hong Kong, together with Bobby and Tina Moore.

Just like everyone else my father viewed Bobby Moore as a true gentleman and had a great deal of time and respect for him.

My dad joined West Ham United in December 1973 and although Bobby left for Fulham soon afterwards, he did go on to spend more time with him socially, in the 1980s. Bobby was coaching a team called Eastern AA in Hong Kong by then and my dad spent a year out there playing for him. Graham always told the story about Christmas one year, when they decided to celebrate on a big Chinese junk. All the English speaking players followed Bobby onto this boat and they floated out to sea for a big knees-up. Unfortunately, someone dropped the turkey overboard and there was Bobby and my dad trying to retrieve it from the South China Sea!

As a lad, I went out to see my dad in Hong Kong and actually stayed at Bobby's apartment. I was good friends with his son Dean who was a couple of years older than me. We used to kick about together when our dads were staying at hotels, away trips, that sort of thing. Bobby was very kind, very generous and very giving.

Both West Ham and Fulham stayed in hotels on Park Lane prior to the 1975 FA Cup final. My dad left the Hilton and walked down the road to the Grosvenor to catch up with Bobby.

Recalling the Cup final itself, my dad always said it wasn't the most exciting game that he had ever played in and the two quick goals from Alan Taylor finished off Fulham. He much preferred the two semi-final games against Ipswich Town. He thought they were really thrilling encounters, even though winning the FA Cup was the highlight of his career. He sometimes mentioned a couple of goals that he scored – one against Eintracht Frankfurt in Germany during the semi-final of the European Cup Winners Cup in 1976. His favourite goal, however, was one he scored against Wolverhampton Wanderers at Molineux in September 1975 – a 45-yard strike which sadly wasn't captured by the cameras. Thankfully, we do have a DVD of the Eintracht goal.

My dad was quite a private man and kept a lot of things to himself. He went to Bobby's funeral to pay his respects but came straight home once it was over. That was just his way. He was greatly affected by Bobby's death and later in life he lost two other men he had a great deal of time and respect

The cultured midfielder.

for – Peter Osgood in 2006 and Alan Ball a year later. I think he felt that everything that was any good was behind him and his mood was affected as a result. It was a shame because he was usually a very upbeat, lively and energetic individual.

I believe my father was highly respected as a player. He was a players' player. He absolutely loved football and really struggled to come to terms with life outside of the game. He took various coaching and scouting jobs just to stay in touch but it hit him hard when he couldn't get a regular position. It was sad really because he travelled to places like Brunei and Michigan to participate in coaching camps for two or three months just to stay in touch. But it was being in football on a full-time basis which was the one thing in life that kept him focused. When that was gone there wasn't a great deal left for him. Football was his life and he took it very seriously. He often put it before his family and we all understood and accepted that.

Illuminating the post-Bobby Moore era. When class and elegance flourished. Graham is Runner-up to Trevor Brooking in the 1975-76 Hammer of the Year awards.

He had a tremendous amount of respect for both Ron Greenwood and John Lyall and he often spoke about them in the very highest regard.

Graham, Billy Bonds and Frank Lampard were among the first topless 'Page 7 Fellas' in The Sun newspaper. They were stripped off to the waist bearing their chests!

His years at West Ham were the best years of his life. He embraced being in the East End, respected the people and they really warmed to him. He was very close to Frank Lampard, Keith Robson and Pat Holland. He always used to say that Lampard, himself and Robson was one of the best left-sided combinations at West Ham. He thought it had been particularly strong during the European games.
Graham Paddon

There were plenty of recollections of Graham Paddon…

We were very similar really in that we were both very private people. I used to visit him a lot at his home in Loughton. There was a real class about Graham He was so stylish

on the pitch and we built up a good understanding on the left-side. We used to stay behind and practise together and attempted all kinds of different skills and techniques. Some West Ham fans will remember a goal I scored at home to Wolves when Graham flicked up the ball for me to volley home. We had practised that at Chadwell Heath. He was so good in some of the matches, that sometimes I'd even stop to watch him play!
Frank Lampard

When I first came down to West Ham I was all on my own and Graham took me under his wing. West Ham was a team of humble players. There were no superstars or massive egos. He was a fantastic player, very underestimated and he was the bridge between Frank Lampard and myself on that left side. He was a lovely bloke, who helped me out when I was in trouble and he was the type of person that would assist anybody. I was lucky enough to play with him at both West Ham and, later, Norwich. He was a pleasure to be with.
Keith Robson

Graham (top row, second left) with Eastern AA of Hong Kong in 1982-83. Coach, Bobby Moore in the front row.

Christmas 1982 – Postcard from Hong Kong. Graham enjoying life with Bobby and Tina, Alan Ball and Trevor Brooking.

Graham was a good mate of both myself and Frank Lampard. He came from Norwich and fitted in very well. He had a left foot that could do pretty much anything.
Clyde Best

I really liked Graham. He was a fantastic guy. I played with him in the England Under-23s.
Kevin Lock

What a player! What a left peg!
Ken Brown

We called him Jersey Joe, but don't ask me why. He was at Coventry City as a kid when I was there. He played in the youth team at Highfield Road with my brother, Trevor. Then all of a sudden we came together at West Ham. He was so stylish on the ball – the complete opposite to me!
Bobby Gould

I knew Graham when he played for Norwich City. He would come into the Bell Hotel which my husband ran so that was where I really got to know him.

When Graham and his wife, Pam, ran a pub called The Ship in South Walsham, I went and worked for them. The pub life didn't really work out for them and Graham began drinking far too much.
Patsy Dashwood (friend of Graham and his ex-wife, Pam)

Bobby Moore went to Hong Kong from Australia for the 1982-83 season and took over a team called Eastern AA. Both Graham and I went over from Norwich City and stayed for one year. We always called Graham 'Budgie' which was a nickname he had before he re-joined Norwich so it must have come from his time at West Ham. He was softly spoken and never had an argument with anyone. Graham was a gentleman and his character was very much like Bobby Moore. You will never hear anything bad about Graham Paddon. Bobby and Graham were great mates and spent all their time together in Hong Kong.

I was only 20-years-old so it was a very special time to be with men of their stature. I have a great photo of me, Graham, Bobby and a few other players from Europe, when we first arrived at the airport over there. We were with the club owners of Eastern Athletic and I can't imagine there are too many photos from Bobby's time in Hong Kong. Both Trevor Brooking and Alan Ball also came over and joined us for a little while. Bobby was a great person and a perfect gentleman and Graham Paddon fitted the same mould.

Greig Shepherd (Former Norwich City striker)

We got on really well with Bobby and Tina, particularly when we spent some time together in Hong Kong in the early 1980s. Bob was so unassuming, very kind and not at all affected by anything. He was very down-to-earth and had a great sense of humour.

Both Alan Ball and his wife, Lesley, were there and George Best joined us later. That was a bit of a sham really because George was supposed to be off the drink but would always be in a hurry to get back to his room early and we all knew he was drinking heavily until the early hours. It was a shame to see such a man end up that way.

I met Graham in Coventry around the time of the 1966 World Cup. He was an apprentice with Coventry City and my father ran a building company. The story goes that Graham saw me swinging on some scaffolding and came over and started talking to me. My dad said he could pop round anytime for a chat and we became friends. When he was transferred to Norwich City we both started to panic about being separated so he asked my dad if we could get engaged.

The Norwich manager at the time was Ron Saunders and he didn't like his players to be single which nudged us towards marriage that bit quicker and we were married on December 7, 1969.

The football years were such fun and the trips to Wembley with Norwich and West Ham were terrific times. Football was everything to Graham and he simply couldn't cope when he wasn't part of it anymore. He suffered from bouts of depression and it was difficult to reach him when he was like that. Drink took him over really and I remember going with him to hospital and the surgeon telling him that he must simply stop drinking. He told Graham straight, that another year continuing as he was and his body just wouldn't survive. Unfortunately for Graham, if there was no football there was no life and he ignored all the warnings and his body shut down in the end. His life was football and there was nothing else. He was such a great player and so exciting to watch. We were all devastated to lose him.

Graham's first wife, Pam

With former team-mates, Billy Jennings (left) and Keith Robson (right). They were the first two West Ham United signings after the Bobby Moore era.

Signatures of those who played with Bobby Moore.

BOBBY MOORE – WEST HAM UNITED FACTFILE

1. League, FA Cup, League Cup, European Cup Winners Cup, Charity Shield appearances

Total Appearances = 643 (including one substitute appearance): Scored 27 goals (Division One 24, League Cup 3)

			Won	Drawn	Lost	For	Against
League	–	544	183	144	217	875	889
FA Cup	–	36	17	8	11	59	53
League Cup	–	49	28	7	14	115	66
ECWC	–	13	7	4	2	23	5
Charity Shield	–	1	0	1	0	2	2
Total		643	235	164	244	1074	1025

2. Opponents

Bobby Moore played more League games against Manchester United (29) than he did against any other team. He played most overall games against West Bromwich Albion (31).

League		FA Cup		League Cup	
Manchester United	29	Hereford United	3	Cardiff City	4
West Bromwich Albion	27	Stoke City	3	Stoke City	4
Everton	26	Swindon Town	3	West Bromwich Albion	4
Tottenham	26	Blackburn	2	Coventry City	3
Arsenal	25	Burnley	2	Leeds United	3
Chelsea	25	Fulham	2		
		Huddersfield	2		
		Leyton Orient	2		
		Oldham Athletic	2		

3. First Appearances

1) Queens Park Rangers: at Northolt on 6th October 1956. South East Counties League. Won 5-1 (scorers: Tony Banfield (2), John Cartwright (2), Charles Rowlands)

Team: Goymer, Kirkup, Cripps, Lewis, Moore, Lyall, Rowlands, Smillie, Banfield, Cartwright, Norcott
(NB. Four of this team subsequently played with Bobby Moore in the first team – Kirkup, Lyall, Smillie and Cartwright)

2) Briggs Sports: at the Boleyn Ground: 6th November 1956. FA Youth Cup. Won 14-0 (scorers: George Fenn (5), Terry McDonald (4), John Smith (3), John Cartwright, and Charles Rowlands).
   Team: Goymer, Kirkup, Howe (A), Lewis, Moore, Lyall, Rowlands, Smith (J), Fenn, Cartwright, McDonald

3) Birmingham City: at Upton Park, 7th December 1957, Football Combination, Won 4-2, (scorers: Mick Newman (2), Mike Grice, George Fenn).
   Team: Wyllie, Wright, Cooper, Moore, Pyke, Morley, Wragg, Neville, Fenn, Newman, Grice

4 Manchester United: Boleyn Ground, 8th September 1958, Division One (Home), Won 3-2 (scorers: John Dick, John Smith, Malcolm Musgrove)
   Team: Gregory, Bond, Cantwell, Malcolm, Brown, Moore, Grice, Smith, Keeble, Dick, Musgrove

5) Nottingham Forest: City Ground, 13th September 1958, Division One (Away), Lost 0-4
   Team: Gregory, Bond, Cantwell, Malcolm, Brown, Moore, Grice, Smith, Keeble, Dick, Musgrove

6) Charlton Athletic: Boleyn Ground, 26th September 1960, League Cup 1st Round, Won 3-1 (scorers: John Dick, Malcolm Musgrove, Bobby Moore – First ever League Cup Match)
   Team: Rhodes, Bond, Lyall, Malcolm, Brown, Moore, Woodley, Cartwright, Dunmore, Dick, Musgrove

7) Stoke City: Boleyn Ground, FA Cup – 3rd Round, 7th January 1961, Drew 2-2 (scorers: Dave Dunmore, John Dick)
   Team: Rhodes, Bond, Lyall, Malcolm, Brown, Moore, Smillie, Woosnam, Dunmore, Dick, Musgrove

8) Liverpool: Anfield, Charity Shield, 15th August 1964, Drew 2-2 (scorers Geoff Hurst, Johnny Byrne)
   Team: Standen, Bond, Burkett, Bovington, Brown, Moore, Brabrook, Boyce, Byrne, Hurst, Sissons

9) La Gantoise (Belgium): Ghent Stadium, 23rd September 1964, Cup Winners Cup 1st Round 1st Leg. Won 1-0 (scorer: Ron Boyce)
   Team: Standen, Bond, Peters, Bovington, Brown, Moore, Sealey, Boyce, Byrne, Hurst, Sissons

4. First Goals

1) Reading (Away), 5th January 1957, FA Youth Cup, 2 goals – Won 4-2
2) Cardiff City (Away), 30th August 1958, Football Combination – Won 4-2
3) Charlton Athletic (Home), 26th September 1960, League Cup – Won 3-1
4) Wolverhampton Wanderers (Home), 17th December 1960, Division One – Won 5-0
5) Chelsea (Away), 3rd February 1962, Division One – Won 1-0

Bobby Moore scored most goals against…
Wolverhampton Wanderers (5 goals) and Fulham (3 goals).

5. Reserve team matches

Played in 54 reserve matches: 27 (Home): 27 (Away): Scored 3 goals
Won: 21 Lost: 21 Drawn: 12 Goals for: 93 Goals against: 111

74 different team-mates: 45 also played in the first team with Bobby Moore.

9 reserve team-mates did not play in the first-team with Bobby Moore:
Allison, Bleanch, Brooks, Cooper, Cripps, Curry, Dryden, Fenn, Harvey, Hayward, Higgins, Hills, Lewis, McDonald, Morley, Mountford, Nelson, Neville, Newman, Orhan, Pike, Pope, Pyke, Reader, White, Wooler*, Wragg, Wright, Wyllie.

Most reserve team appearances with Bobby Moore:

		Top reserve team goal scorers:	
Doug Wragg	38		
John Lyall	33	Doug Wragg	13
Joe Kirkup	32	Billy Dare	12
Brian Rhodes	30	Ron Brett	7
Bill Lansdowne	29	Andy Smillie	7
John Cartwright	28	John Cartwright	5
Tony Scott	28	Vic Keeble	5
Andy Smillie	28		

Alan Wooler played three first team games during the Bobby Moore era but on all three occasions Moore did not play. Wooler also played in Bobby Moore's last ever game for West Ham United – against Plymouth Argyle in a reserve team match on March 9, 1974. Team: Grotier, Charles (Clive), Wooler, Lutton, White, Moore, Ayris, Boyce, Robson, Pike, Orhan. Pop Robson scored West Ham's goal in a 1-1 draw.

6. Captaincy (League, FA Cup, League Cup, European Cup Winners Cup, Charity Shield games)

Bobby Moore captained West Ham United on 520 of the 643 occasions he played in the first team.

First captaincy: 20th April 1962 v Cardiff City (Home): Won 4-1 (Martin Peters' debut).

	Played	Captain
Division One	544	430
FA Cup	36	33
League Cup	49	45
European Cup Winners Cup	13	11
Charity Shield	1	1

7. '89 Club' – The 89 Hammers who played in the first team with Bobby Moore

The following 10 players made more than 200 appearances with Bobby Moore in Division One / FA Cup / League Cup / European Cup Winners Cup / Charity Shield games.

1)	Geoff Hurst	455	6)	John Sissons	236
2)	Martin Peters	327	7)	Bobby Ferguson	229
3)	Ron Boyce	301	8)	Trevor Brooking	218
4)	Billy Bonds	287	8)	Frank Lampard	213
5)	Ken Brown	275	10)	Jim Standen	205

'Selected Team' based on most appearances by position (Division One / FA Cup / League Cup / European Cup Winners Cup / Charity Shield)

Goal	Bobby Ferguson (229)	Outside Right	Harry Redknapp (159)
Right Back	Joe Kirkup (154)	Inside Right	Ron Boyce (254)
Left Back	Frank Lampard (206)	Centre Forward	John Byrne (143)
Right Half	Martin Peters (208)	Inside Left	Geoff Hurst (273)
Centre Half	Ken Brown (274)	Outside Left	John Sissons (224)
Left Half	Bobby Moore (618)		

Remarkably, Geoff Hurst has the highest number of appearances in two positions as he also played on 143 occasions at centre-forward.

Billy Bonds played 287 games with Bobby Moore. The fourth highest Hammer behind Geoff Hurst (455), Martin Paters (327) and Ron Boyce (301) However, Billy is not included in the 'Selected Team' which is based on the most appearances by position.
Billy played 143 games at right back compared to Joe Kirkup's 154 appearances and 133 games at right half compared to Martin Peters' total of 208.

Bobby Moore made a total of 643 appearances (including his one substitution). In addition to the 618 appearances he made at left-half, Bobby also made a further 6 appearances at right-half (five in the League and one in the Cup Winners Cup) and 18 appearances at centre-half in the League.

8. Goalscorers

A total of 1074 goals were scored during the Bobby Moore era: Division One (875), FA Cup (59), League Cup (115), European Cup Winners Cup (23) and Charity Shield (2)

Top six goal scorers:

		Division One	FA Cup	League Cup	ECWC	Charity Shield	Total
1)	Geoff Hurst	171	21	40	2	1	235
2)	Martin Peters	785	10	4	0	0	97
3)	Johnny Byrne	66	6	13	6	1	92
4)	John Dick	4	1	2	0	0	48
5)	Bryan Robson	43	1	4	0	0	48
6)	John Sissons	34	7	5	2	0	48

22 players scored two goals in a match: Geoff Hurst on 38 occasions, Martin Peters 10, John Dick/Bryan Robson nine each.
10 other players scored two goals on more than one occasion.

Clyde Best	8	Trevor Brooking	3	Players (8) scoring 2 goals on one occasion only	
Johnny Byrne	8	Malcolm Musgrove	3	Ron Boyce	Harry Obeney
Brian Dear	5	Ian Crawford	2	Martin Britt	Graham Paddon
John Sissons	5	Jimmy Greaves	2	Dave Dunmore	Alan Sealey
Peter Brabrook	4	Mike Grice	2	Ted MacDougall	Ron Tindall

10 players scored three goals in a match: Geoff Hurst on six occasions: (twice in Division One, twice in the FA Cup and twice in the League Cup), Johnny Byrne on four occasions: (twice in Division One, twice in the League Cup) and Bryan Robson on two occasions: (Once in Division One and once in the League Cup).

Seven other players also scored a hat-trick: John Bond, Trevor Brooking, Brian Dear, Dave Dunmore, Malcolm Musgrove, Martin Peters and John Sissons.

Hat-trick heroes:

Division One:
1)   6th February 1960   John Bond   v   Chelsea   4-2
2) 22nd October 1960   Malcolm Musgrove   v   Preston   5-2
3) 5th November 1960   Dave Dunmore   v   Arsenal   6-0
4) 22nd February 1964   Johnny Byrne   v   Sheffield Wednesday   4-3
5) 12th September 1964   Johnny Byrne   v   Tottenham Hotspur   3-2
6) 11th December 1965   Geoff Hurst   v   Newcastle United   4-3
7) 26th December 1967   Brian Dear   v   Leicester City   4-2
8) 6th April 1968   Trevor Brooking   v   Newcastle United   5-0
9) 31st August 1968   Martin Peters   v   West Bromwich   4-0
10) 3rd October 1970   Geoff Hurst   v   Burnley   3-1
11) 20th April 1973   Bryan Robson   v   Southampton   4-3

FA Cup:
1) 28th January 1967   Geoff Hurst   v   Swindon Town   3-3 (3rd Round)
2) 14th February 1972   Geoff Hurst   v   Hereford United   3-1 (4th Round Replay)

League Cup:
1) 26th September 1962   Johnny Byrne   v   Plymouth Argyle   6-0 (1st Round)
2) 16th December 1963   Johnny Byrne   v   Workington Town   6-0 (5th Round)
3) 7th November 1966   John Sissons   v   Leeds United   7-0 (4th Round)
4) 7th November 1966   Geoff Hurst   v   Leeds United   7-0 (4th Round)
5) 4th September 1968   Geoff Hurst   v   Bolton Wanderers   7-2 (2nd Round)
6) 17th November 1971   Bryan Robson   v   Sheffield United   5-0 (Quarter Final)

Interestingly, every hat-trick during the Bobby Moore era was scored at the Boleyn Ground.

Geoff Hurst also scored four goals on two occasions: 5th November 1966 v Fulham at the Boleyn Ground (Division One) and 11th October 1967 v Bolton Wanderers at the Boleyn Ground (League Cup).

Brian Dear scored 5 goals – 16th April 1965 v West Bromwich Albion at the Boleyn Ground (Division One).

Geoff Hurst scored 6 goals – 19th October 1968 v Sunderland at the Boleyn Ground (Division One).

9. Scoring debutants in the Bobby Moore era

1) 24th September 1960   Mike Beesley   v   Everton   (Away)   Lost 1-4
2) 27th February 1965   Eddie Presland   v   Liverpool   (Home)   Won 2-1
3) 13th October 1965   Dennis Burnett   v   Mansfield Town   (Home)   Won 4-0   League Cup
4) 21st March 1970   Jimmy Greaves (2)   v   Manchester City   (Away)   Won 5-1
5) 24th February 1971   Bryan Robson   v   Nottingham Forest   (Home)   Won 2-0
6) 30th October 1971   Ade Coker   v   Crystal Palace   (Away)   Won 3-0

* It should be noted that Roger Hugo did score on his West Ham United debut – at Leicester City in March, 1964 – but Bobby Moore did not play. He also scored in his first game with Bobby Moore in the line-up: 28th March 1964 v West Bromwich (Away) Won 1-0.

10. Penalties

A total of 66 penalties were awarded to West Ham with 54 being converted and 12 saved or missed.

	League		FA Cup		League Cup		Total		Total
	Scored	Missed	Scored	Missed	Scored	Missed	Scored	Missed	
Geoff Hurst	18	1	0	3	4	1	22	5	27
Johnny Byrne	15	2	2	0	1	0	18	2	20
John Bond	6	4	0	0	0	0	6	4	10
Martin Peters	3	1	0	0	0	0	3	1	4
Bryan Robson	2	0	0	0	0	0	2	0	2
Billy Bonds	1	0	0	0	0	0	1	0	1
Noel Cantwell	1	0	0	0	0	0	1	0	1
Malcolm Musgrove	1	0	0	0	0	0	1	0	1
Total	47	8	2	3	5	1	54	12	66

A total of 54 penalties were awarded against West Ham with 40 being conceded and 14 saved or missed.

	League		FA Cup		League Cup		Total		Total
	Conceded	Saved	Conceded	Saved	Conceded	Saved	Conceded	Saved	
Jim Standen	12	6	0	1	1	0	13	7	20
Bobby Ferguson	10	3	0	0	1	0	11	3	14
Peter Grotier	4	1	0	0	2	0	6	1	7
Lawrie Leslie	5	0	0	0	0	0	5	0	5
Brian Rhodes	2	1	0	0	0	0	2	1	3
Peter Shearing	1	0	0	0	0	0	1	0	1
Alan Dickie	1	0	0	0	0	0	1	0	1
Colin Mackleworth	1	0	0	0	0	0	1	0	1
Bobby Moore	0	0	0	0	0	1	0	1	1
Mervyn Day	0	1	0	0	0	0	0	1	1
Total	36	12	0	1	4	1	40	14	54

11. Substitutions

A total of 103 substitutions were made during the Bobby Moore era featuring 33 different players including Bobby Moore: (89 Division One, eight FA Cup and six League Cup).

Highest number of substitutions in a single season: 19 (1970-71)

Top six substitute appearances:
10 – Bobby Howe
9 – Kevin Lock
7 – Pat Holland, Trevor Brooking
6 – Ron Boyce
5 – Paul Heffer

Top six most substituted players:
8 – John Ayris, Trevor Brooking, Frank Lampard
7 – John Charles
6 – Clyde Best, Ron Boyce

Bobby Moore played as substitute goalkeeper on two occasions for the first team.

1) 16th September 1961   v   Chelsea at Boleyn Ground, Lawrie Leslie stretchered off with head injury.
2) 26th January 1972   v   Stoke City at Old Trafford, League Cup Semi-Final 2nd Replay, Bobby Ferguson concussion.

12. Players sent off

Four Hammers were sent off during the Bobby Moore era:

1) Bobby Moore: 4th November 1961   v   Manchester City (Away)
2) Harry Redknapp: 12th October 1968   v   Leeds United (Away)
3) Billy Bonds: 9th September 1970   v   Hull City (Home) (League Cup)
4) Ted MacDougall: 6th October 1973   v   Burnley (Home)

13. Division One appearance milestones

1) – 100th League Appearance: 25th August 1962 v Tottenham Hotspur   Boleyn Ground
2) – 200th League Appearance: 16th April 1965 v West Bromwich Albion   Boleyn Ground (Brian Dear scores five)
3) – 300th League Appearance: 23rd December 1967 v Tottenham Hotspur   Boleyn Ground (Billy Bonds scores his first goal for the club)
4) – 387th League Appearance: 10th January 1970 v Sheffield Wednesday   Hillsborough (Post War Club Record League Appearance)
5) – 400th League Appearance: 2nd April 1970 v Leeds United   Boleyn Ground
6) – 500th League Appearance: 2nd December 1972 v Newcastle United   Boleyn Ground
7) – 509th League Appearance: 10th February 1973 v Norwich City   Carrow Road (Club Record League Appearance)

Bobby Moore's most consecutive first team League and Cup appearances: 72 (58 League, four FA Cup and 10 League Cup) from 6th February 1971 v Derby County at the Boleyn Ground until 15th April 1972 v Liverpool at the Boleyn Ground).
Based on available records, Bobby Moore made a total of 913 appearances for West Ham United across all competitions and levels, scoring 53 goals.

Statistics kindly provided by Richard Miller: October 2014.

1964 FA Cup Winners medal   *1965 European Cup Winners Cup medal*   *1966 World Cup Winners medal*

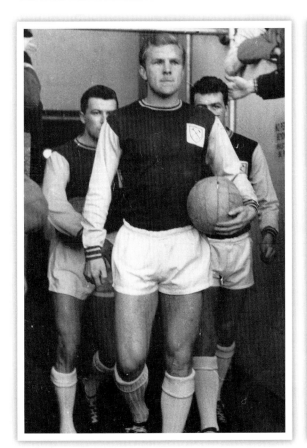

There will never be another...

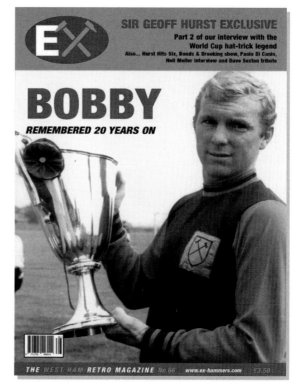